Reforming Primary Elections

Reforming Primary Elections

Edited by
Robert G. Boatright and Richard Barton

DE GRUYTER

ISBN (Paperback) 978-3-11-165985-5
ISBN (Hardcover) 978-3-11-166461-3
e-ISBN (PDF) 978-3-11-166170-4
e-ISBN (EPUB) 978-3-11-166366-1
DOI https://doi.org/10.1515/9783111661704

Library of Congress Control Number: 2025945710

Bibliographic information published by the Deutsche Nationalbibliothek
The Deutsche Nationalbibliothek lists this publication in the Deutsche Nationalbibliografie; detailed
bibliographic data are available on the Internet at http://dnb.dnb.de.

© 2026 with the author(s), editing © 2026 Robert G. Boatright and Richard Barton, published by
Walter de Gruyter GmbH, Berlin/Boston, Genthiner Straße 13, 10785 Berlin.
This book is published with open access at www.degruyterbrill.com.

Cover image: wildpixel / iStock / Getty Images Plus

www.degruyterbrill.com
Fragen zur allgemeinen Produktsicherheit:
productsafety@degruyterbrill.com

Contents

About the Authors

The Editors

Robert G. Boatright is a Professor of Political Science at Clark University and Director of Research for the National Institute for Civil Discourse, the University of Arizona.

Richard C. Barton is an Assistant Teaching Professor in the Maxwell School of Citizenship and Public Affairs at Syracuse University and a Senior Research Fellow at Unite America.

The Authors

Zachary Albert is an Assistant Professor of Politics at Brandeis University.

Hayley M. Cohen is a Postdoctoral Fellow at the Watson School of International and Public Affairs at Brown University, and an incoming Assistant Professor of Political Science at the University of Houston.

Mike Cowburn is a Research Fellow in the European Research Council project on the Design, Creation and Survival of Democratic Laws in the Department of Political and Social Sciences at Zeppelin University Friedrichshafen.

Jesse Crosson is an Associate Professor of Political Science at Purdue University.

Tom Daschle was a Senator from South Dakota from 1987 to 2005. He served as Senate minority leader from 1995 to 2001 and from 2003 to 2005, and as the majority leader from 2001 to 2003. He is the founder and chairman of The Daschle Group and a Co-Chair of the National Institute for Civil Discourse's National Advisory Board.

Ceili Fallon is a student at the University of Wyoming.

Edward B. Foley is the Charles W. Ebersold and Florence Whitcomb Ebersold Chair in Constitutional Law at the Moritz College of Law, Ohio State University and the Director of the Election Law at Ohio State Program.

Jeremy Gelman is an Associate Professor of Political Science at the University of Nevada, Reno.

Rachel Hutchinson is a Senior Policy Analyst at FairVote.

Caitlin E. Jewitt is an Associate Professor of Political Science at Virginia Tech University.

Raymond J La Raja is a Professor of Political Science ate the University of Massachusetts, Amherst, and Co-Director of UMass-Amherst Poll.

Trent Lott was a Senator from Mississippi from 1989 to 2007. He served as Senate majority leader from 1996 to 2001, and as the minority leader from 2001 to 2003. He is the Principal and Director of Crossroads Strategies and a Co-Chair of the National Institute for Civil Discourse's National Advisory Board.

David Lublin is a Professor and Department Chair in the Department of Government at American University.

Carlo Macomber is the Senior Policy Manager at Unite America.

Derek Monson is the Chief Growth Officer at the Sutherland Institute.

Hans Noel is an Associate Professor of Government at Georgetown University.

Deb Otis is the Director of Research at FairVote.

Evan Pritsos is a Ph.D. candidate at the University of Nevada, Reno.

Benjamin Reilly is a Non-Resident Senior Fellow at the United States Studies Centre and Adjunct Senior Fellow at the East-West Center.

Michael Ritter is an Assistant Professor of Political Science at Washington State University.

Marius Sältzer is an Assistant Professor of Digital Social Science at the University of Oldenburg.

Caroline Tolbert is a Distinguished University Professor of Political Science at the University of Iowa.

Sarah A. Treul is a Professor of Political Science at the University of North Carolina, Chapel Hill.

Ryan Williamson is an Assistant Professor of Political Science at the University of Wyoming.

Glenn Wright is a Professor of Political Science at the University of Alaska Southeast.

Acknowledgments

Most of the chapters of this book were originally presented at the Primary Election Research Symposium held by Unite America and the National Institute for Civil Discourse in Washington, DC on May 2–4, 2024. We thank Tyler Fisher, Beth Hladick, Jessica Leven, Carlo Macomber, and Nick Troiano from Unite America for putting on this event and for the financial support they provided for many of the projects included here. We also thank Keith Allred and Timothy J. Shaffer from the National Institute for Civil Discourse for co-hosting the event and helping with the production of this edited volume.

Senators Tom Daschle and Trent Lott

Preface

National Advisor Board Co-Chairs, National Institute for Civil Discourse

The two of us served in Congress for a total of fifty-nine years, sixteen of them as Senate majority or minority leaders. When we came to Congress in the 1970s, Congress was far less polarized than it is today. By the mid-1990s, when we became the leaders of our respective parties in the closely divided Senate, the rise in partisan rancor was already on full display, including during the fraught impeachment proceedings of President Clinton.

Nonetheless, we count our time as Senate leaders as one where the two parties could seek common ground. We take pride that we were able to come together on many important pieces of legislation during the Clinton and Bush presidencies. Even when we disagreed, we kept lines of communication open.

The growing polarization since we left Congress led us to come together to warn the nation of its perils in 2016. In *Crisis Point*, we wrote, "The center can no longer hold under such mindless and unprecedented partisanship: it is no exaggeration to say that the state of our democracy is as bad as we've ever seen it" (1). In noting that, "Congress is being reshaped in sharper, more discrete divisions," we observed that "primaries only encourage this" (45). These critical elections, by which candidates make it to the general election ballot, give an advantage to the extremes over moderates and alienate voters with their negativity.

As alarmed as we were when we published *Crisis Point*, the dysfunction of extreme partisanship has grown substantially in the decade since. In this climate, primaries play even more important and troubling roles. Fearing they will be "primaried," members of Congress believe even more strongly now that they have more to gain from standing their ground and blocking reasonable legislation entirely than making the necessary compromises to enact solutions that serve their constituents' interests. Today, it is almost unheard of for a Democrat to win elections in our home states of Mississippi or South Dakota, just as it is rare for Republicans to win elections in New England or in America's larger cities, making primary elections more important for members of Congress. Many lawmakers clearly believe that primary election outcomes are not driven by what one can do for their district, but by how successfully they demonize the opposing party. Even saying a kind word or appearing in public with members of the opposing party can cause trouble in a primary campaign.

In this climate of playing to the base of one's party, the voters who dominate in primary elections, too many Americans are shut out of the process of choosing their elected leaders. When primary turnout hovers below twenty percent of the electorate, and when the primary is, in many parts of the country, the only election that matters, it is no wonder that politicians stop listening to the full range of citizens they are elected to represent and that their constituents, in turn, feel disenfranchised.

Something needs to be done. That is why we wrote our 2016 book and were proud to lead a Bipartisan Policy Center Taskforce in 2014 to consider ways of governing in our polarized era. For example, our report urged states to adopt open or semi-open primaries to encourage candidates to reach out to voters who are not reflexive partisans. We also suggested the establishment of a single-day national primary.

The magnitude of the problem is such that we cannot stop at primary reforms. We believe they must be undertaken along with changes to the way we draw congressional districts, to our campaign finance laws, and to how Congress operates.

Distressing as the current state of our politics is, we take genuine encouragement from states experimenting with reforms designed to increase the participation and representativeness of primary elections. We are also impressed by the growing sophistication of research investigating these reforms. The chapters in this book document how primary elections have changed over the past decade, examine the impacts of reforms already implemented, and consider promising but as-yet-untested ideas.

Our experience working together demonstrates that election reform need not be a partisan issue. It is in the interest of all Americans to ensure that our politicians represent us. Substantial, bipartisan majorities of Americans agree that our government has lost their trust and that political compromise is important. When partisan cues are not present, Americans of both parties agree on many political reforms. The imperative to reform our elections is more important than ever. The task before us is to understand what is wrong, what might work, and how to get there.

Our democracy is worth fighting for, and the power to fortify it is in our hands. The chapters that follow help identify promising ways to do that. We hope this book will prompt readers, whether they are citizens, scholars, or policymakers, to think and act constructively when it comes to reforming our political system and strengthening the bond between elected leaders and the people.

Bibliography

Bipartisan Policy Center. 2014. "Governing in a Polarized America: A Bipartisan Blueprint to Strengthen our Democracy." Bipartisan Policy Center. bipartisanpolicy.org/report/governing-polarized-america-bipartisan-blueprint-strengthen-our-democracy/.

Lott, Trent, and Tom Daschle. 2016. *Crisis Point: Why we Must – and How we Can – Overcome our Broken Politics in Washington and Across America.* Bloomsbury Press.

Robert Boatright and Richard Barton

Chapter 1
Introduction

Abstract: This introductory chapter examines the evolving role of primary elections in American politics. As political polarization increases, primaries have become central to understanding political dysfunction, with recent high-profile races demonstrating how primaries can influence candidate selection and legislative behavior. We explore three key components of the primary system: voters, candidates, and electoral rules. Despite longstanding debates about whether primaries contribute to polarization, recent evidence reveals that primary electorates are unrepresentative of the general public, moderates increasingly avoid running for office, and reforms like nonpartisan primaries show promise in reducing extremism. Nonetheless, some scholars argue for alternative reforms that strengthen parties and have more transformative effects, including consolidated national primary days, proportional representation, and fusion voting. By situating contemporary debates within a historical context, this chapter provides a foundation for understanding whether America's century-old primary system requires modest adjustments or fundamental restructuring to address current democratic challenges.

After every election cycle, authoritative studies are written explaining the results of the presidential election. Scholars also tend to come to agreement on the meaning of each cycle's House and Senate elections. There are well-accepted models about how to predict changes in the number of seats the two parties hold, based on the geographic strength of the parties and the state of the economy. Yet it is much harder to predict or interpret primary elections, in which partisanship is not a differentiating characteristic between candidates. It is natural that we would want to have such a story—after all, in a typical year barely ten percent of House general elections and twenty percent of Senate general elections are truly competitive, so in most elections the "winners" are really chosen in the primary. But in telling this story it is difficult for political junkies to avoid being distracted by the catnip of the occasional odd result.

Consider some of the most salient examples from the 2024 House and Senate primaries: While the Israeli-Palestinian conflict may not have played a major role in general election politics, two Democratic House incumbents, Jamaal Bowman of New York and Cori Bush of Missouri, lost their primaries after facing a barrage of over $10 million in advertisements from groups supportive of Israel. In Colorado, controversial Republican Congresswoman Lauren Boebert, facing a likely defeat in her congressional race, moved across the state to another district where the incumbent was retiring, won a six-candidate primary, and triumphantly returned to Congress. In Senate primaries in Arizona and Montana, Donald Trump's endorsement elevated political outsiders to the nomination and, in Ohio, to Congress. In California and Washington, David Valadao and Dan Newhouse, the two remaining Republican House members who supported Donald Trump's second impeachment, survived their primaries and won re-election, in part due to these states' nonpartisan top-two primaries. And in Alaska, the surprise winner of the 2022 House race, Democrat Mary Peltola, was narrowly defeated after state Republicans successfully persuaded the third-place finisher in the state's top four primary to drop out of the race, leaving Peltola with only a single Republican opponent in the general election.

Do these stories exemplify systemic trends in recent congressional primary elections? As American politics and governance have grown more polarized, uncivil, and dysfunctional in recent years, many people have pointed to primary elections as an important institutional contributor to these pathologies. Some have placed blame on challenges to incumbent members of Congress, calling attention to instances where ideological challengers such as David Brat or Alexandria Ocasio-Cortez defeated party leaders such as House Majority Leader Eric Cantor or House Democratic Caucus Chair Joseph Crowley, and to more systemic evidence that ideological primary candidates increasingly pose credible challenges against incumbents. It is noteworthy that Jamaal Bowman and Cori Bush, the only two Democratic incumbents to lose primaries in 2024, had originally won their seats by ousting more conventional Democratic incumbents. Their initial foes were not as well-known as Crowley or Cantor, but the dynamic was the same.

Others have taken note of the victories of ideologically extreme and norm-breaking candidates such as Marjorie Taylor Greene, Matt Gaetz, or Andy Biggs, all of whom initially won their House seats with less than a majority of the primary vote in lopsidedly partisan districts. Primary elections, it is said, favor more ideological candidates in open-seat elections, and they may even dissuade more moderate and representative candidates from running for office in the first place. Taylor Greene's district in Georgia has a history of electing very conservative representatives, but its prior representatives did not attract attention the way Greene has. Gaetz's predecessor in Florida and Biggs' predecessor in Arizona were both staunch Republicans, but they were relatively conventional politicians. Perhaps there is something about open-seat primaries today, or about the fact that a very small minority of even the Republican voters in these districts chose these candidates, that is of concern. Perhaps the lesson we can take from these cases, and from Lauren Boebert's 2024 victory as well, is that primaries reward extremism and provocation today.

Others have observed that our increasingly polarized parties can deny voters the opportunity to vote for the candidates who would best represent them. In Ohio, there is ample evidence that in the past two Senate elections, moderate Republican candidates who could have won the general election easily did not make it to the general election ballot; instead, more polarizing Republican candidates such as J.D. Vance and Bernie Moreno eked out wins in multi-candidate Republican primaries but fared far worse in the general election (although both did win) than some of the candidates they defeated in the primary would have.

Those with a more reform-oriented mindset have seized upon the examples of Valadao, Newhouse, and Peltola to tout the potential for nonpartisan primaries (as in California) or top-four primaries with ranked-choice general election voting (as in Alaska) to reduce political polarization. Critics point out, however, that highly ideological candidates continue to win office in these states. Even if primary reforms work in these Western states, it is hard to prove that the same models would work equally well in the rest of the country.

It is by no means clear that any of these observations are anything more than anecdotes about idiosyncratic election results. While ideological primary challengers are more common today than they were two or three decades ago, incumbents still rarely lose primary elections. Further, while it is easy to find examples of ideologically extreme or unrepresentative candidates winning multi-candidate primaries, the United States has used primary elections for over a century, so the victories of extremists may well be a consequence not of our primary election system but of (to give just a few examples) the media environment, our campaign finance system, the gerrymandering of congressional districts, the failure of political parties to act as gatekeepers, or the growing polarization among the general public.

Whether or not such claims about primaries are justified, we do know that legislators regularly acknowledge that the fear of getting "primaried" impacts their behavior. If legislators draw such conclusions from their colleagues' experiences or from media accounts of primary elections, the result can be a legislature full of members who prioritize ideological purity (whether out of principle or fear of a future primary challenger) over compromise, making bipartisan cooperation and consensus-building very difficult. Conversely, if legislators feel empowered by their state's primary system to reach across the aisle or to break with their party on matters of concern to their district, they may provide an example to others.

In short, stories about primary elections are compelling. They are quite possibly more interesting to tell than to recap the story of two presidential candidates facing each other again in a battle over incremental changes in the electorate, or the two parties scrimmaging near the fifty-yard-line for control of the House and Senate. It is important for us to determine whether these stories do in fact contain truths about the state of American politics today, or whether they contain lessons on how to improve our politics.

In the past two decades, the study of primary elections has gone from an obscure backwater in American politics to a central concern of politicians, journalists, and reform advocates. As the political parties have moved apart from each other and basic norms of electoral politics and governance have deteriorated, it has become apparent that primary elections provide an important venue for understanding these changes.

Yet there is much we do not know about primaries. Most accounts of primaries are built on claims about three basic components of the electoral process: the voters, the candidates, and the rules. Because so few people vote in primaries, however, it has been difficult to measure the characteristics of primary voters or to determine why people vote in primaries. It is also evident that recent changes in primaries have encouraged some candidates to run and deterred others, and that these changes have in turn influenced how parties recruit candidates or intervene in primaries. It is hard, however, to identify potential candidates who do not run, or to determine what characteristics of the candidates who do run matter. Further, the most recent innovations in primary election rules, such as those in Alaska, are relatively new and untested, so we know little about how parties will adapt to these rules over time.

Our intent in this book is to provide an overview of what we know about primary voters, candidates, and rules today. The authors in this book have taken advantage of new innovations in the study of each of these aspects of primaries to fill in many of the gaps in our knowledge of primaries. This is, as far as we know, just the third edited volume this century of research on primaries, and it is written with an eye toward helping readers understand whether, in fact, the primary system America has had for over a century is irreparably broken, and what options there might be for change. Before we explore these three features of this book, however, it is important to offer the reader a bit of context on the history of primaries, primary reform, and primary research.

A Brief History of Primaries, Primary Reform, and Primary Election Research

No other country is as dependent on the use of primary elections as the United States. Some American cities and counties experimented with party primaries in the late nineteenth century; they were first introduced at the state level in 1902. By 1917, all but three states had mandatory primaries, and by the 1960s all states were using them. Today, most American accept that primary elections are an essential component of democratic elections.

There is some disagreement among scholars about why primary elections caught on so quickly. In their 1928 book surveying the quick spread of primaries, political scientists Charles Merriam and Louise Overacker argued that primaries were simply a good idea—they appealed to the public, and there were few compelling arguments against them. Nearly a century later, the British scholar Alan Ware (2002) proposed that primaries did not spread because of public appeal but because they solved a problem for political parties—American parties had tired of trying to balance factions against each other when they chose candidates, and it was easier to give this responsibility to the voters. Primaries were an easy way for politicians to satisfy Progressive Era calls for more democracy because they looked like a way of breaking the power of party bosses and giving the public a voice in elections.

Primary elections were established during a period of extraordinary change in the conduct of American elections. Many things that we take for granted in our politics today, including the secret ballot, the direct election of Senators, nonpartisan local elections, and the participation of women in politics, were all established at the time of the Progressive Movement, in the late nineteenth and early twentieth century. Many ideas that are on the wish list of contemporary progressives (small "p"), including proportional representation, campaign finance regulations, and limits on the power of businesses and other wealthy interests in politics, were also under consideration at this time. An easy way to understand this is that the Progressive Era arose as a response to dramatic economic inequality and particularly stark polarization between the two major parties.

Yet some scholars of the era warned that primaries would make matters worse—in part because they gave political parties somewhat of an official role in American politics. The political scientist Henry Jones Ford (1909) warned that the establishment of primaries would simply replace one set of party bosses with another; other political scientists asked whether primaries would reduce the quality of politicians, make campaigning more important than governing, weaken efforts to represent diversity within states' populations, or enable small, unrepresentative minorities within the parties to wield outsized power in choosing candidates. Former president William Howard Taft (1922) contended that primaries would place control of the parties in the hands of people who had no real reason to care about the long-term health of the parties or the political system.

In the short run, it is safe to say that these warnings went unheeded, and that American politics did not, in fact, suffer the ills these critics predicted. In many states, however, party organizations were able to control the primary process while still giving the public the illusion of choice. For much of the twentieth century, parties at the state level experimented with a range of reforms that allowed them to exert some control over nominations. These included preprimary endorsing conventions, rules about who could vote in primaries, rules about how candidates could get their names on the ballot, provisions for run-off elections if no candidate won a majority of the primary vote, changes to the date of the primary, and rules about whether candidate descriptions were allowed on the ballot (for a summary see Boatright 2024). Most of the evidence we have suggests that voters liked primaries, and in the rare instances where states sought to abolish them entirely, voters resisted. However, those Progressive Era reformers who thought that primaries would limit the power of parties were disappointed—most of the time, party leaders got the candidates they wanted, when they wanted to play a role in choosing candidates (Hassell 2018).

Today, there are many types of primaries used to elect state and federal lawmakers across the country. These include: nonpartisan primaries in which all candidates compete in the same primary open to all voters; open primaries in which all voters can choose which partisan primary to participate in; semi-open primaries in which independent voters can choose which partisan primary to participate in, but partisan voters must participate in the primary of the party they are registered with; and closed primaries in which only voters registered with parties may participate in primaries. To make matters more complicated, some states, such as Illinois, Indiana, Ohio, and Iowa, hold semi-open primaries where voters are allowed to cross party lines but are subsequently registered in the party whose ballot they have taken. Because of small variations across states, it is hard to develop rigid categories for primary types.

As Boatright (2024) argues in his history of primary reforms, this complex tapestry of state primary laws is the consequence of nearly a century of experimentation. These state experiments were not undertaken in pursuit of any clear vision of what a good primary system would look like. In many cases, these were changes implemented for short-term goals—to, for instance, block the candidacies of particular candidates or factions, or to aid a candidate with an appeal to particular types of voters. The evolution of different primary laws also reflects variation in political culture across the United States—states that have historically had weaker political parties, such as California, Alaska, or Washington, have experimented with open primaries, nonpartisan primaries, or other unorthodox rules. States which once had strong party machines, such as Ohio, Illinois, or Massachusetts, have tended to place more restrictions on who can vote in primaries or to require people to register as members of one party or the other.

Primary elections were an exciting innovation in the 1900s, 1910s, and 1920s. Researchers of the era explored many different features of the new laws, but they quickly lost interest. Between 1928 and the early 2000s, there were no book-length studies of American primaries, although there are some excellent studies of how primaries developed in the South, in New England, and in some individual states. This all has changed in the past twenty years. As scholars became alarmed about the growth of polarization, within Congress and among American voters, they began to raise many of the same arguments that were raised at the dawn of the twentieth century. Do primaries encourage polarization? Do extreme or demagogic candidates have an advantage? Are compromise-oriented politicians being replaced by amateurs?

In addition to historical studies by Alan Ware (2002) and John Reynolds (2006), several studies of contemporary primaries have been published in the past two decades, including work by many of the authors included in this volume. A very partial list of contributions to the literature on primaries of the past decade includes Shigeo Hirano and James Snyder's *Primary Elections in the United States* (2019), a history of primaries; Danielle Thomsen's *Opting out of Congress* (2017), an exploration of why moderate candidates do not run in primaries; Andrew Hall's *Who Wants to Run?* (2019), also a study of why moderates do not seek office; Hans Hassel's *The Party's Primary* (2018), a discussion of the role political parties play in choosing primary winners; and Sarah Anderson, Daniel Butler, and Laurel Harbridge-Yong's *Rejecting Compromise* (2020), a study of the effect of the threat of primaries on legislators. More recently, Mike Cowburn's *Party Transformation in Congressional Primaries* (2024) shows that primary candidates have increasingly behaved in more ideologically extreme ways in primaries despite the very limited evidence that primary voters themselves have become any different.

Many of the authors included in this volume have contributed to the new scholarship on primaries, and many of the chapters discuss new surveys or other data collection efforts. There is much that we now know about primaries that we didn't know a decade or two ago. Much of that knowledge is summarized below. We still do not agree, however, on how much primaries contribute to political polarization, extremism, or dysfunction. Nor is there a consensus on whether there is one superior alternative to the current system of primaries, or on what the roadmap would be to reform. As we shall see, this is in part because primary voters are difficult to study; it is hard to separate the effects of primaries on candidates from the effects of other changes in the political environment, in part because we have very few examples of what reforms look like in practice. This book seeks to advance our understanding of each of these things.

Contemporary Primary Elections

Contrary to the intuition of many people who work on Capitol Hill, a substantial number of political scientists believe that primaries are *not* a significant contributor to polarization and political dysfunction. As we detail in the previous section, most states have used primary elections to decide congressional nominees for well over a century, yet hyper-polarization and partisanship are more recent phenomena. Moreover, other scholars have convincingly argued that the rise of congressional partisanship around the turn of the twenty-first century was largely driven by strategic party elites (Lee 2016; Theriault 2013). Nonetheless, it could be the case that dynamics within primary elections have changed in recent decades, and that partisan primaries function as an independent force pushing elites to act more partisan and ideological than they would in an alternative institutional setting. Before we describe the contents of this book, we summarize the state of political science literature on primaries.

Primary Voters

Roughly twenty percent of the American electorate participates in non-presidential federal primary elections (Ferrer and Thorning 2023). Primary turnout has declined substantially over the past fifty years. These very low turnout rates are especially concerning given that the majority of nominees advance to an entirely uncompetitive general election contest. A very small share of Americans are meaningfully participating in electoral democracy, and this problem is more acute if primary voters are distinct from the broader electorate. Put differently, if primary voters were a representative sample of the voting eligible population, then presumably higher levels of turnout would not change electoral outcomes or governing behavior.

Are primary voters really that different from the general electorate? If so, how? Because primary voters are such a small percentage of the overall electorate, it has historically been very hard to study them, but the results we do have are surprisingly mixed. We do know that compared to the general electorate as a whole, primary voters are older, whiter, wealthier, and more educated (Kamarck and Podkul 2018). In short, the factors that make political participation more difficult for younger and more marginalized voters are especially pronounced in low-salience and awkwardly timed primary elections.

Unsurprisingly, we also know that people who identify as Democrats or Republicans are more likely to vote in primaries than independents. While independent and unaffiliated voters now represent a majority of the voting eligible population, they are grossly underrepresented in the primary electorate (Reilly, Salit, and Ali 2023; Macomber and Fisher 2024). Across twenty-two states, a total of 23.5 million independent voters are fully excluded from (presidential, and in many cases other federal and state) primary elections (Macomber and Fisher 2024). In other states, independents turnout at far lower rates than partisans for a number of reasons.

However, when researchers employ vote validation techniques, the policy attitudes of primary voters are very similar to the attitudes of co-partisan voters who only vote in the general election (Sides et al. 2020). It is not clear that co-partisan general election voters are the appropriate baseline with which to compare the primary electorate. Primary electorates may be more distinct from the general electorate as a whole (and not just other mainstream party identifiers) on ideology, policy preferences, and other key dimensions. In other words, are primary voters representative of the entire electorate when we consider independents and third party voters? The importance of this question has grown as independent voters have emerged as the dominant affiliation since 2010 (Jones 2024). Until recently, political scientists have largely dismissed independents as either "shadow partisans" or ideologically "innocent" Americans who know and care very little about politics. However, recent research finds that a significant share of independent voters are relatively informed, have a more balanced media diet, and thoughtfully reject the ideological, divisive, and uncompromising politics of the major parties (Reilly, Salit, and Ali 2023).

There are many other ways in which primary voters might be distinct from the general electorate other than descriptive characteristics or partisanship. We know little about whether primary voters are distinct from their co-partisans who do not turn out for primaries on other important non-ideological dimensions such as negative partisanship, conspiratorial thinking, distrust, and populism.

In short, the questions that have animated studies on primary voters are whether primary voters are distinctive, whether they have become more (or less) distinctive in recent years, and whether variations in their distinctiveness have anything to do with features of the elections themselves, such as the rules about who can vote and the choices voters are given.

Primary Candidates

A second well-established line of research pertains to how primary elections shape who runs for public office, who wins office, and how they behave in government. This is of course not possible to study without some understanding of the voters. Candidates succeed, and potential candidates choose to run, based on the electorate and their beliefs about the electorate.

Much of the research on candidacies has had to do with ideology and with candidates' choices about whether to run. It has been established in recent years that ideological moderates are increasingly less likely to run for public office in the first place (Hall 2019). There is evidence, as well, that many moderates in office are choosing to retire because of the increased ideological polarization of Congress and within the electorate (Thomsen 2017).

In large part, contemporary media and the nature of campaigning and governing make running for and holding public office especially undesirable jobs for moderates and pragmatists (Hall 2019). Beyond these factors, moderate prospective candidates (at least Republicans) also believe that they will perform worse in a primary election (Thomsen 2017). Is this belief well-founded? Do more ideological and partisan primary candidates outperform moderates in primary elections? While the motivations for primary challengers were historically diverse, recent competitive primary challengers disproportionately come from the ideological extreme (Boatright 2013; Barton 2022). Nevertheless, despite some salient examples, successful primary challengers from the ideological extreme remain rare (Boatright 2013). The incumbency advantage remains very strong, even in the era of "getting primaried."

The electoral advantage of extremism is more evident in open-seat primary elections. While political party organizations are sometimes able to clear the field for their preferred candidates in open-seat primaries, in recent cycles open-seat primaries have been more competitive (Hirano and Snyder 2019). Analysis on congressional elections held during the second half of the twentieth century finds that primary voters prefer more extreme candidates, and that candidates adjust accordingly (Brady, Hahn, and Pope 2007). More recent research on state legislative races finds that ideological extremism provides a sizable electoral benefit, and that benefit is greater than the benefit of ideological moderation in general elections (Rogers 2023).

These electoral dynamics appear to impact legislative behavior. In surveys, many state legislators admit to rejecting "half-loaf" compromises out of fear of being primaried by an ideological challenger (Anderson, Butler, and Harbridge-Yong 2020). Republican state legislators are nearly equally likely to say that they are more afraid of losing a primary than a general election, and about a fifth of Democrats are more worried about losing a primary (Skovron 2018). Perhaps more importantly, overall, twice as many state legislators believe that primary voters will punish them for their voting record than general election voters (Anderson, Butler, and Harbridge-Yong 2020).

While these dynamics may push some legislators to retire and some potential legislators not to run, those who remain may change their behavior. A number of earlier studies find no statistically significant effect of primaries on polarization in roll call voting (Ansolabehere et al. 2010; Hirano et al. 2010; Boatright 2013; McGhee et al. 2014). However, several recent studies do find an effect. Members of Congress who face an ideological primary challenge are more ideological or more partisan in their voting behavior (Jewitt and Treul 2014) and in their bill sponsorship (Barton 2022). Even the mere threat of an ideological primary challenge appears to dissuade members from cosponsoring with members from the opposing party (Barton 2022). Legislators are less partisan in the months after a primary election (Fowler 2024).

Political Parties

A longstanding concern about primaries is that they have the potential to weaken political party organizations. For the original proponents of primaries, this was the point, and this is the point for many advocates of open, nonpartisan, or top four primaries. Scholars disagree, however, on the merits of weakening parties and on the question of whether weakening parties will benefit voters. Writing about the democratization of the nomination process, prominent scholars warned that weaker political parties were more likely to be captured by well-organized and well-resourced interest groups (American Political Science Association 1950; Ranney 1975; Polsby 1983; Shafer 1983). However, despite the recent rise in ideological primary challenges, political party organizations maintain considerable control over the nomination process. The political parties almost always support (informally and indirectly, at least) incumbents, and despite some high-profile defeats, incumbents continue to win primaries at an extremely high rate (Boatright 2013). In open-seat contests, Hassell (2018) finds that the party establishments' preferred candidates win House primary elections at a rate of about sixty-seven percent, and Senate primaries at a rate of eighty percent. Influential interest groups and activists advance their policy demands by collaborating with party leaders and members, in a collective effort to win general elections (Cohen et al. 2008; Karol 2009; Masket 2011; Bawn et al. 2012; Schlozman 2015).

Nonetheless, more recent research suggests that outside groups are acquiring greater power independent of political party organizations, and, in fact, are increasingly using their growing power to challenge party organizations in primary elections. While the parties' preferred candidates still win in the majority of open-seat primary contests, the parties' success rate decreased during the 2010s. In the 2000s, Republicans' preferred candidates in open-seat primaries won about seventy-five percent of the time, and in the 2010s that their success rate dropped closer to nearly sixty percent. The success rate of the Democratic Party's preferred candidate fell from over ninety percent to less than eighty-five percent (Manento 2021). More recent empirical work finds that the weakening influence of political parties coincides with the growing influence and prominence of ideological donors and activist groups (Manento 2021; Oklobdzija 2024; Skocpol and Hertel-Fernandez 2016; Hertel-Fernandez, Skocpol, and Sclar 2018). However, the evidence in these studies does not suggest that reforms will reduce this problem. These findings suggest that we have entered a period characterized by a problematic combination of "weak parties and strong partisanship" (Azari 2016). The parties are increasingly unable to strategically control who represents the party and how those representatives behave in government. In the void of party influence, it may be that unrepresentative activist groups and donors are better able to exploit low salience and low turnout primary elections to advance their policy goals, sometimes at the expense of the political party to which they are aligned.

Alternatives to Partisan Primaries

One reform idea that has circulated for decades is to expand voter access to primaries. By definition, open partisan primaries, in which independent and unaffiliated voters are free to participate in any party's primary election, expand access. However, studies find that making partisan primaries more open only modestly boosts turnout (Ferrer and Thorning 2023; Micatka, Tolbert, and Boatright 2024) and has a negligible effect on polarization (McGhee et al. 2014).

By contrast, the evidence on open nonpartisan primaries is more promising. Nonpartisan primaries allow all voters, regardless of party affiliation, to participate in a single primary election where candidates from all parties compete against each other. Proponents argue that this approach encourages candidates to appeal to a broader electorate, fostering a more centrist and pragmatic approach to policymaking. By reducing the influence of ideological and partisan primary voters, donors, and activist groups, nonpartisan primaries can potentially produce candidates who are more representative of the broader population and better equipped to govern effectively (Troiano 2024).

Empirical studies examining the impact of nonpartisan primaries on polarization and governing dysfunction have produced mixed results. Early research on

Top-Two nonpartisan primaries found that this reform had minimal impact on polarization and the quality of governance (McGhee et al. 2014; Kousser et al. 2016; McGhee and Shor 2017; Drutman 2021). However, more recent research applying similar methods to more (and more current) data finds that Top-Two nonpartisan primaries have a statistically and substantively significant mitigating effect (Grose 2020; Barton 2023). Other studies find that nonpartisan primaries also result in better governance and societal outcomes (Barton 2022, 2023), and modestly increase descriptive diversity (Alvarez and Sinclair 2015; Centeno, Grose et al. 2021). In their comprehensive book on primary elections, Hirano and Synder (2019) assert that, unlike more open partisan primaries, the Top-Two system appears to have more substantial effects.

The strongest mitigating effects on polarization come from same-party general elections (Crosson 2021; Anderson et al. 2023). Consequently, we might expect a larger impact from Final Four/Five Voting (FFV) systems, in which four or five candidates advance, because the likelihood of same-party general elections increases with the number of nonpartisan primary candidates who advance to the general election (Gehl and Porter 2020; Lee 2022). Nonpartisan primaries that advance more than two candidates require ranked choice voting (RCV) if they are to ensure a majoritarian outcome. Although some opponents have expressed concerns that voters would find ranking candidates exceedingly difficult, research finds that voters are generally able to figure out RCV and prefer it once they have used the system (Drutman and Strano 2022).

Still, even if nonpartisan primaries do curb polarization, both political scientists and party leaders cite a deeper concern with nonpartisan primaries: such primaries, they say, weaken political parties. Such fears seem well-founded, if reformers themselves were to be believed: advocates of the Top Two framed the system as a means to undermine party organizations, which they identified as a source of polarization, gridlock, and dissatisfaction with politics.

However, recent research examining all House primaries from 2004 to 2018 finds that the preferred candidates of the extended party networks perform better (not worse) in nonpartisan primary elections. Compared to direct partisan primaries, parties may enjoy greater control under nonpartisan primaries. Party leaders appear better able to nominate competitive candidates who optimize the party's general election prospects in a radically open system in which all candidates compete directly against each other regardless of their party, and the entire electorate can determine nominees (Barton and Crosson 2024).

Outline of the Book

The research in this volume uses new data and theoretical frameworks and methodological innovations to advance the study of primary elections. The first section of this book considers the current state of primaries—how voters, candidates, and parties have behaved in recent years. In Chapter 2, Richard Barton and Carlo Macomber explore data from the new Primary Election Study, the first public opinion survey aimed at primary voters. Barton and Macomber compare Democratic and Republican primary voters to the general public. The Democratic and Republican primary electorates diverge from the general public on most policies issues, with Democratic primary voters slightly more closely aligned with the full electorate on policy. However, on attitudes towards government institutions (e. g. populism, liberalism, democracy), Republicans are significantly closer to the public. In Chapter 3, Raymond La Raja and Zachary Albert draw on their own survey work to show that Democratic primary voters support candidates who are willing to compromise but Republican primary voters do not. In Chapter 4, Caitlin Jewitt and Sarah Treul show that primary turnout is higher and voters look more like the public when competitive presidential primaries happen at the same time as congressional primaries. The subsequent two chapters discuss primary candidacies—one with an eye toward non-incumbents, and the other with a focus on incumbents. In Chapter 5, Mike Cowburn and Marius Sältzer describe their dataset on the characteristics of primary candidates, and show that primary reforms do not seem to change the types of candidates who run. In Chapter 6, Hayley Cohen explores the behavior of incumbents preparing for primaries; she shows that incumbents raise substantial sums of money shortly before candidate filing deadlines in order to deter potential challengers.

The second section of this book discusses recently implemented reforms. If primary elections do contribute to polarization and governing dysfunction, then what institutional responses can mitigate these problems? Proposals for changes to primary rules are as old as primaries themselves, but in the past decade several organizations, such as Unite America and Open Primaries, have made renewed calls for reform as a means of increasing voter choice and limiting polarization. Other, older groups such as Fair Vote have included primary rule changes as part of broader agendas for changes to American elections.

In this book we have sought to provide a range of perspectives on primary reforms and their effects on political parties. In Chapter 7, David Lublin, Glenn Wright, and Ben Reilly use an expert survey about Alaska legislative candidates, arguing that the new system influenced candidate behavior, leading successful candidates to take more moderate views on a range of issues. In Chapter 8,

Ryan Williamson and Ceili Fallon analyze election results in Alaska, showing that the reforms at least temporarily increased competition and the number of candidates running. Chapter 9, by Jeremy Gelman, Evan Pritsos, and Ben Reilly, uses a series of survey experiments to consider what the effects of establishing a Top-5/ RCV system in Nevada might have been. They show that moderates would have been advantaged but that minor party and independent candidates would likely have been shut out of the general election. In Chapter 10, Jesse Crosson offers a defense of Top-Two nonpartisan primaries, on the grounds that it increases turnout and competition and mitigates polarization.

While using distinct data and methods, all of the studies in these chapters find evidence that nonpartisan primaries—whether Top Two or Final Four or Final Five with ranked choice voting—benefit more moderate candidates. Williamson and Fallon provide the most mixed results on this polarization—they find that Final Four in Alaska only resulted in more moderate Republicans winning state legislative races, with no change among Democrats. However, the measure they use for candidate ideology, Adam Bonica's campaign finance scores, provide a constant ideal point over the course of an individual's career, and is thus less likely to capture immediate change after an institutional reform. By contrast, the expert assessments and student-coded campaign platforms used by Lublin, Wright, and Reilly indicate that Final Four had moderating effects among Republicans and Democrats.

That said, if one is concerned with political polarization, political dysfunction, political extremism, declining trust in government, demagoguery, populism, or any of the other ills that have been said to plague contemporary democracy, it is not necessarily the case that the range of reforms analyzed in this book are the only answers. While the history of changes in primary rules is quite old, the reform ideas discussed in the second part of this book do not exhaust all possible options. Many of these reforms are relatively recent, and it is by no means clear that those who care about primary elections over the next decade or two will simply try to build upon what has already been done. It is also not clear that the stated goals of the past decade's reform advocates are the only plausible goals that should be invoked in discussing changes to primary elections.

There may well be future work done on the relationship between different types of reforms. We know little, for instance, about the relationship between nonpartisan primaries and institutional reforms such as independent redistricting commissions, multimember districts, proportional representation, campaign finance reform, and fusion voting. Some studies of existing reforms suggest that there are tensions between them—for instance, Albert et al. (2024) caution that the establishment of new primary laws in Alaska may substantially increase political spending, thus perhaps disappointing proponents of campaign finance regulation. At the conference from which many of these papers were drawn, Spencer Overton argued that primary reforms that encourage moderation may well conflict with the goal of encouraging politicians to reach out to voters of color. In a Substack piece published after that conference, Seth Masket (2024) reviewed several of the chapters included here and argued that he saw three goals to the work in this book: increasing government effectiveness, empowering voters, and limiting the power of parties. Masket expressed some hesitation about the prospect that primary reforms could fulfill all of these goals.

Building on these concerns, the third section of this book contains six chapters that explore relatively untested ideas about changes to primary election laws. Each of these chapters seeks to situate ideas about primary elections within a broader democratic reform agenda, and to engage trade-offs such as those just mentioned. In Chapter 11, Hans Noel surveys the possible effects of reforms on political parties and contends that primary reformers should seek to strengthen parties, not to encourage moderation. In Chapter 12, Michael Ritter and Caroline Tolbert show that open primary rules can increase voter participation more when combined with voting by mail and other election administration reforms. In Chapter 13, Deb Otis and Rachel Hutchison, both of Fairvote, argue that changes to primary election laws should be pursued as part of a larger agenda—that primary reforms are best understood in conjunction with general election reforms such as proportional representation. In Chapter 14, Derek Monson of the Sutherland Institute cautions that those who advocate for primary reforms focus too much on how reforms might bring about the election outcomes they desire. Sutherland argues that reforms will be more broadly accepted if reformers focus on how primaries fit with the vision of democracy articulated in the *Federalist Papers*. In Chapter 15, Edward Foley proposes that it would be more democratic if primary elections were conducted as round robin tournaments. Finally, in Chapter 16, Robert Boatright and Caroline Tolbert make the case that primary turnout would increase dramatically were we to consolidate the dates of primaries to create a single National Primary Day. All of these proposals are relatively untested but might fuel future efforts to modify primaries.

Closing Thoughts

Finally, it is important to pause to discuss the timing of this book and the current period of upheaval in American politics. This manuscript was submitted to our publisher in May 2025, barely over one hundred days into Donald Trump's second presidential term. At this moment it is evident to us, as it is to many Americans, that the second Trump presidency promises to profoundly disrupt the American political system. This has two implications for how this work is read. On the one hand, it is evident that the politics of contemporary congressional primaries have influenced how Congress responds to President Trump. Already, there have been news accounts of the unwillingness of Republican members of Congress to vote against any of Trump's agenda items or cabinet nominations because of their fear of facing a primary challenger. In a few instances, prominent senators have been publicly threatened with challenges over votes on whether to confirm Trump's nominees, and presidential consigliere Elon Musk announced his willingness to spend substantial amounts of money in the 2026 Republican primaries. On the Democratic side, Senate Minority Leader Charles Schumer also encountered threats of a primary challenge following his decision not to block a continuing resolution in March 2025. Some other senior Democrats encountered threats about primary challenges for not being vigorous enough in opposing Trump, and as of this writing some senior Democrats and Republicans who were anticipating primary opponents have already announced their plans to retire in 2026. These cases provided vivid evidence that congressional decision-making was being driven by anticipation of primary, not general election, competition. They may have made it more urgent to address primary election reforms.

On the other hand, much of the political reform agenda in America over the past two decades has been driven by the priorities of a small set of party activists and donors. Much of the research on political reform has been shaped by a small number of philanthropic foundations. These activists and organizations may well change their priorities in the upcoming years in response to the actions of the Trump Administration. To put matters bluntly, there are many new and immediate problems for those concerned with democracy, there may be some funders who are intimidated about spending money on political reform causes at all, and federal funding for political science research may well dry up entirely. Those who are reading this book may well have the ability to judge whether the concerns raised here seem as pressing as they did when these chapters were written. We would contend, however, that the history of primary elections suggests that primary election reform has been a perennial concern. The research collected here suggests that we know much more about primary elections than at any other point in American history, and we are at a point where we can use this knowledge to improve our nation's candidate selection methods if we so choose.

References

Abramowitz, Alan. 2011. *The Disappearing Center: Engaged citizens, Polarization, and American Democracy.* Yale University Press.

Albert, Zachary, Robert G. Boatright, Lane Cuthbert, Adam Eichen, Wouter van Erve, Raymond J. La Raja, and Meredith Rolfe. 2024. "Election reform and campaign finance: Did Alaska's top 4 nonpartisan primaries and ranked-choice general elections affect political spending?" *Social Science Quarterly* 105: 1668–1690

Alvarez, R. Michael, and J. Andrew Sinclair. 2015. *Nonpartisan Primary Election Reform: Mitigating Mischief.* Cambridge University Press.

American Political Science Association, Committee on Political Parties. 1950. "Toward a More Responsible Two-Party System." American Political Science Review 44 (3): Part 2 (Supplement).

Anderson, Sarah E., Daniel M. Butler, and Laurel Harbridge-Yong. 2020. *Rejecting Compromise: Legislators' Fear of Primary Voters.* Cambridge University Press.

Anderson, Sarah. E., Daniel M. Butler, Laurel Harbridge-Yong, and Renae Marshall. 2023. "Top-Four Primaries Help Moderate Candidates via Crossover Voting: The Case of the 2022 Alaska Election Reforms." In *The Forum* 21 (1). De Gruyter.

Ansolabehere, Stephen, John Mark Hansen, Shigeo Hirano, and James M. Snyder, Jr. 2010. "More Democracy: The Direct Primary and Competition in U.S. House Elections." *Studies in American Political Development* 24 (2): 190–205.

Azari, Julia. 2016. "Weak Parties and Strong Partisanship are a Bad Combination." *Vox*, November 3. www.vox.com/mischiefs-of-faction/2016/11/3/13512362/weak-parties-strong-partisanship-bad-combination.

Barton, Richard, and Jesse Crosson. 2024. "Party Power in Nonpartisan Primaries." Paper prepared for the Annual Meeting of the Midwest Political Science Association, April 4–8. drive.google.com/file/d/1scy3ERnUmruzmjfRUuIxqkEyOhFLjUAV/view.

Barton, Richard. 2022. *Louisiana's Long-Term Election Experiment: How Eliminating Partisan Primaries Improved Governance and Reduced Polarization.* Unite America Institute. docsend.com/view/5ckehrx8vxdm95me.

Barton, Richard. 2023. "The Primary Threat: How the Surge of Ideological Challengers is Exacerbating Partisan Polarization." *Party Politics* 29 (2): 248–259.

Barton, Richard. 2023. *California's Top-Two Primary: The Effects on Electoral Politics and Governance.* Unite America Institute. docsend.com/view/hnmec525w7bzy48p.

Bawn, Katherine, Martin Cohen, David Karol, Seth Masket, Hans Noel, and John Zaller. 2012. "A Theory of Political Parties: Groups, Policy Demands and Nominations in American Politics." *Perspectives on Politics* 10 (3): 571–597.

Boatright, Robert G. 2013. *Getting Primaried.* University of Michigan Press.

Boatright, Robert G. 2024. *Reform or Retrenchment? A Century of Efforts to Fix Primary Elections.* Oxford University Press.

Brady, David W., Hahrie Han, and Jeremy C. Pope. 2007. "Primary Elections and Candidate Ideology: Out of Step with the Primary Electorate?" *Legislative Studies Quarterly* 32 (1): 79–105.

Butler, Daniel M., Laurel Harbridge-Yong, and Sarah E. Anderson. 2020. *Rejecting Compromise: Legislators' Fear of Primary Voters.* Cambridge University Press.

Centeno, Raquel, Christian R. Grose, Nancy Hernandez, and Kayla Wolf. 2021. "The Demobilizing Effect of Primary Electoral Institutions on Voters of Color." papers.ssrn.com/sol3/papers.cfm?abstract_id=3831739.

Cohen, Martin, David Karol, Hans Noel, and John Zaller. 2008. *The Party Decides: Presidential Nominations Before and After Reform.* University of Chicago Press.

Cowburn, Mike. 2024. *Party Transformation in Congressional Primaries.* Cambridge University Press.

Crosson, Jesse. "Extreme districts, moderate winners: Same-party challenges, and deterrence in top-two primaries." *Political Science Research and Methods* 9 (3): 532–548.

Drutman, Lee. 2021. "What we know about Congressional primaries and Congressional Primary Reform." https://www.newamerica.org/political-reform/reports/what-we-know-about-congressional-primaries-and-congressional-primary-reform/

Drutman, Lee, and Maresa Strano. 2022. *Evaluating the Effects of Ranked-Choice Voting.* New America. https://www.newamerica.org/political-reform/reports/evaluating-the-effects-of-ranked-choice-voting/introduction-lee-drutman-and-maresa-strano/

Ferrer, Joshua, and Michael Thorning 2023. *2022 Primary Turnout: Trends and Lessons for Boosting Participation.* Bipartisan Policy Center.

Fiorina, Morris P., Samuel J. Abrams, and Jeremy C. Pope. 2004. *Culture War?: The Myth of a Polarized America.* Longman.

Ford, Henry Jones. 1909. "The Direct Primary." *North American Review* 190 (644): 1–14.

Fowler, Anthony, Seth J. Hill, Jeffrey B. Lewis, Christopher Tausanovitch, Lynn Vavreck, and Christopher Warshaw. 2023. "Moderates." *American Political Science Review* 117 (2): 643–660.

Fowler, Anthony. 2024. "Partisan Constituencies and Congressional *Polarization." Journal of Political Institutions and Political Economy* 5 (3): 335–361.

Gehl, Katherine M., and Michael E. Porter. 2020. *The Politics Industry: How Political Innovation Can Break Partisan Gridlock and Save Our Democracy.* Harvard Business Review Press.

Grose, Christian R. 2020. "Reducing legislative polarization: Top-two and open primaries are associated with more moderate legislators." *Journal of Political Institutions and Political Economy* 1 (2). https://doi.org/10.1561/113.00000012.

Hall, Andrew B. 2019. *Who wants to run?: How the Devaluing of Political Office Drives Polarization.* The University of Chicago Press.

Hassell, Hans. J. G. 2018. *The Party's Primary: Control of Congressional Nominations.* Cambridge University Press.

Hertel-Fernandez Alexander, Theda Skocpol, and Jason Sclar. 2018. "When Political Mega-Donors Join Forces: How the Koch Network and the Democracy Alliance Influence Organized U.S. Politics on the Right and Left." *Studies in American Political Development* 32 (2): 127–165.

Hirano, Shigeo, James M. Snyder Jr., Stephen D. Ansolabehere, and John M. Hansen. 2010. "Primary elections and partisan polarization in the U.S. Congress." *Quarterly Journal of Political Science* 5 (2): 169–191.

Hirano, Shigeo, and James M. Snyder, Jr. 2019. *Primary Elections in the United States.* Cambridge University Press.

Jewitt, Caitlin E., and Sarah A. Treul. 2014. "Competitive Primaries and Party Division in Congressional Elections." *Electoral Studies* 35 (1): 140–149.

Jones, Jeffrey M. 2024. "Independent Party ID tied for high; Democratic ID at New Low." *Gallup.* January 12. news.gallup.com/poll/548459/independent-party-tied-high-democratic-new-low.aspx.

Kamarck, Elaine, and Alexander R. Podkul. 2018. "The 2018 Primaries Project: The Demographics of Primary Voters." Brookings Institute. www.brookings.edu/articles/the-2018-primaries-project-the-demographics-of-primary-voters/.

Karol, David. 2009. *Party Position Change in American Politics.* Cambridge University Press.

Kousser, Thad, Scott Lucas, Seth Masket, and Eric McGhee. 2015. "Kingmakers or Cheerleaders? Party Power and the Causal Effects of Endorsements." *Political Research Quarterly* 68 (3): 443–456.

Lee, Frances E. 2016. *Insecure Majorities: Congress and the Perpetual Campaign.* University of Chicago Press.

Lee, Jeannette. 2022. "Why Alaska's Top-Four Open Primaries are Better Than Top-Two." Sightline Institute.

Macomber, Carlo, and Tyler Fisher. 2024. Not Invited to the Party Primary. Unite America. www.uniteamerica.org/articles/new-research-not-invited-to-the-party-primary

Manento, Cory. 2019. "Party Crashers: Interest Groups as a Latent Threat to Party Networks in Congressional Primaries. *Party Politics* 27 (1): 137–148.

Masket, Seth E. 2024. "The Reformers' Agenda." *Tusk.* May 9. smotus.substack.com/p/the-reformers-agenda.

Masket, Seth. E. 2011. *No Middle Ground: How Informal Party Organizations Control Nominations and Polarize Legislatures.* University of Michigan Press.

McGhee, Eric, and Boris Shor. 2017. "Has the top two primary elected more moderates? *Perspectives on Politics* 15 (4): 1053–1066.

McGhee, Eric, Seth Masket, Boris Shor, Steven Rogers, and Nolan McCarty. 2024. "A primary cause of partisanship? Nomination systems and legislator ideology." *American Journal of Political Science* 58 (2): 337–351.

Merriam, Charles, and Louise Overacker. 1928. *Primary Elections.* University of Chicago Press.

Micatka, Nathan K., Caroline J. Tolbert, and Robert G. Boatright. 2024. "All Candidate Primaries, Open Primaries, and Voter Turnout." *Journal of Political Institutions and Political Economy* 5 (3): 363–385.

Oklobdzija, Stan. 2024. "Dark Parties: Unveiling Nonparty Communities in American Political Campaigns." *American Political Science Review* 118 (1): 401–422.

Polsby, Nelson. 1983. *Consequences of Party Reform.* Oxford University Press.

Ranney, J. Austin. 1975. *Curing the Mischiefs of Faction.* University of California Press.

Reilly, Thom, Jacqueline Salit, and Omar Ali. 2023. *The Independent Voter.* Routledge.

Reynolds, John F. 2006. *The Demise of the American Convention System, 1880–1911.* Cambridge University Press.

Rogers, Steven. 2023. *Accountability in State Legislatures.* University of Chicago Press.

Schlozman, Daniel. 2015. *When Movements Anchor Parties: Electoral Alignments in American History.* Princeton University Press.

Shafer, Byron E. 1983. *Quiet Revolution: The Struggle for the Democratic Party and the Shaping of Post-Reform Politics.* Russell Sage Foundation.

Sides, John, Christopher Tausanovitch, Lynn Vavreck, and Christopher Warshaw. 2020. "On the Representativeness of Primary Electorates." *British Journal of Political Science* 50 (2): 677–685.

Skocpol, Theda, and Alexander Hertel-Fernandez. 2016. "The Koch Network and Republican Party Extremism." *Perspectives on Politics* 14 (3): 681–699.

Skovron, Christopher. 2019. "What Politicians Believe About Electoral Accountability." SSRN. papers.ssrn.com/sol3/papers.cfm?abstract_id=3309906.

Taft, William Howard. 1922. *Liberty Under Law.* Yale University Press.

Theriault, Sean M. 2013. *The Gingrich Senators: The Roots of Partisan Warfare in Congress.* Oxford University Press.

Thomsen, Danielle M. 2017. *Opting Out of Congress: Partisan Polarization and the Decline of Moderate Candidates.* Cambridge University Press.

Troiano, Nick. 2024. *The Primary Solution: Rescuing Our Democracy from the Fringes.* Simon & Schuster.

Ware, Alan. 2002. *The American Direct Primary: Party Institutionalization and Transformation in the North.* Cambridge University Press.

Part I: **Contemporary Primary Elections**

Richard Barton and Carlo Macomber

Chapter 2
How Distinct are Primary Voters? Insights from the 2024 Primary Election Survey

Abstract: This chapter examines the distinctiveness of primary electorates using original survey data from the 2024 Primary Election Survey in three states. We find that when analyzed separately, Democratic and Republican primary electorates are unrepresentative of the general public on most policy issues. Republican primary voters show particular extremism on immigration policy, while both parties significantly deviate from public preferences on EPA funding, minimum wage, and abortion. Beyond traditional ideology, Democratic primary voters exhibit less conspiratorial thinking, populism, and openness to political violence than Republican voters, while showing stronger commitment to democratic liberalism. Notably, the general public aligns more closely with Republican primary voters on these non-policy dimensions, suggesting that Democratic primary voters are uniquely detached from broader public sentiment regarding institutional trust. Our findings indicate that partisan primary electorates may contribute to polarization, particularly in safe districts where primary elections effectively determine representation.

Despite their crucial role in American democracy, we know surprisingly little about the distinctiveness of primary voters. Extant research on the ideological distinctiveness of primary voters is mixed. Moreover, scholars pay less attention to how primary electorates vary in their support for democratic institutions, trust in government, and acceptance of political violence. Are primary voters, compared to the general electorate, distinctively populist or conspiratorial, or less committed to democratic liberalism? If so, partisan primary elections (and primary voters in particular) may contribute to the changing attitudes and beliefs among elected officials.

In this chapter, we present new evidence on the attitudinal distinctiveness of primary voters using original survey data collected during the 2024 primary elections in California, Michigan, and Nevada. We find little evidence that primary voters, in the aggregate, are more extreme than general elections voters. However, as we argue below, this comparison provides limited insight, since in most states Democratic and Republican primary voters function as two distinct electorates.

Rather than simply comparing primary voters to general election voters, we argue that examining Democratic and Republican primary electorates separately provides deeper insight into how nomination contests may contribute to ideological polarization and democratic backsliding. On most issues, we find that the partisan primary electorates are highly unrepresentative of the general public. In particular, we find that Republican primary voters are highly extreme and misaligned with the general public on immigration policy. Moreover, both parties deviate from the general public considerably on EPA funding, the federal minimum wage, and abortion policy.

We also find compelling evidence that Democratic and Republican primary voters are systematically distinct in their political attitudes beyond traditional left-right ideology. We find that Democratic primary voters are significantly less conspiratorial, less populist, less open to political violence, and more committed to the principles of democratic liberalism than Republican primary voters.

Moreover, and most interestingly, Democratic primary voters (more so than Republicans) are especially distinctive from the general public in their non-policy political attitudes. That is, on the whole, members of the broader electorate who do not participate in primary elections share Republican primary voters' distrust of and cynicism about elites and institutions, and they are similarly open to more aggressive and unorthodox reactions against liberal democracy. While some will interpret these findings to suggest that Democratic primary voters are more moderate in these non-ideological attitudinal dimensions, they also appear more out of touch with broader public sentiment.

What We Know About Primary Voters

During the current era of hyperpolarization in American politics, many political observers have offered an array of causal explanations for the current predicament. One such theory is that the subset of voters who participate in primary elections (the "primary electorate") holds more ideologically extreme views than the much larger group of voters who participate in general elections. Indeed, the primary electorate is undoubtedly a small minority of the general public, with voter participation averaging around twenty percent of eligible voters in recent midterm elections (Ferrer and Thorning 2023).

If the primary electorate, despite its size, is representative of the broader pool of voters, candidates that reflect the views of most voters should reach the general election and win office. On the other hand, if the voters selecting the dominant party's candidates hold more extreme views than the broader voting public, then primary elections may distort representation.

Concerns about the effectiveness of primary elections as a nomination procedure and the representativeness of primary electorates are not new. For example, in 1956, V.O. Key Jr. worried that "the most improbable sorts of characters" could potentially serve in office after winning a party's nomination in a primary (Key 1956, 166). However, early research that analyzed the 1976 and 1980 elections failed to find evidence that presidential primary voters were more extreme than their co-partisans who voted in the general election (Geer 1988; Norrander 1989).

But much has changed about American politics since 1980, perhaps most notably the increasingly distinct ideologies of the two major parties. As the parties sort, has the ideological makeup of primary voters shifted away from that of general election voters? The relative power of primary electorates in determining who serves in office has grown, as well. The number of districts that are "safe" for either the Democrats or Republicans has increased considerably in recent years (Wasserman 2023). In safe districts, the primary election is "the only game in town," effectively granting the primary electorate of the dominant party the ability to choose the district's representative. In 2024, eighty-seven percent of congressional districts were uncompetitive, and collectively the primary voters who determined representatives in these districts comprised a mere seven percent of the American electorate (Unite America, 2024). Has the growing power of primary electorates in safe districts distorted representation in legislative bodies?

Recent research on the representativeness of primary voters is fairly mixed. Studies that analyze survey data from a single election cycle and rely on respondents to self-report their participation in primary and general elections have found evidence that primary electorates are more ideologically extreme than general election voters who did not vote in the primary (Jacobson 2012; McDonald and Merivaki 2015). Hill (2015) builds on prior research by using vote validation techniques rather than relying on self-reported turnout and by incorporating both 2010 and 2012 CCES data. Employing a hierarchical model of policy positions, Hill finds significant ideological differences between a party's primary voters and their co-partisans who do not participate in primaries, ultimately concluding that primary electorates are more extreme.

However, the most recent and comprehensive study on this subject pushes back on these findings. Sides et al. (2020) used validated vote data and analyzed findings from five surveys that cover four election cycles (2008–2014). The broad dataset not only ensured a larger sample size that is not constrained by the idiosyncrasies of a single election, but it also ensured the inclusion of competitive congressional and presidential primaries for both major parties. Sides et al. (2020) compared primary voters to two sets of co-partisans: voters who identify with the party or who voted for the party's candidate in the presidential election, and voters who identify with the party and voted in the general election but not the primary. Ultimately, the authors found that primary voters are not demographically distinct or ideologically extreme compared to either of the above groups of co-partisans. The only substantial difference was that primary voters reported more interest in politics. These findings held for both presidential and midterm elections, and they also held across different types of partisan primaries (i.e., closed, semi-closed, and open).

Given these findings, and the polarized and extreme nature of Congress and many state legislatures across the country, it would seem to follow that the electorate as a whole must be quite ideologically extreme. The literature, however, tends to find that a considerable share of Americans hold moderate views or, at least, a mixture of liberal and conservative views. For example, Fowler et al. (2023) found that "a large proportion of the American public is neither consistently liberal nor consistently conservative," and they estimated that many of those voters who report such views "hold genuine views in the middle of the same dimension of policy ideology that explains the views of consistent liberals and consistent conservatives."

With high levels of polarization and ideological extremity among elected officials, it is difficult to reconcile the findings of Sides et al. (2020) and Fowler et al. (2023). First, since the findings of Sides et al. rely on surveys covering 2008–2014, it is possible that primary (and/or general) electorates have changed in the past decade and are now distinct and more extreme. Second, it is possible that primary voters are distinct from their co-partisans on important non-ideological dimensions, such as negative partisanship, conspiratorial thinking, distrust, and populism. Third, it is unclear that co-partisan general election voters are the appropriate baseline with which to compare the primary electorate (as Sides et al. do). Primary electorates may be more distinct from the general electorate as a whole (and not just other co-partisans) on ideology, policy preferences, and other key dimensions. Are primary voters representative of the electorate when compared to a broader group that includes the growing share of voters who do not identify with the major parties (Jones 2024)?

In democratic theory, the median voter in the decisive election should determine representation, ideally reflecting the preferences of the median voter in the overall electorate. However, given that the vast majority districts are "safe" and general elections are overwhelmingly uncompetitive, the primary election of the dominant party is, in effect, the most commonly decisive contest that determines who serves in office. This raises the possibility that the median voter in a partisan primary, rather than the median voter in the overall electorate, is driving governance decisions and distorting representation. Our analysis examines whether there are meaningful differences between median primary voters and median general election voters. If no significant differences exist, then we might reasonably conclude that primary voters do not distort representation—or, put differently, if primary elections distort representation, it is not because primary voters are systematically distinct from the broader public. However, if substantial differences are found, this presents the possibility that primary voters contribute to misrepresentation. In this case, a critical follow-up question is whether polarization among primary voters corresponds to polarization among elected officials. If the behavior of legislators reflects the unrepresentative attitudes of their co-partisan primary voters, then this suggests that primary election rules exacerbate polarization and governing dysfunction.

Data and Methods

In this chapter, we analyze data from an original public opinion survey of voters. Our survey was part of the Primary Election Survey (PES) organized by scholars Sarah Anderson, Laurel Harbridge-Yong, and Daniel Butler. The purpose of the PES is to better understand the primary electorate by oversampling likely primary voters in a handful of strategically selected states. For comparative purposes, the PES also samples non-primary voters in these states.

The inaugural PES surveyed participants during the weeks immediately preceding the 2024 congressional primary elections in California, Nevada, and Michigan. These states were selected because each contained competitive U.S. Senate elections, and altogether these states provide variability in primary election rules. California uses a top-two all-candidate primary system. The seat was open and multiple viable Democrats (e.g., Adam Schiff, Katie Porter, Barbara Lee) sought office, which set up a competitive primary in which all voters could participate. Nevada has a closed partisan primary system in which only voters registered with a political party can participate. While incumbent Democrat Senator Jacky Rosen did not face a credible primary challenge, the Republican primary was competitive. Michigan has an open partisan primary system; voters in the state do not register with a party affiliation, and every registered voter can choose to vote in any one party's primary. The U.S. Senate seat was open, and both parties' primaries had multiple candidates on the ballot.

We surveyed 615 voters from Michigan, 574 from California, and 405 from Nevada. The primary voters in our study are a representative sample of the primary electorate in a given state. The PES oversamples primary voters to gain more information about this population. Primary voters compromise roughly seventy-five percent of our sample. We use general population weights to estimate findings for the general electorate.

To identify likely primary and general election voters in the sample, we employed a conservative coding approach that reflects established research practices on voter turnout. For primary election participation, we coded respondents as likely voters only if they selected "10 (Definitely will vote)" on a 1–10 scale measuring their likelihood of voting in the upcoming primary election. For general election participation, we adopted a slightly more inclusive approach, coding respondents as likely voters if they selected either "10 (Definitely will vote)" or "9" on a similar scale measuring their likelihood of voting in the November general election. This coding strategy reflects the well-documented phenomenon that survey respondents tend to overreport their likelihood of voting (Silver et al. 1986; Rogers and Aida 2014), and thus using only the highest response categories helps identify those most likely to turn out. The more stringent criterion for primary election voting acknowledges the consistently lower turnout rates in primary elections compared to general elections, while the inclusion of both 9 and 10 responses for general election voting reflects the higher baseline turnout in these contests.[1]

As a simple validity check, in Table 2.1 we compare the estimated primary and general election turnout using the responses to the primary and general election participating questions described above, as well as the population weights. The alignment with actual voter turnout data from the 2024 election gives us confidence in the representativeness of the PES sample, the validity of responses to the primary and general election participation questions, and the accuracy of its weighting scheme.

Table 2.1: PES estimated and actual election turnout by state.

	Primary Turnout (%)		General Turnout (%)	
State	PES Estimate	Actual	PES Estimate	Actual
California	33.0	28.0	61.3	60.3
Michigan	24.3	24.0	68.7	74.7
Nevada	17.1	14.0	53.6	72.8

The PES slightly overestimates primary turnout in California and Nevada, and is remarkably close for Michigan. Modest overestimations in some cases are consistent with well-documented social desirability bias, where respondents overreport their likelihood of voting, particularly in low-turnout elections. Despite this, the

---

1 The results that follow do not significantly change if we lower or raise the threshold for determining a likely primary or general election voter.

PES estimates provide a reliable approximation of primary turnout, indicating that the survey design and weights capture the primary electorate effectively.

If the primary electorate as a whole is ideationally distinct from the general public, such distinctions might be a source of elite polarization and misrepresentation. However, the ideational distinctiveness of the entire primary electorate, relative to the general population, might not be the most important comparison. Indeed, in most legislative districts, it is not the entire primary electorate that determines who serves in office but exclusively primary voters in the district's dominant party. Since the vast majority of congressional and state legislative districts are uncompetitive in the general election, and only the electorate of the dominant party truly determines outcomes, it is worth analyzing the extent to which Democratic primary voters and Republican primary voters are individually distinct from the general public.

Consequently, in the analysis below, we summarize the responses from Democratic primary voters and Republican primary voters separately, and compare these groups to each other and the general public in that state.

The Distribution of Policy Preferences Across Electorates

We asked participants a series of policy-specific questions to compare the ideology of primary voters to the general public. We include four questions on economic and administrative issues that were salient in 2024: corporate taxation, Social Security funding, funding for the Environmental Protection Agency (EPA), and the federal minimum wage. We also include three questions on divisive cultural issues: immigration, abortion, and gun control.

These questions, which are borrowed from Fowler et al. (2023), are designed to enable respondents to select "extreme" answer choices on either side of the ideological spectrum. Rather than offering incrementally spaced ordinal response options, each question is structured to capture true ideological extremity by providing dramatically different policy alternatives anchored around the status quo.

For example, on corporate taxation, rather than offering options that move in regular five or ten percentage point increments from the current twenty-one percent rate, the question presents respondents with stark alternatives: "A big increase to forty percent" on one extreme and "A big decrease to five percent" on the other. We use a similar approach for the other policy areas. These large jumps in the response options allow us to clearly identify respondents who support the most extreme policy changes. This approach also addresses the potential problem of ceiling effects, whereby many respondents may cluster at the ends of an incremental scale. If, for example, the corporate tax question only offered options up to thirty percent at the high end, we might find many Democratic primary voters selecting this highest available option even though they would prefer an even higher rate, which may compress the observed ideological distribution and mask true differences between Democratic primary and general election voters.

This measurement approach improves upon traditional binary agree/disagree questions in several ways. First, by anchoring each question with the current policy status quo and offering multiple reform options in both liberal and conservative directions, it allows respondents to express not just the direction but also the intensity of their policy preferences. Second, the response options that deviate considerably from the status quo enable identification of truly extreme positions.

Figure 2.1 displays the full distribution of responses from participants in Michigan. The histograms display the proportion of respondents from each electorate group (Democratic primary voters, Republican primary voters, and the general public) who selected each answer choice. We present results from Michigan since it is the only state in our sample with open partisan primaries, making it the "midpoint" of our three states in terms of openness of the primary system. The distributions are strikingly similar in Nevada and California.[2]

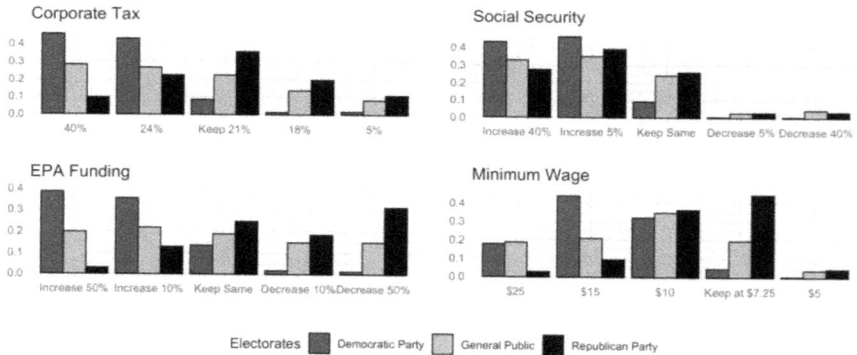

Figure 2.1: Proportion of economic/administrative policy positions by Michigan electorates.

As one might expect, Democratic and Republican primary voters are deeply polarized on many issues. The median and modal Democratic primary voter wants to

---

2 In California, which uses open, all-candidate primaries, we asked respondents which party primary they would have voted in if it had been a partisan primary. We treat these voters as the partisan primary electorate in California.

increase the federal minimum wage to $15 per hour, while the median and modal Republican primary voter wants it to remain at $7.25. The primary electorate is the most polarized on EPA funding, with the plurality of Democratic primary voters preferring a massive fifty percent increase in funding, and the median Democrat preferring a ten percent increase, while Republican primary voters prefer the mirror opposite (a plurality supports a fifty percent cut, and the median a ten percent cut). Meanwhile, the median member of the general public prefers a more modest increase in the minimum wage to $10 per hour, and to maintain the EPA's current funding level.

On other issues, Democratic and Republican primary voters are more closely aligned. The plurality of Democrats supports a massive increase in the federal corporate tax rate, to forty percent, while the plurality of Republicans would prefer to keep it at twenty-one percent. The median Democrat and median Republican are less polarized, with the former preferring a corporate tax rate of twenty-four percent and the latter twenty-one percent. The median member of the general public shares the median Democrat's preference for a rate of twenty-one percent.

Moreover, a large majority of Democratic and Republican primary voters alike support increasing social security—although the plurality of Democratic primary voters supports a drastic forty percent increase, while the plurality of Republican primary voters prefers a more modest ten percent increase. The general public is more closely aligned to Republican primary voters on this issue.

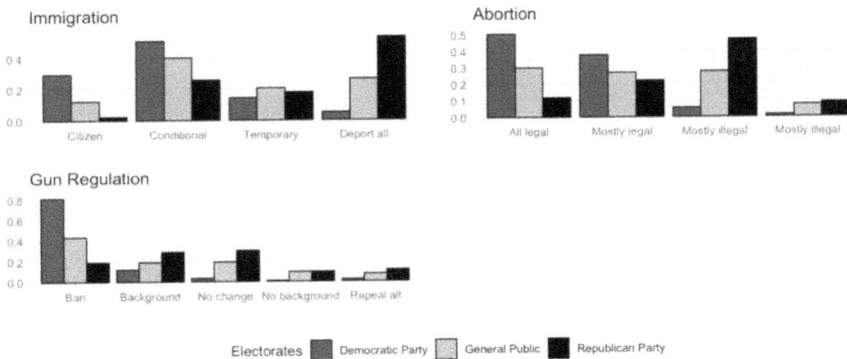

Figure 2.2: Proportion of social policy positions by Michigan electorates.

Figure 2.2 displays results on cultural issues across each electorate. On immigration policy, a near majority of Republican primary voters selected the very conservative policy option to immediately deport all undocumented immigrants, while eighty percent of Democratic primary voters selected the liberal or very liberal policy options. The general public, by contrast, is considerably more moderate on immigration but more closely aligned to Democratic primary voters. The median and modal response from Democratic primary voters and the general public was that undocumented immigrants should be granted a conditional pathway to citizenship.

On abortion, Democratic and Republican primary voters are similarly polarized, but in this case, the majority of Democrats (not the Republicans) prefer the most extreme policy option. The general public supports more nuanced (or conditional) abortion policy. Both primary electorates deviate roughly equally from the median general election voter on this issue.

Democratic and Republican primary voters appear less polarized than one might expect on gun policy. The vast majority (over eighty percent) of Democratic primary voters supports the most liberal option of federal mandatory background checks and an assault weapons ban. The median (and modal) Republican primary voter prefers to maintain the status quo, rather than further entrenching federal gun regulations. The median member of the general public supports mandatory background checks without an assault weapons ban.

Altogether, the primary electorates are much more deeply polarized than the general public on most (but not all) policy questions. The distinctiveness of the primary electorates on key policy questions, combined with the reality that general elections are predictively and consistently uncompetitive in most districts, may contribute to extremism and misrepresentation in government. To the extent that candidates and legislators cater to the median primary voter, the findings here suggest that this tendency may incentivize them to take positions on many issues (i.e. minimum wage, environmental protection, immigration, abortion, and gun control) that deviate from the preferences of the general public. On other issues (i.e. corporate taxation and social security), primary voters are less polarized, and in particular Republican efforts to reduce corporate taxes and cut social security spending do not reflect the preferences of the median Republican primary voters.

Defining Concepts Beyond Ideology

The PES also included questions that allow for comparisons between primary voters and the general public on concepts beyond ideology and policy preferences. These concepts include support for i) conspiracist thinking; ii) populism; iii) political violence; iv) democratic principles; and v) support for liberalism or liberal democratic institutions.

Conspiracist thinking, defined as the tendency to explain significant political and social events as the product of secret plots by powerful malevolent actors, has emerged as an important force in contemporary American politics (Uscinski and Parent 2014; Oliver and Wood 2014). Some scholars have suggested that primary voters may be particularly susceptible to conspiracist narratives, as these voters tend to be more engaged with political content on social media where conspiracy theories often flourish (Bail et al. 2020).

Populism, characterized by anti-elite sentiment and claims to represent "the true will of the people," has become increasingly prominent in American politics (Müller 2016; Oliver and Rahn 2016). Primary electorates may be especially drawn to populist appeals, as these voters often express stronger ideological views and greater dissatisfaction with political institutions than general election voters.

Support for political violence represents a concerning trend in American democracy, with recent research documenting rising acceptance of violence to achieve political goals (Kalmoe and Mason 2022). Given that primary voters tend to hold stronger partisan identities and express more extreme ideological views than general election voters, they may be more likely to justify political violence.

Democratic support, or commitment to democratic principles and processes even when they conflict with partisan interests, is fundamental to democratic stability (Dahl 1971; Levitsky and Ziblatt 2018). Primary voters' strong partisan attachments and ideological views may make them less willing to prioritize democratic processes over preferred outcomes.

Liberal democracy requires not just majority rule but also institutional constraints on power and protection of basic rights (Diamond 1999). Primary voters' tendency toward ideological extremity may correspond with weaker support for liberal democratic institutions that limit majority power.

Operationalization and Analysis of Non-ideological Measures

We constructed indices to measure each of the five non-ideological concepts defined above. The conspiratorial thinking index uses four questions that assess respondents' beliefs about hidden power structures and secret control over political events. The questions probe whether respondents believe "a few people will always run things" despite democratic structures, whether the true power-holders are unknown to voters, whether major events like wars and elections are controlled by secretive groups working against the public interest, and whether people's lives are broadly controlled by "plots hatched in secret places." Responses to each item were coded on a five-point scale from 0 (strongly disagree) to 4 (strongly agree). The final index sums responses across all four items, creating a scale ranging from 0 to 16, with higher values indicating stronger conspiratorial thinking.

We constructed a populism index utilizing four questions that measure key populist attitudes. The first question directly assesses a core populist belief by asking whether "the opinion of ordinary people is worth more than that of experts and politicians." The remaining questions capture related populist sentiments: distrust of official government accounts; viewing politics as a battle between good and evil; and believing strong leaders sometimes need to "bend the rules" to achieve their goals. Each question was coded on a five-point scale from 0 (strongly disagree) to 4 (strongly agree), and responses were summed to create an index ranging from 0 to 16, with higher scores indicating stronger populist attitudes.

Our results, shown in Figure 2.3, reveal substantial differences between Democratic and Republican primary voters in their levels of conspiratorial and populist thinking. In all three states, Republican primary voters exhibit markedly higher levels of conspiratorialism and populism than their Democratic counterparts. Across the three states in our study, the average conspiratorialism score for a Democratic primary voter hovers around six on conspiratorialism and 6.5 on populism, while the average Republican score is about nine on conspiratorialism and 9.5 on populism. Notably, the general public is considerably closer to the typical Republican primary voter, with a typical score of around 8 to 9 on both metrics.

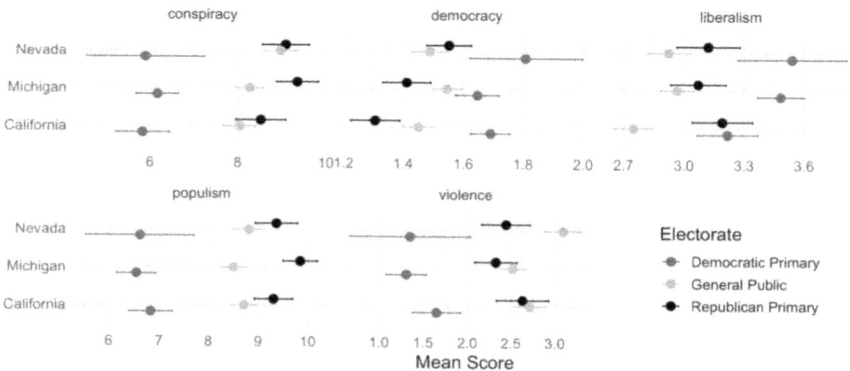

Figure 2.3: Non-ideological attitudes across electorates and states.

To contextualize a score of 9 on the sixteen-point conspiratorial thinking scale, consider a few possible ways a voter can achieve that score. An average Republican primary voter or member of the general public may, for example, score themselves as a 2—"neither agree nor disagree"—on three of the four questions mentioned above, and, on the fourth question, they may rate themselves a 3, thus indicating that they agree with the statement. An average Democratic primary voter (who has a score of 6) would score themselves a 1—which indicates active disagreement—on any two of these questions, while selecting the middle option on the other two. For example, an average Democratic primary voter may actively disagree that "a few people always run things" and "the true power-holders are unknown to voters" in a way that the average member of the general public does not.

These findings suggest that Democratic primary voters' high level of institutional trust represents a departure from broader public sentiment, and is opposed to Republican primary voters' institutional skepticism, which is uniquely high. Indeed, Democratic primary voters demonstrate a uniquely low level of conspiratorial and populist thinking among the American public, indicating substantially higher levels of trust in traditional political and social institutions.

The data on support for political violence tells a similar story. We constructed a measure to operationalize this concept through two questions that directly assess respondents' views on the legitimacy of violence in the American political context. The first asks whether violence is sometimes acceptable for Americans to express disagreement with the government. The second probes whether respondents believe people must "take charge" through violence if elected leaders fail to protect America from perceived threats. As with the other indices, responses were coded on a five-point scale from 0 to 4 and summed to create a scale ranging from 0 to 8, with higher values indicating greater support for political violence.

There are notable differences in support for political violence between Democratic and Republican primary voters across all three states, as well as between primary electorates and the general public. Across all three states, Republican primary voters consistently express higher support for political violence than Democratic primary voters. Furthermore, Republican primary voters (typical score around 2.5) are consistently closer to the general public (typical score around 2.8) in their scores, whereas Democratic primary voters (typical score around 1.4) report substantially lower levels of support for political violence compared to the broader electorate. To contextualize these scores, the average Democratic primary voter strongly disagrees with at least one of the two statements related to political violence: More often than not, Democratic primary voters select 0 for at least one question (given that the average score is under 2). Republican primary voters and the general public, on the other hand, are far less likely to select a 0 and also much more likely to indicate agreement (a score of 3 or 4) on at least one of the political violence questions.

These findings reinforce the pattern observed in conspiratorialism and populism: Republican primary voters tend to align more closely with the broader public sentiment, while Democratic primary voters represent a distinct subset with lower levels of support for political violence. This dynamic highlights the ideological divergence between primary electorates and underscores the closer alignment of Republican primary voters with the general public on this dimension.

Interestingly, the average citizen expresses a greater openness to political violence than both the average Democratic and Republican primary voter—although they are only slightly more accepting of it than the average Republican primary voter.

Furthermore, we constructed measures of democratic support using two questions that forced respondents to choose between democratic processes and preferred outcomes. One asks whether America would be better off with universal participation or restricted participation based on being "informed and responsible." The other asks whether respondents prioritize maintaining fair democratic processes or achieving their preferred policy outcomes. These questions effectively measure commitment to democratic principles when they conflict with partisan interests. The democracy index scores range from 0 to 2 (with higher scores indicating stronger support for democratic principles).

Democratic primary voters consistently demonstrate stronger support for democratic principles (1.72) than both Republican primary voters (1.42) and the general public (1.49). Again, the general public's democratic support aligns more closely with Republican primary voters than Democratic primary voters in all three states. This suggests that Democratic primary voters' higher likelihood of supporting democratic principles—such as supporting universal participation in elections and prioritizing democratic processes over preferred outcomes—represents a departure from typical public attitudes.

Finally, we constructed liberalism measures to assess support for key liberal democratic institutions—specifically separation of powers and press freedom. One question asks whether it would be helpful or harmful for presidents to work without regard for Congress and courts, while the other asks about restricting journalists' access to government information. These items capture support for fundamental liberal democratic constraints on executive power and commitment to press freedom as a check on government. The liberalism index scores range from 0 to 4.

The data on support for liberalism reveals narrower differences between Democratic and Republican primary voters compared to other indices, though distinct patterns remain. In each state, Democratic primary voters (average score of 3.4) express slightly stronger support for liberalism than Republican primary voters (3.1). However, again, in each state, Republican primary voters align more closely with the general public than Democratic primary voters on liberalism. With an average score of 2.9, the general public actually scores lower on this index than both sets of primary voters.

To further contextualize these differences, one could think of half of Democratic primary voters as scoring themselves a 2—indicating clear support for the democratic principle—on both questions, and the other half placing themselves as a 2 on one question and a 1 on the other. Republican primary voters and the general public, however, are far more likely to take a neutral position on one of the two questions.

These findings reveal a consistent trend across all states: while Democratic primary voters tend to report marginally higher support for liberal democratic principles, their scores are less representative of the broader electorate compared to Republican primary voters. Republican primary voters consistently align more closely with the general public, suggesting that their views on liberal democratic principles, though slightly lower than their Democratic counterparts, are more reflective of the average voter. This alignment reinforces the broader pattern that Democratic primary voters are distinct from the general public, while Republican primary voters are more ideationally proximate to the broader electorate.

What is Driving the Divide in Liberal Democratic Attitudes?

On the non-ideological measures, we consistently find that the general public is more closely aligned with Republican primary voters than Democratic primary voters across all three states. No matter what one may think is normatively best, our data suggests that it is Democratic primary voters who are more significantly misaligned with the broader public on these measures. This begs the question: Are our findings identifying a stable and reliable difference, or are our measures simply picking up on something more temporary and context dependent?

It is possible that respondents' perceptions of the current party in power impacted their choices. At the time of the survey, President Biden was in the White House, and the Democrats controlled the U.S. Senate; the party was widely viewed as being in power. Did Democratic primary voters express greater institutional trust and support for democratic principles simply because their party was in power? Were Republican primary voters' views just the result of negative partisanship? If this premise is true, it may also make sense that the general public leaned closer to the Republicans on this measure: Given the outcome of the November election, the general public certainly swung against the party in power in 2024. Perhaps, now that President Trump is back in office and the Republicans control the federal government, partisan responses to these measures will flip in 2026.

However, based on a deeper look at our data, this explanation appears insufficient. While partisanship likely plays a role in shaping attitudes, the consistent trends across states and the specific patterns of support suggest deeper ideological and cultural divides between Democratic and Republican primary voters. For example, even on a question measuring support for a "strong leader" bending the rules—a measure one might expect to be especially influenced by the party in power—Republican primary voters still express higher levels of support than their Democratic counterparts (see Table 2.2).

Table 2.2: Share of respondents who support strong leader bending the rules.

	Democrats (% Agree or Strongly Agree)	Republicans (% Agree or Strongly Agree)
California	28.67	27.77
Michigan	18.62	39.14
Nevada	29.70	36.36

The alignment of the general public with Republican primary voters on democratic liberalism (see Figure 2.3) further challenges the idea that these results are driven by the partisan dynamics of the moment. If partisanship was the dominant factor, we might expect Democratic primary voters to display higher levels of illiberalism in response to their party holding the presidency. Instead, our findings reveal a more structural trend: Republican primary voters consistently report higher support for illiberal measures, even when their positions are relatively more reflective of the broader public.

Primary Reform and Electorate Policy Preferences

While we find minimal evidence that primary voters as a whole are distinct from general election voters, this masks a critical underlying dynamic: in most states, Democratic and Republican primary voters constitute two separate electorates. Each partisan primary draws on a unique slice of the voting public, shaped by party registration rules, political culture, and differential mobilization strategies. When we compare all primary voters to the general electorate, we are averaging across two very different populations, which can obscure the ideological distinctiveness of each group.

This is precisely why electoral system design matters. In most states, nomination contests functionally take place within partisan silos. But in all-candidate primaries—like those used in California—there is only one primary election, and all voters, regardless of party affiliation, participate in the same contest. In these systems, Democratic and Republican primary voters are no longer separate groups selecting their own nominees: they are part of a single, mixed electorate choosing from the same set of candidates.

California's all-candidate primary system allows us to examine what happens when partisan primary electorates are pooled into a unified primary electorate. As Figure 2.4 shows, the distribution of social policy preferences among California primary voters looks much more like that of the general electorate. Because all voters participate in the same contest, the median primary voter in California is also much closer to the median general election voter—particularly on divisive issues like immigration and abortion.

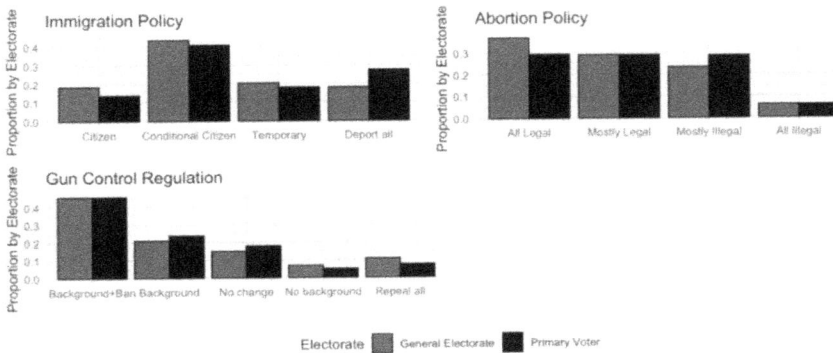

Figure 2.4: Proportion of social policy positions by California electorates.

The mechanism by which reform reduces polarization is not about changing the overall composition of the primary electorate but making primary voters a single electorate. Candidates in these systems must appeal to a wider range of voters—not just their partisan base—at the most critical stage of the electoral process. The act of pooling distinct primary electorates into one makes the primary more competitive, more representative, and more aligned with general election outcomes.

Conclusion

In this chapter, we contribute to the study of primary voters in two ways. First, we compare the views of Democratic and Republican primary voters both to each other and to the entire general electorate, rather than simply to the views of their co-partisans who only vote in general elections. This approach allows us to isolate the differences among the groups of voters who may participate in the consequential election. Second, we move beyond measuring how different electorates differ on policy preferences and develop measures of non-ideological attitudes, including conspiratorialism, populism, support for political violence, and support for liberal democratic principles.

Across our policy measures, the primary electorates are more polarized than the general public. On most policy issues, the median member of the general public is more moderate than the median voter from both party primary electorates. With the exception of Social Security spending, on which the median voters from all three electorates (Democratic primary, Republican primary, and the general) are aligned, we find that the median voter from at least one primary electorate deviates from the median voter of the general public.

Of course, this does not prove that primary voters are a key source of elite polarization. However, the findings in this chapter strongly indicate that catering to their primary electorate typically requires candidates to deviate—on some issues, substantially—from the general public. To the extent that candidates and legislators are incentivized to cater to their primary electorate, relative to their general electorate, then the ideological distinctiveness of primary voters distorts representation. Moreover, there is reason to believe that politicians often (and should) gravitate more towards the center of their primary electorate than their general electorate. General election margins are typically stable, predictable, and only modestly sensitive to candidate platforms and legislative behavior, while primary elections are more volatile and less predictable, and more sensitive to the positions of candidates. Given these dynamics, it seems plausible—if not likely—that partisan primaries (and partisan primary voters) encourage candidates and legislators to take less moderate and less representative (of the general public) policy positions.

On the non-ideological measures, we find that Democratic primary voters are less likely than Republican primary voters to express conspiratorial or populist views or support for political violence, while they report slightly higher support for liberal democratic principles. However, across all of these measures, we find that the general public is actually more closely aligned with Republican primary voters than Democratic primary voters. This indicates that it is Democratic primary voters' higher levels of trust in government institutions that is out of line with the general public. We also argue that our findings are not simply the result of partisans reacting to which party was in power at the time of the survey.

Future research should investigate the relationship between Democratic primary voters' pro-system political attitudes and the legislative behavior of Democratic elected representatives. Do Democratic officials take less populist, more pro-system positions to appease their primary voters?

More generally, future research should investigate whether legislators from partisan primary states are more likely to support less representative policies in an effort to align with their primary electorate. Conversely, do legislators from all-candidate primary states gravitate more toward the policy position of median voters in their state or district?

References

Bail, Christopher A., Brian Guay, Emily Maloney, Aidan Combs, D. Sunshine Hillygus, Friedolin Merhout, Deen Freelon, and Alexander Volfovsky. 2020. "Assessing the Russian Internet Research Agency's Impact on the Political Attitudes and Behaviors of American Twitter Users in Late 2017." *Proceedings of the National Academy of Sciences* 117 (1): 243–250. https://doi.org/10.1073/pnas.1906420116.

Dahl, Robert A. 1971. *Polyarchy: Participation and Opposition.* Yale University Press.

Diamond, Larry. 1999. *Developing Democracy: Toward Consolidation.* Johns Hopkins University Press.

Ferrer, Joshua, and Matthew Thorning. 2023. "2022 Primary Turnout: Trends and Lessons for Boosting Participation." Bipartisan Policy Center, March. https://bipartisanpolicy.org/download/?file=/wp-content/uploads/2023/03/Primary-Turnout-Report_R03.pdf.

Fowler, Anthony, Seth J. Hill, Jeffrey B. Lewis, Chris Tausanovitch, Lynn Vavreck, and Christopher Warshaw. 2023. "Moderates." *American Political Science Review* 117 (2): 643–660. https://doi.org/10.1017/S0003055422000818.

Geer, John G. 1988. "Assessing the Representativeness of Electorates in Presidential Primaries." *American Journal of Political Science* 32 (4): 929–945. https://doi.org/10.2307/2111195.

Hill, Seth J. 2015. "Institution of Nomination and the Policy Ideology of Primary Electorates." *Quarterly Journal of Political Science* 10 (4): 461–487.

Jacobson, Gary C. 2012. "The Electoral Origins of Polarized Politics: Evidence from the 2010 Cooperative Congressional Election Study." *American Behavioral Scientist* 56 (12): 1612–1630. https://doi.org/10.1177/0002764212463352.

Jones, Jeffrey M. 2024. "Independent Party ID Tied for High; Democratic ID at New Low." Gallup. January 12. https://news.gallup.com/poll/548459/independent-party-tied-high-democratic-new-low.aspx.

Kalmoe, Nathan P., and Lilliana Mason. 2022. *Radical American Partisanship: Mapping Violent Hostility, Its Causes, and the Consequences for Democracy.* University of Chicago Press.

Key, V.O. 1956. *American State Politics: An Introduction.* Knopf.

Levitsky, Steven, and Daniel Ziblatt. 2018. *How Democracies Die.* Crown Publishing Group.

McDonald, Michael P., and Thessalia Merivaki. 2015. "Voter Turnout in Presidential Nominating Contests." *The Forum* 13 (4): 597–622. https://doi.org/10.1515/for-2015-0041.

Müller, Jan-Werner. 2016. *What Is Populism?* University of Pennsylvania Press.

Norrander, Barbara. 1989. "Ideological Representativeness of Presidential Primary Voters." American *Journal of Political Science* 33 (3): 570–587. https://doi.org/10.2307/2111063.

Oliver, J. Eric, and Wendy M. Rahn. 2016. "Rise of the Trumpenvolk: Populism in the 2016 Election." *The ANNALS of the American Academy of Political and Social Science* 667 (1): 189–206. https://doi.org/10.1177/0002716216662639.

Oliver, J. Eric, and Thomas J. Wood. 2014. "Conspiracy Theories and the Paranoid Style(s) of Mass Opinion." *American Journal of Political Science* 58 (4): 952–966. https://doi.org/10.1111/ajps.12084.

Rogers, Todd, and Masahiko Aida. 2014. "Vote Self-prediction Hardly Predicts Who Will Vote and is (Misleadingly) Unbiased." *American Politics Research* 42 (3): 503–28.

Sides, John, Chris Tausanovitch, Lynn Vavreck, and Christopher Warshaw. 2020. "On the Representativeness of Primary Electorates." *British Journal of Political Science* 50 (2): 677–685. https://doi.org/10.1017/S000712341700062X.

Silver, Brian D., Barbara A. Anderson, and Paul R. Abramson. 1986. "Who Overreports Voting?" *American Political Science Review* 80 (2): 613–24.

Unite America Institute. 2024. "The Primary Problem." https://www.uniteamericainstitute.org/research/the-primary-problem.

Uscinski, Joseph E., and Joseph M. Parent. 2014. *American Conspiracy Theories.* Oxford University Press.

Wasserman, David. 2023. "Realignment, More Than Redistricting, Has Decimated Swing House Seats." Cook Political Report. https://www.cookpolitical.com/cook-pvi/realignment-more-redistricting-has-decimated-swing-house-seats.

Zachary Albert and Raymond La Raja

Chapter 3
Who Votes in Primaries and What Are Their Attitudes Toward Compromise?

Abstract: Political scientists disagree about whether and how primary voters differ from non-voters. We believe the costs associated with participating in an additional election, often with limited public attention, make primary voters unique. Through this electoral costs framework, we test theories about the impact of individual resources, motivation, and mobilization on primary turnout. We also test theories about candidate selection in primaries, specifically the willingness to vote for those who oppose compromise with political opponents. Drawing on two surveys, one an original study of 2022 Ohio citizens and the other a nationally representative sample from the 2022 Cooperative Election Study (CES), we find that primary voters are more strongly partisan, politically knowledgeable, and politically interested than non-voters. Republican primary voters are far more opposed to compromise than Democrats, especially those who are strongly ideological, have strong negative feelings toward Democrats, and have more hostile racial attitudes. The findings have important implications for primary election outcomes and help explain the growing role of hardliners within the GOP. The findings also help explain why elected officials may fear compromising in the legislative process.

Are primary voters in congressional elections different from rank-and-file partisans? Research to date shows mixed findings (Drutman 2021). Yet primary voters play a crucial role in shaping parties through candidate selection (Albert and Costa 2024; Hall 2019; Porter and Steelman 2023; Thomsen 2017) and influencing how legislators behave once in office (Anderson, Butler, and Harbridge-Yong 2020; Ansolabehere, Hirano, and Snyder 2007; Hirano, Snyder, and Ting 2009). In this chapter, we examine how partisans who vote in primaries differ from those who do not. Using established theories of general election participation, we show that these models are even more predictive in explaining who votes in primaries. We then investigate whether primary voters hold distinctive attitudes—especially toward political compromise. Legislators often fear that primary voters oppose compromise (Anderson, Butler, and Harbridge-Yong 2020), which could exacerbate polarization and gridlock. We test whether this fear is justified and explore which types of voters are most opposed to working with the other side.

Although primary turnout has increased slightly in recent cycles, it remains low: Approximately one-fifth of registered voters participated in recent House primaries (Ferrer and Thorning 2023). That means a small, possibly unrepresentative slice of the electorate helps decide nominees, especially in safe districts where the primary winner is virtually guaranteed victory (Leaverton 2023). Primary elections add an extra cost to participation, beyond eligibility rules, shaping the partisan voter pool in ways that may skew political representation (Doherty, Dowling, and Miller 2022; Brady, Han, and Pope 2007; Burden 2001). If this pool is more extreme in its attitudes, we risk selecting leadership that fails to adequately represent relatively moderate general electorates (Bafumi and Herron 2010).

We start with the premise that the extra costs of primary voting are not equally borne. Voters with more resources and stronger partisan attachments are more likely to show up (Verba et al. 1995; Campbell et al. 1960; Green, Palmquist, and Schickler 2002). Habitual voters are also more likely to be mobilized, reinforcing turnout gaps (Brady, Schlozman, and Verba. 1999; Rosenstone and Hansen 1993).

Our findings confirm that primary voters stand out for their partisan intensity, political knowledge, and news interest. We then explore what kinds of candidates they prefer—specifically, whether they support compromise in the legislative process. This matters because compromise is a democratic good widely supported in principle (Gutmann and Thompson 2010) but potentially less so by highly engaged subgroups. Legislators may avoid compromise to avoid alienating their base (Anderson, Butler, and Harbridge-Yong 2020; Boatright 2013), but we know little about which voters are driving this dynamic.

We find that the most ideological primary voters are opposed to compromise; this is especially the case with Republicans. We do not observe the same relationship among partisans who do not vote in the primary. We also find that opposition to compromise is strongest among Republican voters with strong negative feelings toward Democrats and hostile racial attitudes. These dynamics, however, appear present for both Republican primary and general election voters. We do not find the same resistance to compromise—either for primary or general election voters—among most subgroups within the Democratic Party. These findings lend support for research that demonstrates politicians are reluctant to compromise in the legislature, claiming they fear the wrath of some primary voters (Anderson, Butler, and Harbridge-Yong 2020). More specifically, they suggest why elements of the Republican Party in government have become hardliners against compromise.

Our study draws on two sources of data. The first is a survey of Ohio voters, conducted just before the 2022 primaries, and the second is a national sample of validated voters from the Cooperative Election Study in 2022. These sources have contrasting strengths and weaknesses. While the Ohio sample is distinct from the national primary electorate and relies on self-reported turnout, we are able to draw a sizable sample that avoids having to control for cross-state differences in primary rules and political context. Furthermore, we included original questions about primary mobilization and voter attitudes to directly test our theories. The national CES sample, on the other hand, allows us to generalize to the U.S. population and has validated voter turnout data, but it does not include questions related to voter attitudes about compromise. By relying on both sources, we hope to provide more robust findings. Unlike previous research that looked at aggregate voters, we model voters at the individual level to predict who tends to vote in primaries, and how these same voters tend to think about political compromise.

Primary Electorates

As partisan and ideological polarization deepens, scholars are looking at primaries as one potential underlying cause. Several studies look at whether primary voters have a different profile than the general electorate. Jacobson's (2012) work suggests they possess more ideological constraint in their issue preferences and that primary electorates are more polarized ideologically than general election voters. This appears especially true among Republican primary constituencies, as well as among the high proportion of party activists who participate in primaries. A subsequent study by Hill (2015) examines district-level data to show clear differences between the two electorates, finding that "not a single district in either party, election year, or type of primary has a primary electorate more centrist than the general electorate." He adds for emphasis that, "Even the general electorates in even the safest districts are not as ideological as the primary electorates in most districts around the nation." However, more recent research using large sets of survey data on primary electorates suggests minimal differences, in the aggregate, between primary voters and partisans who do not vote in these elections (Sides et al. 2020). Primary voters appear to share similar demographics, although they reveal a much stronger interest in politics and are somewhat more educated and older. They also are more likely to give money, confirming that they tend to be activists.

We believe these demographic differences are important. They illustrate that primary constituencies tend to have more resources (e. g., education, age, money), they follow politics more intensely, and they have more coherent ideological views. All of this means they are better able and more motivated to participate relative to those who do not vote in primaries. Such differences should not be overlooked casually, since they imply that primary voters may have different priorities and may be more willing to hold politicians accountable for issues they care about deeply and for which they believe the party stands. This dynamic may lead to the kind of rigid "issue ownership" that primary voters prioritize, rather than actual performance on the policy area that a broader set of voters might prefer (see Egan 2013). Notably, previous studies have not modeled the characteristics that tend to predict who votes in primaries, nor have they examined attitudes that primary voters deploy to evaluate politicians compared to general election voters.

Expectations about Who Votes in Primaries

In predicting who votes in primaries, we draw on theories about who votes in the general election. These theories have even greater weight in primaries because they are pre-elections that require additional effort beyond the general election. Primary electorates might be understood to be made up of "super voters," which suggests they possess all the qualities we see in the general electorate, only more so. Our model of primary voter turnout draws on three factors that tend to predict political participation: resources, motivation, and mobilization. We expect primary voters to tally higher on these factors than rank-and-file partisans who do not vote or only vote in the general election. These factors are included in our model using the following measures:

Resources: Abundant research shows individual levels of resources matter in predicting turnout in the general election (e. g., Wolfinger and Rosenstone 1980). We expect resources to matter even more for turnout in subsidiary elections, such as primaries, which are less salient than general elections. Those who are more educated, wealthy, and older also tend to have the knowledge, skills, and time that make one more likely to participate in primaries.

Motivation: Citizens who are more motivated by an election tend to turn out. Motivation is obviously related to political interest. It is also powered by individual identities, the most salient one being the strength of partisan allegiance. Strong partisans are more likely to view elections as important and to care about the party picking a good candidate and winning. We also expect the strongest ideologues to be more motivated to participate in primaries because these voters care about what the party stands for. We might expect motivation to be especially strong among voters who perceive a larger ideological distance between themselves and their own party, which they see as more moderate.

Mobilization: Citizens participate more when politicians and groups mobilize them (Rosenstone and Hansen 1993). We expect primary voters to be contacted by groups more frequently. Beyond the costs and benefits, the social networks one belongs to (e.g., churches, social clubs, etc.) may stimulate participation in ways that subsidize the costs of participation (e.g., by providing information about who to vote for), or increase the psychological benefits of voting. Political actors are strategic in who they mobilize, looking for voters who support their causes and who have resources that make them more likely to engage (Brady, Schlozman, and Verba 1999; Rosenstone and Hansen 1993). We expect those who participate in politics beyond voting (e.g. donating money, attending meetings, or working on campaigns) to participate at higher rates because these acts indicate that they have been mobilized more broadly.

Primary Voters' Attitudes Toward Compromise

Given these theories about the factors that motivate voting, we expect a different pool of voters to show up in primaries. The next question is whether these differences extend to their political attitudes. We focus on one particular attitude—about politicians who compromise—rooted in the academic literature. Do primary constituencies prefer politicians who "stick to their guns" more than the general electorate? And what are the underlying characteristics of these primary voters? We know from previous research that opposition to compromise is not the dominant position in the electorate. Indeed, the public widely supports bipartisanship and may even hold hardliners accountable in Congress for their votes (Canes-Wrone et al. 2002; Carson et al. 2010; Wolak 2020). Legislators who refuse to compromise often receive negative evaluations (Pew Research Center 2012; Wolak 2020).

On the other hand, attitudes about compromise are not uniform across the electorate (Arceneaux et al. 2016). One study found that as many as one-third of voters in their survey wanted their legislator to vote against a compromise on a bill, and that primary voters made up a greater proportion of those willing to punish officeholders for compromising (Anderson, Butler, and Harbridge-Yong 2020). Some voters—especially strong partisans—may be more likely to favor aggressive partisanship from their side, even if they disavow conflict in the aggregate (Harbridge and Malhotra 2011; Harbridge, Malhotra, and Harrison 2014), and they may reward officeholders who engage in such behaviors in the primary (Pyeatt 2015). This is especially true in states with high intra-party competition and low inter-party competition (Burke et al 2021). Given the growing divide between engaged and unengaged voters (Krupnikov and Ryan 2022) and changes in technology (e.g., social media like Twitter/X), legislators and party officials may increasingly oppose compromise and believe voters feel the same.

Opposition to Compromise Among Primary Voters: Ideology and Status Threat

Our main expectation is that primary voters will be more opposed to compromise than non-voters, due mainly to the motivational differences between the two groups. We expect primary voters to possess a number of traits—like ideological extremity or negative feelings toward the opposing party—that both motivate them to turn out and make them predisposed to resist compromise. However, one motivational factor that is unlikely to predict attitudes about compromise is the strength of partisanship. While we expect strong partisanship to be a major factor in predicting turnout in primaries, research indicates that partisanship is not necessarily associated with opposition to compromise, although there is evidence that strong ideologues are less keen on democratic norms (Graham and Svolik 2020) and that ideologues are less supportive than moderates on compromise (Wolak 2022).

For this reason, we expect voters who are highly ideological, i.e. those who self-describe as being very liberal or very conservative, to be most likely to oppose compromise. The self-labeling may reflect strong issue preference or a symbolic identity (likely both). Regardless, these voters put a premium on politicians who uphold ideological commitments. Research shows that ideologues are more likely to root worldviews in moralistic terms, which makes them more likely to oppose compromise, punish compromising politicians, and forsake material gains (Ryan 2017). According to Arceneaux (2019), strong ideologues hold "more intense and implacable opinions that take on an absolutist quality" (n.p.). He demonstrates they are more likely to be intolerant of political disagreement and reprove candidates who make compromises.

We expect ideology to be a stronger motivating factor for Republicans than Democrats. Arceneaux also finds that conservatives (especially social conservatives) tend to score higher on absolutism than liberals, which suggests the strongest conservatives will be especially likely to oppose compromise. Recent research on local party recruitment supports the view that conservative parties might have more voters who dislike compromise. Republican Party chairs—and voters in their districts—appear to view a candidate who is willing to compromise as unlikely to win a primary. In contrast, Democratic chairs and voters appear to seek candidates that are open to compromise (Doherty, Dowling, and Miller 2022). There may be a strategic premise in play as well that applies uniquely to conservative partisans. Such voters may view any compromise with the liberal party as necessarily shifting policy in a more progressive direction. To practice compromise as a norm is to "give in" repeatedly to a less conservative society.

The second kind of voter opposed to compromise should include those who feel a heightened threat from the rival party coalition. This threat includes several dimensions. One of them reflects perceptions of difference. Those who see greater ideological distance between themselves and the other party are more likely to see compromise as threatening or giving away too much. A second dimension of difference is affective. Voters who have more negative feelings about the rival party relative to their own party are more likely to dislike politicians who compromise with the other side. Negative affective orientations towards those in the opposing party may lead voters to believe the other party is not worthy of negotiation and compromise (Iyengar et al. 2012; Kalmoe 2020; Mason 2018).

A third kind of voter opposed to compromise is one that experiences deep status threat. Status threat is the perceived loss of one's group's dominant position in the social, cultural, or political hierarchy. It is not just about actual material decline—it's about the fear or belief that "people like me" are losing ground, influence, or respect in society. We expect groups that previously held dominant positions in American society but who are experiencing rapid change to be the most opposed to democratic norms like compromise (Bartels 2020; Craig and Richeson 2014; Mutz 2018). These groups are primarily in the Republican Party. They include whites, especially those with negative views of blacks. Such voters are likely to oppose compromise with a Democratic party that is supportive of expanded civil rights for racial minorities. They also include religious Republicans who might feel threatened by a Democratic Party that is viewed as highly secular and unfriendly to religious traditions. On the Democratic side, we do not expect the same dynamics because the party tends to represent marginalized groups—women, blacks, and LGBTQ—that benefit from democratic norms of compromise (Brown 2014).[1]

Data and Methods

We draw on two different datasets to test these hypotheses. First, we use an original survey of 1,990 respondents fielded in the state of Ohio in the weeks before the primaries for congressional and statewide offices on May 3, 2022. The sample contains nearly equal numbers of Democrats (894) and Republicans (888), defined

---

1 Indeed, we evaluate the impact that the importance Democrats place on racial, gender, and sexual identities has on compromise attitudes in separate models (which we do not show) and find null results, as expected.

based on the party primary a respondent said they had or would vote in.[2] The sample is weighted to reflect Ohio population statistics for gender, education, race, and age using figures from the American Community Survey. This data allows us to examine the nature of primary participation in a state with substantively important nomination contests—including contested races to determine nominees for governor and an open US Senate seat—that would have drawn substantial interest in the state.[3] We believe Ohio represents a "hard" case when it comes to identifying differences between primary voters and non-voters, and testing hypotheses about opposition to compromise among the former, because these fairly competitive nomination contests attracted higher voter turnout than states with more lopsided races. By using data on individuals from a single state, we also avoid the need to account for the influence of factors that vary across jurisdictions (like partisan competition, participation rules, and polarization).

The most important distinction within this sample is whether or not the respondent is a primary voter. The survey relies on self-reported primary participation, with respondents selecting that they already voted (early or absentee), definitely will vote, probably will vote, are undecided, probably will not vote, or definitely will not vote. Thus, there are several ways to define a primary voter. We opt for two methods: a strict definition that defines primary voters as those who said they already voted or would definitely vote, and a more lenient definition that also includes those who said they probably would vote. The weighted percentage of primary voters is 65.4 percent based on the strict definition and 84.1 percent based on the lenient definition. Because our findings are consistent regardless of the definition used, in the pages that follow we present only the results from the strict definition.[4]

The second survey we use is the 2022 Cooperative Election Study (CES). The full survey contains 60,000 respondents but, because we again remove true independents, the final sample size is 49,520 respondents (29,210 Democrats and 20,310

---

2 Respondents who did not plan to vote were asked which party's primary they would participate in if they were to vote. We exclude those who did not pick a major party primary from our analysis.

3 At the gubernatorial level, incumbent Republican Mike DeWine faced two challengers who garnered twenty-eight and 21.8 percent of the vote in the primary, while the Democratic nominee fended off one opponent with sixty-five percent of the vote. For the open Senate race, four Republicans earned at least eleven percent of the vote, and the eventual nominee, J.D. Vance, earned just 32.2 percent. The Democratic primary was less competitive, with former US House member Tim Ryan earning seventy percent and two others splitting the remaining vote.

4 There is also some evidence, based on a comparison of self-reports and validated primary voting in the 2020 CES survey, that the strict definition minimizes overreporting (when a respondent claims they voted but did not) and better approximates true turnout.

Republicans). We use the built-in CES weights to generalize our findings to the American population. Because the CES sample has validated primary participation, we adopt a single definition for the primary voter variable that is equal to 1 if the person has a valid voting record in the 2022 congressional primaries and 0 otherwise. The weighted percentage of primary voters is thirty-eight percent. These validated turnout figures, in addition to the larger sample size, represent the main benefits of using the CCES sample. However, the two samples have different coverage (state versus national), and as such we expect some minor differences when comparing our results.

Comparing Primary Voters and Non-voters in the Two Samples

Table 3.1 shows descriptive statistics for the Ohio and CES samples. We are interested in comparing not only primary voters and non-voters in each sample but also the Ohio and CES samples to better understand how our two data sources differ. To that end, statistics in Table 3.1 that differ significantly (i. e. by more than ten percentage points) across the two samples are bolded.

Within each party, there are clear differences between primary voters and non-voters with respect to resource advantages. In both parties in Ohio, as expected, primary voters are older, more educated (especially in the Republican Party), and wealthier than Ohio non-voters. We also observe that primary voters have characteristics that would make them more motivated to vote in a primary. They have higher levels of political knowledge; more of them self-describe as "strong partisans"; and more call themselves "very ideological." With respect to identities such as gender and race, we see that primary voters tend to be men in both parties, but we do not observe significant differences by race.

Many of these broad patterns apply to the validated primary voter pool nationwide, seen on the right side of the table. We once again observe that primary voters in both parties tend to be older, better educated, and wealthier. At the national level, primary voters are also more likely to be white compared to their party overall, especially for Democrats. With regard to motivation, we find that primary voters are much more politically interested and knowledgeable than non-voters, and more likely to identify as strong partisans and ideologues.

Our Ohio sample differs in key (but mostly understandable) ways from the national sample. In both parties, non-white, college educated, and wealthier respondents are more common in the US than in Ohio. The gaps for college education and income are particularly large for Democratic primary voters. Democrats

Table 3.1: Comparing primary voters and non-voters in the 2022 Ohio and CES samples.

	Ohio Sample				CES Sample			
	Democratic Non-Voters	Democratic Voters	Republican Non-Voters	Republican Voters	Democratic Non-Voters	Democratic Voters	Republican Non-Voters	Republican Voters
Age (mean)	43.7	50.2	44.8	53.7	42.6	54.4	48.1	60.9
Female	64%	52%	53%	41%	54%	57%	49%	49%
Non-white	28%	32%	10%	8%	45%	29%	20%	11%
College-educated (bachelors +)	25%	29%	20%	34%	35%	58%	27%	41%
Income greater than $80k	14%	18%	18%	28%	27%	40%	27%	35%
High news interest	5%	24%	6%	25%	36%	68%	39%	69%
High political knowledge	10%	18%	8%	19%	23%	42%	26%	46%
Strong partisan	29%	55%	29%	52%	46%	64%	45%	57%
Very ideological	13%	22%	11%	26%	24%	30%	25%	36%

who vote in nominating contests in Ohio are much less educated and wealthy than Democratic primary voters overall, likely due to the demographics of the state, and, perhaps, because the competitive nature of Ohio elections draws a wider swath of voters to turn out. Indeed, there are also very large gaps between the CES and Ohio samples in terms of political interest and knowledge, with the latter seeing a larger share of less interested and knowledgeable voters. Lastly, both voters and non-voters in Ohio are less likely to identify as strong partisans or ideologues, though the gap is smaller among primary voters.

What are the Predictors of Primary Turnout?

To more rigorously test our hypotheses about primary participation, we model turnout at the individual level using logistic regression models. We build models separately for Democrats and Republicans in order to assess cross-party differences, and we compare results from our state sample to the national CES sample. The terms in our models test our main theories about differences between primary voters and non-voters based on resources, motivation, and mobilization.

To account for resource-based explanations of participation we include the respondent's age, their income level, and their education level.[5] To operationalize motivational considerations, we include measures of each respondent's news interest and several measures of the strength of their political identities, namely whether they are a strong partisan or very ideological.[6] We also hypothesize that citizens who view their own party as more moderate than themselves will be motivated to turn out in primaries to help move the party nominee toward their own preferences. Thus, we include a binary term called "own party more moderate" that is set to 1 if the respondent rates their party's ideology as more moderate than their own and 0 otherwise. Lastly, we include measures of three

---

5 Income and education levels are measured using ordinal variables (transformed to numeric values) representing family income brackets and educational attainment levels; larger values indicate higher income/educational attainment.

6 News interest is an ordinal variable (ranging from 1 to 4) with larger values indicating that the respondent follows political news more often. The strong partisan and very ideological terms are both binary variables set to 1 if the respondent identifies as a strong Democrat/Republican (on a seven-point partisanship scale) or very liberal/conservative (on a five-point ideology scale), respectively.

non-political identities that could spur participation: whether the respondent is female or non-white and their church frequency (as a proxy for religiosity).[7]

Our final terms account for the effects of mobilization on primary participation. We include a binary term indicating whether someone took part in political activity beyond voting, set to 1 if they did at least one of the following: donated money, contacted elected officials, protested, volunteered on a campaign, or attended a political meeting. This term provides an indicator of whether a respondent has been mobilized to participate in more substantial political activities, which should be correlated with mobilization to vote in primaries. To examine primary mobilization more specifically, the Ohio models also include a term for the number of groups contacted, which measures the number of organized interests that contacted the respondent to encourage them to vote in the 2022 primaries.[8] This question was not asked on the CES survey.

Figure 3.1 uses coefficient plots to show the results of our models predicting participation in the Democratic (top) and Republican primaries (bottom). The underlying regression tables can be found in the Appendix. Estimates for which the whiskers do not intersect the dashed vertical line represent statistically significant effects at $p < 0.05$. Positive coefficients suggest that a given factor increases the odds of voting in a primary, while negative coefficients decrease the odds.

As expected, individual resources matter for getting people to turn out in this additional election. In all models, older and wealthier people are more likely to vote. Additionally, for members of both parties, education appears to be a powerful predictor in the national sample but not the Ohio sample.

Regarding motivation, it is clear from both samples that having an interest in news and solid political knowledge is associated with primary turnout. When it comes to identities as motivators, being a strong partisan is a powerful predictor of participation. This is particularly true in a state like Ohio in 2022, with competitive statewide primaries: respondents there who said they were "strong Democrats" had a seventy-six percent predicted probability of voting in the primary compared to sixty percent for those who did not consider themselves strong partisans at the time. Similarly, on the Republican side, Ohio respondents who said they were "strong Republicans" had an eighty percent predicted probability of voting in the Republican primary compared with sixty-seven percent for those who

---

7 The church frequency variable ranges from 1 to 5, with higher values indicating more frequent church attendance.

8 We asked respondents how many of the following types of groups contacted them in the 2022 election cycle: environmental, women's, guns, abortion, religious, animal rights, ethnic/racial, civil liberties, economic, union, or veterans. The group contact term ranges from 0 (no group contact) to 8 (contacted by all of these types of groups).

Democrats

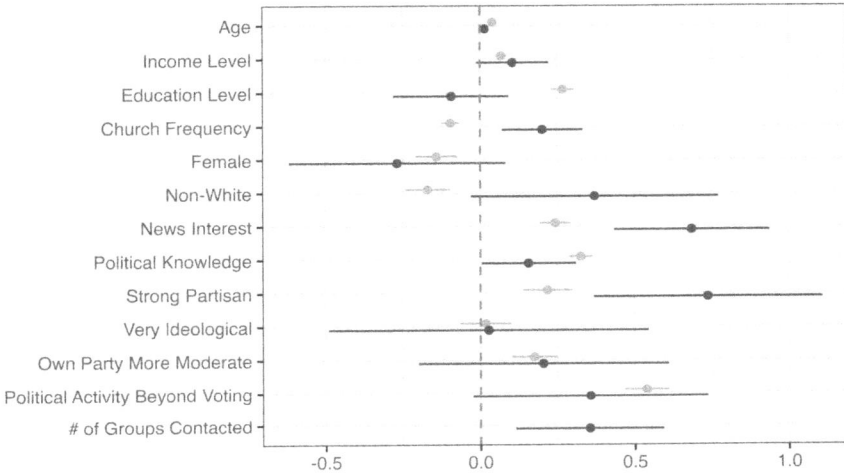

Republicans

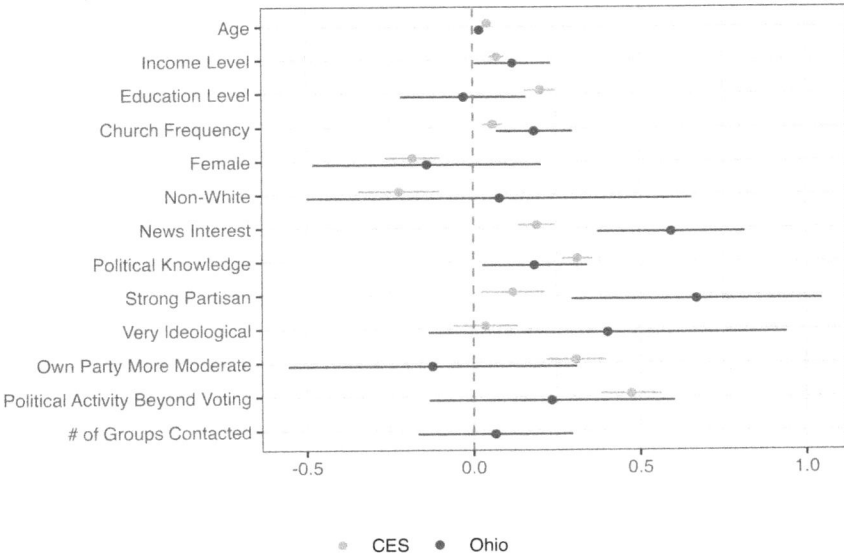

CES • Ohio

Figure 3.1: coefficient plots for logistic regression models predicting primary turnout.

were not strong partisans. The national CES sample has much lower predicted probabilities—about thirty-six percent for strong partisans and thirty-one percent for all others—because so many races are uncontested or uncompetitive.

Somewhat surprisingly, those who are very ideological are no more likely to vote in primaries than everyone else, in both Ohio and nationally. In the case of Ohio, this may have something to do with the state having relatively fewer respondents identifying as very ideological, as well as the fact that their competitive primaries attracted a broader set of voters. But when we dig deeper into the nationwide results, it appears that ideology does play a role in motivating participation. For both parties, respondents who perceive their own party as too moderate are expected to vote at higher rates, with an increased turnout probability of four percentage points for Democrats and seven points for Republicans. This perception term soaks up the explanatory power of self-identified ideology.[9] In models where we drop the own party perception term (not shown), we find that being very ideological is a statistically significant predictor of turnout, increasing the probability by about three percentage points in each party.

These are not especially large effects, but they demonstrate that ideology plays a role in motivating turnout even after accounting for other demographic and political factors. Importantly, however, it is not ideological self-identification alone that motivates primary voting. Rather, what seems to matter is how a potential voter perceives their party relative to their own ideological beliefs. This provides some evidence that primary voters use their participation in nominating contests to move their party toward their own preferences by selecting more liberal or conservative candidates.

Regarding our arguments about the importance of mobilization in generating primary turnout, we find several factors in play. We observe that being contacted by multiple groups matters for Democrats. We also see that those who are active in politics in other ways are also more likely to vote in the primary, in both parties in the national survey but only in the case of Democrats in the Ohio survey. Finally, church attendance is highly predictive of voting in the Democratic primary in Ohio, but it is negative in the national sample (with a relatively small coefficient). These differences remind us that the makeup of the Democratic Party coalition in Ohio is somewhat different from the nation. For Republicans, church attendance is found to increase the odds of turning out in both Ohio and nationally.

---

9 Importantly, while these concepts are related, the two variables tap into distinct concepts, reducing concerns about biases introduced by high correlations. Of those who said they were very ideological, 59% said their own party was too moderate, compared to 21% for all others.

Overall, our results confirm our argument that the additional primary election appears to draw on a unique set of voters. Compared to partisans who fail to show up in primaries, primary voters appear to be associated with having more individual resources, more motivation, and more external mobilization.

What Predicts Opposition to Compromise?

Beyond resources, motivations, and mobilization, we also believe primary voters possess unique attitudes that exert strong (and often negative) effects on political outcomes. Here we explore one manifestation of this: attitudes toward compromise.

We again find evidence that primary voters are unique. Table 3.2 shows the weighted percentage of Democratic and Republican voters and non-voters who oppose or support compromise, as well as the total sample statistics, within the Ohio sample (the CES did not include questions about compromise). Overall, the weighted percentage of respondents who oppose compromise is 56.8 percent. This level of opposition is higher than some other studies (e. g. Wolak 2020) and may reflect the binary nature of the question. However, if this is the case, it would likely mute our findings regarding the distinctiveness of those who oppose compromise; as such, this is a difficult test of our theory.

Table 3.2: Voter attitudes toward politicians who stick to positions or compromise.

	Democratic Non-Voters	Democratic Voters	Republican Non-Voters	Republican Voters	Total
I like elected officials who stick to their positions.	51.9%	45.0%	64.8%	66.3%	56.8%
I like elected officials who make compromises with people they disagree with.	48.1%	55.0%	35.2%	33.7%	43.2%

With regard to partisan differences, Democrats are less opposed to compromise (and more open to making agreements with political opponents) than the sample as a whole. This is especially true of Democratic primary voters, who were seven percentage points more supportive of compromise than Democratic non-voters, twelve percentage points more supportive of compromise than the sample, and nearly twenty-two percentage points more supportive than Republican primary voters. Support for compromise is quite low among both types of Republicans, with two-thirds of both GOP primary voters and non-voters opposing compromise.

To further understand the factors associated with these attitudes, we developed additional logistic models where the dependent variable represents whether a respondent selected that they "like elected officials who stick to their positions" (1) or that they "like elected officials who make compromises with people they disagree with" (0). We model opposition to compromise separately for the two parties and for primary voters and non-voters.

The compromise models include the same demographic and political variables to control for age, income level, education level, church frequency, gender (i. e., being female), race (i. e., being non-white), news interest, and political knowledge. The remaining terms aim to test our main theoretical predictions about the effects of ideology, out-party threat, and identity threat on opposition to political compromise. We again include a term for whether the respondent is very ideological. We also include additional terms that assess the effects of attitudes toward the out-party, with the expectation that those who view members of the out-party in more distant and negative ways will be less likely to support compromising with them. The affective polarization term measures the difference between in-party and out-party warmth to test whether negative feelings toward the out-party are associated with heightened resistance to compromising with these opponents.[10] And the out-party distance term, representing the distance between a respondent's own ideology and their perceptions of the out-party's ideology, assesses whether those who see the opposing party as quite ideologically distant are more likely to oppose compromise.[11]

Our last set of theoretical predictions suggests that identity threat should undermine prospects for compromise with an opposing party that represents people and causes perceived as threatening to one's most important identities. As noted, this status threat should be particularly acute among respondents who belong to groups that once held dominant positions in society but are now experiencing rapid changes that threaten their standing. Such respondents are mostly found within the GOP, and especially among those with negative racial attitudes. For this reason, we take advantage of the *FIRE battery* (DeSante and Smith 2020), a

---

10 This is measured using in-party and out-party feeling thermometers on a scale from 0 (entirely cold) to 100 (entirely warm). Larger, positive values for this variable suggest greater affective polarization. Conversely, negative values indicate that the respondent has warmer feelings toward the out-party than their own party (which is quite rare).

11 This term represents the absolute value of the difference between two ordinal scales (self-declared ideology and out-party ideology), with higher values indicating greater ideological distance.

parsimonious measure of racial animus with negative values indicating greater racial prejudice and higher, positive values indicating greater racial sympathy.[12] We expect Republicans high in racial prejudice to be especially opposed to compromising with a Democratic Party that represents the interests of racial minorities.

In both parties, we also expect respondents who place a premium on their partisan identity to be more likely to oppose compromise with the out-party. And for Republicans, we expect those who emphasize their religious identity to oppose compromise with an increasingly secular Democratic Party. To speak to these identities, we leverage a question asking respondents to rank the importance of various identities—gender, partisan, racial or ethnic, religious, occupational, sexual, and socio-economic—when it comes to political attitudes and behaviors. We also create two binary variables indicating whether the respondent ranked as most important their partisan identity (party ID most important) or religious identity (religious ID most important).[13]

Figure 3.2 presents the results from these models, again using separate coefficient plots for respondents from each party (see the full model results in the Appendix). In support of previous research, we also fail to find a relationship between partisan strength and opposition to compromise. Partisan loyalty, per se, does not appear to be an obstacle to committing to this democratic norm. We do find, however, that opposition to compromise appears heightened among Republicans who declare that the Republican identity is the most important one informing their political attitudes and behaviors. And we know that, overall, Republicans—both voters and non-voters—are more opposed to compromise than Democrats.

Aside from this partisan asymmetry, the key finding is that the ideological commitments of primary voters in both parties are the principal factors in opposing compromise, and this is especially true for Republicans. For Republican pri-

---

12 The index, which ranges from -6 to +6, represents the level of agreement with the following statements: "White people in the US have certain advantages because of the color of their skin"; "Racial problems in the US are rare, isolated situations"; and "I am angry that racism exists." Respondents who strongly agree with a racially prejudiced statement (or strongly disagree with an unprejudiced statement) are assigned a value of -2, those who somewhat agree a value of -1, those who neither agree nor disagree a value of 0, those who somewhat disagree a value of 1, and those who strongly disagree a value of 2.

13 In separate models, we also included binaries for whether a racial, gender, or sexual identity was most important, with null effects. We also examined interaction terms to see whether these identity importance effects hinge on a respondent identifying with a particular identity group (e.g. female x gender ID most important). The effects were largely insignificant and did not change the takeaways from our models.

Democrats

Republicans

Non-Voters ● Voters

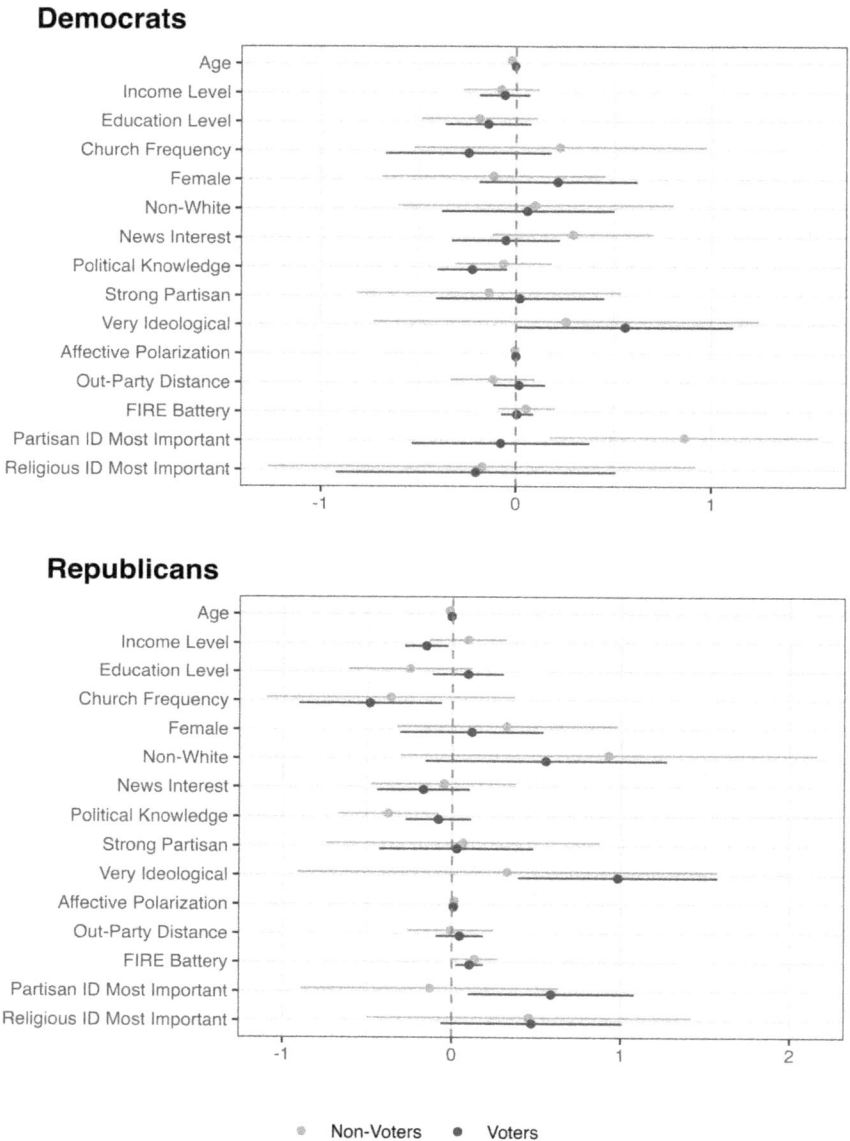

Figure 3.2: Coefficient plots for logistic regression models predicting opposition to compromise.

mary voters who are "very conservative," the predicted probability of opposing compromise is eighty percent, compared to sixty-three percent for those who fall below the most extreme ideology. For Democrats, a primary voter who is "very liberal" has an expected probability of fifty-four percent, while a primary voter who is not at the extreme lies at forty percent. Importantly, we only observe a statistically significant result among primary voters in both parties, suggesting the strongest ideologues in primary electorates may have a unique preference within the party for nominees who profess they will not compromise. At the same time, we find that perceptions that the other party is ideologically very distant did not seem to affect attitudes toward compromise for any group.

Instead, what appears to matter is affective partisanship—the distance in feelings one has for one's own party relative to the other. In this case, the effect was only among Republicans. Moreover, the dynamic is relevant for both primary voters and non-voters, so we cannot say that primary voters are unique along this dimension. To visualize this finding, Figure 3.3 illustrates the predicted probability of opposing compromise for primary voters and non-voters in both parties based on their levels of affective polarization. As negative feelings toward the other side increase for Republican voters—including those who don't vote in primaries—the predicted probability of opposition to compromise escalates significantly. For non-voters, the probability increases from fifty-five percent to eighty-three percent, while for primary voters the jump is from fifty-eight percent to seventy-six percent. There is no apparent relationship for Democratic primary voters. These findings suggest, at least for Republican primary voters, that affective partisanship plays a role in attitudes toward compromise with Democrats.

With regard to our hypotheses about individual identities and partisan coalitions, we find evidence that GOP primary voters who hold negative racial attitudes, view their partisan identity as the most important, and view their religious identity as most important are more likely to oppose compromise. However, the effect of being racially antagonistic is a strong predictor of disliking political compromise for both Republican primary voters and non-voters, suggesting it is not a uniquely motivating factor among primary electorates. There is also a partisan asymmetry when it comes to the importance of party ID: while Democratic non-voters who rank this identity as most important are more opposed to compromise, there is no effect for primary voters, while the opposite is true for Republicans.

Perhaps the biggest surprise is related to religiosity. While ranking a religious identity as most important marginally increased opposition to compromise for Republican primary voters (at $p < 0.1$), attending church had the *opposite* effect. Those who attend church more frequently are more likely to support compromise. Recall that our theory was that Republican primary voters who are strongly religious would fear compromise with the Democratic party, which champions secular positions on a range of issues. Our identity variable provides some support for

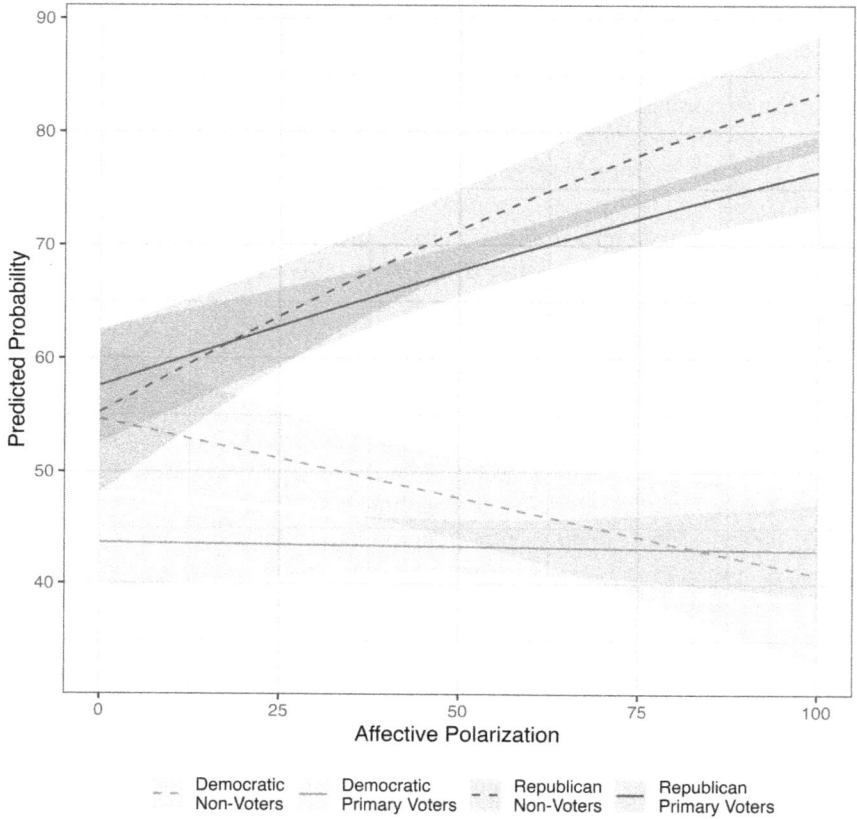

Figure 3.3: Predicted opposition to compromise by affective polarization.

this hypothesis, but our church frequency finding makes us consider countervailing theories to explain the opposite result. One possibility is that churchgoers (especially in a politically diverse state like Ohio) spend a lot of time with other people and gain experience with the need for compromise. They engage with fellow congregants who may disagree with them on a range of issues. They help run organizations where compromise might be necessary to get things done.

We should point out that Ohio's religious landscape is largely representative of the broader United States. According to one 2023–2024 survey, 64 percent of Ohioans identify as Christian, about the same as the rest of the nation at 62 percent (Pew Research Center 2025). And among Christian sects, Ohioans are only slightly more likely to be Evangelical Protestants and somewhat less likely to be Catholic than the overall US population.

Discussion and Conclusion

Our goal in this chapter was to improve understanding of electoral participation in primaries. Using two separate datasets, we asked a basic question about whether primary voters differ from rank-and-file partisans who do not vote in primaries. Our underlying premise is that an additional pre-election winnows participation to an exclusive set of "super" voters. Drawing on existing theories of political participation, we theorized that what distinguishes primary voters from partisans who vote only in the general election is that they possess *even more* of the characteristics that studies show predict general election turnout. That is to say, they possess more individual resources, more underlying motivations, and receive more mobilization than those who vote only in the general election. Our results substantiate this expectation.

Beyond having resources like education, wealth and experience (age), we find that motivations such as strong partisanship and political interest are powerfully associated with voting in primaries. There is also evidence that extreme ideology motivates turnout in primaries. We did not find, however, that voters who perceive the party as more moderate than themselves were more likely to vote. We expected that such voters might show up in primaries because they want to pull the party toward their more extreme positions. Regardless, our central finding about these super voters requires more attention to see how the highly engaged differ along other dimensions from the less engaged (Krupnikov and Ryan 2022).

To gain traction on such a question, we also examined attitudes toward an important norm in democratic politics: whether voters prefer candidates who would compromise with those they disagree with, or not. Previous research illustrates that officeholders fear compromise in legislating, and that such behaviors diminish the potential for passing broadly supported policies (Anderson, Butler and Harbridge-Yong 2020). Our analysis probed differences between primary voters and partisans who did not vote in the primary on attitudes toward compromise. We expected and confirmed that a disposition toward compromise has less support among the most extreme ideological primary voters in both parties. As expected, these dynamics were more powerful among Republican primary voters who, we argued, belonged to a more ideologically narrow party, which attenuates incentives to compromise. We also found that affective polarization and hostile racial attitudes reduced support for compromise among Republican voters, but this was not limited to primary voters.

The findings support previous research about partisan asymmetries among party elites regarding willingness to follow democratic norms of bargaining and compromise (Mann and Ornstein 2012). Our study illustrates the potential linkage stemming from a subset of very ideological voters in the Republican primary electorate who disfavor compromise. Additionally, our findings suggest why Republican party elites tend to pick more conservative candidates than most Republican partisans would prefer, and why these elites believe that candidates who compromise will not do well (Doherty, Dowling, and Miller 2022). These elites may be getting strong signals from the subset of ideological and affective voters we identify in this analysis. These signals are not only sent in primaries: in another analysis we conducted (Albert and La Raja 2025), we find that primary voters opposed to compromise are more active in donating to elected officials than those who support compromise.

Additional research might explore our finding that those who attend church more frequently are more open to compromise from politicians. This finding may go against the conventional view of churchgoers as rigid moralists. But if viewed through the framework of social networks and associational life, it becomes more understandable why this may be so. Religious congregants—and those embedded intensely in any social organization—have experience with the need to compromise with members in their group. We might apply insights about primary voters' attitudes from other areas of research regarding how group-based memberships and networks affect attitudes about democratic norms.[14]

Lastly, this work has some implications for potential reforms. Given concerns about how primaries may favor extremist candidates, much of the focus on remedies (as we shall see in the next part of this book) has been on changing the nomination rules by adopting open or nonpartisan primaries. However, a helpful reframing of the problem might be to consider how merely having a pre-election shapes the electorate more powerfully than most sets of primary rules. If the purpose is to make nominations more representative of the partisan electorate, this would imply either focusing on significant expansion of participation in primaries, or eliminating them.

---

14 This work starts with Tocqueville and his insights about how associational life develops democratic habits.

Appendix

Table 3.3: Logistic models predicting primary voting.

	(1) Democrats (Ohio)	(2) Democrats (CES)	(3) Republicans (Ohio)	(4) Republicans (CES)
(Intercept)	-3.606***	-5.366***	-3.376***	-5.489***
	(0.482)	(0.116)	(0.484)	(0.135)
Age	0.015**	0.041***	0.020***	0.043***
	(0.006)	(0.001)	(0.005)	(0.001)
Income Level	0.106+	0.069***	0.120*	0.072***
	(0.060)	(0.010)	(0.059)	(0.012)
Education Level	-0.093	0.268***	-0.028	0.203***
	(0.095)	(0.019)	(0.096)	(0.024)
Church Frequency	0.202**	-0.095***	0.185**	0.058***
	(0.067)	(0.015)	(0.059)	(0.016)
Female	-0.267	-0.141***	-0.138	-0.181***
	(0.179)	(0.035)	(0.175)	(0.042)
Non-White	0.370+	-0.170***	0.079	-0.222***
	(0.204)	(0.037)	(0.295)	(0.062)
News Interest	0.684***	0.244***	0.594***	0.192***
	(0.129)	(0.025)	(0.113)	(0.028)
Political Knowledge	0.157*	0.325***	0.185*	0.312***
	(0.078)	(0.020)	(0.081)	(0.023)
Strong Partisan	0.737***	0.219***	0.670***	0.119*
	(0.189)	(0.041)	(0.192)	(0.049)
Very Ideological	0.027	0.018	0.403	0.036
	(0.264)	(0.043)	(0.274)	(0.050)
Own Party More Moderate	0.205	0.176***	-0.122	0.308***
	(0.206)	(0.039)	(0.221)	(0.045)
Political Activity Beyond Voting	0.356+	0.538***	0.235	0.472***
	(0.194)	(0.037)	(0.188)	(0.047)
# of Groups Contacted	0.354**		0.065	
	(0.122)		(0.118)	
Observations	773	19,477	801	12,693
Akaike Inf. Crit.	843.1	21,313.5	850.0	14,044.4
Log Likelihood	-407.553	-10,643.752	-410.991	-7,009.190

Notes: + $p < 0.1$ * $p < 0.05$ ** $p < 0.01$ *** $p < 0.001$

Table 3.4: Logistic models predicting opposition to compromise.

	(1) Democratic Voters	(2) Democratic Non-Voters	(3) Republican Voters	(4) Republican Non-Voters
(Intercept)	1.035+	1.661*	1.159+	1.918*
	(0.549)	(0.742)	(0.598)	(0.827)
Age	-0.006	-0.025**	-0.007	-0.017+
	(0.006)	(0.009)	(0.006)	(0.010)
Income Level	-0.061	-0.078	-0.154*	0.092
	(0.067)	(0.100)	(0.065)	(0.116)
Education Level	-0.145	-0.190	0.092	-0.250
	(0.113)	(0.152)	(0.108)	(0.188)
Church Frequency	-0.245	0.224	-0.486*	-0.364
	(0.217)	(0.382)	(0.215)	(0.375)
Female	0.212	-0.118	0.115	0.324
	(0.207)	(0.292)	(0.217)	(0.333)
Non-White	0.058	0.098	0.555	0.925
	(0.225)	(0.360)	(0.365)	(0.629)
News Interest	-0.055	0.290	-0.170	-0.049
	(0.142)	(0.211)	(0.140)	(0.220)
Political Knowledge	-0.227*	-0.067	-0.081	-0.377*
	(0.091)	(0.128)	(0.099)	(0.152)
Strong Partisan	0.020	-0.141	0.028	0.064
	(0.220)	(0.345)	(0.233)	(0.413)
Very Ideological	0.557*	0.256	0.982**	0.329
	(0.283)	(0.504)	(0.300)	(0.634)
Affective Polarization	0.000	-0.006	0.009**	0.014*
	(0.003)	(0.005)	(0.003)	(0.006)
Out-Party Distance	0.016	-0.120	0.046	-0.008
	(0.069)	(0.110)	(0.071)	(0.130)
FIRE Battery	0.006	0.052	0.103*	0.134+
	(0.043)	(0.075)	(0.042)	(0.073)
Partisan ID Most Important	-0.079	0.861*	0.589*	-0.128
	(0.232)	(0.352)	(0.251)	(0.390)
Religious ID Most Important	-0.207	-0.174	0.474+	0.460
	(0.366)	(0.559)	(0.274)	(0.488)
Observations	464	240	539	211
Akaike Inf. Crit.	634.5	336.5	640.8	270.8
Log Likelihood	-301.273	-152.231	-304.386	-119.383

Notes: + p < 0.1 * p < 0.05 ** p < 0.01 *** p < 0.001

Bibliography

Albert, Zachary, and Mia Costa. 2024. "Winning At All Costs? How Negative Partisanship Affects Voter Decision-Making." *Political Behavior* 47 (3): 963–989.

Albert, Zachary, and Raymond La Raja. 2025. "Insurgency in Republican Primaries." In *The Changing Character of the American Right, Volume II: Ideology, Politics and Policy in the Era of Trump*, edited by Joel D. Aberbach, Bruce E. Cain, Desmond King, and Gillian Peele, 129–165. Springer.

Anderson, Sarah E., Daniel M. Butler, Laurel Harbridge-Yong, and Renae Marshall. 2023. "Top-Four Primaries Help Moderate Candidates via Crossover Voting: The Case of the 2022 Alaska Election Reforms." *The Forum* 21 (1): 123–136.

Anderson, Sarah E., Daniel M. Butler, and Laurel Harbridge-Yong. 2020. *Rejecting Compromise: Legislators' Fear of Primary Voters.* Cambridge University Press.

Ansolabehere, Stephen, Shigeo Hirano, and James M. Snyder Jr. 2007. "What Did the Direct Primary Do to Party Loyalty in Congress?" In *Party, Process, and Political Change in Congress, Volume 2*, edited by David W. Brady and Mathew D. McCubbins, 21–36. Stanford University Press.

Arceneaux, Kevin, Martin Johnson, Rene Lindstädt, and Ryan J. Vander Wielen. 2016. "The Influence of News Media on Political Elites: Investigating Strategic Responsiveness in Congress.: *American Journal of Political Science* 60 (1): 5–29.

Arceneaux, Kevin. 2019. "The Roots of Intolerance and Opposition to Compromise: The Effects of Absolutism on Political Attitudes." *Personality and Individual Differences* 151: 109498.

Bafumi, Joseph, and Michael C. Herron. 2010. "Leapfrog Representation and Extremism: A Study of American Voters and Their Members in Congress." *American Political Science Review* 104 (3): 519–542.

Bartels, Larry M. 2020. "Ethnic Antagonism Erodes Republicans' Commitment to Democracy." *Proceedings of the National Academy of Sciences* 117 (37): 22752–22759.

Bipartisan Policy Center. 2018. *2018 Primary Election Turnout and Reform.* Bipartisan Policy Center Report. bipartisanpolicy.org/report/2018-primary-elections-turnout-and-reforms/.

Boatright, Robert G. 2013. *Getting Primaried the Changing Politics of Congressional Primary Challenges.* University of Michigan Press.

Brady, David W., Hahrie Han, and Jeremy C. Pope. 2007. "Primary Elections and Candidate Ideology: Out of Step with the Primary Electorate?" *Legislative Studies Quarterly* 32 (1): 79–105.

Brady, Henry E., Kay Lehman Scholzman, and Sidney Verba. 1999. "Prospecting for Participants: Rational Expectations and the Recruitment of Political Activists." *American Political Science Review* 93 (1): 153–68.

Brady, Henry E., Sidney Verba, and Kay Lehman Schlozman. 1995. "Beyond SES: A Resource Model of Political Participation." *The American Political Science Review* 89 (2): 271–294.

Brown, Nadia E. 2014. *Sisters in the Statehouse: Black Women and Legislative Decision Making.* Oxford University Press.

Burden, Barry C. 2001. "The Polarizing Effects of Congressional Primaries." In *Congressional Primaries and the Politics of Representation*, ed. Peter F. Galderisi, Marni Ezra, and Michael Lyons. Lanham, MD: Rowman and Littlefield, pp. 95–115.

Burke, Richard, Justin H. Kirkland, and Jonathan B. Slapin. 2021. "Party Competition, Personal Votes, and Strategie Disloyalty in the U.S. States." *Political Research Quarterly* 74 (4): 1024–36.

Campbell, Angus, Philip E. Converse, Warren E. Miller, and Donald E. Stokes. 1960. *The American Voter.* University of Chicago Press.

Canes-Wrone, Brandice, David W. Brady, and John F. Cogan. 2002. "Out of Step, Out of Office: Electoral Accountability and House Members' Voting." *American Political Science Review* 96 (1): 127 – 140.

Carson, Jamie L., Gregory Koger, Matthew J. Lebo, and Everett Young. 2010. "The Electoral Costs of Party Loyalty in Congress." *American Journal of Political Science* 54 (3): 598 – 616.

Craig, Maureen A., and Jennifer A. Richeson. 2014. "On the Precipice of a 'Majority-Minority' America: Perceived Status Threat From the Racial Demographic Shift Affects White Americans' Political Ideology." *Psychological Science* 25 (6): 1189 – 1197.

DeSante, Christopher D., and Candis Watts Smith. 2020. "Fear, Institutionalized Racism, and Empathy: The Underlying Dimensions of Whites' Racial Attitudes." *PS: Political Science & Politics* 53 (4): 639 – 45.

Doherty, David, Conor M. Dowling, and Michael G. Miller. 2022. *Small Power: How Local Parties Shape Elections*. Oxford University Press.

Drutman, Lee. 2021. "What We Know about Congressional Primaries and Congressional Primary Reform." *New America*. newamerica.org/political-reform/reports/what-we-know-about-congressional-primaries-and-congressional-primary-reform/.

Egan, Patrick J. 2013. *Partisan Priorities: How Issue Ownership Drives and Distorts American Politics*. Cambridge University Press.

Ferrer, Joshua, and Michael Thorning. 2023. "2022 Primary Turnout: Trends and Lessons for Boosting Participation." Washington, DC: Bipartisan Policy Center.

Graham, Matthew H., and Milan W. Svolik. 2020. "Democracy in America? Partisanship, Polarization, and the Robustness of Support for Democracy in the United States." *American Political Science Review* 114 (2): 392 – 409.

Green, Donald P., Bradley Palmquist, and Eric Schickler. 2002. *Partisan Hearts and Minds: Political Parties and the Social Identities of Voters*. Yale University Press.

Grose, Christian R. 2020. "Reducing Legislative Polarization: Top-Two and Open Primaries Are Associated with More Moderate Legislators." *Journal of Political Institutions and Political Economy* 1 (2): 267 – 287.

Gutmann, Amy, and Dennis Thompson. 2010. "The Mindsets of Political Compromise." *Perspectives on Politics* 8 (4): 1125 – 1143.

Hall, Andrew B. 2019. *Who Wants to Run? How the Devaluing of Political Office Drives Polarization*. University of Chicago Press.

Harbridge, Laurel, and Neil Malhotra. 2011. "Electoral Incentives and Partisan Conflict in Congress: Evidence from Survey Experiments." *American Journal of Political Science* 55 (3): 494 – 510.

Harbridge, Laurel, Neil Malhotra, and Brian F. Harrison. 2014. "Public Preferences for Bipartisanship in the Policymaking Process." *Legislative Studies Quarterly* 39 (3): 327 – 355.

Hill, Seth J. 2015. "Institution of Nomination and the Policy Ideology of Primary Electorates." *Quarterly Journal of Political Science* 10 (4): 461 – 487.

Hirano, Shigeo, James M. Snyder, and Michael M. Ting. 2009. "Distributive Politics with Primaries." *The Journal of Politics* 71 (4): 1467 – 1480.

Iyengar, Shanto, Gaurav Sood, and Yphtach Lelkes. 2012. "Affect, Not Ideology: A Social Identity Perspective on Polarization," *Public Opinion Quarterly* 76 (3): 405 – 31.

Jacobson, Gary C. 2012. "The Electoral Origins of Polarized Politics: Evidence From the 2010 Cooperative Congressional Election Study." *American Behavioral Scientist* 56 (12): 1612 – 1630.

Kalmoe, Nathan P. 2020. *With Ballots and Bullets: Partisanship and Violence in the American Civil War.* Cambridge University Press.

Krupnikov, Yanna, and John Barry Ryan. 2022. *The Other Divide.* Cambridge University Press.

Leaverton, Chris. 2023. "Three Takeaways on Redistricting and Competition in the 2022 Midterms." Brennan Center for Justice. January 20, 2023. www.brennancenter.org/our-work/analysis-opinion/three-takeaways-redistricting-and-competition-2022-midterms.

Mann, Thomas E., and Norman J. Ornstein. 2012. *It's Even Worse than It Looks: How the American Constitutional System Collided with the New Politics of Extremism.* Basic Books.

Mason, Lilliana. 2018. *Uncivil Agreement: How Politics Became Our Identity.* 1st edition. University of Chicago Press.

McGhee, Eric, Seth Masket, Boris Shor, Steven Rogers, and Nolan McCarty. 2014. "A Primary Cause of Partisanship? Nomination Systems and Legislator Ideology." *American Journal of Political Science* 58 (2): 337–351.

Mutz, Diana C. "Status Threat, Not Economic Hardship, Explains the 2016 Presidential Vote." 2018. *Proceedings of the National Academy of Sciences* 115 (19): E4330–39.

Pew Research Center. 2012. "Trends in American Values: 1987–2012. The Pew Research Center for People and the Press." https://www.pewresearch.org/dataset/1987-2012-values-survey-combined-dataset/ Pew Research Center. 2025. "Religious Landscape Study." www.pewresearch.org/collections/religious-landscape-study/.

Porter, Rachel, and Tyler S. Steelman. 2023. "No Experience Required: Early Donations and Amateur Candidate Success in Primary Elections." *Legislative Studies Quarterly* 48 (2): 455–466.

Pyeatt, Nicholas. 2015. "Party Unity, Ideology, and Polarization in Primary Elections for the House of Representatives: 1956–2012." *Legislative Studies Quarterly* 40 (4): 651–76.

Rosenstone, Steven J., and John Mark Hansen. 1993. *Mobilization, Participation, and Democracy in America.* Macmillan.

Ryan, Timothy J. 2017. "No Compromise: Political Consequences of Moralized Attitudes." *American Journal of Political Science* 61 (2): 409–23

Sides, John, Chris Tausanovitch, Lynn Vavreck, and Christopher Warshaw. 2020. "On the Representativeness of Primary Electorates." *British Journal of Political Science* 50 (2): 677–685.

Thomsen, Danielle M. 2017. *Opting Out of Congress: Partisan Polarization and the Decline of Moderate Candidates.* Cambridge University Press.

Verba, Sidney, Kay Lehman Schlozman, and Henry E. Brady. 1995. *Voice and Equality.* Cambridge, MA: Harvard University Press.

Wolak, Jennifer. 2020. *Compromise in an Age of Party Polarization.* Oxford University Press.

Wolak, Jennifer. 2022. "The Social Foundations of Public Support for Political Compromise." *The Forum* 20 (1): 193–215.

Wolfinger, Raymond E, and Steven J. Rosenstone. 1980. *Who Votes?* Yale University Press.

Caitlin E. Jewitt and Sarah Treul

Chapter 4
The Influence of Presidential Primary Elections on Congressional Primary Turnout

Abstract: While the date of the general election is codified in federal statute to be held on the first Tuesday after the first Monday in November, the timing of congressional primary elections varies considerably, typically ranging from March until September. Furthermore, in years with a presidential election, there is variation in whether the congressional primary is held on the same day as the presidential primary. In this chapter, we explore the effects of the variation in the congressional primary date and the synchronizing of congressional and presidential primary dates on voter turnout. We find that when congressional primaries are aligned with the presidential primary and the latter is competitive, significantly more people turn out and cast ballots in the congressional primary.

In 2016, North Carolina planned to hold its primary elections for the U.S. House of Representatives on the same date as its statewide and presidential primary elections, as it had done in 2008 and 2012. The date for the primaries was set for March 15, 2016. However, in early February federal judges deemed the congressional districts drawn by the North Carolina General Assembly racially gerrymandered—meaning the race of eligible voters was over-emphasized in drawing the district maps. The state did not have enough time to redraw the maps, issue a new candidate filing period using those new maps, print new ballots, and mail absentee ballots before the March primary date. Therefore, the state legislature passed a bill, signed by Republican Governor Pat McCrory, setting the new congressional primary date for June 7, 2016, thereby separating the congressional primary from the presidential primary date by several months.

This example from 2016 in North Carolina is illustrative because it is both common and unusual. As we show in this chapter, states regularly move around the dates they hold congressional and/or presidential primaries on for several reasons, and sometimes these dates are concurrent[1] with one another and other

---

1 This chapter uses the term "concurrent" to refer to those congressional primaries that are held

times they are not. In fact, from 2000 to 2020, states switched from aligning their party primaries to separating their primaries (or vice versa) forty-seven times.[2] What is less typical about this example is that the moving of primary dates is often the decision of the state in consultation with the political parties, and not the decision of courts, as it was in North Carolina in 2016. North Carolina intended to align its primaries, but for logistical and legal reasons was unable to do so. Typically, states enjoy great discretion in selecting the date to hold congressional primary elections, which leads to congressional primary dates ranging from March until September.

In addition to choosing the date for the congressional primary, in presidential election years states and state parties can also opt to align the primary with the presidential nominating contest or hold the primaries on separate dates. Over the past several decades, approximately forty percent of states have conjoined their presidential and congressional primaries. Yet, given the wide variation in congressional primary dates, and the sequential nature of the presidential nomination season with primaries and caucuses held over the course of several months, it is sometimes the case that even when the primaries are concurrent, the presidential nominee is already decided by the time the state's congressional primary is held.

This chapter is a first step in investigating how synchronizing a congressional primary with the presidential primary—and how the competitiveness of the presidential primary—might increase voter turnout at the congressional level. As explained below, there is reason to suspect that a competitive presidential primary occurring on the same day as a congressional primary could increase a voter's propensity to engage with the congressional primary. Thus, we expect that holding the congressional and presidential primaries on the same day will greatly increase congressional turnout, especially if the presidential nomination is still undecided

---

on the same date as the state's presidential primary. Other literature occasionally uses "aligned," "conjoined," and "synched" as synonyms.

2 This statistic represents states switching their congressional and presidential primaries from being aligned to separate or separate to aligned between 2000 and 2020. Each party is considered separately. For instance, North Carolina held aligned congressional and presidential primaries for both the Democratic and Republican parties in May 2000 but then separated them in 2004 (the congressional primary was held in July, the presidential primary was held in February). This represents two changes. Then North Carolina aligned both parties' primaries once again in May 2008, which equates to two more changes. The state stayed constant between 2008 and 2012, holding congressional and presidential primaries on the same date in May 2012, before hosting the primaries on separate dates in 2016, as described in the text above. In 2020, the state switched again, returning to holding the congressional primaries and presidential primaries on the same date in March.

at the time of the primary. We find that states that hold their congressional primaries alongside their presidential primary experience higher turnout in the congressional primary. This is particularly the case when the presidential primary is competitive.

Assessing turnout in congressional primaries is an important first step toward better understanding how the timing of primaries influences primary results. If certain types of candidates benefit from changes in turnout, then the question of whether or not the primaries are aligned could drastically affect the success of particular types of primary candidates. This, in turn, may affect who represents a district in Congress. Given the small number of congressional districts that have competitive general elections, it is important to better understand primary elections, where much of the competition occurs, and the factors that contribute to success in these elections. Furthermore, because states frequently adjust primary dates and couple and uncouple them from presidential primaries, it is important for policymakers to understand the potential implications of these adjustments for democratic participation.

Variation in Congressional Primary Timing

Article I, Section 4, Clause 1 of the Constitution notes that the "Times, Places and Manner of holding Elections for Senators and Representatives, shall be prescribed in each State by the Legislature thereof... ." This gives each state great discretion over when, where, and how its voting eligible population (VEP) casts ballots for its representative to the U.S. Congress. This includes state control over the administration of primary elections. Although congressional primary elections are intraparty affairs designed to allow voters a say in choosing the party's nominee, these contests are also run through the state in consultation with each party (Boatright 2014). Establishing the date for a primary, the type of primary held (e. g. open, closed, semi-open), and whether the congressional primary will be held concurrently with the presidential primary is based on a state's statutes, party constitutions, and party rules and regulations. When allowable by law, states can make changes to congressional primary dates, which leads to both variation across states as well as variation within states over time.

To illustrate, Figure 4.1 depicts the timing of the Republican congressional primaries (for each state) in 2000.[3] This figure shows that there were several states that held their congressional primaries in March and early April, a sizable num-

---

3 Data from the National Conference of State Legislatures (www.ncsl.org).

ber that held them throughout May and June, and many that held them in late summer/early fall.[4] All in all, there was considerable variation and spread in the timing of when congressional primaries were held in 2000.

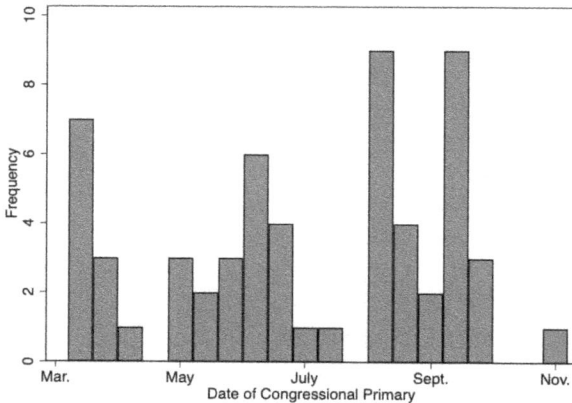

Figure 4.1: Timing of the Republican congressional primaries by state in 2000.
Note: The date each state held its Republican congressional primary in 2000.

It is also the case that the dates states choose to hold congressional primaries on do not remain constant. States move their congressional primary dates with some frequency for a variety of reasons, including accommodating religious holidays, allowing enough time for overseas and military voters, and delaying due to the COVID-19 pandemic (Han 2024; Sullivan, Levy, and Stark 2020; Foderaro 2018). Table 4.1 shows the dates of congressional primaries between 2000 and 2020 in selected states. For instance, North Carolina has held its congressional primary in March, May, and July across this period for twenty years. New York and Connecticut started out with congressional primaries in September before Connecticut moved to an August primary in 2004 where it has remained ever since, whereas New York shifted to a June primary in 2012 (and stuck with that thereafter).

---

4 Typically, the congressional primaries begin in March, but the earliest date of a congressional primary in our data was a primary in Illinois on February 2, 2010. The November primaries in Figure 4.1 are in Louisiana. Prior to 2026, Louisiana conducted all local, state, and congressional primary elections on the same day. In a presidential election year, these primaries were on the same date as the presidential general election. If a congressional primary candidate won a simple majority on Election Day, the candidate won the election outright. If no one received a simple majority, there was a second round of elections in December.

Illinois has consistently held a March congressional primary except for 2008, when it held an early February primary. New Jersey, however, has remained consistent, holding its primary in early June throughout this time period.

Table 4.1: Congressional primary dates from 2000 to 2020 in selected states.

	North Carolina	New York	Connecticut	Illinois	New Jersey
2000	May 2	Sept. 12	Sept. 12	March 21	June 6
2004	July 20	Sept. 14	Aug. 10	March 16	June 8
2008	May 6	Sept. 9	Aug. 12	Feb. 5	June 3
2012	May 8	June 26	Aug. 14	March 20	June 5
2016	March 15	June 16	Aug. 9	March 15	June 7
2020	March 3	June 23	Aug. 11	March 17	June 7

Note: A sample of five states and their respective congressional primary dates from 2000 to 2020.

The decisions states make about the timing and the type of the primary have the potential to influence outcomes. Political scientists have examined how the type of primary influences turnout and candidate extremism (e. g. Micatka, Boatright, and Tolbert 2024; Hall 2015; Grose 2020) and how the date of the primary affects candidate entry, fundraising, and interest group activity (Anzia 2014; Hassel 2018). What is less well studied is how other elections, particularly top-of-the-ballot contests including presidential primaries, influence voter interest and outcomes in congressional primaries.

We are particularly interested in utilizing the variation in concurrent primaries across years and parties to assess how turnout in congressional primaries shifts as states move primaries to (off) presidential primary dates. We also leverage the fact that over the time period studied (2000–2020) states occasionally switch from holding concurrent primaries to holding nonconcurrent primaries and vice versa. From 2000 to 2020, approximately thirty-seven percent of states held their party's congressional primaries on the same date as the presidential primary.[5] The other sixty-three percent of state parties' primaries were held on a different date than the state party's presidential primary.

---

5 Throughout this analysis, we focus on congressional primaries held between 2000 and 2020. Thus, our typical unit of analysis is each party's congressional primary in each state in each election year. Given that states have varying numbers of congressional districts, this dramatically

Table 4.2 shows there is also variation across years in the percent of states holding congressional primaries aligned with the presidential primaries. In 2000 and 2020, more than forty percent of states synchronized their congressional primaries and presidential primaries; however, in 2008, less than thirty percent of primaries were concurrent.

Table 4.2: States with congressional primaries sharing a date with presidential nomination contests, by year.

	2000	2004	2008	2012	2016	2020
Same Date	41.18%	34.34%	27.45%	38.24%	36.27%	41.84%
	(42)	(34)	(28)	(39)	(65)	(41)
Different Date	58.82%	65.66%	72.55%	61.76%	63.73%	58.16%
	(60)	(65)	(74)	(63)	(65)	(57)
Total	100.00%	100.00%	100.00%	100.00%	100.00%	100.00%
	(102)	(99)	(102)	(102)	(102)	(98)

Note: The unit of analysis in this table is the state/party/year because all congressional districts within a state have the same primary date. Thus, in each presidential election year, there are a maximum of fifty-one cases for each party (the fifty states and the District of Columbia), or 102 cases per year. In some years, there are missing cases due to states canceling presidential primaries when an incumbent president is running for re-nomination.

There is reason to suspect that a concurrent presidential and congressional primary will increase turnout. Anderson (2023) finds that when there are multiple elections on a ballot, citizens find it easier to engage with less effort, as concurrent elections can reduce some of the costs of voting. Boatright, Moscardelli, and Vickrey (2020) find that primary turnout decreases as the election cycle progresses, but it is hard to isolate the effect of timing because primaries are more likely to be concurrent earlier in the election cycle. This leads us to expect that congressional primaries held on the same day as presidential primaries will see greater turnout. Of course, the costs and benefits of voting will also depend on how competitive the presidential primary is at the time voters cast their ballots.

---

affects the sample size. Thus, at times, it also makes sense to look at the data from the presidential primary level, with the unit of analysis being the state/party/primary in each state in each year.

The Effect of Concurrent Presidential Primaries on Turnout

Whereas congressional primaries take place over the course of several months, these are all discrete events. The presidential nomination differs in that it is a sequential process where voters head to polling places and caucus sites over the course of several months (typically February to June) to voice a preference for the candidate of their choice. These events, which take place in each state and some territories, culminate in the nomination of a candidate for each party. As a result, the competitiveness of the nomination is not constant over the course of the nomination season. At some point during the nomination season, a candidate typically emerges as the de facto nominee. This happens for one of two reasons: either the candidate has secured a majority of delegates, the necessary threshold to win the party's nomination;[6] or all of the candidate's serious competitors have withdrawn from the race and it is clear that it is just a matter of time before the candidate secures enough delegates to become the de facto nominee (Jewitt 2019).

Given this, we consider a presidential nomination to be competitive when there is still a meaningful choice to be made between candidates. Once a candidate has secured the necessary delegates or no longer faces any competition from other serious candidates, we consider the presidential nomination from that point forward to no longer be competitive. Table 4.3 lists the dates on which each presidential nomination since 2000 shifted from the competitive phase to the uncompetitive phase (Jewitt 2019).

Voter participation in the presidential nomination process varies depending on the length of time the nomination remains competitive (Jewitt 2019). For instance, in 2004 (Republicans), 2012 (Democrats), and 2020 (Republicans), an incumbent president was running uncontested for his party's nomination, and there was no meaningful competition. As a result, there was little incentive for voters to head to the polls—in fact, some states and state parties canceled the presidential nominating contests, either as a show of support for the incumbent president or as a cost-saving measure (Isenstadt 2019; Wong 2011). In other years, the presidential nomination is competitive for the entire season and voters in all of the states have the opportunity to vote when there is a meaningful choice to be made on the outcome (e. g. 2008 Democrats). A robust literature on the timing of presidential

---

6 Once a candidate secures a majority of delegates, he or she is considered the de facto nominee. However, a candidate does not officially become the nominee until the summer Convention.

primaries indicates that states with primaries early in the calendar benefit from increased attention and that voters in these early primary states, especially if the race is still competitive, are more likely to participate (e. g. Mayer and Busch 2004; Jewitt 2019).

Table 4.3: Date presidential nominations shifted from competitive to uncompetitive.

Year	Party	Date Nomination Shifted from Competitive to Uncompetitive
2000	Republican	March 9, 2000
2000	Democratic	March 9, 2000
2004	Republican	Uncontested - uncompetitive for entire season
2004	Democratic	March 4, 2004
2008	Republican	March 4, 2008
2008	Democratic	June 3, 2008
2012	Republican	April 11, 2012
2012	Democratic	Uncontested - uncompetitive for entire season
2016	Republican	May 4, 2016
2016	Democratic	June 7, 2016
2020	Republican	Uncontested - uncompetitive for entire season
2020	Democratic	April 8, 2020

Note: The presidential nomination is considered uncompetitive once a candidate has either secured a majority of delegates or all other serious candidates have withdrawn from the race, leaving one candidate as the *de facto nominee*. The nominations listed as uncontested had an incumbent president running for renomination with no serious competition. Data from Jewitt (2019).

We expect this variation in the timing and competitiveness of presidential primary dates to not only influence turnout in the presidential primaries but to also influence voter turnout in congressional primaries when they share a date. Thus, while Figure 4.1 above shows the spread of the 2000 Republican congressional primaries across the calendar between March and November, it is also necessary to consider the timing of the presidential primaries, which began in late January, and concluded in early June, as well as the competitiveness of the presidential nomination race.

Building on Figure 4.1, Figure 4.2 displays the timing of the Republican presidential and congressional primaries in 2000 and also indicates whether the primaries were conjoined or separate. From this, it is clear that early on in the calendar year, there were a handful of standalone presidential primaries. Then in March, we start to see congressional and presidential primaries held concurrently, with a smattering of presidential primaries that were not linked up with the congressional primary. Finally, once the presidential nomination season concluded in June through the fall, there were congressional primaries that were not linked with the presidential primary.

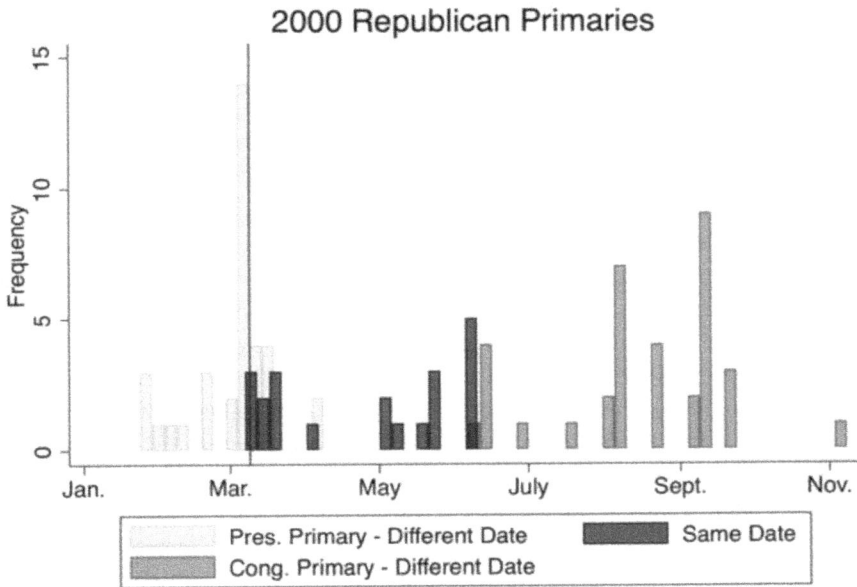

Figure 4.2: Timing of the Republican congressional and presidential primaries, by state in 2000. Note: this figure depicts the date of the Republican congressional and presidential primaries in 2000, indicating whether or not they had different dates within a state or shared the same date. The vertical line indicates March 9, the date that the presidential nomination shifted from competitive to uncompetitive.

In the 2000 Republican presidential nomination, George W. Bush became the presumptive nominee on March 9, 2000, meaning that after that date, the presidential nomination was no longer competitive. This date is indicated by a vertical black line on Figure 4.2. Thus, from this point on, we would expect lower interest and thus turnout in the presidential nomination, as there was no meaningful choice to be made (Jewitt 2019). In 2000, only states that held their congressional primaries on March 7 (the earliest date for congressional primaries that season) had the possibility of sharing a date with a competitive presidential primary.

There were no concurrent primaries earlier. All congressional primaries that were held in conjunction with presidential primaries after this date were linked up with an uncompetitive presidential primary.

This stands in contrast to the 2008 Democratic presidential nomination. As discussed above, there were far fewer conjoined primaries in 2008 than in other years. However, all of these conjoined primaries occurred when the presidential nomination was still competitive because the Democratic presidential nomination race between Barack Obama and Hillary Clinton was competitive until after all of the states held their presidential nomination contest. Figure 4.3 displays the timing of the Democratic presidential and congressional primaries in 2008 and also indicates whether the primaries were conjoined or separate. Although there are more presidential primaries earlier on the Republican side in 2000 (see Figure 4.2) than for the 2008 Democrats, Figure 4.3 shows a handful of early presidential primaries that were not conjoined with congressional primaries. Once the concurrent primaries began, they lasted until early June. The black line on Figure 4.3 indicates June 3, 2008 at the date when Barack Obama secured enough delegates to become to presumptive nominee. Thus, on the Democratic side all of the congressional primaries that were aligned in 2008 were conjoined with a competitive Democratic presidential primary. After this date, the presidential nomination was no longer competitive. Additionally, the congressional primaries held after this date were not conjoined with presidential primaries, as they were all held prior to this date.

Thus, when we consider whether or not the congressional and presidential primaries are aligned, it is also vital that we consider the competitiveness of the presidential nomination. We expect that synchronizing the congressional primary with the presidential primary will stimulate interest in the congressional primary, but only if the presidential primary is still competitive.

Congressional Primary Turnout

Having established that there is variation across states and years in primary date (congressional and presidential), presidential competitiveness, and whether the congressional primary is held on the same date as the presidential primary, we turn back to our overarching question: does aligning a congressional primary with a competitive presidential primary increase interest in the congressional contest? Although there are certainly other ways to operationalize interest, here we measure interest as the turnout of eligible voters.

Scholarship on voter turnout is vast (see Geys 2006 for a review), but most of the literature focused on the United States addresses general election turnout or

2008 Democratic Primaries

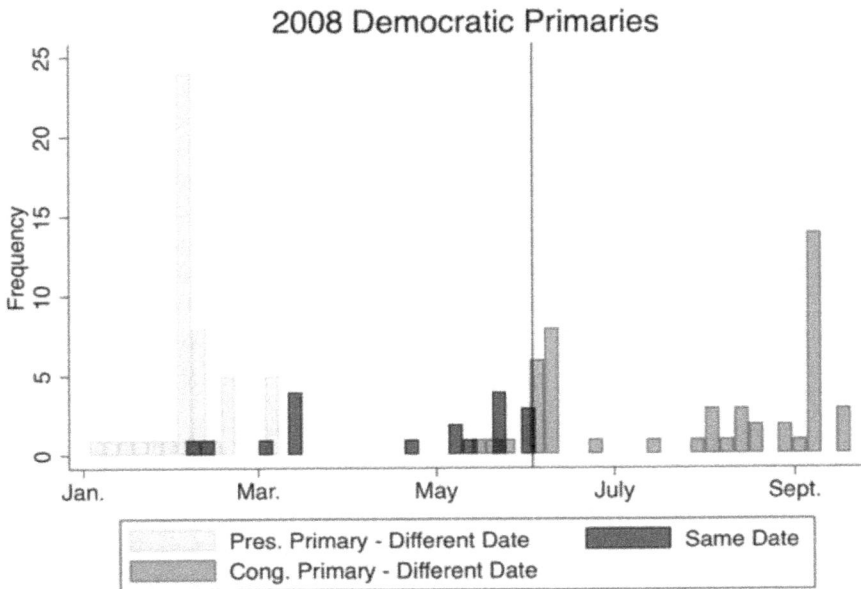

Figure 4.3: Timing of the Democratic congressional and presidential primaries, by state in 2008. Note: This figure depicts the date of the Democratic congressional and presidential primaries in 2008, indicating whether or not they had different dates within a state or shared the same date. The vertical line indicates June 3 as the date that the presidential nomination shifted from competitive to uncompetitive.

presidential primary turnout. Likely part of the reason for the lack of scholarly attention to congressional primary turnout is that many primaries are not that competitive (Boatright 2013) and turnout is typically under twenty percent of the voting eligible population.

The limited work that has explored turnout in congressional primary elections demonstrates that while low competition and turnout are the norm, there remains significant variation in both competition and turnout across districts and in the same district over time (Kenney and Rice 1986, Micatka, Boatright, and Tolbert 2024). Low primary turnout is cause for concern if the small number of people voting in primaries is not representative of the electorate as a whole (Burden and Ezra 1999). If it is the case that the twenty percent of people selecting the party nominee have more extreme preferences, the candidates in the general election might be more extreme than those who would be selected with greater turnout (Brady, Han, and Pope 2011; King, Orlando, and Sparks 2016; Ferrer and Thorning 2023). This is of particular concern in today's gerrymandered districts, where winning a primary frequently serves as the de facto general election in many districts (Drutman 2021; Hill and Tausanovitch 2018). Thus, turnout in congressional primaries is of interest to political scientists because it is thought that partisan primaries are one of the drivers of elite polarization (Hall 2015; Alvarez and Sinclair 2012). Given that low congressional primary turnout might be one of the factors contributing to polarization, it is important that we understand the conditions under which turnout increases or decreases. If conjoining a congressional primary with a competitive presidential primary helps drum up interest in the congressional race—or at least increases turnout—it might help reduce polarization or at least decrease the chances of inexperienced (see Porter and Treul 2025) or ideologically extreme (Boatright 2013) candidates winning elections.

V. O. Key (1956) noted early on that variation in turnout in gubernatorial primaries "...depends on the time, place, and circumstances" (134). Building on Key's finding, other scholars have found contextual variation also influenced turnout in presidential (Ranney 1977; Kenney and Rice 1985), senatorial (Kenney 1986), and congressional primaries (Kenney and Rice 1986). These studies found that turnout significantly increased when the senatorial or gubernatorial primary was held in conjunction with the presidential primary. In their 1986 piece, the first to examine congressional primary turnout, Kenney and Rice showed that district specific variables, election specific variables, and socioeconomic variables influenced congressional primary turnout. Moreover, one of the biggest contributing factors to increased congressional primary turnout was whether the congressional primary coincided with the presidential primary. According to Kenney and Rice (1986), congressional primaries held on the same date as presidential primaries increased turnout by 12.6 percent compared with those primaries not held in conjunction.

Much of the more recent work on congressional primary turnout focuses on the effects of primary reforms (e.g. type of congressional primary) or ballot initiatives that increase turnout (see for example Micatka, Boatright, and Tolbert 2024; Hill 2015, 2022). It is also the case that competitive primaries increase turnout. Although these studies clearly show how reforms, competition, and ballot initiatives influence turnout, we still need to update how presidential primaries might affect congressional primary turnout. Here, and building on the discussion above, there are two important factors we contend affect turnout to consider: 1) in years with a presidential primary, is the congressional primary held concurrently or on a different date; and 2) if the primaries are concurrent, is the presidential primary still competitive?

Data and Methods

In order to assess the relationship between the timing of the congressional prima-ry and its alignment with (or separation from) the presidential primary and the competitiveness of the presidential nomination, we assembled an original data set. The unit of analysis is the congressional primary (for the Republican and Democratic parties) between 2000 and 2020. Among other information about the congressional and presidential primaries in this period, our dataset notably contains information about the date of the congressional primary, the date of the presidential primary, when the presidential primary was decided, and the turnout rate in the congressional primary.[7] Our dependent variable, turnout in the congressional primaries, is calculated by taking the total number of votes cast in the primary (by summing each primary candidate's vote total) and dividing that by the voting-age population in the congressional district,[8] and then convert-ing that value into a percentage. We exclude congressional primaries that were uncontested for theoretical and methodological reasons. Theoretically, we do not expect that those congressional primaries with no competition—with only one candidate—will draw voters to the polls. Methodologically, it is challenging to obtain vote totals in some instances for these uncontested primaries. In the analyses that follow, we focus on congressional primaries held in presidential election years and exclude midterm years, as we are interested in the impact of sharing a date with a (competitive) presidential primary.

To begin exploring the impact of a shared primary date and competitive pres-idential nomination on turnout in congressional primaries, we present a con-trolled mean comparison in Table 4.4. To review, we expect that the congressional primaries that occur alongside a competitive presidential primary will see greater interest and, thus, have higher levels of turnout than those congressional pri-maries that occur on a different date from the presidential primary.

---

7 We calculated the turnout rate by adding together the vote totals for each candidate in the congressional primary and dividing by the voting age population. This information was gathered from Robert Boatright's extensive dataset on congressional primaries.

8 We recognize that using the voting age population (VAP) is not ideal for several reasons (see Burden and Ezra 1999). For one, there are most certainly people living in a district who meet the age requirements for voting but are not eligible for other reasons. However, the voting-eligible population is only available at the state level, not the district level. Thus, while not ideal, it is methodologically possible. When studying turnout in congressional primaries, other scholars (notably Boatright, Moscardelli, and Vickrey 2020; Geras and Crespin 2018; and Flavin and Nelson 2017) also use the voting-age population.

Table 4.4: Controlled mean comparison table of turnout in congressional primaries, by competitiveness of presidential nomination race and shared date.

Status of Presidential Nomination Race	Same Date	Different Date
Competitive	14,01	8.71
	(883)	(577)
Not Competitive	7.97	8.01
	(1,237)	(1,264)

Note: Cell entries in this table are mean values of turnout in contested congressional primaries with the number of cases in parentheses. We calculate turnout by taking the total number of votes cast in the primary (by summing each primary candidate's vote total) and dividing that by the voting-age population in the congressional district, and then converting that value into a percentage.

Our findings provide support for our hypothesis; our analysis shows that among contested congressional primaries, if the congressional primary shares a date with a competitive presidential primary, we expect the turnout rate to be, on average, about fourteen percent. In contrast, congressional primaries sharing a date with the presidential primary, but occurring once the presidential nomination race is no longer competitive, do not see elevated levels of turnout. These congressional primaries have an expected turnout rate of just under eight percent, which is very similar to congressional primaries held on a different date than the presidential primary.

To further investigate this relationship, we also fit an ordinary least squares regression model, with turnout in the congressional primary as our dependent variable. The results are presented in Table 4.5. Our key independent variables include a dichotomous variable for "same date" where a value of one indicates that the congressional and presidential primary shared the same date, a value of zero indicates that they were scheduled on different dates, and there is a dichotomous independent variable for a "competitive presidential race", indicating whether the presidential nomination race was still in the competitive phase when the congressional primary was held. We also include an interaction term, same date * competitive presidential, indicating whether the primaries were aligned during the competitive portion of the presidential nomination race. Our control variables are "congressional primary competitive," which is a dummy variable with a value of one indicating that the difference between the primary winner and the second place candidate was twenty percentage points or less;[9] "month of

---

9 Literature in political science suggests contested races can be classified as uncompetitive if the

the congressional primary,"[10] where a value of three indicates the primary was held in March, a value of four indicates the primary was held in April, and so on; and "incumbent in primary," indicating that there was an incumbent competing in the congressional primary.

The results of this multivariate analysis further confirm our expectations that when a congressional primary shares a date with a competitive presidential primary, congressional turnout is increased. More specifically, the positive, statistically significant coefficient for "same date" indicates that controlling for other factors, congressional primaries that share a date with an uncompetitive presidential primary have a turnout rate that is just over one percentage point higher than turnout in congressional primaries that do not share a date with a presidential primary and occur when the presidential race is no longer competitive. The coefficient for "competitive presidential race" suggests that congressional primaries held on a different date than the presidential primary, but during the competitive phase of the presidential nomination, have a slightly lower turnout rate (approximately 0.9 percentage points less) than congressional primaries held on a different date than the presidential primary during the uncompetitive phase of the presidential nomination. The interaction term, "same date * competitive presidential," indicates that congressional primaries that are on the same date as the presidential primary and happen during the competitive phase of the presidential nomination have an increase in turnout about seven points higher than just one of those conditions being fulfilled.

In order to assess our hypothesis fully, that congressional primaries sharing a date with a competitive presidential primary will have higher turnout than competitive primaries on a different date during the uncompetitive phase, we need to calculate the linear combination of our interaction term. When we do so, we uncover a positive, statistically significant coefficient of 7.72 (p<.0001). This indicates that congressional primaries scheduled on the same date as a competitive presidential primary have a turnout rate that is almost eight percentage points higher than congressional primaries scheduled on a different date than the presidential primary when the presidential nomination race is no longer competitive. We contend that this is not only statistically significant, but also substantively significant, especially given the low levels of turnout in congressional primaries. An increase

---

winning candidate captures more than twenty to twenty-five percent of the vote (see Burden 2004; Jewitt and Treul 2018; Jewitt and Treul 2014). We selected twenty percent to capture as many congressional primaries as possible.

10 As coded, the variable "month of congressional primary" does not capture difference within a month, but it is an approximation for where in the electoral cycle the primary fell.

Table 4.5: Impact of shared date and competitiveness of presidential nomination race on turnout in congressional primaries, 2000–2020.

	β
	(Std. Error)
Same date	1.10*
	(0.490)
Competitive presidential race	-0.89*
	(0.376)
Same date * competitive presidential	7.51*
	(0.505)
Congressional primary competitive	1.33*
	(0.294)
Month of congressional primary	0.606*
	(0.096)
Incumbent in primary	-4.68*
	(0.251)
Constant	10.78*
	(0.912)
N	3.942
F(6, 3935)	143,44
Adj. R-Squared	0,1782

Note: Cell entries in this table are OLS regression coefficients, with the standard error in parentheses. The dependent variable is turnout percentage in the congressional primary. *p<.05

of almost eight percentage points in turnout is sizable and has the potential to be impactful.

The results also suggest that, all else equal, competitive congressional primaries have higher levels of turnout than uncompetitive congressional primaries, that congressional primaries held later in the calendar year have higher levels of turnout than congressional primaries held earlier, and that turnout is lower when there is an incumbent in the congressional primary.

Conclusion

From 2000 to 2020 voter turnout in contested congressional primaries ranged from less than one percent to over forty percent. The highest turnout during this time period was, unsurprisingly, in Louisiana since that state used to hold congressional primaries during the November general election. Congressional primaries in Louisiana have had high turnout because the primaries happened on the same day as the national general election. The theory underlying our research question is encapsulated by the Louisiana example. That is, congressional primary turnout is likely to increase when there are competitive, national elections on the ballot. Although the Louisiana example is unique, there are plenty of states that synchronize their congressional primaries with their presidential primaries. We expect that states that hold their congressional and presidential primaries on the same day experience higher turnout in their congressional primaries, especially when the presidential primary is competitive.

Our results indicate that this is the case. States that synchronize their congressional primaries with the presidential primaries experience significantly higher levels of turnout. Supporting our hypothesis, we find that congressional primaries see a significant increase—about eight percentage points on average—in turnout when the primary is synchronized with the presidential one and when the latter remains competitive. Given the American electorate's interest in presidential campaigns, it is not surprising that a competitive presidential primary gets voters to the polls and engaged with the other down-ballot, federal contests.

The finding that a competitive presidential primary occurring on the same day as the congressional primary can significantly increase turnout has potentially serious consequences for democracy. First, congressional primaries are already low turnout elections. Thus, any finding showing that turnout can be increased under certain circumstances is likely to draw the attention of states and parties who decide primary rules and dates. Second, if higher turnout favors particular types of candidates, as we would expect, synchronizing these primaries and moving them early during in the presidential nomination season could result in particular congressional candidates doing better than other types of candidates.

Of course, there are other potentially confounding factors that may be influencing this relationship. Presidential candidates and their campaigns make choices about what states to spend resources in. It could be the case that when presidential candidates spend more time and resources in particular states with concurrent primaries, these are the states that see the greatest boost to congressional turnout. In addition to looking into the role of presidential candidate resources, future research should examine what types of candidates might benefit the most from higher turnout and how this varies by district level factors. Additionally, in competitive, congressional districts, if one party's presidential primary is competitive, but the other's is not, it could be the case that the party with the competitive primary could drum up more interest in the congressional election, including turnout. This elevated interest and turnout might help the winner of the congressional primary that came from the party with the competitive presidential primary on Election Day. After all, if more voters showed their support during the primary, they might feel compelled to continue that support on Election Day.

Given the variation in timing of congressional and presidential primaries that exists across states and across years, with some states frequently shifting the date of their primaries, it is important that we continue to explore the impact of this timing. It is a consequential, yet underexplored, area that has the potential to have significant impacts on our understanding of congressional primary elections, where, in the modern era, much of the competition happens and decisions are made.

Bibliography

Alvarez, Michael B., and Betsy Sinclair. 2012. "Electoral Institutions and Legislative Behavior: The Effects of Primary Processes." *Electoral Studies* 65 (3): 544–557.

Anderson, David. 2023. "Crowded Out: The Effects of Concurrent Elections on Political Engagement, Candidate Evaluation, and Campaign Learning in the United States." *Journal of Representative Democracy* 60 (2): 325–344.

Anzia, Sarah F. 2014. *Timing and Turnout: How Off-Cycle Elections Favor Organized Groups.* University of Chicago Press.

Boatright, Robert G., Vincent G. Moscardelli, and Clifford Vickrey. 2020. "Primary Election Timing and Voter Turnout." *Election Law Journal* 19 (4): 472–485.

Boatright, Robert G. 2013. *Getting Primaried: The Changing Politics of Congressional Primary Challenges.* University of Michigan Press.

Boatright, Robert G. 2014. *Congressional Primary Elections.* Routledge.

Brady, David W., Hahrie Han, and Jeremy C. Pope. 2011. "Primary Elections and Candidate Ideology: Out of Step with the Primary Electorate?" *Legislative Studies Quarterly* 32 (1): 79–105.

Burden, Barry C. 2004. "Candidate Positioning in U.S. Congressional Elections." *British Journal of Political Science* 34 (1): 211–221.

Burden, Barry C., and Marni Ezra. 1999. "Calculating voter turnout in U.S. House primary elections." *Electoral Studies* 18 (1): 89–99.

Drutman, Lee. 2021. "What We Know about Congressional Primaries and Congressional Primary Reform." https://www.newamerica.org/political-reform/reports/what-we-know-about-congressional-primaries-and-congressional-primary-reform/

Ferrer, Joshua, and Michael Thorning. 2023. *2022 Primary Turnout.* Bipartisan Policy Center. bipartisanpolicy.org/report/2022-primary-turnout/

Flavin, Patrick, and Julie Nelson. 2017. "District Voter Turnout and Dyadic Representation in Congress." *Congress & the Presidency* 44 (2): 201–211.

Foderaro, Lisa W. 2018. "Only in New York: Where Primary Day Comes Twice a Year." *The New York Times.* June 25, 2018. www.nytimes.com/2018/06/25/nyregion/new-york-primary-congress-state-federal.html.

Geras, Matthew J., and Michael H. Crespin. 2018. "The Effect of Open and Closed Primaries on Voter Turnout." In *Routledge Handbook of Primary Elections*, edited by Robert Boatright. Routledge.

Geys, Benny. 2006. "Explaining voter turnout: A view of aggregate-level research." *Electoral Studies* 25 (3): 637–663.

Grose, Christian R. 2020. "Reducing Legislative Polarization: Top-Two and Open Primaries Are Associated with More Moderate Legislators." *Journal of Political Institutions and Political Economy* 1: 1–21.

Hall, Andrew B. 2015. "What Happens when Extremists Win Primaries." *American Political Science Review* 109 (1): 18–42.

Han, Daniel. 2024. "Governor, Legislative Leaders Plan to Move 2025 Primary to June 10." *Politico.* December 12, 2024. subscriber.politicopro.com/article/2024/12/governor-legislative-leaders-plan-to-move-2025-primary-to-june-10–00194132.

Hassell, Hans J. G. 2018. *The Party's Primary: Control of Congressional Nominations.* Cambridge University Press.

Hill, Seth J. 2022. "Sidestepping Primary Reform: Political Action in Response to Institutional Change. Political Science Research and Methods 10 (2): 391–407.

Hill, Seth J. 2015. "Institution of Nomination and the Policy Ideology of Primary Electorates." Quarterly Journal of Political Science 10 (4): 461–487.

Hill, Seth J., and Chris Tausanovitch. 2018. "Southern Realignment, Party Sorting, and the Polarization of American Primary Electorates, 1958–2012." *Public Choice* 176 (1–2): 107–132.

Isenstadt, Alex. 2019. "Republicans to Scrap Primaries and Caucuses as Trump Challengers Cry Foul." *Politico.* September 6. www.politico.com/story/2019/09/06/republicans-cancel-primaries-trump-challengers-1483126.

Jewell, Malcom E. 1977. "Voting Turnout in State Gubernatorial Primaries." *Western Political Quarterly* 30 (2): 236–254.

Jewitt, Caitlin E., and Sarah A. Treul. 2018. "Ideological Primaries and Their Influence in Congress." In *Routledge Handbook of Primary Elections*, edited by Robert Boatright. Routledge.

Jewitt, Caitlin E. 2019. *The Primary Rules: Parties, Voters, and Presidential Nominations.* University of Michigan Press.

Jewitt, Caitlin E., and Sarah A. Treul. 2014. "Competitive Primaries and Party Divisions in Congressional Elections." *Electoral Studies* 35: 140–153.

Kenney, Patrick J. 1983. "Explaining Turnout in Gubernatorial Primaries." *American Politics Quarterly* 11 (2): 315–326.

Kenney, Patrick J. 1986. "Explaining Primary Turnout: The Senatorial Case." *Legislative Studies Quarterly* 11 (1): 65–73.

Kenney, Patrick J., and Tom W. Rice. 1985. "Voter Turnout in Presidential Primaries: A Cross-Sectional Analysis." *Political Behavior.* 7 (1): 101–112.

Kenney, Patrick J., and Tom W. Rice. 1986. "The Effect of Contextual Forces on Turnout in Congressional Primaries." *Social Sciences Quarterly* 67 (2): 329–336.

Key, V.O., Jr. 1956. *American State Politics: An Introduction.* Knopf.

King, A. S., F. J. Orlando, and D. B. Sparks. 2016. "Ideological Extremity and Success in Primary Elections: Drawing Inferences From the Twitter Network." *Social Science Computer Review* 34 (4): 395–415.

Mayer, William G., and Andrew E. Busch. 2004. *The Front-loading Problem in Presidential Nominations.* Brookings Institution Press.

Micatka, Nathan M., Robert G. Boatright, and Caroline J. Tolbert. 2024. "Nonpartisan Primaries, Open Primaries, and Voter Turnout." *Journal of Political Institutions and Political Economy* 5: 363–385.

Porter, Rachel, and Sarah A. Treul. 2025. "Evaluation (in)experience in congressional elections." *American Journal of Political Science* 69 (1): 284–298. https://doi.org/10.1111/ajps.12854.

Ranney, Austin. 1977. *Participation in American Presidential Nominations.* American Enterprise Institute.

Sullivan, Kate, Adam Levy, and Liz Stark. 2020. "Here are the States that Postponed Their Primaries Due to Coronavirus." CNN. June 4. www.cnn.com/2020/03/16/politics/state-primaries-postponed-coronavirus/index.html.

Wong, Queenie. 2011. "Lawmakers Vote to Cancel 2012 Presidential Primary." *The Seattle Times.* April 19. www.seattletimes.com/seattle-news/politics/lawmakers-vote-to-cancel-2012-presidential-primary/.

Mike Cowburn and Marius Sältzer

Chapter 5
Candidate Characteristics in Primary Elections: An Analysis of U.S. House Candidates in 2024

Abstract: Organizations promoting primary reforms contend that non-partisan primaries are an effective mechanism to increase candidate diversity and reduce polarization in Congress. We examine this question empirically in terms of the backgrounds and identities of candidates. Using an original dataset of 2,354 Democratic and Republican primary candidates for the U.S. House of Representatives in 2024, we assess variation in candidate characteristics (gender, race, and "quality") in terms of primary type, partisanship, geographic region, and outcome. Having done so, we empirically test whether non-partisan primaries are associated with substantively different primary and general election candidates in terms of these characteristics. We show that non-partisan primaries are not associated with more diverse or experienced candidates. We complement these descriptive findings with in-depth qualitative analyses of several important House primaries. We conclude by discussing how primaries relate to questions of candidate identity and party control of the nomination process, positing that one reason for the minimal effects of reform is that parties quickly adapt to them.

Partisan primaries are frequently said to be a cause of problems in U.S. democracy, most prominently in terms of contributing to a lack of diversity and as a driver of partisan polarization in the U.S. Congress (Fiorina, Abrams, and Pope 2005). Non-partisan primaries, where all candidates run on a single primary ballot regardless of party affiliation, are said to improve descriptive representation and produce less polarized outcomes (Alvarez and Sinclair 2015; but see Ahler, Citrin, and Lenz 2016). In this chapter, we empirically investigate the relationship between primary elections and candidate backgrounds in terms of gender, race, and previous elected experience ("quality"). Our goal is to better understand the characteristics of challengers, incumbents, and candidates in open-seat primaries; differences between Democrats and Republicans; regional variation; and candidate outcomes, i.e., how successful different types of candidates were. We then pay specific attention to the question of difference between candidates in non-partisan and partisan primaries.

To do so, we collected data on all candidates who ran for the U.S. House of Representatives as a Republican or Democrat in 2024. In total, our dataset includes 2,354 candidates across all fifty U.S. states. We first identify descriptive differences in each type of candidate in our data and then present a series of t-tests to identify the differences between candidates in states that use various forms of non-partisan primaries (Alaska, California, Louisiana, Washington) and those that use partisan primaries. We complement these descriptive findings with a series of in-depth case studies of notable primary contests.

In our descriptive associations, we find that minority candidates and quality non-incumbents disproportionately ran in open-seat primaries. This pattern was not true for women, who ran at similar rates across all types of primaries. We show that women and minorities were about twice as likely to run as a Democrat than as a Republican, with a much smaller difference in candidate quality. We identify little in the way of regional differences, with slightly more minority candidates in the South and West, and more quality candidates in the Midwest and West. In terms of outcomes, we show that women were less likely to withdraw once they threw their hat in the ring, and were slightly better able to advance to the general election from the primary. Minority candidates were more likely to withdraw, be disqualified from, or lose their primary election.

We find limited differences between candidates in partisan and non-partisan primaries. In terms of gender and prior experience we find no difference between candidates running under different primary systems. We do observe some descriptive differences in terms of candidates' racial identities but demonstrate that this association is connected to state demographics rather than the primary system, with no relationship when the percentage of non-white population is controlled for. Overall, our descriptive associations suggest little in the way of difference in outcomes in terms of candidate identity or background.

Our qualitative cases suggest some further potential challenges in states that use non-partisan primaries. Broadly speaking, we consider these disadvantages to be connected to the limited power that party organizations hold over who can appear on the ballot using the party name in non-partisan primaries. Yet, in some instances we show that non-partisan primaries are more susceptible to party control and backroom engineering in ways that might be considered negative for voters. Despite these concerns, we also do not identify any less diversity in states with non-partisan primaries, suggesting that putting more power in the hands of the primary voters does not result in a Whiter, more male pool of candidates.

We argue that a shift towards non-partisan primaries can, at least temporarily, undermine the formal power of party organizations to influence candidate choices without producing more diverse outcomes in terms of candidate background. Indeed, we posit that there may be districts where party organizations would prefer to nominate women and minorities as a way to align with local de-mographics, yet struggle to do so due to the comparative openness of U.S. candidate selection (see e.g., Cowburn and Kerr 2023). Though it may appear that non-partisan primaries offer citizens more input and are therefore more democratic, we argue that the gatekeeping function for political parties serves as an important power that non-partisan primaries erode. We therefore conclude by offering some further thoughts about the claim that non-partisan primaries serve as effective tools to diversify the range of candidates that voters can choose from.

Candidate Characteristics in Primaries

The design and functioning of primary election systems in the United States, particularly their implications for candidate diversity, polarization, and representation, remains a contested subject among scholars. In particular, non-partisan primaries—where candidates from all parties run in a single nomination contest—are commonly proposed as a reform to mitigate partisan polarization and promote diversity in candidates' backgrounds and identities (see e.g., Troiano 2024).

Partisan primaries are often blamed for exacerbating partisan polarization in Congress. In the House of Representatives, the decline of competitive districts in the general election has heightened the importance of primary elections (Drutman 2021; Fiorina, Abrams, and Pope 2005). It was long theorized that voters in these low-turnout elections were ideologically extreme and unrepresentative (Mann and Ornstein 2008; Polsby 1983), and supported primary candidates in terms of positional proximity. Though empirical data indicate little difference between parties' primary and general electorates (Sides et al. 2020), studies find that candidates in primary elections and elected politicians perceive benefits of non-centrist behavior in primary elections (Anderson, Butler, and Harbridge-Yong 2020; Cowburn 2024). As a result, we have previously identified that, under the right circumstances, primary challenges can incentivize members of Congress to move toward their ideological pole (Blum and Cowburn 2024; Cowburn and Sältzer 2024; Cowburn and Theriault 2025).

One argument in favor of non-partisan primaries is that they have the potential to encourage underrepresented groups to run for office. Structural changes to the primary system may reduce ideological extremism and attract a broader array of candidates (Drutman 2021; Thomsen 2017). Party organizations have been shown to control the outcomes of primary elections at both the presidential (Cohen et al. 2008) and the congressional (Hassell 2018) level. If descriptively underrepresented groups believe that the party no longer determines the outcome of primary elections, they might be more inclined to run for office and become the party nominee. Yet, evidence on the efficacy of these systems in increasing candidate diversity is mixed. Though institutional reforms may influence voter participation, they do not necessarily translate into a shift in the demographic composition of candidates (Grumbach and Sahn 2020), and empirical evidence indicates that states' adoption of more open primary systems has not produced meaningfully different legislators (McGhee et al. 2014).

Though non-partisan nominations might reduce some of the barriers associated with party gatekeeping, broader societal and structural factors—including district demographics and political networks—play a more critical role in candidate emergence (Holman and Schneider 2018). The demographic features of a district, such as its racial composition, largely outweigh institutional factors in shaping the pool of candidates (Canon 1999). Similarly, the partisanship of a district has been shown to be closely associated with the numbers of women running and winning primary elections, where Republican women face additional difficulties in winning conservative districts likely due to attitudinal biases about the role of women in politics, and Democratic women are less likely to win in highly competitive general election districts, likely due to strategic discrimination and electability concerns (Cowburn and Conroy 2025).

Whether non-partisan primaries yield better-qualified candidates has also attracted scholarly attention. Top-two primaries are said to induce more "quality" candidates—with prior elected experience (Jacobson 1989)—to run for political office (Sparks 2020). Research examining a longer period of U.S. history finds that primaries are an effective method of selecting "quality" candidates (Hirano and Snyder 2019). The continued role of party organizations in vetting and supporting candidates has been highlighted as a critical factor. Partisan primaries may, therefore, ensure that candidates with substantive experience and qualifications rise to the general election. In contrast, the diminished influence of party structures in non-partisan systems could lead to the election of less experienced candidates, as these systems rely more heavily on individual campaigns and voter recognition.

To better understand the relationship between candidates and primary elections, we consider variation along three dimensions that we refer to as "candidate characteristics." Given the continued underrepresentation of women in the U.S. Congress—relative both to their male counterparts and to comparative democratic national legislatures (Inter-Parliamentary Union 2023)—and extensive literature indicating that the primary process poses a "higher hurdle" (Shames 2018, 96) for women's descriptive representation, we first consider candidate gender in our analyses. Race and racial attitudes remain the central feature of U.S. politics (Hutchings and Valentino 2004), with "white identity" serving as a highly salient explanation for political outcomes and behavior (Jardina 2019; Takahashi and Jefferson 2021). We therefore consider candidates' race as the second indicator of diversity, identifying the numbers of non-White or minority candidates under different primary systems. Finally, we consider candidate quality as a way to measure whether certain primaries are incentivizing non-traditional candidates to run for office.

Data

To construct our dataset of candidates running in congressional primary elections in 2024, we scraped data from Ballotpedia, a comprehensive and reliable source for U.S. election information. We identified relevant candidate profiles, extracted structured data, and then manually checked the accuracy. The initial data collection included candidate names, party affiliations, incumbency status, campaign priorities, and demographic information where available. Having scraped these data using an automated process, we then confirmed our entries while manually coding candidate gender, race, and quality (this process is detailed later in this section).

We recognize that a few candidates may not have had Ballotpedia pages, but, given that the FEC results are not available at the time of writing, we are unable to cross-reference the full returns for all districts against our dataset. Our expectation is that few primary candidates did not have Ballotpedia pages, and those without them were almost exclusively longshot candidates who raised no money and with little prospect of winning the nomination.

From our initial dataset, we then filtered to only include candidates who ran as a Democrat or Republican. We include all candidates who declared to run and therefore generated a Ballotpedia entry, even if those candidates withdrew or were disqualified before making it onto the primary ballot. If a candidate ran or attempted to run in multiple districts, they appear in our dataset in each district in which they ran for office. We exclude candidates who ran to be a non-voting member in Washington D.C., Guam, American Samoa, Puerto Rico, the Northern Mariana Islands, and the U.S. Virgin Islands. This process produced a dataset of 2,354 candidates across all 435 House districts in all fifty states. Of these, 560 candidates withdrew or were disqualified before the primary election and so never appeared on a primary ballot. Two candidates, Jennifer Pace (R-IN07) and Shelia Jackson Lee (D-TX18), died before the general election, having won the primary. One candidate, Anduin Craighill-Middleton (D-NC06), was disqualified from running in the general due to a "miscommunication from official bodies" (Craighill-Middleton 2024).

Gender: We code candidates' gender using their preferred pronouns as per their Ballotpedia page or campaign website. The small number of non-binary candidates in our dataset all expressed a preference for either male or female pronouns and so were grouped accordingly for the purpose of this study. This approach resulted in us having only two gender categories, allowing us to empirically test differences in the numbers of male- and female-identifying candidates under different primary systems.

Race: Though the 118th Congress (2023–25) was the most racially and ethnically diverse ever, non-Hispanic Whites still comprised seventy-two percent of U.S. Representatives; as recently as the 79th Congress (1945–47) this figure was ninety-nine percent (Schaeffer 2023). Given the overrepresentation of non-Hispanic Whites throughout the entirety of U.S. history, we are interested in whether there is any relationship between non-partisan primaries and the frequency of non-Hispanic Whites running for office and becoming the party's nominee. We therefore code candidates according to this racial category. Wherever possible, we use candidates' stated racial identity on their website or from biographical information. Where this information was not available we used data from alternative publicly available sources Center for American Women and Politics 2024). When these sources were not available, we manually coded whether a candidate appeared to be non-Hispanic White using images on their Ballotpedia, website, and social media profiles.[1] Given the likely relationship between the percentage of non-Hispanic Whites in the state and the percentage of non-Hispanic candidates, we add these data from the most recent census (US Census Bureau 2020).

Quality: We are also interested in whether non-partisan primaries are associated with candidates and congressional nominees with previous experience. To test this, we code all candidates in our dataset using Jacobson's (1989) widely used and applied measure of candidate quality. This is a binary indicator that takes the value 1 (quality) if the candidate has previously been elected to public office previously, and 0 (amateur) otherwise. This process was undertaken manually by one of the authors using data from candidates' Ballotpedia page and the "about me" section of their websites. Where neither of these sources indicated that a candidate had previously been elected to public office, we assumed that they had not previously been elected and so coded them as amateur.

Given our interest in the differences between partisan and non-partisan primaries in this chapter, we clearly delineate between these two types of primary election. The top-four primary in Alaska, the top-two primaries in California and Washington, and the jungle primary in Louisiana are the non-partisan pri-

---

1 We recognize that this approach is subject to potential biases based on the researchers' judgements, but, given the lack of alternative information sources due to the low salience of many of these candidates, this was the only option to estimate the ethnicity of these candidates.

maries in our data. In Alaska (discussed further in Chapters 7 and 8 of this volume), all candidates run in a single non-partisan primary, with the four highest-placing candidates advancing to the November general election which then uses ranked choice voting to order the candidates, with successive lowest-placing candidates being eliminated until one candidate has a majority of preferences. In California and Washington (discussed in Chapter 10), all candidates run in a single primary with the two-highest placing candidates advancing to the general election regardless of party affiliation. In Louisiana, the initial election takes place on the date of the general election, with all candidates running on a single ballot. If a candidate receives fifty percent of the vote, then they are immediately elected to congress, otherwise a run-off between the two highest-placing candidates follows in December. In 2024, the winning candidate in all six of Louisiana's congressional districts received at least fifty percent of the vote, meaning that no run-offs were required. The variety of primary systems present in the other forty-six states are all partisan primaries, meaning that Democratic and Republican candidates initially run on separate partisan ballots to become their party's nominee.

Finally, we also code whether primary elections are contested. Following the extant literature (Boatright 2013, 2014; Cowburn 2022, 2024), we consider primaries as being contested when at least two candidates appear on the ballot. Primaries with multiple candidates who withdraw or are disqualified from the ballot leaving only one candidate are not considered as contested. In non-partisan primaries, we consider primaries as having been contested for a given party when more than one candidate from that party appears on the primary ballot (again following Boatright 2013, 2014; Cowburn 2022, 2024).

A Description of Primary Candidates

Our approach to data collection allows us to identify a larger number of candidates than studies using names on the primary ballot (e. g., Cowburn 2024) or filing with the Federal Election Commission (FEC) (e. g., Bonica 2014). We therefore first provide some descriptives of the candidates that feature in our dataset along our three key variables of gender, race, and quality in terms of primary type, party differences, regional differences, and differences in candidate outcomes. In all of these descriptives except for outcomes we exclude incumbents from our quality category to better understand where non-incumbent quality challengers emerge.

Table 5.1 shows the differences in our three candidate characteristics across different types of primary. The position of the incumbent is one of the most important features of a congressional primary election, and we therefore show descriptive patterns in open-seat (where no incumbent runs in either party), challenger (where the incumbent runs in the alternative party's primary), and incumbent (where the incumbent runs in that party's primary). Table 5.1 indicates that female candidates ran for office at roughly similar rates across all types of primary. This finding runs counter to some studies that suggest that women are particularly strategic in terms of their candidate entry decisions and disproportionately target open seats (Burrell 2014). Conversely, we see that non-white candidates do appear to be more strategic about where they run, running more frequently in open-seat primaries than in challenger or incumbent races. This suggests that non-white candidates are cognizant of the difficulties of displacing incumbent members of Congress either from their own or the alternative party. This pattern is even more true for quality non-incumbents, who disproportionately target open-seat primaries such that they are almost three times as likely to run in these contests than in challenger or incumbent races.

Table 5.1: Differences in primary type.

Primary Type	Candidates	Women	Non-White	Quality
Open-Seat	301	71	106	67
		(23.6%)	(35.2%)	(22.3%)
Challenger	1,012	242	285	81
		(23.9%)	(28.2%)	(8.0%)
Incumbent	1,041	237	283	92
		(22.8%)	(27.2%)	(8.8%)

We next consider differences in candidate characteristics between Republicans and Democrats. Women's representation in Congress has a clear partisan asymmetry, with more women consistently being elected as Democrats and barely increasing levels of Republican women in Congress over the past thirty years (Elder 2021). Similarly, the Democratic House caucus has long been more diverse than its Republican counterpart, with Democrats disproportionately winning majority-minority districts and having a more diverse coalition of voters (Hartig et al. 2023). Consequently, Democrats constitute eight-five percent of minority members of the U.S. House in the current (119th) Congress. Some partisan differences have also been identified in terms of candidate quality (Bond, Fleisher, and Talbert 1997).

In Table 5.2, we demonstrate these descriptive associations in our data. As expected, we see far higher rates of women and non-white candidates running as Democrats, with almost twice as many in both categories compared to Republicans. These differences align with previously observed trends in descriptive representation in terms of gender (Elder 2021; Sanbonmatsu 2006), race (Swers and Rouse 2011), and their intersection (Sanbonmatsu 2015). Democratic women benefit from established party networks and recruitment efforts, such as those led by EMILY's List, which have actively worked to increase female candidacy and representation (Thomsen 2017). In contrast, Republican women often face greater structural and ideological barriers within their party, which has historically prioritized traditional gender roles and demonstrated less institutional support for female candidates (Cowburn and Conroy 2025; Elder 2021). The underrepresentation of minorities in Republican primaries may also be the result of barriers such as the composition of primary electorates and party gatekeeping mechanisms that favor white candidates (Canon 1999). We observe only a small difference between the parties in terms of non-incumbent quality candidates.

Table 5.2: Partisan differences.

Party	Candidates	Women	Non-White	Quality
Democratic	1,092	345	421	119
		(31.2%)	(38.6%)	(10.9%)
Republican	1,262	205	253	121
		(16.2%)	(20.0%)	(9.6%)

In Table 5.3, we consider regional variation in candidate characteristics, dividing the U.S. into four regions as per the census; Midwest, Northeast, South, and West.[2] Though U.S. politics has been nationalizing in the modern era (Hopkins 2018), important regional differences remain. Rates of women running in primary elections were broadly consistent across these four regions. Candidates in the Midwest were, on average, whiter than the other regions, where the South saw the highest number of non-white candidates running for office. Candidates in the West and Midwest regions tended to have previous elected experience slightly more often than those in the Northeast and South.

Next, we consider the differences between candidate outcomes in the different groups with the trends shown in Table 5.4. Here we observe that women were slightly less likely to withdraw before the primary and slightly more likely to advance from the nomination process, aligning with research that indicates that women who run for office tend to be more qualified (Lawless and Fox 2010). Mi-

2 Northeast includes CT, ME, MA, NH, RI, VT, NJ, NY, PA. Midwest includes IL, IN, MI, OH, WI, IA, KS, MN, MO, NE, ND, SD. South includes DE, DC, FL, GA, MD, NC, SC, VA, WV, AL, KY, MS, TN, AR, LA, OK, TX. West includes AZ, CO, ID, MT, NV, NM, UT, WY, AK, CA, HI, OR, WA.

Table 5.3: Regional differences.

Region	Candidates	Women	Non-White	Quality
Midwest	480	109	90	53
		(22.7%)	(18.8%)	(11.0%)
Northeast	337	72	93	27
		(21.3%)	(27.5%)	(8.0%)
South	916	217	301	71
		(23.7%)	(32.9%)	(7.8%)
West	621	152	190	89
		(24.5%)	(30.6%)	(14.3%)

nority candidates were slightly more likely to withdraw, be disqualified from, or lose their primary election. This finding aligns with research showing that non-white candidates struggle to get institutional support in the Republican Party (Mundy 2025). Unsurprisingly, quality candidates (including incumbents) were highly likely to win their general election.

Table 5.4: Outcomes.

Outcome	Candidates	Women	Non-White	Quality
Withdrew before primary	553	96	157	65
		(17.4%)	(28.3%)	(11.8%)
Disqualified from primary	53	14	20	5
		(23.4%)	(37.8%)	(9.4%)
Lost primary	895	193	272	116
		(21.6%)	(30.4%)	(13.0%)
Withdrew before general	13	3	3	5
		(23.1%)	(23.1%)	(38.5%)
Lost general	402	123	105	53
		(30.6%)	(26.1%)	(13.2%)
Won general	435	120	115	412
		(27.5%)	(26.4%)	(94.7%)

Our data also allow us to descriptively compare candidates in partisan and non-partisan primaries. We present the results of a series of two-tailed t-tests of differences between candidates in partisan and non-partisan primaries in Figure 5.1 in terms of their gender (first column), race (second column), and quality (third column). We break these figures down first for all candidates in our dataset (first row), then restrict this to those candidates who were not excluded or withdrew before the primary election (second row). Then we restrict this to those candidates who ran in a contested primary with at least two same-party candidates on the ballot (third row), and finally restrict this to those candidates who won contested primaries and thereby advanced to the general election (fourth row).

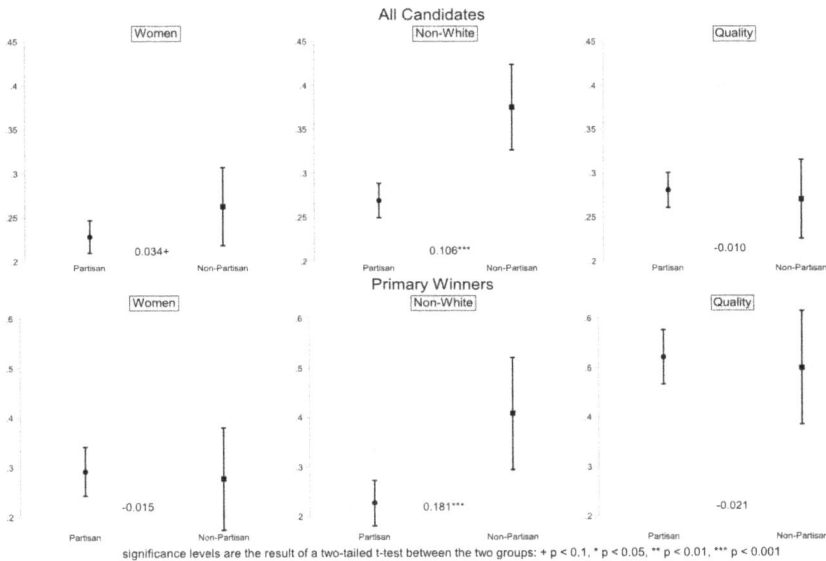

Figure 5.1: Differences between partisan and non-partisan primaries.

Our findings in Figure 5.1 are consistent across candidates and primary winners. We observe little to no difference in the numbers of women in partisan and non-partisan primaries across the four groups (first column), a finding which aligns with research into women's representation under top-two primaries at the state level (Alvarez and Sinclair 2015). Similarly, we see no difference in candidate quality in partisan or non-partisan primaries (third column). The only consistent difference observed across both groups is in the number of non-white candidates in partisan and non-partisan primaries, with non-partisan primaries consistently having more diverse candidates (second column).

Yet, existing literature identifies the main driver of candidate diversity as the diversity of the population from which they emerge (Algara and Hale 2023; Lee 2024; Lublin and Wright 2024). The largest state with non-partisan primaries, California (34.7 percent White), is significantly more diverse than the U.S. average (57.8 percent White), and the differences between partisan and non-partisan primaries in terms of candidates' racial identity are likely connected to state level demographic differences rather than the primary system. This is, in part, because non-partisan primaries do not appear to radically alter the profile of candidates who run (Drutman 2021; Grose 2020; Kanthak and Loepp 2018). Some evidence suggests that under the top-two primary, majority-minority districts in California were the most likely to feature two Democrats in the general election (Alvarez and Sinclair 2015), potentially increasing the opportunities for minority candidates.

We run a logistic regression with an additional control for the percentage of residents in the state that are White. We present the results of this model in Table 5.5, showing that when state demographics are included, we observe no relationship between the presence of non-partisan primaries and non-white candidates in all four groups, suggesting that non-partisan primaries are not associated with more diverse candidates. This finding aligns with studies that found no change in the descriptive representation of minorities following California discontinuing the blanket primary in 2000 (Quinn and Alvarez 2010). Unsurprisingly, our control for percentage of the state population that is White is highly significant and negatively associated in all cases. We note that our approach here, focusing on data from a single election cycle, does not enable us to say anything about whether the establishment of the top-two primary caused any change in the rates of non-white candidates. However, we can say that by 2024 it does not appear to be associated with higher rates than states with partisan primaries.

Table 5.5: Logistic regression of candidate race.

	All Candidates	Candidates on Primary Ballot	Candidates in Contested Primary	Contested Primary Winners
Non-Partisan Primary	-0.136	-0.029	-0.067	-0.000
	(0.136)	(0.154)	(0.171)	(0.319)
State % White	-3.402***	-3.458***	-3.694***	-4.861***
	(0.369)	(0.425)	(0.484)	(0.955)
Observations	2,354	1,748	1,297	402

Note: Standard errors in parentheses *** $p<0.001$, ** $p<0.01$, * $p<0.05$, + $p<0.1$

We also recognize that the comparative lack of part influence or control over nomination processes in states with non-partisan primary does not correspond to lower racial diversity in the candidate pool or among the nominees selected in a primary competition. Given voters' baseline predisposition for candidates of their own race (Barreto 2010; Philpot and Walton 2007; Sigelman and Sigelman

1982), parties with complete control over their candidate selection process would likely see benefits of having a diverse candidate pool, and strategically nominate minorities in districts with more minority voters. Were this happening across enough districts, we might observe a negative relationship between non-partisan primaries and non-white candidates being selected. The absence of such a relationship therefore suggests that—though they do not appear to strengthen the position of non-white candidates—non-partisan primaries do not hinder parties' abilities to recruit diverse candidates.

Qualitative Case Studies

We think that these descriptive quantitative associations are an interesting first step in examining the (lack of) relationship between non-partisan primaries and candidates' backgrounds. To better understand some of the problems and challenges presented by non-partisan primaries we now qualitatively examine some of the important contests in 2024.

We start with the case of Alaska's top-four system. In 2022, Alaska moved from having partisan primaries to having a top-four system with ranked choice voting in the general election. Like California and Washington's top-two system, all candidates now run on the same initial primary ballot regardless of party affiliation. Yet, unlike these states, Alaska's adoption of the non-partisan primary is incredibly recent, with historical evidence that the introduction of reforms to the nomination system can destabilize elections (Boatright 2024), and that the time since introduction of the reform is particularly important because candidates, parties, and other interested groups adapt to the reform's introduction. In application to the Alaska reform, one recent study found that its introduction gave voters a greater diversity of candidates in 2022 (Reilly, Lublin, and Wright 2023; see also Chapter 7 of this volume). The 2024 primary took place on August 20, with incumbent Democratic Representative Mary Peltola placing first with more than half of the votes. Peltola is a particularly interesting candidate in this case as she is a woman, an Alaska Native, had served in the state legislature ("quality") prior to her election to Congress, and her 2022 election victory was likely helped by the state's move to non-partisan primaries in that year.

Republicans Nick Begich, Nancy Dahlstrom, and Matthew Salisbury finished second, third, and fourth respectively in 2024 and were scheduled to advance to the general. Begich previously ran unsuccessfully (in part because the Republican vote was split with Sarah Palin) for the seat in 2022, and Dahlstrom was the state lieutenant governor (a quality female candidate). Salisbury had finished a distant fourth with less than one thousand votes. Yet, because the state Republican Party feared that Begich and Dahlstrom would once again split the Republican vote and allow Peltola to retain the seat, both Dahlstrom and Salisbury were pressured to withdraw their candidacies between the primary and general elections (Samuels 2024). Consequently, the general election ballot featured Peltola, Begich, an Alaskan Independence Party candidate (John Howe) who had finished fifth on the primary ballot, and Eric Hafner, a Democrat and convicted felon who had been imprisoned in New York (Kilgannon 2024) and had never visited the state (Shoaib 2024), who received fewer than 500 votes in the primary.

In response, the state Democratic Party petitioned unsuccessfully to have Hafner removed from the ballot and were opposed by the Republican Party (Samuels 2024). Behind-the-scenes machinations from the state Republican Party—a malady that non-partisan primaries are said to fix—meant that Alaskans chose between two Democrats, one Republican, and an Independence Party candidate in the November general election rather than choosing between one Democrat and three Republicans. Begich went on to displace Peltola in a close-fought general election in November, a result that can be understood as the Republican Party apparatus learning from their mistakes in 2022 and adapting to the reformed electoral system. In short, the temporary increase in diversity can be attributed to the Republican Party's lack of coordination in 2022, a situation they rectified by appropriately gaming the new primary system in 2024. Consequently, Alaska was once again (as it had been since its incorporation as a state until Peltola's 2022 victory) represented by a White man in the House of Representatives.

Similar dynamics were visible in some of the top-two contests in our data. For example, in an open-seat primary for California's 20th District in March, two Republicans—Vince Fong (male, non-white, quality) and Mike Boudreaux (male, white, quality)—advanced as the general election candidates from the primary. Same-party general elections are the arena in which non-partisan primaries are said to be the most beneficial, producing better legislators who are willing to work in a bipartisan manner (Alvarez and Sinclair 2015). Yet, as is common in these instances, the candidate who finished second, Mike Boudreaux, unofficially withdrew his candidacy and did not campaign for the general election, after Fong won a special election between the same two candidates in May to become the incumbent. Fong had received a string of high-profile state and national endorsements, including from Donald Trump. Fong's race may have factored into the Republican Party's support in a district that is less than fifty percent white, with a significant (7.3 percent) Asian population.

Boudreaux's withdrawal meant the Republican Party was spared from spending money on a contest that it knew they could not lose, but left the voters of California's 20th District with a ballot featuring one Republican who campaigned and another who did not. General election voters who did not participate in the primary were given no opportunity to determine who their representative would be, and Democratic voters had no opportunity to support any candidate with their partisan persuasion in the general election.

A similar dynamic sometimes occurs in partisan primaries that feature a run-off if no one candidate reaches a pre-determined threshold.[3] This practice is most common in southern states. The presence of a run-off can similarly incentivize party intervention in the primary process, as seen in the Republican primary in North Carolina's 13th District in 2024. In the initial primary on March 5, Kelly Daughtry (female, white, amateur) finished in first place with Brad Knott (male, white, amateur) finishing in second. Following that initial contest, Donald Trump decided to endorse Knott, and Daughtry unofficially withdrew from the contest (ABC11 Raleigh-Durham 2024). In the run-off on May 14, Knott received more than ninety percent of the votes, suggesting that the party retains a strong ability to determine their nominees in these systems by sending signals to voters and pressuring candidates.

A further challenge of non-partisan primaries is that parties are unable to have any control over who appears on the ballot using their party label. Our data-set features fifty-four candidates who were disqualified from standing in the primary; none of these disqualified candidates came from states with non-partisan primaries. In many of these instances, there appears to be normatively good reasons for parties being able to control who appears on a ballot using the party label. One such example was Daniel Boman (male, white, quality), a former member of the Alabama House of Representatives, who had been elected as a Republican and then switched to the Democratic Party four months into his tenure, and then attempted to run as a Republican for Alabama's 5th District (Cason 2023b). Boman had previously been suspended by the Alabama State Bar for racist and misogynistic language and then disbarred on charges of theft (Cason 2023a).[4] Under a non-partisan primary, the party would have had no recourse to disqualify Boman, illustrating one normative benefit of parties retaining the ability to remove candidates from standing with their label.

More generally, these examples suggest that once a new reform such as a non-partisan primary has been introduced, parties remain both willing and able to game whatever system of nomination they are faced with to try and get their preferred candidate. Though non-partisan primaries do lessen the formal powers of the party to control this process, the party retains a range of tools at their disposal,

---

3 Thirty percent in North Carolina; thirty-five percent in South Dakota; fifty percent in Alabama, Arkansas, Georgia, Mississippi, Oklahoma, South Carolina, and Texas.
4 This example also illustrates a linguistic challenge of the term "quality" in describing such candidates.

such as pressuring unfavored candidates to withdraw, or sending signals to voters through endorsements.

Discussion and Conclusion

In this chapter we have identified several clear descriptive associations between primaries and candidate characteristics. Non-white candidates and quality non-incumbents disproportionately targeted open-seat primaries, likely recognizing them as their best opportunity to enter Congress. Women and minority candidates were nearly twice as likely to run as Democrats than Republicans, reflecting broader partisan trends in representation. Women were less likely to withdraw once they entered the race and had a slightly higher chance of advancing from contested primaries. In contrast, minority candidates were more likely to withdraw, be disqualified, or lose in primary elections.

Our findings for non-partisan primaries were far less conclusive; we suggest that our quantitative results and qualitative cases suggest pause for thought in terms of the benefits of non-partisan primaries. Rather than resulting in more diverse candidates and a more transparent democratic processes, we contend that non-partisan primaries introduce new considerations and challenges into the U.S. electoral system. Most importantly, we contend that non-partisan primaries weaken the power of U.S. political parties, at least temporarily, to determine who runs as their candidate in November general elections. In some cases, major political parties even lose the right to field a candidate in these elections.

Yet, the Alaska example shows that parties are also quick to adapt to reforms, as they had done previously in Washington and California in the election cycles following the introduction of the top-two primary. Following their failure to coordinate in 2022, the Republican Party was able to ensure their preferred candidate in 2024 did not face same-party opponents who would split the vote. Political parties remain central actors in shaping elections, and our qualitative case studies demonstrate that, even in systems designed to reduce their influence, parties adapt by engaging in alternative methods of candidate selection and coordination.

We suggest that the assumed benefits of non-partisan primaries, particularly regarding candidate diversity and the reduction of party influence, are more complex and nuanced than reform advocates sometimes suggest. Despite arguments that these systems increase candidate diversity and improve electoral outcomes by broadening the choices available to voters, non-partisan primaries did not systematically produce more diverse or experienced candidates in 2024.

The reduced formal role of parties in candidate selection can lead to unintended consequences that may not align with the broader goals of democratic representation. By limiting the ability of parties to vet and support candidates, non-partisan primaries create openings for individuals with little political experience, controversial backgrounds, or weak ties to the electorate to enter the race. This is particularly concerning in instances where candidates with problematic histories, such as disbarred or discredited individuals, are able to appear on the ballot under a major party label despite lacking party endorsement or support. However, we also note that non-partisan primaries do not appear to be systematically producing less diverse or qualified candidates either, likely because the parties quickly understand how to influence the outcomes in these systems.

U.S. parties must navigate the most open and inclusive system of legislative candidate selection in the world (Cowburn and Kerr 2023). This system hinders their ability to strategically select women and minority candidates, and appears particularly acute in a comparative perspective. In the United Kingdom, the Labour Party has used all-women shortlists since 1997 to increase the proportion of female members of parliament (Cutts, Childs, and Fieldhouse 2008), with women constituting more than half (51%) of the party's MPs in 2019.[5] Similar approaches have been used by parties in Scandinavia, Latin America, South Korea, and Canada. In many proportional electoral systems a "zipper system" mandates that party lists alternate between male and female candidates. Such systems are legally required in countries including Argentina, Costa Rica, France, Mongolia, and Senegal, while elsewhere some parties—including the Swedish Social Democratic Party (SAP) and the Spanish Socialist Workers' Party (PSOE)—voluntarily implement the system. These reforms have proved highly effective at increasing the numbers of women in national legislatures but are simply not available to U.S. parties due to the openness of their candidate selection processes.

In sum, our findings for the U.S. raise questions about the sustainability and long-term effectiveness of non-partisan primaries as a reform mechanism. It is noteworthy that the 2024 election cycle was accompanied by a raft of efforts to further "open up" the primary process, shifting power away from political parties and towards non-partisan primaries. Initiatives for various types of non-partisan primaries were on the ballot in Arizona, Colorado, Idaho, Montana, Nevada, South Dakota, and Washington D.C. in November 2024. Of these, only the measure in Washington D.C. was successful. The rejection of non-partisan primaries was the result of a combination of factors including voter confusion, issues with high-profile candidates selected under ranked choice voting[6] (West 2024), coordi-

---

5 The party abandoned all-women shortlists in 2022, with the percentage of women MPs falling to 46% after the 2024 election.
6 Most notably, New York Major Eric Adams.

nated opposition, and voter skepticism (Masket 2024). Although reform advocates argued that non-partisan primaries foster greater choice and inclusivity, opposition campaigns successfully framed them as untested and potentially disruptive to existing electoral norms. Rather than creating a more equitable political landscape, our findings suggest that these reforms may instead temporarily reconfigure existing power dynamics until the key actors learn how to navigate the new terrain and reassert themselves.

Bibliography

ABC11 Raleigh-Durham. 2024. "Kelly Daughtry Drops out of Republican Run-off Primary Election against Brad Knott." *ABC11 Raleigh-Durham.*
https://abc11.com/kelly-daughtry-drops-out-republican-run-off-primary-election/14756336/.

Ahler, Douglas J., Jack Citrin, and Gabriel S. Lenz. 2016. "Do Open Primaries Improve Representation? An Experimental Test of California's 2012 Top-Two Primary." *Legislative Studies Quarterly* 41 (2): 237–268.

Algara, Carlos, and Isaac Hale. 2023. "Race, Partisanship, and Democratic Politics: The Role of Racial Attitudes in Motivating White Americans' Electoral Participation." *Journal of Race, Ethnicity, and Politics* 8 (3): 301–323. https://doi.org/10.1017/rep.2023.16.

Alvarez, R. Michael, and J. Andrew Sinclair. 2015. *Nonpartisan Primary Election Reform: Mitigating Mischief.* Cambridge University Press.

Anderson, Sarah E., Daniel M. Butler, and Laurel Harbridge-Yong. 2020. *Rejecting Compromise: Legislators' Fear of Primary Voters.* Cambridge University Press.

Barreto, Matt. 2010. *Ethnic Cues: The Role of Shared Ethnicity in Latino Political Participation.* Illustrated edition. University of Michigan Press.

Blum, Rachel M., and Mike Cowburn. 2024. "How Local Factions Pressure Parties: Activist Groups and Primary Contests in the Tea Party Era." *British Journal of Political Science* 54 (1): 88–109. https://doi.org/10.1017/S0007123423000224.

Boatright, Robert G. 2013. *Getting Primaried: The Changing Politics of Congressional Primary Challenges.* University of Michigan Press.

Boatright, Robert G. 2014. *Congressional Primary Elections.* Routledge.

Boatright, Robert G. 2024. *Reform and Retrenchment: A Century of Efforts to Fix Primary Elections.* Oxford University Press Inc.

Bond, Jon R., Richard Fleisher, and Jeffery C. Talbert. 1997. "Partisan Differences in Candidate Quality in Open Seat House Races, 1976–1994." *Political Research Quarterly* 50 (2): 281–929. https://doi.org/10.1177/106591299705000202.

Bonica, Adam. 2014. "Mapping the Ideological Marketplace." *American Journal of Political Science* 58 (2): 367–386.

Burrell, Barbara. 2014. *Gender in Campaigns for the U.S. House of Representatives.* University of Michigan Press.

Canon, David T. 1999. *Race, Redistricting, and Representation: The Unintended Consequences of Black Majority Districts.* University of Chicago Press.

Cason, Mike. 2023a. "Alabama GOP Congressional Candidate Facing Theft Charge." *Al.com*. https://www.al.com/news/2023/11/alabama-gop-congressional-candidate-facing-theft-charge.html.

Cason, Mike. 2023b. "Alabama GOP Removes Candidate Daniel Boman from Ballot in 5th District." *Al.com*. https://www.al.com/news/2023/12/alabama-gop-removes-candidate-daniel-boman-from-ballot-in-5th-district.html.

Center for American Women and Politics. "Women Elected Officials by Race/Ethnicity." 2024. https://cawpdata.rutgers.edu/women-elected-officials/race-ethnicity?current=1&yearend_filter=All&state%5B%5D=Washington&items_per_page=50.

Cohen, Marty, David Karol, Hans Noel, and John Zaller. 2008. *The Party Decides: Presidential Nominations Before and After Reform*. University of Chicago Press.

Cowburn, Mike. 2022. "Partisan Polarization in Congressional Nominations: How Ideological & Factional Primaries Influence Candidate Positions." Doctoral Thesis. Freie Universität Berlin.

Cowburn, Mike. 2024. *Party Transformation in Congressional Primaries: Faction and Ideology in the Twenty-First Century*. Cambridge University Press. https://doi.org/10.1017/9781009536516.

Cowburn, Mike, and Meredith Conroy. 2025. "Where Do Women Win Primaries? Candidate Gender, District Partisanship, and Congressional Nomination." Journal of Women, Politics, and Policy. https://doi.org/10.1080/1554477X.2025.2552576.

Cowburn, Mike, and Rebecca Kerr. 2023. "Inclusivity and Decentralisation of Candidate Selectorates: Factional Consequences for Centre-Left Parties in England, Germany, and the United States." *Political Research Quarterly* 76 (1): 292 – 307. https://doi.org/10.1177/10659129221081213.

Cowburn, Mike, and Marius Sältzer. 2024. "Partisan Communication in Two-Stage Elections: The Effect of Primaries on Intra-Campaign Positional Shifts in Congressional Elections." In *Political Science Research and Methods*, 1 – 20. https://doi.org/10.1017/psrm.2023.62.

Cowburn, Mike, and Sean Theriault. 2025. "Preventative Polarization: Republican Senators' Positional Adaptation in the Tea Party Era." *American Politics Research* 52 (2): 125 – 139. https://doi.org/10.1177/1532673X241295697.

Craighill-Middleton, Andy. 2024. "Facebook." *Facebook: Andy Craighill-Middleton for US Congress*. https://www.facebook.com/p/Andy-Craighill-Middleton-for-US-Congress-61558385198108/.

Cutts, David, Sarah Childs, and Edward Fieldhouse. 2008. "'This Is What Happens When You Don't Listen': All-Women Shortlists at the 2005 General Election." *Party Politics* 14 (5): 575 – 595. https://doi.org/10.1177/1354068808093391.

Drutman, Lee. 2021. *What We Know about Congressional Primaries and Congressional Primary Reform*. New America. http://newamerica.org/political-reform/reports/what-we-know-about-congressional-primaries-and-congressional-primary-reform/.

Elder, Laurel. 2021. *The Partisan Gap: Why Democratic Women Get Elected But Republican Women Don't*. New York University Press.

Fiorina, Morris P., Samuel J. Abrams, and Jeremy C. Pope. 2005. *Culture War? The Myth of a Polarized America*. Longman.

Grose, Christian R. 2020. "Reducing Legislative Polarization: Top-Two and Open Primaries Are Associated with More Moderate Legislators." *Journal of Political Institutions and Political Economy* 1 (2): 267 – 287.

Grumbach, Jacob M., and Alexander Sahn. 2020. "Race and Representation in Campaign Finance." *American Political Science Review* 114 (1): 206–221. https://doi.org/10.1017/S0003055419000637.

Hartig, Hannah, Andrew Daniller, Scott Keeter, and Ted Van Green. 2023. "3. Demographic Profiles of Republican and Democratic Voters." *Pew Research Center.* https://www.pewresearch.org/politics/2023/07/12/demographic-profiles-of-republican-and-democratic-voters/.

Hassell, Hans J. G. 2018. *The Party's Primary: Control of Congressional Nominations.* Cambridge University Press.

Hirano, Shigeo, and James M. Snyder. 2019. *Primary Elections in the United States.* Cambridge University Press.

Holman, Mirya R., and Monica C. Schneider. 2018. "Gender, Race, and Political Ambition: How Intersectionality and Frames Influence Interest in Political Office." *Politics, Groups, and Identities* 6 (2): 264–280. https://doi.org/10.1080/21565503.2016.1208105.

Hopkins, D. J. 2018. *The Increasingly United States: How and Why American Political Behavior Nationalized.* University of Chicago Press.

Hutchings, Vincent L., and Nicholas A. Valentino. 2004. "The Centrality of Race in American Politics." *Annual Review of Political Science* 7 (1): 383–408.

Jacobson, Gary C. 1989. "Strategic Politicians and the Dynamics of U.S. House Elections, 1946–86." *The American Political Science Review* 83 (3): 773–793. https://doi.org/10.2307/1962060.

Jardina, Ashley. 2019. *White Identity Politics.* Cambridge University Press.

Kanthak, Kristin, and Eric Loepp. 2018. "Strategic Candidate Entry: Primary Type and Candidate Divergence." In *Routledge Handbook of Primary Elections* edited by Robert G. Boatright. Routledge.

Kilgannon, Corey. 2024. "How a Man Imprisoned in New York Could Sway a Key House Race in Alaska." *The New York Times.* https://www.nytimes.com/2024/10/15/nyregion/alaska-house-race-eric-hafner.html.

Lawless, Jennifer L., and Richard L. Fox. 2010. *It Still Takes A Candidate: Why Women Don't Run for Office.* Cambridge University Press.

Lee, Da In. 2024. "Minority Political Ambition and Candidate Supply in the United States." Columbia University. https://doi.org/10.7916/q5f4-c029.

Lublin, David, and Matthew Wright. 2024. "Diversity Matters: The Election of Asian Americans to U.S. State and Federal Legislatures." *American Political Science Review* 118 (1): 380–400. https://doi.org/10.1017/S0003055423000242.

Mann, Thomas E., and Norman J. Ornstein. 2008. *The Broken Branch: How Congress Is Failing America and How to Get It Back on Track.* Oxford University Press.

Masket, Seth. 2024. "Why Primary Reform Took a Hit in 2024." *Substack.* https://substack.com/inbox/post/153030581.

McGhee, Eric, Seth Masket, Boris Shor, Steven Rogers, and Nolan McCarty. 2014. "A Primary Cause of Partisanship? Nomination Systems and Legislator Ideology." *American Journal of Political Science* 58 (2): 337–351.

Inter-Parliamentary Union. "Monthly Ranking of Women in National Parliaments." 2023. *IPU Parline: Global Data on National Parliaments.* https://data.ipu.org/women-ranking.

Mundy, Ryan. 2025. "A Bigger Tent? Nonwhite Republican Candidates and Their Uphill Paths to Office." *Political Research Quarterly:* 10659129251320967. https://doi.org/10.1177/10659129251320967.

Philpot, Tasha S., and Hanes Walton. 2007. "One of Our Own: Black Female Candidates and the Voters Who Support Them." *American Journal of Political Science* 51 (1): 49 – 62. https://doi.org/10.1111/j.1540-5907.2007.00236.x.

Polsby, Nelson W. 1983. *Consequences of Party Reform*. Oxford University Press.

Quinn, Anthony T., and R. Michael Alvarez. 2010. *Primary Process Reform in California*. California Forward.

Reilly, Benjamin, David Lublin, and Glenn Wright. 2023. "Alaska's New Electoral System: Countering Polarization or "Crooked as Hell"?" *California Journal of Politics and Policy* 15 (1). https://doi.org/10.5070/P2cjpp15160081.

Samuels, Iris. 2024. "Judge Rules That Incarcerated U.S. House Candidate Can Remain on Alaska Ballot." *Anchorage Daily News*. https://www.adn.com/politics/2024/09/10/judge-rules-that-incarcerated-us-house-candi-date-can-remain-on-alaska-ballot/.

Sanbonmatsu, Kira. 2006. *Where Women Run: Gender And Party in the American States*. Illustrated edition. The University of Michigan Press.

Sanbonmatsu, Kira. 2015. "Electing Women of Color: The Role of Campaign Trainings." *Journal of Women, Politics & Policy* 36 (2): 137 – 160.

Schaeffer, Katherine. 2023. "The Changing Face of Congress in 8 Charts." *Pew Research Center*. https://www.pewresearch.org/short-reads/2023/02/07/the-changing-face-of-congress/.

Shames, Shauna. 2018. "Higher Hurdles for Republican Women: Ideology, Inattention, and Infrastructure." In *The Right Women: Republican Party Activists, Candidates, and Legislators*, edited by Malliga Och and Shauna Shames, 95 – 107. Bloomsbury.

Shoaib, Alia. 2024. "Who Is Eric Hafner? Jailed Alaska Candidate Could Tip Congress to GOP." *Newsweek*. https://www.newsweek.com/eric-hafner-alaska-candidate-congress-1972047.

Sides, John, Chris Tausanovitch, Lynn Vavreck, and Christopher Warshaw. 2020. "On the Representativeness of Primary Electorates." *British Journal of Political Science* 50 (2): 1 – 9. https://doi.org/10.1017/S000712341700062X.

Sigelman, Lee, and Carol K. Sigelman. 1982. "Sexism, Racism, and Ageism in Voting Behavior: An Experimental Analysis." *Social Psychology Quarterly* 45 (4): 263 – 269. https://doi.org/10.2307/3033922.

Sparks, Steven. 2020. "Quality Challenger Emergence under the Top-Two Primary: Comparing One-Party and Two-Party General Election Contests." *Electoral Studies* 65: 102136. https://doi.org/10.1016/j.electstud.2020.102136.

Swers, Michele L., and Stella M. Rouse. 2011. "Descriptive Representation: Understanding the Impact of Identity on Substantive Representation of Group Interests." In *The Oxford Handbook of the American Congress*, edited by George C. Edwards, Frances E. Lee, and Eric Schickler. Oxford University Press. https://doi.org/10.1093/oxfordhb/9780199559947.003.0011.

Takahashi, Koji, and Hakeem Jefferson. 2021. "When the Powerful Feel Voiceless: White Identity and Feelings of Racial Voicelessness." https://osf.io/preprints/psyarxiv/ry97q_v1.

Thomsen, Danielle M. 2017. *Opting Out of Congress: Partisan Polarization and the Decline of Moderate Candidates*. Cambridge University Press.

Troiano, Nick. 2024. *The Primary Solution: Rescuing Our Democracy from the Fringes*. Simon & Schuster.

US Census Bureau. 2020. "2020 Census Results." *Census.gov*. https://www.census.gov/2020results.

West, Darrell M. 2024. *The Future of the Instant Runoff Election Reform*. Brookings. https://www.brookings.edu/articles/the-future-of-the-instant-runoff-election-reform/.

Appendix

Table 5.6: Types of candidates in partisan and non-partisan primaries.

	Partisan Primaries	Non-Partisan Primaries
All Candidates	**1,973**	**381**
Women	450	100
	(22.8%)	(26.2%)
Non-White	531	143
	(26.9%)	(37.5%)
Quality	554	103
	(28.1%)	(27.0%)
Candidates on Primary Ballot	**1,452**	**296**
Women	356	84
	(24.5%)	(28.4%)
Non-White	381	116
	(26.2%)	(39.2%)
Quality	492	95
	(33.9%)	(32.1%)
Contested Primaries	**1,055**	**242**
Women	240	72
	(22.7%)	(29.8%)
Non-White	282	94
	(26.7%)	(38.8%)
Quality	269	62
	(25.4%)	(25.6%)
Winners	**326**	**76**
Women	95	21
	(29.1%)	(27.6%)
Non-White	74	31
	(22.7%)	(40.8%)
Quality	170	38
	(52.1%)	(50.0%)

Hayley M. Cohen

Chapter 6
Running Scared in the Primary: Campaign Behavior of Safe Incumbents in a Partisan Era

Abstract: Over the last few decades, partisanship in the electorate has strengthened and the number of competitive congressional districts has shrunk. Now, the vast majority of incumbents are overwhelmingly likely to be re-elected in general elections simply because their party affiliation matches that of their district. Despite this decrease in electoral competitiveness, incumbents who are heavily advantaged to win their general elections still campaign vigorously, raising more money each cycle and allocating more time and staff to campaigning. I posit that these "safe" incumbents continue to campaign vigorously to project strength to deter strong candidates from challenging them in the only remaining election that could be competitive: the primary. These incumbents would rather deter these challengers from entering the race than risk facing them in the primary when voters are not tied by partisanship to the incumbent. Using fundraising data from House of Representative elections from 2002 to 2018, I show that these incumbents use fundraising to project strength to outside political actors, are less concerned with projecting strength during the primary and general election campaigns, and are most concerned with projecting strength before the candidacy filing deadline. Using data on primary challenger entry dates, I also show that primary challengers announce their campaigns after receiving cues about incumbents' strength from fundraising data. Incumbents with safe general elections still campaign vigorously because they are "running scared."

With Republicans breathing down my neck – I'll be honest, this wasn't where I wanted to be right now. Can you consider making one last donation to get us all the way there?... I don't want to show any signs of weakness.

(An email from Representative Brad Schneider (IL-10) to supporters, sent on August 1, 2019)

We have 40 days until the most important election in American history. If we don't get across the finishing line, America as we know it may cease to exist... I am a few short days away from the most important fundraising deadline of the year... My campaign funds are depleting... it's getting harder and harder to defend myself. It's now or never.

(An email from Representative Marjorie Taylor Greene (GA-14) to supporters, sent on September 25, 2024)

A voter whose name and contact information have been placed on a fundraising list will recognize phrases in these quotes. In an election year, voters are inundated with texts, emails, pieces of mail, and social media advertisements that communicate a candidate's dire and urgent need for more funds lest the worst happen— their opponent bests them, or, as candidates often put it, the country hurtles toward catastrophe. But these pleas stand in stark contrast to the reality facing most incumbent members of Congress: they are overwhelmingly likely to win re-election. Over the last few decades, as voters' partisanship has come to hold more influence over who they vote for in a general election, the number of congressional districts with competitive general elections has shrunk. Today, the vast majority of incumbents are very likely to win their general elections simply because their party affiliation matches that of their district.

Still, despite their high level of safety, incumbents desperately raise campaign funds, spend hours on the phone calling donors, and travel back to their districts to host events. Importantly, even incumbents who are heavily advantaged to win their general elections (i. e. "safe" incumbents, like the two whose emails are quoted) campaign vigorously, raising more money each cycle and allocating more time and staff to campaigning. In 2020, incumbents who were favored to win their general elections by more than ten percentage points raised $470 million. In 2022, they raised $517 million. Why do safe incumbents campaign so hard for something they're almost certain to win anyway?

This chapter proposes an answer to this question. Safe incumbents continue to campaign vigorously in order to deter strong candidates from challenging them in the only remaining election that could be competitive: the primary. Safe incumbents would rather deter primary challengers from entering the race than risk facing them in the primary, where partisanship is not a determining characteristic. These incumbents deter strong primary challengers by projecting strength, using campaign fundraising, to make themselves seem difficult to beat.

I support this theory using campaign fundraising data for incumbent members of the House of Representatives from 2002 to 2018 and examine when money is raised by safe incumbents as a proxy for when incumbents find it most important to project strength.[1] I find that House incumbents running for re-election in safe congressional districts do not fundraise more vigorously throughout the course of the election season, suggesting these incumbents have not engaged in fundraising only to mount vigorous campaigns. Safe incumbents, in contrast to incumbents who are not heavily favored to win their general elections, raise more money in the days directly preceding the candidacy filing dead-

---

1 All fundraising data used in this paper is adjusted for inflation to 2018 dollars.

line than during any other time in the election cycle. I argue that this shows that safe incumbents are using fundraising to project strength before the electoral field is set, rather than to beat candidates who have entered the race. Furthermore, safe incumbents engage in this behavior more over time, supporting the idea that, as holding a partisan advantage in one's district becomes more predictive of winning a general election, incumbents find it more important to deter the competition that would threaten them: primary challengers.

I also look at the reaction to such posturing by examining the candidacy announcement dates for primary challengers from 2010 to 2014 and 2020 to see whether challengers launch their candidacies only after receiving cues about incumbents' strength.[2] I show that primary challengers who are considered "high quality" announce their campaigns after receiving cues about incumbents from fundraising data. I conclude that incumbents with safe general elections still campaign vigorously because they are "running scared."

This chapter lays out the puzzle of safe incumbents' campaigns, outlines the research method, and uses fundraising data to support the argument of "running scared." It concludes with a discussion of other possible explanations for safe incumbent fundraising and a summary of findings.

The Puzzle

Incumbent legislators are overwhelmingly likely to win re-election, yet they still campaign as if they face a strong threat, raising more money every year and devoting significant amounts of time to campaigning.

Incumbents have been favored to win re-election for decades. Political science scholars began noticing the increasing vote shares received by incumbents in the 1960s and spent the latter half of the twentieth century documenting both the increasing size of incumbents' electoral advantage and its possible causes. Between 1942 and 1950, House incumbents received only a 1.09 percentage point advantage by virtue of their incumbency. By the 1980s, the incumbency advantage had increased at least eightfold, to between eight and twelve percentage points of the general election vote share, by different estimates. (Ansolabehere and Snyder 2002; Gelman and King 1990; Gelman and King 1996).

As their security increased, incumbents campaigned more, raising more money and employing more staff to meet constituent requests (Fiorina 1989; Al-

---

2 Thank you to Hans Hassell and Adam Bonica for providing these datasets. Data collection for intervening and more recent election cycles is ongoing.

bert 2017). Fenno (1978) argued that incumbents campaigned to scare off strong challengers from running for office, rather than facing them in an election. Jacobson (1987) refined this theory further, arguing that incumbents "running scared" rose out of larger trends in American politics in the middle of the twentieth century. Specifically, as partisanship waned among the electorate in the 1950s, voters were less tied to supporting their party's nominee in the general election. This allowed the incumbency advantage to rise, as incumbents took advantage of higher name recognition, access to more resources, and delivery of constituent services. However, the rise of voters not strongly tied to their party's nominee presented a double-edged sword. Though incumbents could more easily win over opposing partisans who were not tied to voting for their party's nominee, voters of an incumbent's party could also be won over by a strong challenger. The only way to ensure success was to campaign vigorously to project strength and scare off strong potential challengers, rather than take the risk of facing them in an election. This explanation was corroborated by later work that found the increase in incumbency advantage could be attributed to incumbents facing lower quality candidates in general elections (Gelman and King 1996).

While this helped explain the vigorous campaigning of incumbents in the mid- to late twentieth century, the dynamics underlying the "running scared" theory have changed. Partisanship has resurged among the electorate. Voters are more likely to strongly identify with a party today than they were in the 1970s or 1980s (Hetherington 2001; Bartels 2000; Bafumi and Shapiro 2009; Iyengar et al. 2012). Voters of all levels of political awareness and party identification are more likely to see important differences between the parties (Smidt 2017). Voters are also more likely to feel animus towards their out-party and affinity for their in-party (Iyengar and Westwood 2015).

With this increase in partisanship among the electorate, straight-ticket voting (i.e. voting for candidates of only one party across multiple offices) has increased and the relationship between partisanship and vote choice has strengthened (Hetherington 2001; Bartels 2000; Smidt 2017). This is true even in races with incumbents, and even among voters who don't strongly identify with a political party.

Subsequently, individual general elections today are less competitive and the incumbency advantage declined to only three percentage points in 2012 (Jacobson 2015). There are more districts that are "safe," effectively one-party districts, and fewer districts that have competitive general elections. According to ratings from FiveThirtyEight.com, the number of swing or lean House districts decreased from forty-three percent in 1992 (188 seats) to twenty-nine percent in 2000 (125 seats), and to just twenty percent in 2012 (87 seats) (Silver 2012). Meanwhile, the number of safe districts where one party is expected to win by a "landslide" grew dramatically, from twenty-eight percent in 1992 (123 seats) to fifty-six percent (242 seats) in 2012. "Landslide" districts live up to their name; though a number of districts remain competitive, the average margin of victory in races for the House was twenty-seven percent in 2024 (Ballotpedia 2025).

But even as the phenomena that underpin the running scared theory fade, and even as general elections become less competitive, incumbents raise more and more money each election, and spend large amounts of time and staff campaigning. Between 1980 and 2016, the amount that congressional candidates raised from individual donors increased over fivefold, from $165 million to $873 million, and the amount that congressional candidates raised via political action committees (PACs) increased sixfold, from $207 million to $1.2 billion (Albert 2017). Incumbent fundraising follows the same dizzying growth, raising more from individual contributors over time, from $36 million in 2002 to $2.3 billion in 2022.

Furthermore, even incumbents in nearly one-party districts who do not face significant competition in general elections raised more money over time. Figure 6.1 displays the total amount of money raised by House incumbents running for re-election over time. Incumbents are separated by how much they are favored to win their general election (by more than ten or twenty percentage points, and less than ten or twenty percentage points). Even incumbents who were favored to win their general elections by more than ten percentage points and those who are favored to win by more than twenty percentage points raised dramatically more money over time, growing by over 833 percent and 750 percent respectively. In 2018, House incumbents who were favored to win their general elections by more than twenty percentage points raised over $34 million and House incumbents who were favored to win their general elections by more than ten percentage points raised over $84 million, compared to only $4 million and $9 million, respectively, in 2002.

Beyond raising more money, incumbents are also devoting more time and staff to their campaigns. Senators, for example, take more trips to their home state than they used to (Kaslovsky 2020). Senators also place more staff in state offices, placing a stronger emphasis on constituent services. In 2018, forty-one percent of Senators' staff worked in state offices, compared to just twenty-five percent in 1978 (Kaslovsky 2020).

Elected officials also spend significant amounts of time campaigning and soliciting donations. A leaked slideshow made by Democratic leadership in 2013 outlining how new members of Congress should spend their day recommended that freshman House members spend forty to fifty percent of any given day fundraising and campaigning (Grim and Siddiqui 2013).

Particularly for those incumbents running in safe districts, who are heavily favored to win the general election, why exert so much effort?

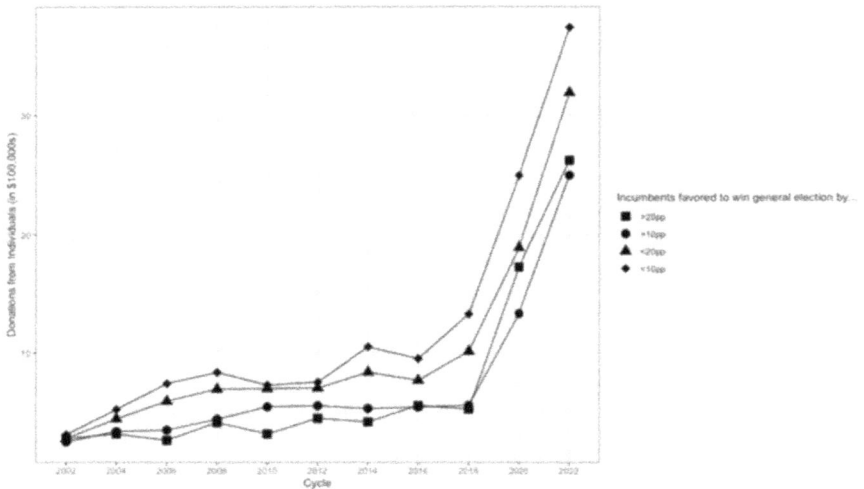

Figure 6.1: Average fundraising of House incumbents running for re-election by cycle.

Theory and Method

This chapter proposes a simple theory to explain the puzzle of campaign efforts by incumbents in safe general election districts. As partisanship has become more prognostic of vote choice in general elections, incumbents in safe general election districts have little reason to fear even strong general election challengers. Today, the primary is where these incumbents are most vulnerable to being unseated. As such, incumbents in "safe" districts still campaign, but they do not campaign in order to deter strong general election challengers. Rather, they seek to project strength in order to scare off strong primary election challengers.

I support this theory using fundraising data for House incumbents running for re-election from 2002 to 2018, collected by the Database on Ideology, Money in Politics, and Elections (Bonica 2023). I focus on fundraising data to reveal incumbents' campaign activity because it is the most visible and accessible campaigning metric, to both researchers and political actors outside of a campaign (such as prospective candidates, PACs, and party officials). Past work argues that public fundraising data serves as a signal of incumbents' vulnerability, specifically for potential challengers (Epstein and Zemsky 1995). Furthermore, other public information about incumbents, especially ones in uncompetitive districts, is hard to come by as media coverage is thin outside of the general election (Huber and Tucker 2024).

I aggregate how much each House incumbent raises on each day in an election cycle (defined as January 1 the year before the election to December 31 the year of the election; for the 2014 cycle, this period is January 1, 2013 to December 31, 2014) to investigate when incumbents are trying hardest to raise money (or at least are most successful in raising money).

I define incumbents in "safe" general election districts as those who are favored to win their general election by a more than a ten percentage point margin by the Cook Political Voting Index. The results shown here also replicate when I define "safe" incumbents as those favored to win the general election by more than twenty percentage points. I use the Cook Political Voting Index rather than actual election results because they are developed and released before all candidates have announced and therefore do not reflect incumbent campaigning effort as much as election results do.

I show that House incumbents in districts with uncompetitive general elections (i. e. "safe" incumbents) fundraise more heavily when it is most important and visible to project strength: around the Federal Elections Commission's quarterly fundraising reporting deadlines and immediately prior to the candidacy filing deadline.[3] In contrast, safe incumbents do not fundraise as heavily over the entire course of the campaign itself, including both the primary and general elections, suggesting these incumbents are using fundraising as a tool to show invulnerability to dissuade potential challengers from entering the race, rather than mounting vigorous campaigns immediately prior to elections.

Finally, I examine whether primary challengers orient their behavior around incumbent fundraising reports, by looking at the dates of Federal Elections Commission candidacy filings for all primary challengers in House races from 2010, 2012, 2014 and 2020.[4] I find that quality challengers who have previously held elected office tend to announce their candidacies immediately following the release of a quarterly fundraising report, when they have received information about their opponents' strength (or lack thereof).

Importantly, this chapter presents only descriptive evidence. I do not account for incumbents who chose to retire because they fear being unseated in the primary or the general. I do not account for when donors may be more likely to give to incumbent campaigns. I also do not delineate incumbents based on whether they end up drawing a primary or general election challenger. I examine incum-

---

3 These deadlines vary by state.
4 Thanks to Adam Bonica and Hans Hassell for providing this data.

bent campaigns in safe general election districts when they face uncertainty about their opponents.

Results

If incumbents in safe general election districts are trying to project strength to deter strong primary challengers, when would we expect them to do so? There are two times throughout an election cycle when incumbents are best positioned to use fundraising to deter potential opponents: FEC quarterly reports, which are the most reliable sources for fundraising totals, and prior to the candidacy filing deadline, when potential opponents are deciding whether to enter the race.

Projecting Strength Quarterly

A key method incumbents have to project strength to outside political actors in an upcoming election is to post strong fundraising reports. Though campaigns can release memos with fundraising totals whenever they think best, the most reliable source of fundraising totals are campaigns' public fundraising reports to the Federal Elections Commission, which are due quarterly.

Furthermore, incumbents and their campaigns attempt to project as much strength to prospective challengers as possible by trying to inflate the size of their quarterly reports. Party leadership explicitly advises campaigns to ramp up fundraising efforts immediately preceding reporting deadlines (Democratic Congressional Campaign Committee 2018). Campaign managers also report efforts to convince large donors to move the timing of their donations to immediately before filing reports (Cohen 2023). These funds, especially those collected in years preceding an election, serve as an indication of strength because the funds are not needed so far in advance of the active campaign.

Do incumbents who expect uncompetitive general elections try to project strength through quarterly fundraising reports? Figure 6.2 displays total donations to House incumbents running for re-election between 2002 and 2018 who are heavily favored to win their general elections. Figure 6.2 plots this donation data across the course of a year, with four dotted lines denoting the weeks of the year that the FEC requires campaigns to file quarterly fundraising reports. Even for incumbents with safe general elections, fundraising receipts clearly spike directly before quarterly reporting deadlines.

Figure 6.3 shows the same data as Figure 6.2, fundraising of safe incumbents over the course of a year, relative to FEC quarterly reporting deadlines. But Figure

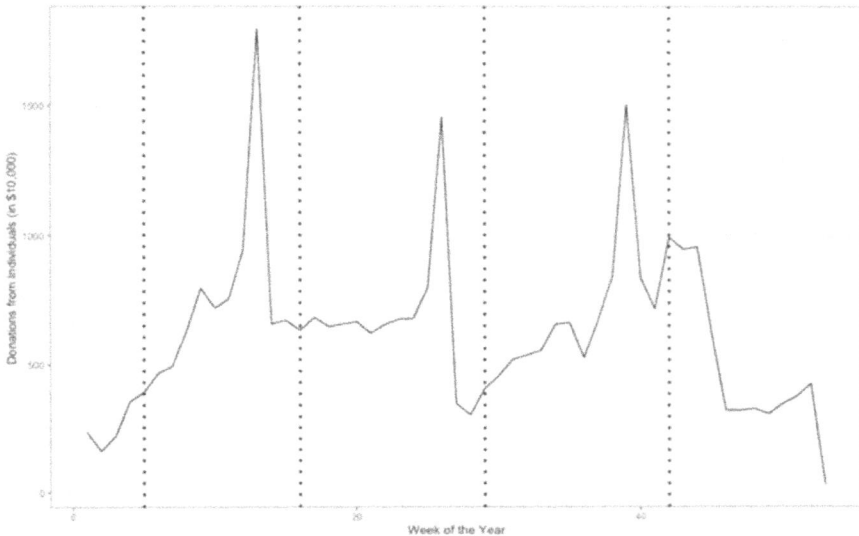

Figure 6.2: Total fundraising of 2002–2018 safe House incumbents running for re-election relative to FEC quarterly reporting deadlines.

6.3 separates this data into election and non-election years. Both election and non-election year funding receipts show spikes before quarterly reporting deadlines. As a result, Figure 6.3 shows that incumbents who are heavily favored to win their general elections raise more money before reporting deadlines even in non-election years, long before incumbents will use the money to mount a campaign.

Finally, Figure 6.4 shows the same data, but separates fundraising from earlier election cycles (between 2002 and 2010) and later election cycles (between 2010 and 2018). As expected, safe incumbents raised more money in later election cycles than earlier ones, consistent with the overall fundraising trends shown in Figure 6.1. In both earlier and later election cycles, safe incumbents raise more money immediately preceding FEC reporting deadlines. However, this trend is significantly more pronounced in later election years. This is what the theory that safe incumbents are "running scared" in the primary predicts; as partisanship among voters becomes more determinant of general election vote choice and incumbency advantage declines, incumbents who have partisan advantages in their district become more certain those advantages will assure them general election victories. However, the lowering incumbency advantage makes these incumbents more vulnerable in primary elections, and so makes it more important for them to

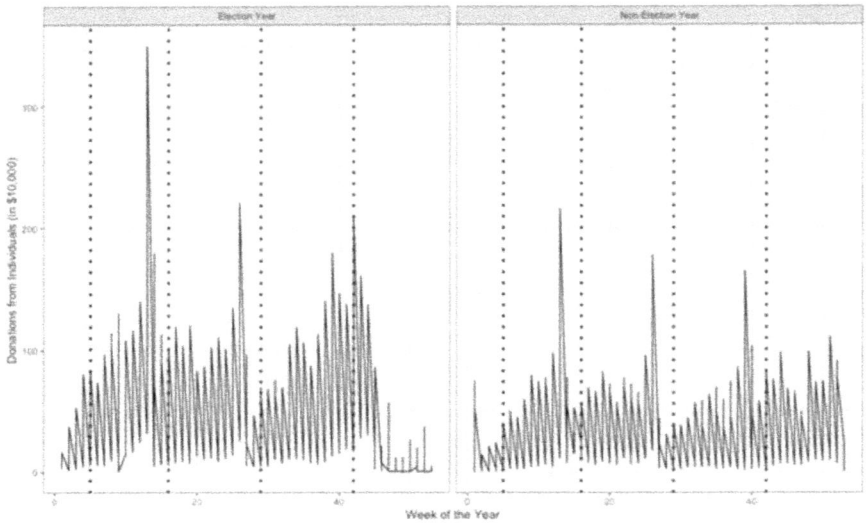

Figure 6.3: Total Fundraising of 2002–2018 safe House incumbents running for re-election relative to FEC quarterly reporting deadlines, separated into election years and non-election years.

project strength to deter strong primary challengers. In response to these trends, safe incumbents work harder to inflate their quarterly fundraising reports.

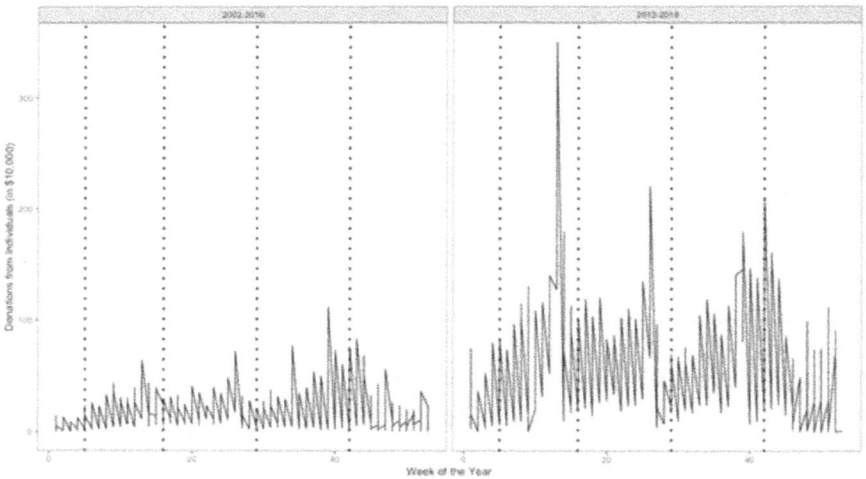

Figure 6.4: Total fundraising of 2002–2018 safe House incumbents running for re-election relative to FEC quarterly reporting deadlines, separated into later and earlier years.

Before the Candidacy Filing Deadline

Projecting strength throughout an incumbent's term in the form of FEC quarterly reports may signal overall strength, but to deter specific challengers in a specific election, an incumbent would also want to demonstrate strength before the candidacy filing deadline.

Figure 6.5 shows fundraising totals for safe incumbents relative to each race's candidacy filing deadline. The filing deadline is denoted by the dotted line; fundraising data to the left of the line occurred before the filing deadline while fundraising to the right of the line occurred after (e. g. day 0 is the day of the filing deadline and day -10 is 10 days before the deadline). Incumbents running for re-election in safe districts exhibit a spike in fundraising just before their candidacy filing deadline, raising more before the deadline then after it.

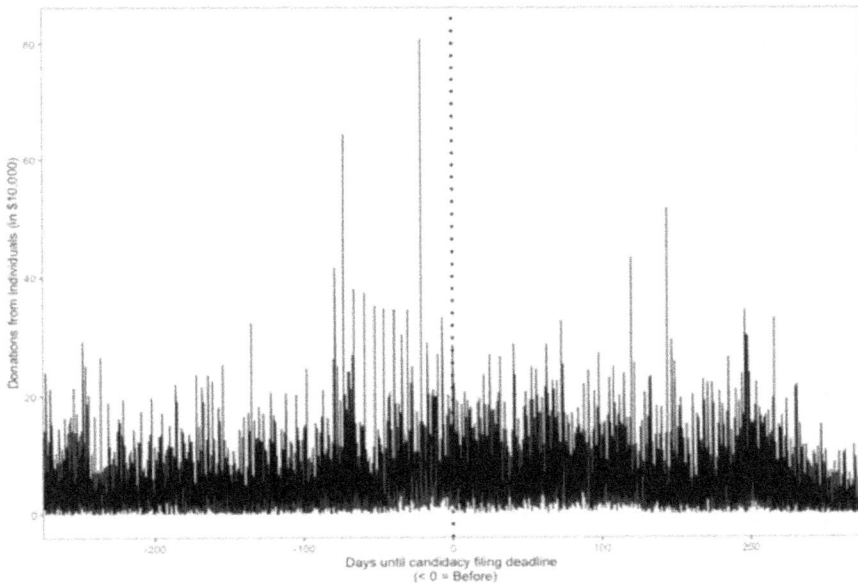

Figure 6.5: Fundraising of safe House incumbents running for re-election, 2002–2018, relative to candidacy filing deadline.

In 2002, safe incumbents raised $1.7 million in the two months before the candidacy filing deadline, compared to $855,000 in the two months afterward. In 2014, they raised $7.5 million in the two months before the filing deadline, compared to $6.5 million afterward. This spike before the filing deadline is the single highest period of fundraising for safe incumbents over the entire election cycle. Incumbents in safe districts do not raise more at any time during the primary or the general election. Incumbents who have no reason to be concerned about general election challengers try hardest to project strength before the candidacy filing deadline rather than at any other time during the election.

Furthermore, this behavior is unique to safe incumbents. Figure 6.6 shows the same fundraising data, total funds raised on each day relative to the candidacy filing deadline, among incumbents with safe general elections (shown on the right; this data is identical to that shown in Figure 6.5) and among incumbents with competitive general elections (shown on the left). Safe incumbents fundraise most and most consistently in the days immediately preceding the candidacy filing deadline. In contrast, incumbents with competitive general elections fundraise much more than safe incumbents but do so throughout the entire election season, with no analogous peak before the candidacy filing deadline. While incumbents facing competitive general elections fundraise throughout the election cycle to keep their seat, safe incumbents focus on fundraising when it would deter opponents.

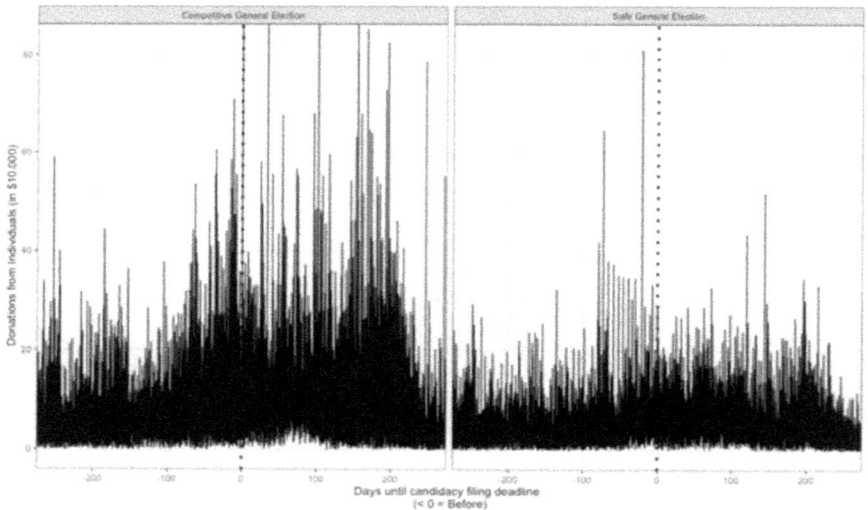

Figure 6.6: Fundraising of all House incumbents running for re-election, 2002–2018, separated by incumbent safety in the general election.

Because the electoral fortunes of safe incumbents are tied to shifting dynamics in American politics, we would expect safe incumbents to engage in efforts to deter primary challengers more over time, just like incumbents' efforts to inflate quarterly fundraising reports. Figure 6.7 shows fundraising data for safe incumbents relative to the candidacy filing deadline, separated into earlier election cycles (between 2002 and 2010) and later election cycles (between 2012 and 2018). Similar to Figure 6.4, we see that safe incumbents raise more in later election cycles than earlier ones. Also like Figure 6.4, safe incumbents concentrate their fundraising efforts directly before the candidacy filing deadline to a greater extent in later years than in earlier election cycles. Over time, as safe incumbents become more vulnerable in their primary elections, they become more concerned with showing strength before candidacy filing deadlines.

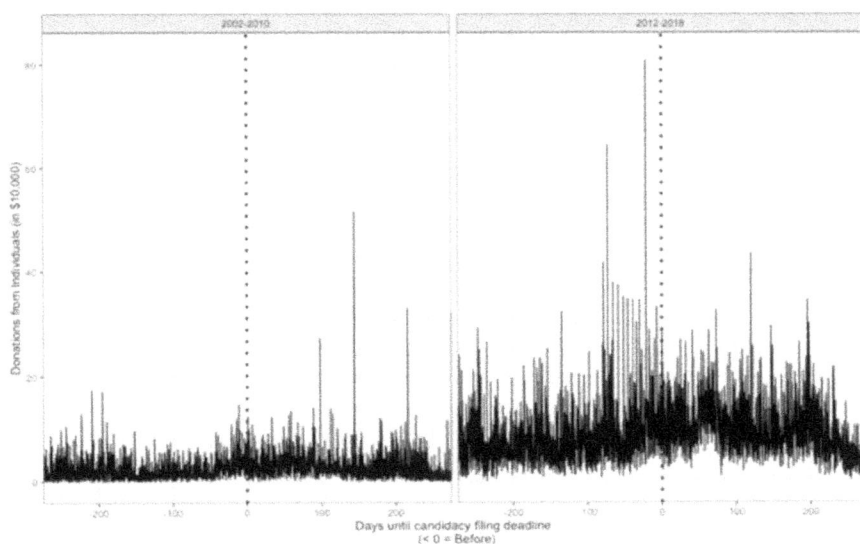

Figure 6.7: Fundraising of safe House incumbents running for re-election, 2002–2018, relative to candidacy filing deadline, separated into later and earlier years.

Republicans Run Scared More than Democrats

Given that Hirano and Snyder (2019) find that the upsurge in primary challengers in the last decade is driven mostly by an increase in Republican primary challengers, we might think that incumbents of different parties place different levels of importance on deterring primary challengers.

Figure 6.8 shows fundraising of safe incumbents (for only later election cycles) relative to the candidacy filing deadline and separated by the incumbent's party. While Democratic incumbents in safe general election districts do raise money more vigorously before the filing deadline than during the rest of the election, the spike in fundraising directly preceding the filing deadline is driven by Republican incumbents. Republican incumbents who face uncompetitive general elections raise money more vigorously before the candidacy filing deadline and exhibit the largest influx of donations directly preceding the deadline than at any other point in the campaign. For example, in 2018, safe Democrats raised $1.2 million in both the two weeks before and the two weeks after the filing deadline. Safe Republicans, though, raised $1.3 million in the two weeks before the filing deadline but only $983,000 in the two weeks following the deadline, a 24% decrease.

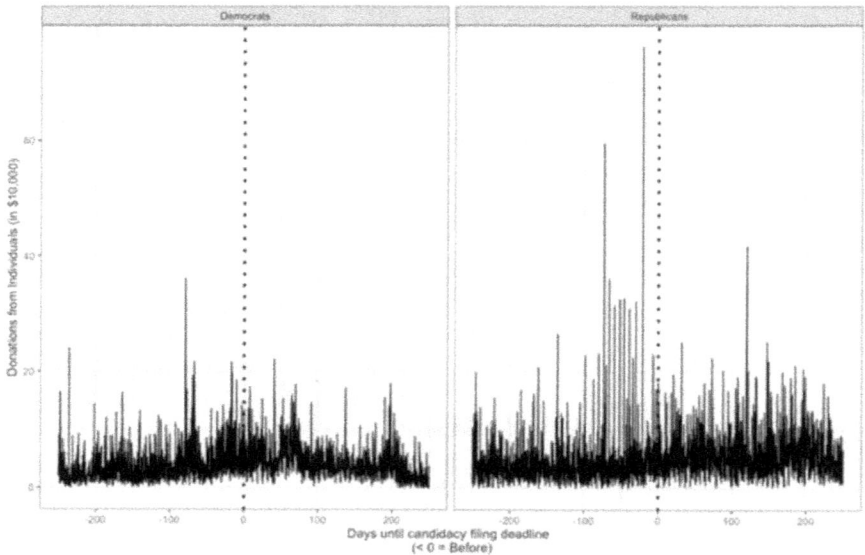

Figure 6.8: Fundraising of safe House incumbents running for re-election, 2012–2018, relative to candidacy filing deadline, separated by party of incumbent.

While there is evidence that safe incumbents in both parties raise money to project strength to deter strong primary challengers, Republican incumbents in safe districts are either more successful in soliciting donations to project strength or exert more effort. Safe Republican incumbents may also focus more heavily on fundraising before candidacy filing deadlines to deter strong primary challengers because they are at a higher risk of facing a well-financed challenger; Republican incumbents are slightly more likely to draw ideologically extreme challengers than Democratic incumbents, and these challengers have easier access to national donors and PACs (Boatright 2013).

Challengers' Candidacy Announcement Timing

Given the time, effort, and money that incumbents in safe general election districts spend projecting strength to outside parties, do these outside actors pay attention to these efforts?

If safe incumbents campaign to deter primary challengers, primary challengers should emerge around the time they receive a signal about an incumbent's weakness. Do primary challengers tend to announce their candidacies following regular releases of incumbent campaign information at quarterly reporting deadlines? Figure 6.9 shows the number of House primary candidates challenging incumbents in safe districts and the week of the year that they announced their candidacies for the 2010, 2012, 2014, and 2020 election cycles. The four dotted lines on the chart denote the four FEC quarterly reporting deadlines. If challengers take into account cues of incumbent strength when deciding whether to enter the race, we would expect to see a spike in entrants after each filing deadline when these cues are made public.

Note that this investigation is far from causal. There may be many other reasons quarters are attractive candidacy announcement dates for primary challengers besides getting a cue to an incumbent's strength. Specifically, challengers who announce following a quarterly reporting deadline give themselves the most time before the next deadline to fundraise to post an impressive report themselves. Further, we cannot observe the challengers who choose not to announce after seeing a strong fundraising report by the incumbent in their district. We can only observe an incumbent's failure to deter a primary challenge, rather than their success.

Figure 6.9 shows little relationship between quarterly reporting deadlines and when challengers tend to announce their candidacies. Perhaps this is because incumbents are so effective at deterring challengers that the few challengers that do announce do so without any regard to an incumbent's strength. Alternatively, incumbents could be working hard to project strength only to find that their intended audience, prospective primary challengers, pays little attention.

But incumbents care not just about primary challengers writ large but specifically strong primary challengers who would prompt a competitive primary. What makes a strong challenger can be hard to determine ex ante, but a common measure for quality challengers is whether they have previously held elected office. These candidates are more likely to succeed, perhaps because they have access

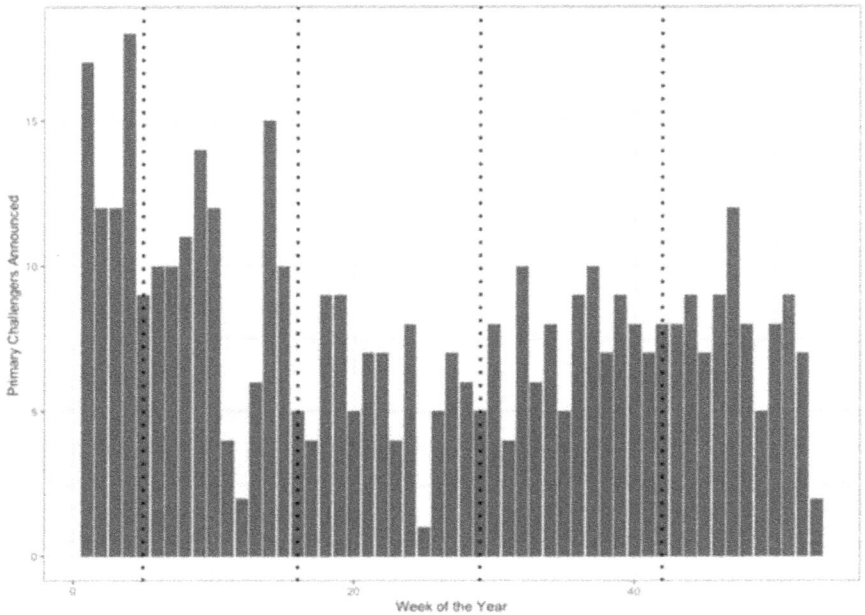

Figure 6.9: Timing of primary challenger announcements in safe districts for 2010–2014 and 2020 house races.

to more resources, experience running campaigns, and higher name recognition (Buttice and Stone 2012; Squire 1992; Jacobson 1978). For this reason, we might expect that prospective quality challengers are the intended audience of a safe incumbent's quarterly fundraising reports. Figure 6.10 shows the number of candidacy announcements by primary challengers in safe districts over the course of the year for the 2010–2014 election cycles but only for those challengers who are "high quality."

Figure 6.10 shows that "high quality" primary challengers are more likely to announce their candidacies directly following a quarterly reporting deadline than before or in between reports. Though we cannot observe those quality challengers who choose not to run, quality challengers who do mount campaigns tend to do so after information is available about an incumbent's strength. That quality challengers for House seats make decisions about joining the race based on an incumbent's strength is congruent with other work that shows that quality challengers are often available for Senate races but rarely choose to run (King 2017).

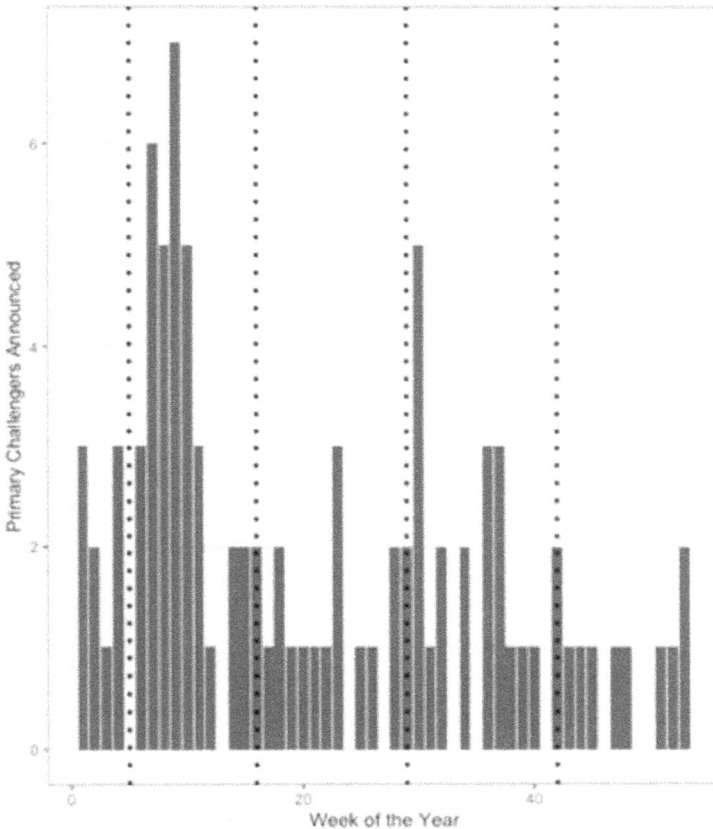

Figure 6.10: Timing of primary challenger announcements in safe districts for 2010–2014 House races, quality candidates only.

Alternative Explanations

Although I have provided descriptive evidence consistent with the theory that safe incumbents fundraise to deter serious primary challengers, other motivations could explain incumbents' campaign behavior. Namely, (1) incumbents could fundraise to finance actual campaigns they mount; (2) incumbents could have little control over when they raise money due to the growing portion of donations from small dollar digital contributions; or (3) incumbents could see fundraising as a way to gain political clout within the party by demonstrating that they can raise money. Though each of these explanations is plausible, donation data does not corroborate them. Instead, using fundraising to deter primary challengers remains the strongest explanation for donation patterns.

Running to Beat Challengers

The first counterargument one might lodge against this chapter's theory is that safe incumbents might still face significant uncertainty and competition, just in the primary election rather than the general. This means they need to engage in fundraising and campaigning to run against primary challengers, rather than to deter them.

But over the period of time I examine, incumbents are not likely to face or lose to a primary challenge. Boatright (2013) catalogues primary competition from 1970 to 2010 and finds no increase in challenges over time; fewer than ten percent of House incumbent primaries were contested from 2000 to 2010. Boatright also finds that even if incumbents do face primary challengers, they are not at great risk of losing. Fewer than two percent of incumbents are unseated in the primary in every election between 2000 and 2010. Moreover, the number of incumbents facing primary challengers and the number of incumbents losing to primary challengers were no higher in the 2000s than during the 1990s or 1970s.[5]

Hirano and Snyder (2019) include more recent elections, cataloging primary competition in House elections through 2016. They find a slight uptick in the number of primary challengers in the 2010s, particularly against Republican incumbents. But Rogers (2023) goes even further, cataloging primary challenges to state house and House of Representative incumbents through 2020. The number of House incumbents facing challengers does increase slightly over the 2010s (driven by the 2012 primaries), but the rate of re-nomination of incumbents remains stable over that time, holding at ninety-eight percent. This is not to say that individual primary challenges do not matter; indeed, with narrowing margins in Congress, each election has more sway over partisan control of the House or Senate. Yet, any individual member of Congress has an exceedingly low probability of facing and losing to a primary challenger.

We can also look to fundraising data to investigate whether incumbents in safe general election districts raise money throughout the primary election to mount campaigns to run against primary challengers. If incumbents in safe general election districts were concerned with both projecting strength to deter pri-

---

5 Primary challenges were particularly rare during the 1980s.

mary challengers and running vigorous campaigns to beat those primary challengers, we should see vigorous fundraising from before the candidacy filing
deadline through the primary campaign, with increased fundraising before the
day of the primary election. If incumbents in safe general election districts
were concerned only with projecting strength to deter primary challengers, but
not with beating them, we should see that fundraising drops off well before the
primary election, when challengers have either been deterred or not.

Figure 6.11 displays donations per day to House incumbents running for re-
election in safe districts oriented relative to the date of each incumbent's primary
election, denoted by the dotted line.[6] Data to the left of the dotted line are funds
raised before the primary election and data on to the right of the line are funds
raised after the primary election. Figure 6.11 focuses on fundraising between 2012
and 2018, when Hirano and Snyder (2019) and Rogers (2023) find slight increases
in primary challengers. Because Hirano and Snyder (2019) find that this uptick is
driven by Republican incumbents facing primary challengers, Figure 6.11 also separates donations by the party of the incumbent.

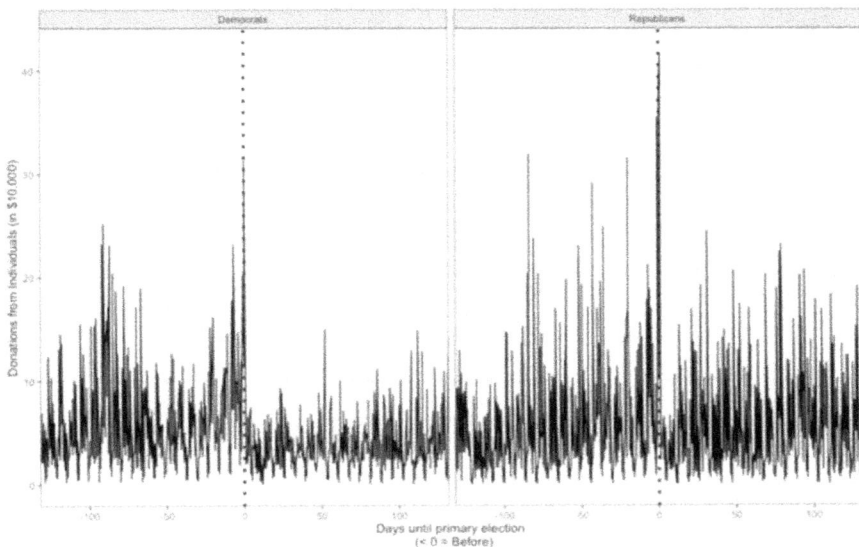

Figure 6.11: Fundraising of safe House incumbents running for re-election, 2012–2018, relative to
the primary election, separated by party.

---

6 The date of the primary election varies by state.

Democratic incumbents in safe general election districts make more effort to raise money about three months before the primary election (consistent with the timing of candidacy filing deadlines) but actually raise less money during the heart of the primary campaign (one to two months before the primary election). These Democrats raise money more vigorously in the few weeks directly before election day, and experience a spike in fundraising when they win the primary. Republican incumbents in safe general election districts, however, raise money consistently throughout the course of the primary campaign, right up to the primary election. They also receive more donations immediately after winning the primary election.

Taken with Figure 6.8, which shows the concentration of fundraising before the candidacy filing deadline is driven by Republicans, Figure 6.11 suggests that safe incumbent Republicans are both more concerned with deterring primary challengers and campaign more heavily throughout the course of the primary campaign when they draw more challengers than Democratic incumbents. In contrast, safe Democratic incumbents, who are less likely to face these challenges, focus more singularly on projecting strength to deter primary challenges. Perhaps Democrats are more successful than Republicans in deterring primary challenges, or perhaps some other aspect of the Republican party is spurring more primary challenges.

Recent work by Porter and Treul (2025) suggests the latter is more likely, as the number of Republican primary challengers who had not previously held elected office rises. As illustrated by Figures 6.9 and 6.10, inexperienced or "low quality" primary challengers are less responsive to information about incumbents' strength and are no more likely to announce their candidacy after incumbents' quarterly fundraising reports. Republican incumbents are working to project strength as much as (or more than) Democratic incumbents, but Republican primary challengers are a different population than Democratic primary challengers. They are more numerous and less concerned with incumbent strength, prompting more competitive primaries and safe Republican incumbents who must raise money throughout the primary campaign.

Donors' Decisions to Give

The running scared theory presumes that incumbents exercise control over how much and when they raise money. But donors also have agency regarding when and how much they want to contribute. One might argue that the trends shown in this chapter reflect when donors want to give, rather than when incumbents want to raise. Particularly, the election years included in the dataset that show the rise in safe incumbent fundraising at strategic times coincides with a period of rapid change among donors. Over these same years, campaigns began to raise money over the internet and email, particularly to solicit small dollar donations (defined as donations of less than $200) from a wide number of people. This is a departure from traditional fundraising strategies, which involve the candidate or a campaign staffer personally soliciting a donation from a high net-worth individual who could give a large donation. As a result of this shift, small dollar donations (and small dollar donors) make up an increasing portion of campaign funds (and donors); in 2020, small dollar donations made up twenty-two percent of campaign funds, an increase from fifteen percent in 2016 (Gratzinger 2020).

The growth of small dollar donations, and the growth in the number of donors, means that campaigns have less control over when they raise money. Instead of campaign staff or candidates deciding when to call big donors and solicit larger sums of money from them, campaigns send out emails and social media ads soliciting $5 donations from thousands of people.

Still, it is not clear that the growth of small dollar donations would explain the spike of funds raised preceding the candidate filing deadline or the FEC quarterly reporting deadlines. If anything, small dollar donors should be less tuned-in to esoteric reporting and filing deadlines, especially in non-election years. That we see incumbents raising more money around these deadlines despite the growth of small dollar donations may mean that incumbents are working even harder than we can see to inflate fundraising at strategic times.

Figure 6.12 shows total donations to safe incumbents between 2012 and 2018 relative to FEC quarterly reporting deadlines, denoted by the four dotted lines, separated by whether the donation is large or small. For large dollar donations that incumbents are more likely to solicit directly, fundraising spikes preceding reporting deadlines. For small dollar donations that result from fundraising efforts that campaigns exercise less control over, Figure 6.12 shows no clear pattern in the timing of small dollar donations. Fundraising from small dollar donations remains relatively flat (albeit erratic) over the course of the year.

Figure 6.12 illustrates that when campaigns have more influence over fundraising, they use it to inflate donations strategically at moments when they can best project strength. When campaigns have less control over fundraising, as with small dollar donations, fundraising is unpredictable and erratic over time. Looking at small and large dollar donations separately bolsters the theory that safe incumbents use fundraising to look strong to outside political actors. But as small dollar donations make up increasing portions of campaign funds, incumbents may lose influence over the timing of their receipts, weakening their ability to present themselves as invulnerable to challenges.

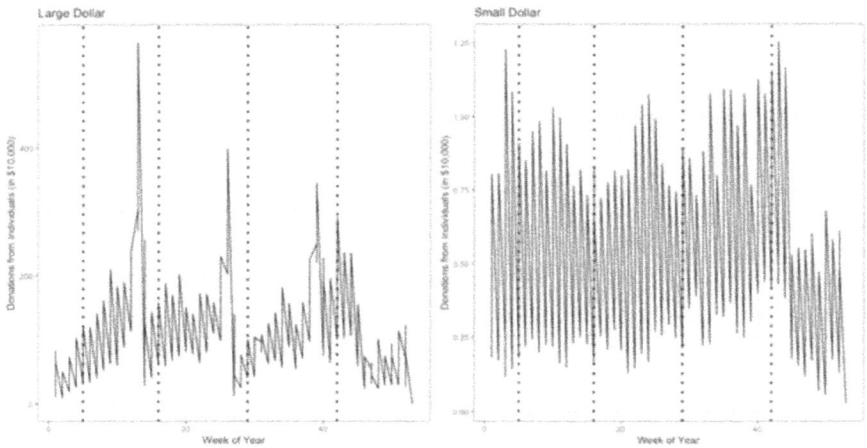

Figure 6.12: Fundraising of safe House incumbents running for re-election, 2012–2018, relative to FEC quarterly reporting deadlines, separated into large and small dollar donations.

Clout within the Party

Finally, safe incumbents seeking re-election may be raising money not for electoral purposes (whether to scare off challengers or mount a campaign against them) but to gain clout within their party by providing help to other party members and support for broader party goals. During the campaign season, that means funding other party members' campaigns and especially contributing to the party's candidate in swing districts and close races.

One way incumbents can try to elevate their status within the party is by creating a leadership PAC, or a political action committee that functions much the same as any other PAC but is affiliated with an incumbent such that the incumbent can solicit donations for the PAC and direct it to spend its funds on races important to the party. Leadership PACs were explicitly created to help incumbents advance within the party; the House incumbent who lobbied the FEC to create this unique type of PAC did so to gain favor within the party to win a subcommittee chairmanship (Beckel and Ratliff 2018).

The use of leadership PACs has grown dramatically over the same period of time safe incumbents have increasingly raised money strategically. From 2002 to 2022, the number of leadership PACs has increased over threefold (from 223 in 2002 to 746 in 2022). The money from leadership PACs donated to candidates has grown similarly over time: from $25.3 million in 2002 to $76.1 million in 2022 (Open Secrets 2025).

But even as incumbents raise more money to further their status in the party through leadership PACs, they are also raising more money for their own campaigns. And as incumbents are limited from transferring more than $5,000 per year from their campaign to their leadership PAC, the growth of leadership PACs does not explain the increase of safe incumbents' fundraising for their own campaigns, nor the timing of that fundraising (Federal Election Commission n.d.).

Another way incumbents could attempt to gain influence in their party is by redistributing the money they raise for their own campaign to other candidates by donating directly from their campaign fund to other campaigns. The total dollar amount donated to other campaigns from the ten highest-giving incumbents has increased over time, from a $1.2 million in 2000 to $3.7 million in 2022 (Open Secrets 2023). But this threefold increase over two decades pales in comparison to the increase in incumbent funding over the same period. Over the same time period, safe incumbents increased their total funds over 5,700 percent from $8.9 million to $517 million. Incumbents who faced competitive general elections increased their funds 6,600 percent from $9.4 million to $628 million.

Incumbents may be fundraising more in part so that they can redistribute funding from their own campaign to other campaigns. But this trend does not explain the vast majority of the increase in incumbent campaign funding. Future work should look at campaign disbursements by all incumbents in order to further investigate how much incumbent fundraising is redistributed to other campaigns.

Conclusion

This chapter argues that the rigorous campaigning of incumbents who are highly favored to win their general elections constitutes a perplexing puzzle. Furthermore, this puzzle has real consequences for American governance. Incumbents in safe districts spend exorbitant amounts of money campaigning for elections they are overwhelmingly likely to win, and spend vast amounts of time campaigning that they could spend governing.

In this chapter I have argued that these incumbents use campaigning and fundraising to project strength to scare off prospective primary challengers. They do so by concentrating fundraising at crucial moments in the campaign, namely, before candidacy filing and FEC quarterly reporting deadlines. In other words, incumbents who have little to worry about in general elections "run scared in the primary."

This chapter also shows that this pattern varies over time and by party. As partisanship has grown stronger among the electorate and general election outcomes have become more predictable, incumbents in safe general election districts appear to have placed more emphasis on using fundraising totals to deter primary challengers. Furthermore, Republican incumbents in safe general election districts appear to have used fundraising totals to deter primary challengers more than Democratic incumbents have in similarly safe districts.

Finally, this chapter suggests that at least some types of primary challengers may be waiting for these signals of strength (or lack thereof) to decide whether to enter the race. Primary challengers who have held elected office before are likely to announce their candidacies directly following quarterly reporting deadlines when they have access to information about incumbents' support.

The evidence presented in this chapter is fundamentally descriptive and does not account for strong prospective primary challengers who decide not to run for office or incumbents who decide to retire rather than face a challenger. Still, other possible explanations for safe incumbents' growing war chests and strategic fundraising timing do not seem to account for the rigorous campaigning of safe incumbents. Republican incumbents who are more likely to face a primary challenge raise money consistently throughout the primary campaign, but they also make particular efforts to raise money shortly before the candidacy filing deadline. Democrats, in contrast, focus overwhelmingly on fundraising around the filing deadline. Furthermore, large dollar donations that the campaigns solicit from individuals (rather than in bulk through email lists and social media advertisements), and therefore have more control over, are concentrated around times when incumbents want to project strength. Finally, though incumbents do increasingly redistribute their campaign funds to other candidates, perhaps to further their status within their party, their own campaign war chests grow at a much faster rate.

As the dynamics of primary elections have changed, incumbents in safe general election districts have shifted their focus away from deterring general election opponents and toward protecting themselves from being unseated in the primary. But primary elections continue to change in ways that make incumbents' efforts to deter primary challengers less effective; namely, primary challengers are more likely to not have held elected office before (and so respond less to esoteric signals of strength like FEC fundraising reports), and small dollar donations make up a higher percentage of campaign funds (reducing the campaign and candidate's influence over when the campaign raises money). Though safe incumbents have spent increasing amounts of time, money, and energy to stave off primary competition, the new dynamics of modern primary elections may blunt incumbents' ability to successfully deter primary challengers and leave incumbents searching for new strategies to keep their seats.

Bibliography

Albert, Zachary. October 12, 2017. "Trends in Campaign Financing, 1980–2016." *Bipartisan Policy Center.*

Ansolabehere, Steven, and James M. Snyder Jr. 2002. "The Incumbency Advantage in U.S. Elections: An Analysis of State and Federal Offices, 1942–2000." *Election Law Journal* 1 (3): 315–340.

Bafumi, Joseph, and Robert Y. Shapiro. 2009. "A New Partisan Voter." *The Journal of Politics* 71 (January): 1–24.

Ballotpedia. February 2, 2025. "Election results, 2024: Congressional margin of victory analysis." https://ballotpedia.org/Election_results,_2024:_Congressional_margin_of_victory_analysis.

Bartels, Larry M. 2000. "Partisanship and Voting Behavior, 1952–1996." *American Journal of Political Science* 44 (1): 35–50.

Beckel, Michael, and Amisa Ratliff. 2018. "Leadership PACs, Inc." Washington, DC: Issue One.

Boatright, Robert. 2013. *Getting Primaried: The Changing Politics of Congressional Primary Challenges.* University of Michigan Press.

Bonica, Adam. 2023. *Database on Ideology, Money in Politics, and Elections*: Public version 3.1 [Computer file]. Stanford University Libraries.

Bonica, Adam. 2020. "Why Are There So Many Lawyers in Congress?" *Legislative Studies Quarterly* 45 (2):253–289.

Buttice, Matthew K., and Walter J. Stone. 2012. "Candidates Matter: Policy and Quality Differences in Congressional Elections." *Journal of Politics* 74 (3): 870–887.

Cohen, Hayley M. 2023. "Who you gonna call? How primary campaigns conduct voter outreach." Working Paper.

Democratic Congressional Campaign Committee. 2018. *Leaders Playbook: A guide to Building, Executing and Winning Democratic Congressional Campaigns.*

Epstein, David, and Peter Zemsky. 1995. "Money Talks: Deterring Quality Challengers in Congressional Elections." *American Political Science Review* 89 (2): 295–308.

Federal Election Commission. N.d. "Leadership PACs." https://www.fec.gov/help-candidates-and-committees/registering-pac/types-nonconnected-pacs/leadership-pacs/

Fenno, Richard. 1978. *Homestyle: House Members in Their Districts.* Longman.

Fiorina, Morris. 1989. Congress: Keystone of the Washington Establishment. Yale University Press.

Gelman, Andrew, and Gary King. 1990. "Estimating Incumbency Advantage without Bias." *American Journal of Political Science* 34 (4): 1142–1164.

Gelman, Andrew, and Gary King. 1996. "Why Did the Incumbency Advantage in U.S. House Elections Grow?" *American Journal of Political Science* 40 (2): 478–497.

Gratzinger, Ollie. 2020. "Small donors give big money in 2020 election cycle." *Open Secrets.* October 30.

Grim, Ryan, and Sabrina Siddiqui. 2013. "Call Time For Congress Shows How Fundraising Dominates Bleak Work Life." Huffington Post. January 8.

Hetherington, Marc J. 2001. "Resurgent Mass Partisanship: The Role of Elite Polarization." *American Political Science Review* 95 (3): 619–631.

Hirano, Shigeo, and James Snyder. 2019. *Primary Elections in the United States.* Cambridge University Press.

Huber, Gregory A., and Patrick D. Tucker. 2024. "House Members on the News: Local Television News Coverage of Incumbents." *British Journal of Political Science* 54: 503 – 513.

Iyengar, Shanto, Gaurav Sood, and Yphtach Lelkes. 2012. "Affect Not Ideology: A Social Identity Perspective on Polarization." *Public Opinion Quarterly* 76 (Fall): 405 – 431.

Iyengar, Shanto, and Sean J. Westwood. 2015. "Fear and Loathing across Party Lines: New Evidence on Group Polarization." *American Journal of Political Science* 59 (3): 690 – 707.

Jacobson, Gary C. 2015. "It's Nothing Personal: the Decline of the Incumbency Advantage in US House Elections." *Journal of Politics* 77 (3): 861 – 873.

Jacobson, Gary C. 1987. "Running Scared: Elections and Congressional Politics in the 1980s." In *Congress: Structure and Policy,* edited by Mathew McCubbins and Terry Sullivan, 34 – 81. Cambridge University Press.

Jacobson, Gary C. 1978. "The Effects of Campaign Spending in Congressional Elections." *American Political Science Review* 72 (2): 469 – 491.

Kaslovsky, Jaclyn. 2020. *District Attentiveness and Representation in the Modern Congress.* Doctoral dissertation, Harvard University, Graduate School of Arts & Sciences.

King, Aaron S. 2017. *Unfolding Ambition in Senate Primary Elections.* Lexington Books.

Open Secrets. 2023. "Which Politicians Give the Most Money to Other Candidates?" June 27, 2023. https://www.opensecrets.org/elections-overview/candidate-to-candidate?cycle=2022&display=cmtes.

Open Secrets. 2025. "Leadership PACs contributions to candidates, 2023 – 2024." February 6, 2025. https://www.opensecrets.org/political-action-committees-pacs/industry-detail/Q03/2024

Porter, Rachel, and Sarah A. Treul. 2025. "Evaluating (in)experience in congressional elections." *American Journal of Political Science* 69 (1): 284 – 298.

Rogers, Steven. 2023. *Accountability in State Legislatures.* University of Chicago Press. Silver, Nate. December 27, 2012. "As Swing Districts Dwindle, Can a Divided House Stand?" *FiveThirtyEight.*

Squire, Peverill. 1992. "Challenger Quality and Voting Behavior in U.S. Senate Elections." *Legislative Studies Quarterly* 17 (2): 247 – 263.

Smidt, Corwin D. 2017. "Polarization and the Decline of the American Floating Voter." *American Journal of Political Science* 61 (2): 365 – 381.

Part II: **The Effects of Primary Reform**

Glenn Wright, Benjamin Reilly, and David Lublin

Chapter 7
Electoral Reform and Political Polarization: The Case of Alaska

Abstract: In recent years, ranked choice voting (RCV) has emerged as a leading electoral reform in the U.S. Currently used for elections in two states, three major cities, and over a dozen smaller jurisdictions, single-member RCV—also known as the instant runoff, alternative vote, or preferential voting—offers a viable alternative to the dominant plurality model of elections. Party primaries have been another reform focus, with "Top-2" or "Top-4" models adopted in several states to choose the best-supported general election candidates. Both systems have attracted strong advocacy from those seeking solutions to democratic malaise and polarization. Despite this, RCV has only been used to elect one state legislature: Alaska. This chapter examines the impact of Alaska's new Top-4/RCV system on political behavior and outcomes. We present a survey of candidate ideological and policy positions in elections before and after Alaska's introduction of the new system in 2020, augmented by case studies of individual electoral rematches. Focusing primarily on the state legislature, this research design allows us to isolate the impact of the Top-4/RCV system compared to the former model of closed party primaries and plurality general elections. We show that the introduction of Top 4/RCV not only changed candidate behavior and electoral outcomes but also appears to have driven changes in public policy, with winning candidates more likely to espouse moderate over extreme positions.

Political science theories suggest that changing institutional rules such as the electoral system can affect candidate behavior, ideology, and outcomes. For example, various electoral systems can encourage politicians and candidates to pursue starkly different avenues to electoral success: civil or hostile campaigns, broad or narrow policy agendas, and cooperative or divided approaches to legislating. This explains the scholarly consensus that "if one wants to change the nature of a particular democracy, the electoral system is likely to be the most suitable and effective instrument for doing so" (Lijphart 1995, 412).

A major issue facing the United States in recent years has been the problem of political polarization. Many political scientists see the most common U.S. electoral arrangements—closed party primaries followed by plurality general elections—as exacerbating political polarization and extremism, by enabling motivated partisan ideologues (who usually comprise only a small share of the overall electorate) to choose a candidate. As most seats are uncompetitive, victory in many cases is a foregone conclusion, giving candidates limited incentive to pitch appeals beyond their core supporters (Gehl and Porter 2020). Instead of broad-based representation, the result is increased partisanship, ideological rigidity, and legislative polarization (Lublin and Reilly n.d.).

By contrast, offering a greater range of options to voters, and giving politicians incentives to seek some level of cross-partisan support, should in theory promote more moderate outcomes (Diamond 2015; Drutman 2021; Horowitz 1991; Lublin and Reilly n.d.; Mann and Ornstein 2016; Reilly 2001). In most cases, the way to attract wider support is to adopt more centrist or "catch all" policy positions which appeal to the median voter. The exception is where more votes are lost by such moderation than are gained, which is always a possibility in very safe districts or in places with deep and entrenched polarization. But in competitive districts where outcomes are uncertain, politicians seeking to gain additional votes from non-core supporters should have an incentive to moderate their political rhetoric and broaden their policy positions to pick up additional voter support (Reilly 2001, 2018).

The Top-4/RCV package first used in Alaska in 2022 follows this logic. The nonpartisan primary is completely open to all comers, with the four best-supported candidates going through to the general election regardless of their partisan affiliation. All primary voters in a given district receive the same ballot with candidates of all parties (i. e. there are no separate Democrat and Republican party ballots). Voters vote for a single candidate and the four highest vote-getters in a given race advance to the general election. While ostensibly similar to the "Top-2" primaries used in California and Washington State, or to two-round runoff elections used widely around the world, the Top-4 model offers more ideological and partisan diversity. Studies of the top-two model diverge, with some scholars finding it reduced polarization (Crosson 2021; Grose 2020; Munger, Jr. 2019; Schwarzenegger and Khanna 2018) but others detailing that it had little impact (Highton et al. 2016; McGhee and Shor 2017; Troxler 2010). Similarly, studies of runoff presidential elections in Latin America (McClintock 2018) indicate a positive impact on legitimacy and moderation, but they are also vulnerable to more extreme candidates who are unattractive to a majority of voters making it to the runoff, as occurred in both Chile and Peru in 2021. Conversely, both systems can sometimes generate two candidates from one party, hampering voter choice.

Under a Top-4 system, by contrast, one-fifth of the primary vote is sufficient to guarantee a spot on the general election ballot, and in practice candidates often need much less (Reilly et al. 2022). This is because a Top-4 primary structurally resembles the single non-transferable vote (SNTV) systems used previously in elections in Japan, South Korea, and Taiwan. Studies of SNTV indicate that they produce a diversity of winners from different parties and often from different factions within the dominant party, which suggests that they should also produce a diversity of choices when used as a primary system for general elections too (Grofman et al. 1999).[1] In line with this, Alaska's first use of the system in August 2022 saw a sharp increase in both overall primary candidature and in minor party candidates going through to the general election (Maguire 2022).

The second part of the Alaska system is a ranked-choice rather than a single-choice ballot for the general election, giving voters the opportunity to express their preferences not just for but also between parties and candidates. Voters rank their preferences from one to four (or one to five if they choose a write-in candidate). If a candidate wins a majority of voters' first-choice votes they are the victor, but if no candidate wins a majority, the least popular candidate is eliminated and that candidate's votes are redistributed to those voters' next choice. This process of elimination and redistribution continues until one candidate has a majority.

The more information that ballots reveal about voters' preferences, in theory, the more accurate their representation should be, especially given that voters do not need to be strategic about expressing their true first choice. In plurality elections, by contrast, voters for smaller parties are often faced with a dilemma: should they vote sincerely for their true choice, even if that party or candidate is unlikely to win? Or should they instead abandon their favorite and strategically vote for least-worst option amongst those who have a chance to win? While RCV doesn't completely eliminate the potential for strategic voting, in general, voters can simply express their preferences honestly in the knowledge that voting sincerely can never hurt their chosen candidate.

The combination of a Top-4 primary with a ranked choice election also prevents voters from being overwhelmed by choice at the general election. While this has not so far been a problem in Maine, which uses RCV for both primary and

---

1 SNTV is vulnerable to voters casting ballots in an inefficient way, which helps explain why it was it was gradually abandoned in all three of these countries (except for elections to the two Aboriginal constituencies in Taiwan). Votes may end up "wasted" if too many voters cast ballots for a single candidate, when transferring some to another candidate would have allowed the party to win an additional seat. On the other hand, splitting votes among two candidates may result in the defeat of both, when combining the votes would allow a single candidate to win. These inefficiencies are likely less problematic when SNTV is being used to winnow candidates in a primary round for a RCV general election, as a smaller party or faction is still more likely to gain access to the general election ballot than under Top-2. In Alaska, virtually all primary candidates made it to the general election in state legislative contests and most major party factions were represented in statewide contests.

general elections (but for its congressional seats only, not for its state house), it was a genuine concern in Alaska, which had forty-eight candidates enter the special election for its only U.S. House seat in the wake of Representative Don Young's death in 2021. A maximum of four or five (with write-in options) rankings optimizes the ability of voters to make choices—an especially important point in the U.S. where voters elect far more offices simultaneously than in most countries (Reilly et al. 2022).

In much of the country today, however, voters often face a difficult choice at the ballot box between "wasting" their vote on a minor party or choosing between major party nominees that are more extreme than the average elector—for instance, between a pro-Trump Republican and a left-wing Democrat. With the "missing middle" creating a feedback loop of ever-increasing polarization (Mason 2018), this has direct consequences for governance, priming elected legislators for partisan conflict, even when they agree on issues, for fear of a primary challenge (Anderson et al. 2020).

By giving candidates incentives to reach beyond their base, RCV potentially undercuts this zero-sum approach, creating the possibility of a positive-sum game: a candidate can benefit from ballots cast initially for someone else, if those votes return to them in the form of second or later rankings. Some studies have argued that this shifts the tone of politics in a more civil and cooperative direction, or at least a less negative and polarising one (Diamond 2017; Donovan et al. 2016; Reilly 2018). Top-4/RCV may thus spur the return of American traditions of bipartisanship and compromise by rewarding electoral moderation—defined here, following Maeda (2016), as a party or candidate moving towards the center and away from the extremes in any policy space.

To test this hypothesis, we adopt a "before-and-after" research design centered around the 2020 adoption of Alaska's Top-4/RCV reforms and the ideological composition of candidates and legislators. We compare the results of the 2022 election under Top 4/RCV with those held in 2020 and 2018 under the old model of closed party primaries and plurality general elections. Though Alaska experienced political changes across this four-year period, many candidates contested elections under both systems, and major political cleavages and policy debates remained the same, giving us some leverage to examine the independent impact of the new election system. Employing two original datasets examining candidate ideology and policy positioning bolstered by case studies of individual districts, our study identifies what impact, if any, the new rules had on ideology, policy, and governance.

In both politics and policy, we find a consistent pro-moderation bias after the introduction of the Top 4/RCV upon key political divisions and policy questions in Alaska. Previous studies of RCV have typically found campaigning to be more accommodative than under plurality rules, as politicians do not wish to alienate rivals' supporters who may offer them a potential second or third preference (Atsusaka and Landsman 2021; Donovan et al. 2016; John et al. 2018; Reilly 2001). While this more accommodative style of campaigning should, in theory, make for more cooperation between legislators too, few studies have examined the effect of such reforms on governance (Drutman and Strano 2021). This chapter represents a first attempt to do so. We first classify candidates based on their ideological positioning, in terms of the moderation-extremism continuum. Then, we examine their expressed policy preferences, ranging from bread-and-butter issues of taxation and appropriations to hot-button questions of abortion rights and education policy, again classifying positions as more or less moderate or extreme. Finally, we aggregate these results across all successful candidates in the pre- and post-reform period, to show the overall impacts of the electoral reforms on policy and governance.

Alaska's Politics and Election Reforms

Alaska is often understood "Outside" as a far-right red state and as a kind of "Last Frontier" wilderness backwater. These stereotypes are an oversimplification and —in the second case—a mischaracterization. Alaska is indeed a geographically large state with a small population and many more Republicans than Democrats. It is also, however, a relatively moderate state where Republicans are outnumbered by Independents (around 55% of Alaskan voters are registered as "Nonpartisan" or "Unaffiliated"), and in which politics revolves around complex fiscal and policy challenges which do not often follow party lines.

Alaska also takes its motto "North to the Future" seriously. The adoption of ranked choice voting and a nonpartisan primary is consistent with a long history of progressive leadership on policy and governance: even as a territory, Alaska banned race-based discrimination long before *Brown vs. Board of Education*, the state constitution was written in careful consultation with political and legal scholars as a "model constitution," marijuana was effectively legalized for personal use in the late 1970s, abortion is recognized as a constitutional right, and the Alaska Permanent Fund Dividend was created as a proto-Universal Basic Income in the early 1980s.

In this respect, in many ways Alaska more resembles purple and blue states like Maine and New Mexico than very conservative places like South Dakota and Kansas. Alaska has more independent voters than other states and a history of electing independent and third-party politicians including Gov. Bill Walker, elected as an independent in 2014, and Gov. Wally Hickel, elected on the Alaska Independence Party ticket in 1990. Although formally party-aligned, Alaska's national-level politicians have typically taken quite independent but also moderate, state-oriented, approaches to their congressional duties (e.g. Lisa Murkowski, Ted Stevens, Frank Murkowski, Don Young, and Mary Peltola). In general, state politicians are center-right or center-left and though there are a few very conservative legislators in state politics, Alaska has very few far-left Democrats and lacks a Bernie Sanders-like left wing.

Like other states, Alaska's politics have been nationalized to some degree, but the most important intra- and inter-party divisions in state-level politics are unique to Alaska and often cut across party lines. The most important of these is the Alaska Permanent Fund. Since Alaska began to export oil in the late 1970s, the state government has been supported with a combination of federal transfers and state taxes on the oil industry, with no broadly based taxes such as income or sales taxes. At times, these revenue sources have been very lucrative with revenue at times greatly exceeding appropriations. Perhaps wisely, state politicians chose to save and invest these excess revenues in sovereign wealth funds—the largest of which, the Alaska Permanent Fund, is currently valued at about $80 billion, or around seven times the size of the state's annual budget. In the early 1980s, politicians chose to appropriate most of the fund's earnings as Permanent Fund Dividends (PFDs)—cash payments transferred to individual Alaskan residents. Today, most Alaskans who have resided in the state for more than a year are eligible for PFDs. Over the years, PFDs have varied in size depending on the Fund's investment earnings but have often exceeded $2000 and occasionally $3000 or more.

Though Alaskans' receipt of large annual dividend payments makes the state appear rich, government (and almost everything else) is expensive in Alaska, and the state's oil-based revenues are now too low to support appropriations without additional taxation or significant budget cuts. Legislators balanced the state government budget for several years by relying on savings and budget cuts but in the last several election cycles, as savings have run out, inflation and population growth have made budget cuts more difficult. Notably, the state university system has seen significant budget cuts since 2018, and public primary and secondary education spending has been flat for around a decade.

Solutions to this budget dilemma are obvious but politically unpopular. To balance the budget, the state could adopt some broadly-based income or sales tax, reduce the size of PFDs to free up revenues from the Permanent Fund, or cut expenditures.[2] Each of these options has been proposed by prominent policymakers

---

2 Spending cuts alone would now likely be too large to be politically tenable; a cuts-alone

but, for now, state politicians have chosen to draw on Permanent Fund earnings rather than introduce new taxes to balance the budget. This may have been the most expedient choice but even so has been very controversial; probably the most salient division in Alaska politics is between politicians (mostly Democrats but also many Republicans) who believe the state should use Permanent Fund earnings to fund government operations and others who believe the state should return to the pre-2015 days of the "Full Statutory PFD," essentially a call for much larger dividend checks. Typically, politicians calling for larger PFDs also oppose other sources of revenue such as taxes; the call for larger PFDs is rarely coupled with coherent positions on other new sources of government revenue and is sometimes combined with support for very large but unspecific budget cuts or populist opposition to any additional taxes or cuts.

These revenue challenges have been the most significant public policy issues in recent state election campaigns and remained paramount in elections in 2022, particularly for the state legislature. The political divisions around this and other policy questions frame our analysis in the remainder of this chapter. First, we briefly outline the impact of the new electoral system on the 2022 statewide races, which included several high-profile politicians. Then, we move on to the less-studied arena of Alaskan state politics, where the most salient policy debates often revolve around fiscal and social policy and the Permanent Fund, via both case-based and quantitative studies of the 2022 election. We conclude with a discussion of the aftermath of this first-ever use of Top-4/RCV to elect a state legislature, including the subsequent repeal campaign and 2024 election, and prospects for the future.

Statewide races in 2022[3]

Alaska's first use of the new system was in the special U.S. House Top-4 primary in June 2022 following the death of Rep. Don Young. Reformers had argued that the nonpartisan primary would bring more diversity and more choice, and it certainly did. A total of forty-eight candidates stood for election, including an unparalleled

---

approach to balancing the budget nearly led to a recall of Governor Michael Dunleavy in 2019 and 2020. Dunleavy was likely saved only by the emergence of the COVID-19 virus and the consequent difficulty of gathering recall petition signatures. Presumably the state could also balance the budget over the short term by issuing bonds, but substantial borrowing is not an option that has been seriously considered by the legislature or governor.
3 This section draws on Reilly et al. (2023).

number of women and four Alaska Natives—one of whom, Mary Peltola, came in fourth and advanced to the general election.

The special RCV general election followed in August 2022—the same day as the first regularly scheduled Top-4 primary for state offices. Following the dropout of the third-placed independent candidate, Peltola faced two high-profile Republicans, Sarah Palin and Nick Begich, and won 40.2 percent of first rankings, with Palin (31.3 percent) and Begich (28.5 percent) splitting the Republican vote between them. In normal circumstances, one might have expected Republican voters to rank both candidates first and second. But the campaign had featured considerable animosity between Palin and Begich, who attacked each other far more than their Democratic opponent. By contrast, Peltola refrained from criticizing her opponents, focusing instead on issues that many Alaskans agree on, like the need to protect fisheries and abortion access (Samuels 2022a).

Voters who ranked Begich first effectively decided the outcome. When he was eliminated as the lowest-polling candidate, one-half of his voters ranked Palin second, but more than one-quarter crossed party lines to support Peltola (with the remainder opting not to give a second choice and hence "exhausting" their vote). As a polarizing figure well-known to Alaskan voters, Palin's inability to win a greater share of her follow Republican's rankings was crucial to the outcome, a narrow majority victory for Peltola, the first Alaska Native to represent the state. Had the race been slightly different with Begich running second, it's likely that the result would have been similar because of the negative feelings between Palin and Begich supporters and the relatively high proportion of Begich voters who failed to indicate a second preference or ranked Peltola as their second choice (Clelland 2024).

Four months later, the same House race was then rerun (with the addition of a fourth minor-party candidate) at the November general election, by which time Peltola had increased her first-preference vote share by a full ten points, to forty-eight percent—a near majority of first choice votes—ending up with a comfortable fifty-five percent margin after rankings were distributed.

How did she do it? Incumbency and increased name recognition were key drivers, but her very accommodative approach to campaigning was also a factor. Peltola consistently expressed personal warmth towards other candidates, including Palin. Her public commitments to lower partisanship extended to cross-endorsing Republican Lisa Murkowski in the Senate—an unusual example of cross-partisan campaigning that, while not explicitly a reaction to electoral incentives, was clearly in line with the shift to more accommodative and civil campaigning that RCV advocates have long touted (Hughes 2022). Peltola continued this bipartisan approach to governing in Congress, as part of her catch-all "pro-jobs, pro-fish, pro-choice, pro-families" profile (Kravinsky 2022). On the Republican side, the two 2024 elections provided hard lessons in the importance of relative moderation and avoiding extreme animosity in intraparty clashes, which served them well in 2024 when Begich ran for a third time and won the seat (see below).

The gubernatorial race also saw candidates make cross-partisan appeals. Former Governor Bill Walker, an independent, struck a public cross-endorsement deal with former state Rep. Les Gara, a Democrat, pledging to each vote for the other second and urging voters to do the same in joint television ads featuring their female running-mates. Both well-known figures with a profile to the left of incumbent Governor Mike Dunleavy, this arrangement was "tailor made for Alaska's new voting system" (Samuels 2022b, n.p.). Nonetheless, the result was a comfortable victory for Dunleavy, a conservative Republican who won an outright majority on first rankings. Dunleavy's victory was in part a result of high global oil prices—driven by Russia's invasion of Ukraine—which increased Alaska state revenues and facilitated a very high Fall 2022 Permanent Fund Dividend. Alaska voters saw Dunleavy, who had campaigned on the need for higher dividend checks, as the driver of larger dividends even though global geopolitics were arguably a better explanation (and, as global oil prices dropped after 2022, so did Alaskans' dividend checks).

Finally, in the Senate, incumbent Lisa Murkowski won a tight RCV election against fellow Republican Kelly Tshibaka, who had been endorsed by Donald Trump. Murkowski was widely seen as a primary beneficiary of the electoral reforms, as she would almost certainly have lost a traditional closed primary to a more hardline Republican. Under the new system she topped both the primary and general election but with less than a majority. Her eventual win was dependent on supporters of the eliminated third-placed Democratic candidate, Patricia Chesbro. Seventy percent of Chesbro's 29,134 votes were transferred to Murkowski, an exceptionally high rate of interparty transfers across the two major parties. Murkowski's profile as a bipartisan legislator and prominent public critic of Donald Trump meant this is not exactly a surprise, but again it emphasizes the rewards from ideological moderation inherent in the electoral reforms.

In summary, the statewide November 2022 elections saw victories for the incumbents—Murkowski, Peltola, and Dunleavy. Dunleavy won his majority outright, while Peltola and Murkowski both won a plurality of first-choice votes but needed two rounds of eliminations to achieve a majority under RCV. As well as the increase in cross-partisan appeals, most notable was the fact that the three statewide victors, despite being elected at the same time by the same electorate under the same voting system, represented very different ideologies: moderate and conservative Republican and centrist Democrat.

2022 State Legislative Elections[4]

Alaska's new election system also had clear impacts on Alaska's State Legislature elected in 2022, with several state legislative contests delivering different results than would have been expected under the old system. Their combined impact led to new legislative coalitions in the 2023–2024 state House and Senate, including cross-party coalitions in both legislative chambers. Two short case studies, below, illustrate the impacts of Top-4/RCV on these races and the subsequent effects on legislative coalition formation and hence on policy outcomes.

Giessel vs. Holland

Former Senate President Cathy Giessel was widely seen as a potential beneficiary of the reforms. Before the 2020 election, Giessel served three terms in the State Senate, representing a center-right district in the city of Anchorage. During her time in the legislature, Giessel has been seen as an extremely effective legislator with a long record of legislative accomplishment and as a strong advocate for women in Alaska politics. Despite that strong record, Giessel was defeated in the 2020 Republican primary by a Trump-endorsed hardliner, Roger Holland; notably, Holland and other more right-wing Republicans attacked Giessel and other establishment Republicans for their support of state government use of Permanent Fund earnings (and for the impacts on Permanent Fund Dividends). But Giessel quickly recognized that the adoption of Top-4/RCV greatly increased her chances in 2022 and she announced her comeback bid in late 2021, saying she "intends to campaign as someone who can work across party boundaries" and form new coalitions in the general elections (Brooks 2021, n.p.). Notably, this included working with both Democratic and Republican legislators to produce a balanced budget while returning a moderately large Permanent Fund Dividend.

This strategy was validated by the election results. After easily making it through the Top-4 primary as one of two Republicans, Giessel benefitted from the allocation of general election preferences at the 2022 contest. First preferences were effectively a three-way tie between Giessel (5,651 votes, 33.8 percent), Holland (5,534 votes, 33.1 percent), and Democrat Roselynn Cacy (5,520 votes, 33.0 percent). Cacy's third place finish resulted in her elimination and the redistribution of her votes to the other candidates, meaning that Democratic voters effectively decided which Republican would be elected.

---

4 This and the following section draw on Wright et al. (2025).

While the first round was a near dead heat, the redistribution of Cacy's votes turned the final tally into a rout. Giessel attracted forty percent of Cacy's second-rank votes compared to less than eight percent for Holland, with the remaining ballots exhausted. As a result, Giessel returned to the Senate with a comfortable (fifty-seven percent) victory. Left-leaning voters expressed a clear preference for Giessel over Holland. Giessel and a small number of other moderate victors then led a new bipartisan governing Senate coalition, with Giessel serving as majority leader and playing a significant role in budget negotiations.

Babcock vs. Bjorkman

A second race demonstrating the impacts of the new election system took place in Senate District D, which includes much of Alaska's Kenai Peninsula, a conservative rural area with historic links to the oil and gas industry.

For many years, this region was represented by a relatively moderate Republican, Peter Micciche. Though not a candidate in 2022, Micciche is notable here because he serves as a demonstration of the incentives created under Alaska's old party primary-based election system. After serving as Mayor of the city of Soldotna, Micciche was elected to the State Senate, serving from 2013 to 2022. For his first several years in the Senate, Micciche was seen by political observers as a moderate and pragmatist willing to work across the aisle and unwilling to engage with culture war issues. In 2018, however, he faced a strong primary challenge from a much more conservative competitor named Ron Gilham.[5] Though Micciche was ultimately victorious, the vote was very close with a margin of only seventy-two votes in a primary with around 5,700 ballots cast. After that near-loss, Micciche's behavior and voting record in the Senate moved to the right, presumably to pre-empt further primary challenges.

Though Micciche would likely have done well under the new election system, he announced his retirement from the State Senate in 2022 to run for Mayor of the Kenai Peninsula Borough—boroughs in Alaska are like counties in other states. Three conservatives filed to run for office as his replacement. The first of these was Tuckerman Babcock, a long-time Republican political activist in Alaska who had served as chief of staff to Governor Mike Dunleavy during the early days of Dunleavy's term in the governor's mansion. At that time, Babcock and the governor advocated extremely deep cuts to state services, including the University sys-

---

5 Gilham later ran and won election to the state house, representing a district centered around the Kenai Peninsula community of Seldovia in 2020, but lost in 2022 and 2024.

tem, the state's ferry system, and a range of social services. Babcock's main competitor was Jesse Bjorkman, a former schoolteacher and borough assembly member who ran a still conservative but more moderate campaign—for example, arguing for more competitive pay for teachers and state employees while still opposing abortion and gun control and supporting a "full PFD." Notably, Bjorkman expressed willingness to work with Democrats in the Senate, while arch-conservative Babcock advocated for a conservative, Republican-only approach. The third candidate in the race was Andy Cizek: a somewhat idiosyncratic campaigner with little campaign infrastructure who may be best understood as an anti-establishment conservative.

Babcock would have certainly won a traditional Republican primary against the relatively moderate Bjorkman, but under the Top-4 primary all three conservative candidates advanced to the general election, where Bjorkman—presumably drawing support from District D's small number of Democrats and centrists—received more votes than Babcock. No candidate received a majority of vote; when the third-placed Cizek's ballots were redistributed about twice as many ballots went to Bjorkman (532) than to Babcock (263)—making Bjorkman the winner with 53.6 percent. After his victory, Bjorkman, like Giessel, went on to become a key member of the moderate Senate majority coalition (discussed next).

Coalition Politics Under Top-4/RCV

The Bjorkman and Giessel victories had significant impacts on the state legislature in their own right but also were good illustrations of the ways in which the new election system moderated legislative politics and policy.

In the wake of the Fall 2022 elections, rumors emerged that Alaska Senate Democrats and moderate Republicans might form a cross-party binding caucus that would control the most powerful policy-making process for the next two years. In Alaska, majority caucuses typically form around agreements as to who takes important leadership roles (key committee seats, the Senate Presidency etc.) and what policies the majority will or will not support. Typically, majority members also cooperate to pass legislation (and to defeat the legislation proposed by chamber minorities). These majorities are often party-based, but bipartisan and cross-partisan majorities are also quite common; in each of the last ten legislatures (i. e. the last twenty years), majorities in at least one of the two chambers have included members of more than one political party. In this case, the emergent Senate majority included nine Republicans and eight Democrats—a large coalition (seventeen of twenty total Senate seats, with three very conservative Republicans excluded) that could effectively control the legislative process. Without the Bjorkman and Giessel victories, it is likely that either a smaller and less powerful Democratic-led majority might have formed or the resulting more conservative Republican faction would have had the weight within the party to organize a narrow Republican-led majority.

The policy basis of this bipartisan majority was an agreement to avoid divisive culture-war issues on both the left and right and focus on building a state government budget structured around a smaller PFD and revenues to fund government. Left-leaning legislators agreed not to pursue more progressive policies on (for example) abortion rights, while conservatives agreed to avoid legislating on transgender rights or so-called "Critical Race Theory" in schools. Both groups agreed on the need to use some Permanent Fund revenues to fund state government. Critically, leadership was split between Democrats and Republicans; for example, membership of the powerful Finance committee, which controls both revenue and appropriations, was almost equally divided between parties (three Democrats and four Republicans), with three Co-Chairs including two Democrats and one Republican.

While outcomes in the State House were less dramatic and links to the new election system less salient, post-election negotiations also led to bipartisan coalition there; Republicans coalesced with rural Democrats in order to control a majority of seats.[6] This meant that although Alaska's House majority was heavily weighted towards Republicans (twenty Republicans with two Democrats and two Independents of forty total seats),[7] Republicans were a minority on the powerful House Finance Committee (five Republicans with three Independents and three Democrats), which was also co-chaired by a conservative Republican (Delena Johnson-Palmer), a rural Democrat (Neal Foster-Nome), and a rural Independent (Bryce Edgmon).

Legislative outcomes in 2023 were about what one would expect given this bipartisan control of both legislative chambers, with Finance Committees in both chambers heavily weighted to moderates. The 2023 legislative session proceeded in a workmanlike fashion with relatively little public controversy, though with oc-

---

6 Similar majorities have formed many times since the 1980s. Rural Democrats agree to vote with Republicans on many policy issues and, in return, they receive seats on finance committees, which allows them to steer badly needed infrastructure spending to their underdeveloped districts, which often lack sewage services, reliable electricity, and clean water.

7 The House minority was also a cross-party coalition, with eleven Democrats, one Republican and three Independents. One Representative, David Eastman (R-Wasilla), was something of a pariah and not permitted to caucus with either group. Within the House Finance Committee, the majority held seven seats including the three co-chairs (R, D, and I) and four other Republicans. The minority held four seats (two Democrats and two Independents).

casional rumors of strife within the two majorities, especially the House majority. Alaska's 2023 budget (for Fiscal Year 2024) held few surprises—it included moderate budget increases for most state government agencies—but was striking compared to the extreme budget reduction proposals of just a few years before. Final operating budget votes (the largest and most important of Alaska's budget bills) were bipartisan in both chambers, with the Senate voting seventeen to three on coalition lines and the House vote dividing parties and legislative coalitions. Both chambers of the legislature also largely avoided public debates on contentious social issues, and those which did emerge (including proposals to undo Top 4-RCV) were jettisoned early on because they stood no chance of passing through the Senate. In general, then, legislative outcomes were noticeably less contentious and more moderate in ideological terms.

Testing the Effects of Reform

In addition to making the legislature more workable, the new electoral system also affected key policy cleavages. To show how, we compared attitudes and positions of candidates and legislators before and after the electoral reform using two new quantitative datasets that allow us to drill down into the effects of the new election system on Alaska state politics. First, we conducted an expert informant survey to measure candidate ideology. Alaska political professionals (mostly state legislative aides with lobbyists, legislators and other political professionals mixed in) were asked to complete a short survey rating the partisan ideology of candidates in their home regions (i. e., Southeast Alaska, Anchorage, Fairbanks, Matanuska-Susitna valley, etc.) on a five-point scale, from very liberal to very conservative. Most respondents were legislative staff, with others including a small number of sitting legislators as well as a few other political workers and interested observers. We received 74 responses, with at least two sets of responses for each candidate in 2020 and 2022 and all State Senate candidates in 2018—a total of 222 candidates.

We also gathered a second dataset assessing candidate positions on salient issues before and after the adoption of Top-4/RCV in 2020, enabling the use of simple descriptive statistics of measurable differences between the pre-reform and post-reform periods. Undergraduate students at the University of Alaska Southeast reviewed campaign materials for the 2022 and 2020 primary elections for State House and State Senate and the 2018 State Senate primary, and selected a set of issues on which many candidates expressed opinions. Students collectively developed a description of common issue positions, and then categorized individual candidates according to their positions on abortion rights, state budgeting issues, culture war issues, education and gun rights. The students carrying out this data-gathering were broadly representative of Alaska voters; varying in political knowledge and relatively unfamiliar with candidates for state legislative office. This allowed us to determine whether victorious candidates under the pre-reform and post-reform election systems were more likely to publicize particular positions; in other words, the data were intended to capture what positions candidates campaign on rather than what they necessarily believe or will do if elected to office.

Candidate Ideology

One of the clearest effects of reform was the ideological positioning of successful candidates. To examine the impact of the new election system on the ideology of winners versus losers, we used our expert survey data rating on the ideology of legislative candidates. As shown in Figure 7.1, the new election system did not narrow the range of ideological choices available to voters, with more extreme candidates from both left and right standing in the post-reform period.

We then re-normed these average scores for candidate ideology, generating a scale from 0 to 2 with "true moderates" at 0 and with extreme liberals and extreme conservatives at 2.

This "extremism" measure served as the critical independent variable in a logistic regression model of state legislative election victory (Table 7.1), with the dependent variable coded 1 for winners and 0 otherwise. The model includes a dummy variable representing the new electoral system ("post-RCV") that also interacts with extremism. The model uses robust standard errors clustered on the election district (Table 7.1).[8]

Figure 7.2 illustrates these results in substantive terms, with ideology on the x-axis and a candidate's probability of winning on the y-axis. Two sets of solid lines reveal predicted probabilities of victory under Alaska's old system (the grey solid line) and under the new system (the black solid line) with ninety-five percent confidence intervals (the dotted lines) around each also shown.

Prior to the introduction of Top-4/RCV, more extreme candidates were significantly more likely to be elected. The predicted probability of winning ranged from .18 for a "true moderate" to .50 for an "extreme liberal or conservative." Under the new system in 2022, however, moderates were considerably more likely

---

8 Due to redistricting prior to the 2022 elections, this is an imperfect adjustment, but we lack the ability to control for intragroup correlation in a more robust way. This may be irrelevant, however, as we are evaluating the full before/after population of candidates.

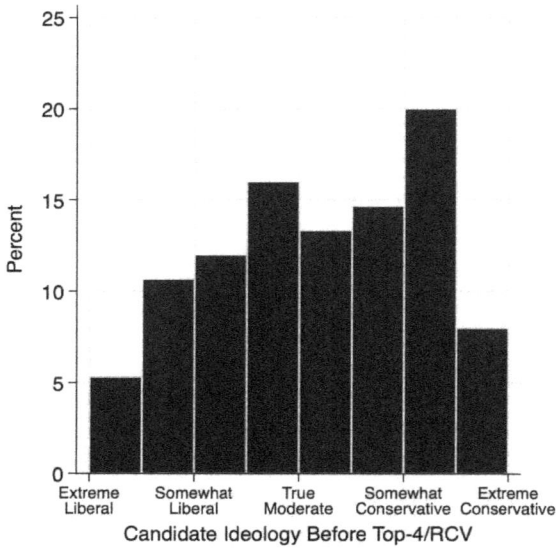

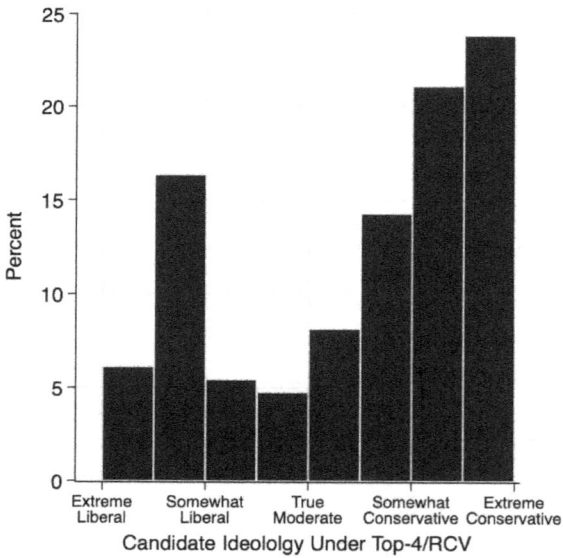

Figure 7.1: Candidate ideologies before and after the Top-4/RCV reform.

Table 7.1: Logistic regression, probability of victory.

	Coefficient (Robust standard error)
Extremism	.817
	(.476) +
Post-RCV	2.14
	(.642) ***
Extremism X Post-RCV	-1.28
	(.603)*
Constant	-1.71
	(.478)***
N	222
Number of clusters	63

+ $p < .1$; * $p < .05$; ** $p < .01$; *** $p < .001$

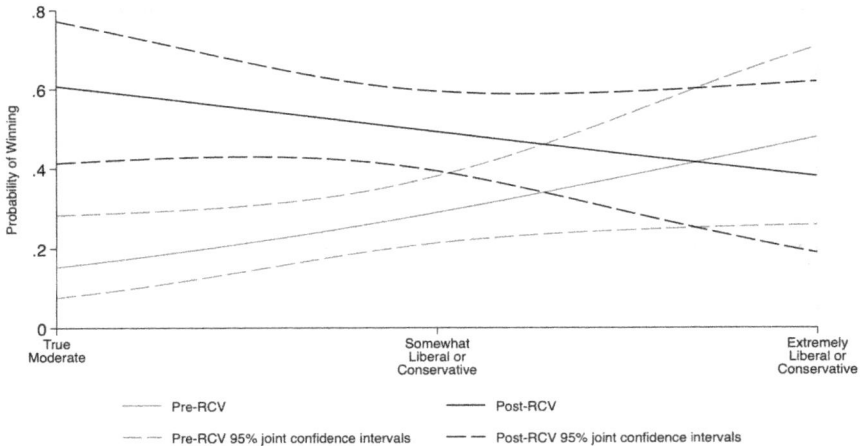

Figure 7.2: Ideology and probability of winning pre and post Top-4/RCV.

to be elected. The predicted probability of victory of a true moderate rose to .60 under Top-4/RCV, albeit with wide confidence intervals.

Taken together, then, the descriptive data in Figure 7.1 and our regression results in Table 7.1 and Figure 7.2 suggest that the new election system seems to be generating incentives for candidates from a wider range of ideologies to run for office, while electing a more moderate set of politicians. In Alaska, at least, this means that voters are facing a wider range of choices and electing politicians who are more representative of Alaska's relatively moderate voters.

Issue Positions

This trend continued when we examined the relationship between position-taking and election victory under the old and new election systems. In most areas, Alaska's new election system favored candidates who took more moderate positions on salient issues, despite the larger number of more extreme candidates overall in the 2022 election.

Questions having to do with Alaska's budget and Permanent Fund Dividend are among the most salient for Alaska voters. Consequently, we have the most information on candidate positions on this issue. In our survey, students placed candidates into four categories: (1) support the use of all Permanent Fund earnings for government spending; (2) favor the 75/25 ratio (25% for PFDs); (3) support the 50/50 ratio; and (4) back the large dividend "full, statutory PFD." Figure 7.3 combines all candidates who supported government use of some permanent fund earnings into a single category. In both the pre- and post-reform periods, support for the most extreme position—the full PFD—was most common, but success rates changed greatly with the introduction of Top-4/RCV. In line with the model presented in Figure 7.2, full-PFD advocates were much less likely to win under the new system but somewhat more likely to win before its adoption.

These changes are substantively important for Alaska: the new election system not only led to a larger proportion of candidates with responsible positions on revenue but (as discussed earlier) also enabled relatively moderate candidates to triumph over more extreme opponents in key races, allowing fiscal moderates to form a cross-party majority caucus in the State Senate. The result was a much more responsible budget, as well as more moderate policy outcomes in most other areas. Notably, Alaskans received a $1,800 PFD in 2023—far lower than the $5,500 dividend advocated by more extreme candidates for office, which would have required unfeasibly large cuts in government services as Alaska's fiscal situation has tightened.

Many candidates for state legislative office also expressed opinions on new taxes, typically broad-based state sales or income taxes. Students tabulated whether candidates: (a) supported income taxes; (b) supported sales or value-added taxes; (c) supported taxes for a specific purpose, such as education; (d) implied that some taxes might be acceptable, for example with voter approval in a referendum; or (e) expressed opposition to taxes under any circumstances. As detailed in Fig-

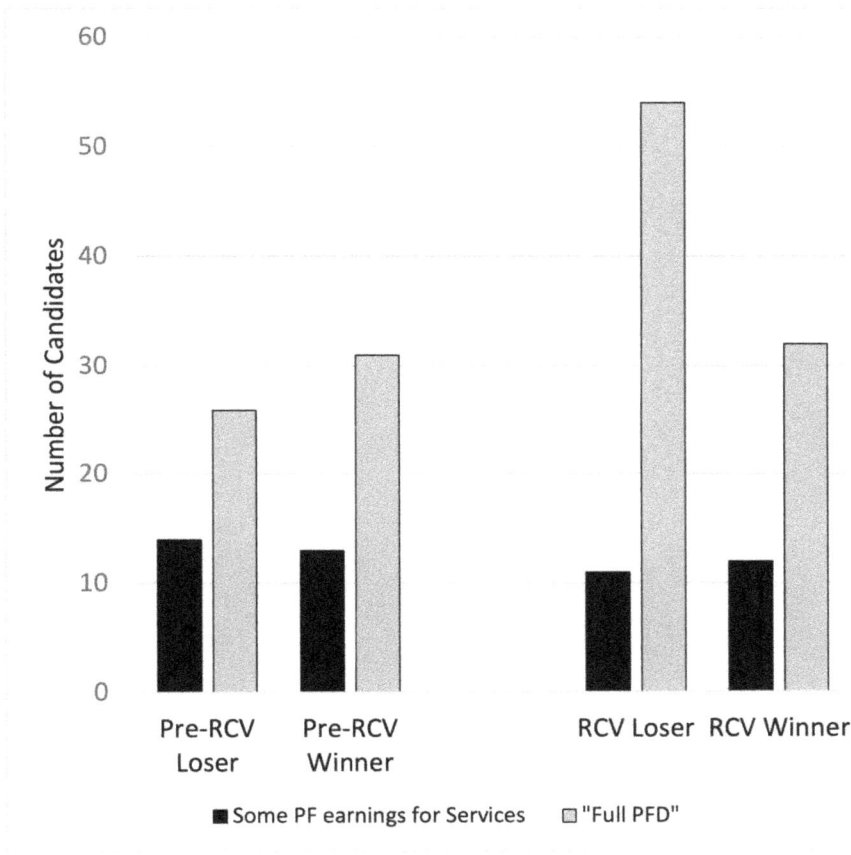

Figure 7.3: Positions on the Alaska permanent fund dividend.

ure 7.4, support for the most extreme position, opposition to all taxes under any circumstances, declined after the introduction of Top-4/RCV, with opponents of taxes under any circumstances now more likely to be losers and less likely among winners.

Many candidates also expressed clear opinions on appropriations.[9] Our student coders noted whether candidates campaigned on: (a) more funding in general; (b) more funding for some specified areas or agencies; (c) no further cuts (i.e.,

---

9 Because these positions were ordinal with several categories we found them difficult to graph clearly and therefore have only described them in the text.

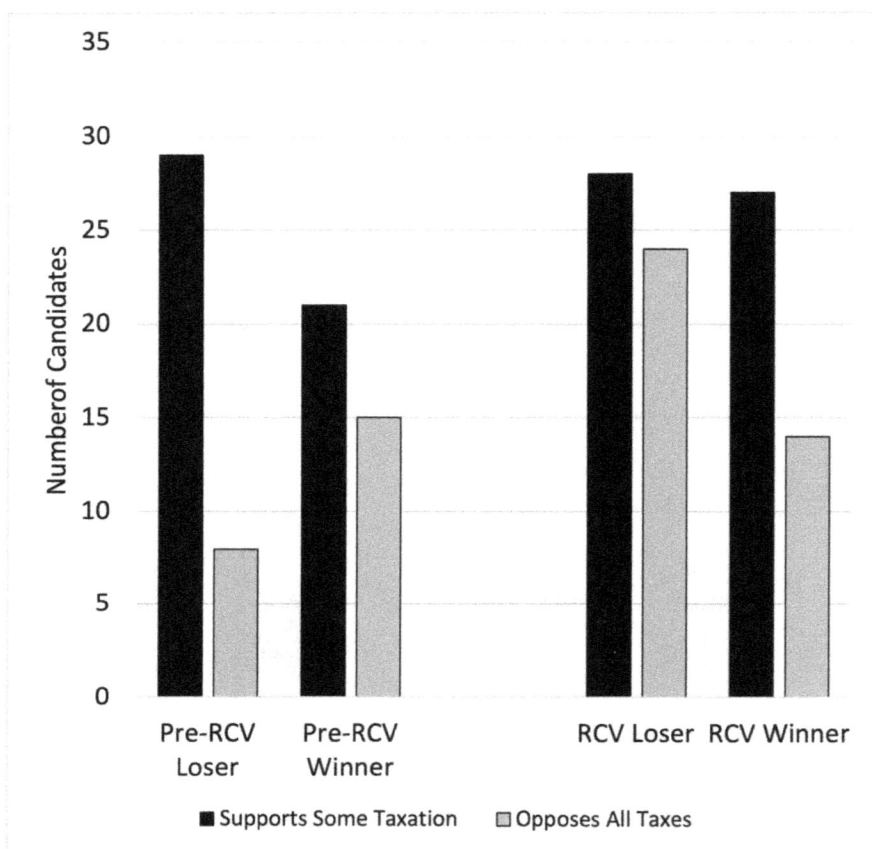

Figure 7.4: Electoral reform and positions on taxation.

the status quo); (d) further unspecified cuts; or (e) specific agency cuts. The coders' intuition was that the most extreme left-wing position was generalized funding increases, while the most extreme right-wing position was specific agency cuts, as these indicate a willingness to alienate particular interest groups or stakeholders. On average, pre-reform positions were more extreme than post-reform—winners were more likely to advocate funding increases and unspecified cuts relative to losers. Status-quo positions were unusual, though more common among winners than losers. On the other hand, winners in the post-reform period were more likely to hold status-quo positions ("no more cuts"). No victorious candidates advocated for general budget increases and only a very small number advocated for specific budget cuts. The greater likelihood of victory for candidates holding pro-status-quo positions in the post-reform period may help explain Alaska's relatively quiet legislative budgeting process in 2023, when the legislature developed a relatively uncontroversial budget with small increases for most agencies (Reilly et al. 2023).

Beyond appropriations in general, spending on education—especially public primary and secondary education—has been hotly debated over the last several years. Students categorized candidates based on their support for: (a) greater funding for education; (b) a status-quo position (i.e., "no further cuts"); or (c) policies that implied cuts to education spending (i.e., "reduce education bureaucracy," "fire bad teachers," advocating school choice, or opposing teachers' unions). Only three candidates advocating further cuts won in 2022, down from eight prior to the reform, while support for the status quo among winners jumped from eight to seventeen legislators after the introduction Top-4/RCV. Reflecting these changes, the 2023 legislature adopted a modest one-time funding increase for primary and secondary education rather than cuts or permanent increases to Alaska's per-student funding formula, the positions of more extreme legislators.

Finally, in addition to these budgetary issues, we gathered data on some social issues. Students categorized positions on abortion rights: candidates either (a) support greater protections for abortion rights; (b) support the Alaska status quo under which abortion rights are protected under state constitutional protections on the right to privacy; (c) express support for abortion but also express ambivalence (i.e., personally pro-life but support *Roe v. Wade*); (d) oppose abortion but with some possible exceptions (rape, incest, life and health of the mother etc.); or (e) oppose abortion without exceptions. Overall, more candidates supported the status quo than other options (thirty in 2022 and twelve in 2020), while opposition to abortion without exception was the second most common category (twenty-eight in 2022, fourteen in 2020 and three in 2018). Figure 7.5 shows the number of candidates taking the most extreme position: opposing abortion without exception. Though more candidates expressed opinions on abortion overall in 2022—and more candidates opposed abortion without exception—winners were less likely to hold these positions than losers in 2022, whereas winners were more likely than losers to oppose abortion without exception before the implementation of Top-4/RCV.

We also gathered data on "culture war" positions related to education policy, for example opposition to transgender athletes and "critical race theory." Relatively few candidates expressed positions on these issues, but as shown in Figure 7.6, such positions are now more identified with losers than winners, whereas they were as likely to be associated with winners as losers under the old election system.

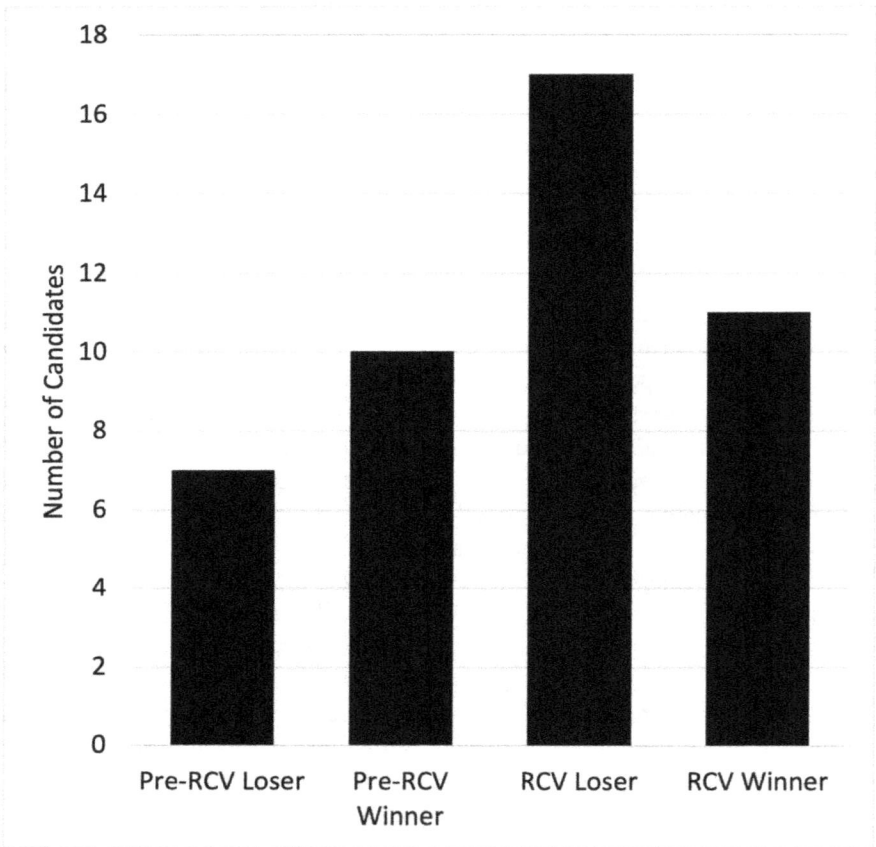

Figure 7.5: Electoral reform and extreme abortion positions.

One area in which we could find no differences across candidates in either the pre-reform or post-reform period was gun control. We were unable to find any significant evidence of anti-gun or pro-gun control legislative candidates in 2018, 2020, or 2022, probably reflecting Alaska's widespread firearm ownership and opposition to gun control regulation.[10] We also found no clear impact of the reforms on candidates' preferences on questions related to internal legislative dynamics: bipartisanship and binding legislative majority caucuses.

---

10 Though public opinion data on gun control is not available in Alaska, we can infer very high support for gun rights from Alaska's high firearm ownership rate, estimated to be the third highest in the country at around sixty-five percent (Schell et al. 2020)

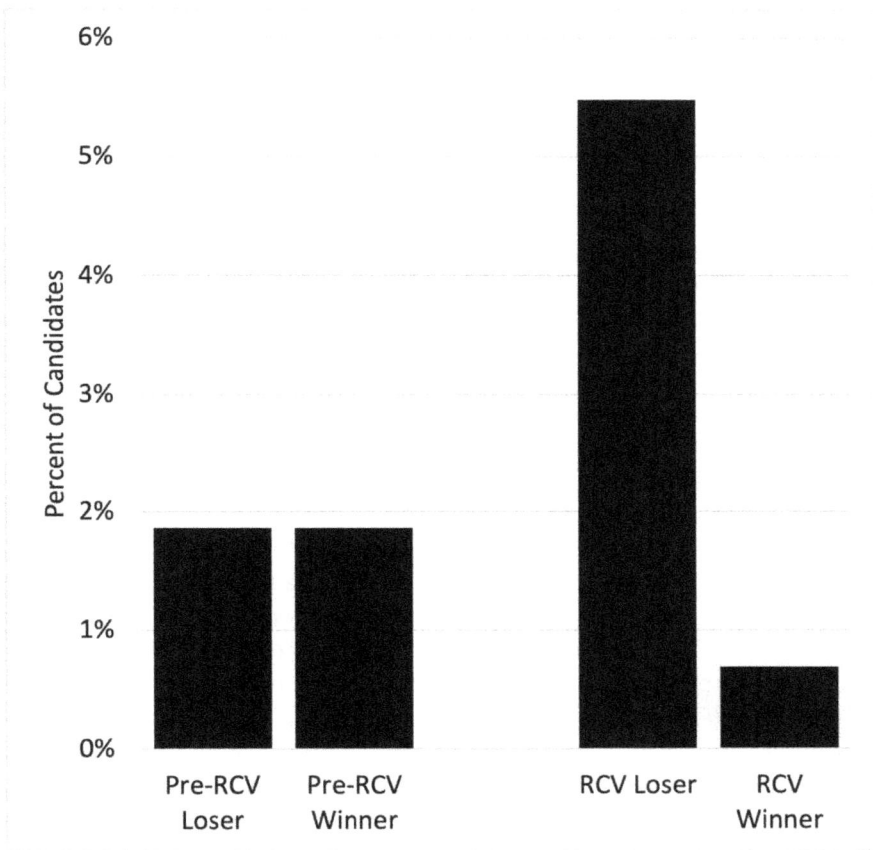

Figure 7.6: Election reform and education "culture war."

Elections in 2024

Alaska's 2024 election cycle, the second using the Top-4/RCV election system, generated results which were broadly similar to those from 2022. In state legislative elections, incumbents and moderates did well, leading to Democratic-led cross-party coalitions in both the State House and State Senate. In the post-election period, House Democrats coalesced with independents and moderate Republicans to form a majority, moving the House to the left. In the State Senate, the Democratic-led majority lost three seats, giving the Republican minority more power and moving the Senate slightly to the right. Cathy Giessel, whose seat was not up for election in 2024, continued as Senate president, and Jesse Bjorkman again prevailed over a more conservative opponent after the second-choice votes of the third-place finisher (a Democrat) were tabulated.

As this book goes to press, the post-2024 Senate majority coalition controls fourteen seats; in the conservative Matanuska-Susitna valley, conservative Republican Robert Yundt defeated David Wilson, the relatively moderate incumbent. Yundt chose to caucus with the Republican minority rather than the cross-party majority caucus and this led two other Republicans to join the minority. As a result, the cross-party majority no longer holds the three-quarters of seats needed to exclude the Republican minority from committee assignments. Consequently, politics will likely move to the right in 2025 and 2026, though policy control remains firmly in the hands of the Senate's center-left majority based on an informal agreement to avoid controversial policy proposals like new state taxes and socially conservative "culture war" legislation.

In the House, Democrats gained control of enough seats that they were able to assemble a twenty-four-seat majority that included all seventeen Democrats in the chamber plus five independents and two moderate Republicans. This is a leftward shift for the State House from the prior majority coalition of Republicans and rural legislators, including some Democrats and independents. The new majority seems poised to take a page out of the Senate majority's book in explicitly avoiding controversial topics while focusing on moderate budget policy, avoiding both large PFDs and new taxes. One notable race saw controversial, extreme-Right Representative David Eastman ousted by conservative Republican Jubilee Underwood. Though Underwood lost the 2024 Top-4 primary by thirty-eight percent to Eastman's sixty-two percent—and likely would have lost a traditional party primary by even more—she advanced to the general election and with the support of relatively moderate Republicans plus Independents and Democrats was able to win a narrow victory with just over fifty percent of the vote in their Wasilla district. As a newcomer, Underwood is untested but appears to be a more conventional politician than Eastman, who was often seen as an agent of chaos in past legislatures and became something of a pariah in the prior two legislative sessions. Underwood's victory is in keeping with the trend towards sensible policymaking and away from the public relations circus of some past legislatures.

Federally, Alaska's sole state-level race in 2024, absent the complicated Republican personality conflicts of 2022, saw Republican Nick Begich successfully challenge incumbent Democrat Mary Peltola for Alaska's sole U.S. House seat. Begich positioned himself as a moderate, similar to 2022, and ran as the only well-known Republican on the ballot after the withdrawal of third-place finisher Nancy Dahlstrom, Alaska's Lieutenant Governor, possibly as a result of some Republican pressure to clear the field. Neither Begich nor Peltola earned an outright majority, but Begich led in the first round, 48.4 percent to 46.4 percent. Rankings from the two other minor candidates, Democrat Eric Hafner—a federal prison inmate—and Alaska Independence Party John Wayne Howe, broke for Begich over Peltola, giving him a narrow victory. Time will tell whether Begich, also untested, governs as a moderate and whether he is able to retain his seat after having fought three sets of elections to gain it.

Probably the most important result in 2024 was the failure of an effort to repeal the Top-4/RCV system by ballot initiative. Sponsored by a conservative political action committee, that effort at one time was mired in scandal including allegations of fraud and violations of state election law (Brooks 2023; Samuels 2023). However, the referendum to repeal Top-4/RCV gathered enough signatures to appear on the general election ballot and came very close to succeeding. The "no" votes opposed to repeal outnumbered "yes" votes for repeal by just over 700 votes out of about 340,000 cast ballots, keeping Alaska's experiment in electoral system reform alive for at least one more election cycle.

Conclusion

In general, Alaska's new election system seems to be living up to the promises of election reformers. In 2022 and 2024, under the new election system, voters selected relatively moderate candidates, bucking the national trend. The success of moderates in statewide and state legislative races like Mary Peltola, Lisa Murkowski, Cathy Giessel, and Jesse Bjorkman was particularly notable when compared to past elections. At the state level, these results led to the formation of relatively moderate cross-party coalitions in both legislative chambers in the 2022–2024 and 2024–2026 legislatures. So far, these coalitions have governed stably, with few public controversies and—arguably—more sensible policymaking than the prior several legislatures.

Our results suggest that the new Top-4/RCV election system played a role in this by eliminating advantages for more extreme candidates under party-based primaries and first-past-the-post general elections. The new system provided a greater diversity of choice to voters via the Top-4 primary, albeit at the cost of further factionalizing Alaska's already weak and divided political parties. Then, the ranked choice general election ballot allowed voters to aggregate these factions into new coalitions. In most but not all cases, when given the opportunity, voters preferred moderates over partisan diehards and hardliners—even when that preference came via second rankings on the ballot.

The best way to view the impact of the reform is that of marginal differences leading to meaningful impacts on campaigning, election results, and legislative behavior. The reform did not greatly change the partisan composition of the legislature but, in some key races, led to the replacement of comparatively extreme by more moderate legislators who provided critical glue for forming cross-party coalitions. Their election also provides visible and powerful evidence of the impact of the elimination of closed party primaries, which reduced the need to hew to the views of more extreme primary electorates (and the subsequent risk of losing to more moderate candidates in the RCV general election). As a result, Alaskan candidates today have more incentive to build coalitions both inside and outside the legislature. Even when winners and losers have similar views on issues, Top-4/RCV rewarded candidates willing to work with other legislators to reach the compromises critical to governing under the American separation of powers as opposed to the refusal to move from extreme positions.

While still in its early stages, the Alaskan experiment thus offers a potential route to combatting the polarization spiral in U.S. politics. To the extent that the "standard" model of closed party primaries and plurality general elections incentivizes extremism over moderation, hardline partisanship may be less baked-in than often assumed, and more a result of the polarized choices on offer. But despite its apparent success, and the increasing number of commentators who see it as relevant to the rest of the United States (Barabak 2023; Foley 2022; Fukuyama 2022; Olsen 2022; Pildes 2022), the survival of Alaska's election system remains in doubt. While the 2024 repeal initiative ballot barely failed, a state Political Action Committee has already begun the process of filing another repeal bid for the 2026 election. Although many Alaskans are proud of their role in election system reform and like the new system, others view it as illegitimate and a tool of left-leaning ideologues. Only time will tell if support for the new system grows and if Top-4/RCV survives in Alaska.

Bibliography

Anderson, Sarah E., Daniel M. Butler, and Laurel Harbridge-Yong. 2020. *Rejecting Compromise: Legislators' Fear of Primary Voters.* 1st ed. Cambridge University Press.

Atsusaka, Yuki, and Theodore Landsman. 2021. "Does Ranked-Choice Voting Reduce Racial Polarization? Evidence from Agent-Based Modeling and Bay Area Mayoral Elections." *SSRN Electronic Journal.* https://doi.org/10.2139/ssrn.3800237.

Barabak, Mark Z. 2023. "Think Our Politics Stink? Look North — To Alaska." *Los Angeles Times.* https://www.latimes.com/politics/story/2023-07-02/alaska-ranked-choice-voting-solution-to-political-polarization.

Brooks, James. 2021. "Former Anchorage Sen. Cathy Giessel, Defeated in 2020, Will Run Again in 2022." *Anchorage Daily News.*

https://www.adn.com/politics/2021/12/01/former-anchorage-sen-cathy-giessel-defeated-in-2020-will-run-again-in-2022.

Brooks, James. 2023. "Report from Alaska Campaign Regulator Says Tshibaka-Linked Group Violated State Law." *Alaska Public Media*. https://alaskapublic.org/2023/08/28/report-from-alaska-campaign-regulator-says-tshibaka-linked-group-violated-state-law/.

Brown v. Board of Education of Topeka. 347 U.S. 483 (1954).

Clelland, Jeanne N. 2024. "Ranked Choice Voting And Condorcet Failure in the Alaska 2022 Special Election: How Might Other Voting Systems Compare?" https://arxiv.org/html/2303.00108v2.

Crosson, Jesse. 2021. "Extreme Districts, Moderate Winners: Same-Party Challenges, and Deterrence in Top-Two Primaries." *Political Science Research and Methods* 9 (3): 532–548.

Diamond, Larry. 2015. "De-Polarizing." *The American Interest* 11 (2). http://www.the-american-interest.com/2015/10/10/de-polarizing/.

Diamond, Larry. 2017. "How to Reverse the Degradation of Our Politics." *The American Interest*. https://www.the-american-interest.com/2017/11/10/reverse-degradation-politics/.

Donovan, Todd, Caroline Tolbert, and Kellen Gracey. 2016. "Campaign Civility under Preferential and Plurality Voting." *Electoral Studies* 42: 157–163.

Drutman, Lee. 2021. "What We Know about Congressional Primaries and Congressional Primary Reform." https://www.newamerica.org/political-reform/reports/what-we-know-about-congressional-primaries-and-congressional-primary-reform/.

Drutman, Lee, and Maresa Strano. 2021. "What We Know About Ranked-Choice Voting." https://www.newamerica.org/political-reform/reports/what-we-know-about-ranked-choice-voting/.

Foley, Edward B. 2022. "Can Alaska Save Democracy?" *Washington Post*. https://www.washingtonpost.com/opinions/2022/02/10/alaska-ranked-choice-voting-senate-murkowski/.

Fukuyama, Francis. 2022. "Paths to Depolarization." *Persuasion. August 3*. https://www.persuasion.community/p/fukuyama-paths-to-depolarization.

Gehl, Katherine M., and Michael E. Porter. 2020. *The Politics Industry: How Political Innovation Can Break Partisan Gridlock and Save Our Republic.* Harvard Business Review Press.

Grofman, Bernard, Sung-Chull Lee, Edwin Winckler, and Brian Woodall, eds. 1999. "SNTV: An Inventory of Theoretically Derived Propositions and a Brief Review of the Evidence of the Evidence from Japan, Korea, Taiwan, and Alabama." In *Elections in Japan, Korea, and Taiwan under the Single Non-Transferable Vote: The Comparative Study of an Embedded Institution*, 375–416. University of Michigan Press.

Grose, Christian R. 2020. "Reducing Legislative Polarization: Top-Two and Open Primaries Are Associated with More Moderate Legislators." *Journal of Political Institutions and Political Economy* 1 (2): 267–287.

Highton, Benjamin, Robert Huckfeldt, and Isaac Hale. 2016. "Some General Consequences of California's Top-Two Primary System." *California Journal of Politics and Policy* 8 (2).

Horowitz, Donald L. 1991. *A Democratic South Africa? Constitutional Engineering in a Divided Society*. University of California Press.

Hughes, Zachariah. 2022. "At AFN, Murkowski Says She'll Vote for Longtime Friend and Democrat Mary Peltola for U.S. House." *Anchorage Daily News*.

https://www.adn.com/politics/2022/10/21/at-afn-murkowski-says-shell-vote-for-long-time-friend-and-democrat-mary-peltola-for-us-house/.

John, Sarah, Haley Smith, and Elizabeth Zack. 2018. "The Alternative Vote: Do Changes in Single-Member Voting Systems Affect Descriptive Representation of Women and Minorities?" *Electoral Studies* 54: 90–102.

Kravinsky, Nancy. 2022. "Mary Peltola Talks Salmon, Bipartisanship and Winning Alaska's U.S. House Race." https://alaskapublic.org/2022/09/01/mary-peltola-talks-salmon-bipartisanship-and-winning-alaskas-u-s-house-race/.

Lijphart, Arend. 1995. Electoral Systems and Party Systems: A Study of Twenty-Seven Democracies, 1945–1990. Oxford University Press.

Lublin, David, and Benjamin Reilly. "Encouraging Cooperation And Responsibility." In *More than Red and Blue: Political Parties and American Democracy*. American Political Science Association and Protect Democracy. https://protectdemocracy.org/work/more-than-red-and-blue/.

Maeda, Ko. 2016. "What Motivates Moderation? Policy Shifts of Ruling Parties, Opposition Parties and Niche Parties." *Representation* 52 (2–3): 215–226.

Maguire, Sean. 2022. "Alaska Moderates See Success in Legislative Primary Results." *Anchorage Daily News.* https://www.adn.com/politics/2022/08/17/alaska-moderates-see-success-in-legislative-primary-results/.

Mann, Thomas E., and Norman J. Ornstein. 2016. *It's Even Worse than It Looks: How the American Constitutional System Collided with the New Politics of Extremism.* New and expanded edition. Basic Books.

Mason, Lilliana. 2018, *Uncivil Agreement: How Politics Became our Identity*. University of Chicago Press.

McClintock, Cynthia. 2018. *Electoral Rules and Democracy in Latin America.* Oxford University Press.

McGhee, Eric, and Boris Shor. 2017. "Has the Top Two Primary Elected More Moderates?" *Perspectives on Politics* 15(4): 1053–66.

Munger, Jr., Charles. 2019. "California's Top-Two Primary: A Successful Reform." *USC Schwarzenegger Institute.* https://schwarzenegger.usc.edu/institute_in_action/californias-top-two-primary-a-successful-reform/.

Olsen, Henry. 2022. "Lisa Murkowski Is Showing the Limits of Political Extremism." *Washington Post.* https://www.washingtonpost.com/opinions/2022/08/18/murkowski-alaska-senate-results-ranked-choice/.

Pildes, Richard H. 2022. "More Places Should Do What Alaska Did to Its Elections." *New York Times.* https://www.nytimes.com/2022/02/15/opinion/alaska-elections-ranked-choice.html.

Reilly, Benjamin. 2001. *Democracy in Divided Societies: Electoral Engineering for Conflict Management.* 1st ed. Cambridge University Press.

Reilly, Benjamin. 2018. "Centripetalism and Electoral Moderation in Established Democracies." *Nationalism and Ethnic Politics* 24 (2): 201–21.

Reilly, Benjamin, David Lublin, and Rachel Levin. 2022. "Final-Five Voting: Comparative Evidence on a Novel Election System." https://political-innovation.org/research-articles/comparative-analysis-france-runoff/.

Reilly, Benjamin, David Lublin, and Glenn Wright. 2023. "Alaska's New Electoral System: Countering Polarization or 'Crooked as Hell'?" *California Journal of Politics and Policy* 15 (1). https://doi.org/10.5070/P2CJPP15160081.

Samuels, Iris. 2022a. "Results in Alaska's Special U.S. House Race Expected Wednesday after Candidates Are Set to Share a Stage." *Anchorage Daily News.* https://www.adn.com/politics/2022/08/30/results-in-alaskas-special-us-house-race-expected-wednesday-when-candidates-are-set-to-share-a-stage/.

Samuels, Iris. 2022b. "Walker, Gara Running Mates Release Joint Ad in Late-Campaign Effort to Replace Dunleavy." *Anchorage Daily News.* https://www.adn.com/politics/2022/10/28/walker-and-gara-campaigns-release-joint-ad-in-last-minute-effort-to-replace-dunleavy/.

Samuels, Iris. 2023. "Complaint Alleges Opponents of Alaska's Ranked Choice Voting Formed Church to Skirt Disclosure Laws." *Anchorage Daily News.* https://www.adn.com/politics/2023/07/05/complaint-alleges-opponents-of-alaskas-ranked-choice-voting-formed-church-to-skirt-disclosure-laws/.

Schell, Terry L. Samuel Peterson, Brian G. Vegetabile, Adam Scherling, Rosanna Smart, and Andrew R. Morral. 2020. "State-Level Estimates of Firearm Ownership." Rand Corporation, https://www.rand.org/pubs/tools/TL354.html.

Schwarzenegger, Arnold, and Ro Khanna. 2018. "Don't Listen to the Establishment Critics. California's Open Primary Works." *Sacramento Bee.* https://www.sacbee.com/opinion/article213415464.html.

Troxler, Howard. 2010. "Let the Top Two Run, Regardless of Party?" *Tampa Bay Times.* https://www.tampabay.com/archive/2010/06/13/let-the-top-two-run-regardless-of-party/.

Wright, Glenn, Benjamin Reilly, and David Lublin. 2025. "Assessing Alaska's Top-4 Primary and Ranked Choice Voting Electoral Reform: More Moderate Winners, More Moderate Policy." *Journal of Political Institutions and Political Economy* 6 (1).

Ryan D. Williamson and Ceili Fallon

Chapter 8
Re-evaluating the Effects of the Top Four System in Alaska

Abstract: This chapter analyses descriptive trends in state legislative elections over time within Alaska. Our focus lies in discerning any significant variability in the electoral landscape within the state after the implementation of the Top-4 system compared to decades prior. Our evaluation centers on several key metrics: the prevalence of unopposed races, the competitiveness of races, incumbent success rates, the correlation between votes and seats secured, differences in candidates' ideological positions, and voter turnout. Our findings indicate significant shifts induced by the Top-4 system in certain domains, while its influence remains negligible in others. We conclude with a discussion of the tradeoffs inherent in the Top-4 system as well as what they might mean for the future of elections in Alaska and elsewhere.

As discussed in the previous chapter, Alaska's adoption of the Top-4 electoral system, initiated by the approval of Ballot Measure 2 in November 2020, represented a significant shift in the state's approach to elections. The Top-4 system replaces the previous closed primaries with a nonpartisan primary, where all candidates appear on a single ballot available to every voter, irrespective of party affiliation. From this primary, the top four vote-getters advance to the general election, regardless of their political party or the number of votes received. In the general election, voters employ ranked-choice voting (RCV), a system that enables them to rank candidates in order of preference. This mechanism ensures that if no candidate garners a majority of first-choice votes, the one with the fewest votes is eliminated, and their votes are redistributed according to the subsequent preferences indicated on the ballot. This process continues until a candidate secures a majority.

This reform was a response to widespread concern about the limitations of the traditional closed primary system, which have been found to exacerbate partisanship and stifle competition (Gerber and Morton 1998; Grose 2020). By allowing voters to select candidates regardless of party affiliation, proponents argued, this system could enhance voter choice and ensure that elected officials better reflect the will of the broader electorate (Macomber 2024). Supporters argue that the structure of the primary broadens the spectrum of candidates and encourages participation from independents and those affiliated with smaller parties (Hamilton 2021). By fostering a more inclusive candidate pool, the system aims to dilute the polarization typical in a traditionally two-party dominated political landscape, offering voters a wider array of choices (John et al. 2018). Advocates believe that the use of RCV in the general election encourages candidates to appeal to a wider voter base, including those who may rank them as a second or third choice, thereby promoting moderation and collaboration over extreme partisan positions (FairVote 2025).

The anticipated benefits of the Top Four system, including enhanced voter choice and reduced polarization, were put to the test during the 2022 election cycle. Many proponents praised the system for the advantage it might provide independent and non-traditional candidates, noting a shift in focus from strict party allegiance to substantive issues and policies. This shift encouraged candidates to engage with a diverse electorate, aiming for both primary and secondary rankings from voters. However, critics expressed concerns over the complexity of RCV and the potential for voter confusion. Furthermore, they argued that it might dilute party influence, thereby sparking broader debates over electoral reforms' effectiveness (FGA 2022).

Despite these mixed reactions, the 2022 election cycle provided a practical demonstration of the Top-4 system's impact on electoral dynamics. It facilitated the election of more diverse candidates, such as Mary Peltola, the first Alaska Native to serve in Congress. Her victory highlighted the system's ability to bring new voices into political arenas, challenging long-standing partisan strongholds. Peltola's election to the U.S. House upset Republicans who had previously maintained control of the state's sole congressional seat. Her victory was seen not only as a significant shift in representation but also as an illustration of the changing political landscape under Alaska's Top-4 electoral system and ranked-choice voting (Herz 2022). Many Republicans expressed dissatisfaction, arguing that the system allowed a Democrat to win despite the state's historical Republican lean. They contended that the ranked-choice voting mechanism, which requires candidates to appeal to a broader constituency for secondary choices, diluted their traditional base's influence (Evensen 2024). This sentiment underscored broader Republican concerns about the impacts of electoral reforms perceived to weaken partisan strongholds and complicate party-organized election strategies. Peltola's case was not particularly anomalous. For example, other work has found that Senator Lisa Murkowski would have likely not been able to retain her seat under the old system (Sinclair et al. 2024), and numerous state legislative races saw more moderate candidates somewhat unexpectedly prevail (Leven and Fisher 2023).

In 2024, the electoral landscape was once again tested by an attempt to repeal the system through Ballot Measure 2, as referenced in the previous chapter. The measure was defeated by a margin of only 737 votes with over 320,000 ballots cast. This outcome was largely due to significant support from Alaska's Native communities. These communities, which often face logistical voting challenges, played a pivotal role in upholding the system. Organizations like Get Out the Native Vote emphasized the importance of open primaries, arguing that such a system empowers voters to choose candidates without the confines of party constraints, fitting better with the unique political landscape of Native regions where political allegiances are diverse and fluid (Sabino 2024).

The response to the 2024 repeal attempt underscores the enduring appeal and perceived fairness of the Top-4 system among Alaska's voters. Particularly in Native-majority districts, there was robust grassroots support that overcame logistical obstacles and highlighted the role of community-driven efforts in fostering democratic participation. This situation showcased the critical ability of local communities to influence electoral outcomes, demonstrating the system's practical advantages in broadening political representation and engagement in remote and traditionally underrepresented areas.

These developments call for a critical examination of the Top-4 electoral system's impacts. The system's ability to alter voting behavior, influence political campaign strategies, and ultimately shape governance in Alaska requires thorough investigation. This chapter therefore explores the question of whether and how the Top-4 electoral system impacts political representation, voter engagement, and partisan dynamics in Alaska. As such, we show that the introduction of the Top-4 electoral system in Alaska represented a significant reform, intended to expand voter choice, boost competition, and decrease partisanship. Analyzing state legislative elections from 1990 to 2024, the reform led to more races with multiple candidates and narrower margins. It also decreased incumbency reelection success and increased Republican candidacies, though Republican winners decreased as Democratic success rose. The anticipated moderation of candidate ideology and increased voter turnout did not materialize, and there were no significant ideological shifts among candidates. Nevertheless, this reform marks a transformation in Alaska's political landscape, suggesting the need for further research into its effects on voter satisfaction and representative outcomes as the dynamics evolve over time.

How did the Top-4 Primary Change State Legislative Elections in Alaska?

In order to assess the impact of Top-4 in Alaska, we build on prior work (Williamson 2023) to evaluate several aspects of elections within the state and to compare races under the reform to races in the decades prior. Specifically, we use election results over time in order to understand changes in the competitiveness of elections (as demonstrated by both the number of unopposed races as well as races with narrow margins of victory), the disruption to the existing political establishment (captured by the incumbent reelection rate and the relative proportion of wins by major party candidates), the impact on candidate positions (which we evaluate by comparing the ideologies of winning and losing candidates), and the impact on voters (measured by turnout in primaries and the general election).

Top-4 and Competitiveness

While state legislative elections are notoriously uncompetitive affairs (Squire 2000), advocates of the new system nevertheless suggested that implementation of Top-4 in Alaska would foster a more competitive environment. To test this, we measure competition in three different ways.[1] First, we examine the proportion of uncontested races—those in which only one candidate appears on the ballot—for all state legislative elections from 1990 to 2024. The results are presented in Figure 8.1. No discernible pattern emerges from this data. In 2022, the first cycle under the new system, there were relatively few uncontested races. However, this proportion is comparable to years prior (such as 1992–1996, 2004, and 2018), and the second cycle under the system, in 2024, saw the proportion nearly double. From 1990 to 2020 nearly twenty-three percent of elections were uncontested, but from 2022 to 2024 that percentage dropped to 16.5. However, a difference of means test before and after implementation does not yield a statistically significant result.

Next, we measure competition as the proportion of state legislative elections with more than two candidates. Under the new system, up to four candidates can advance from the primary election to the general, which creates an incentive for more candidates to run. This appears to be true based on the results as presented

---

1 Our data was collected from the Alaska Division of Elections. Available at: www.elections.alaska.gov/election-results/.

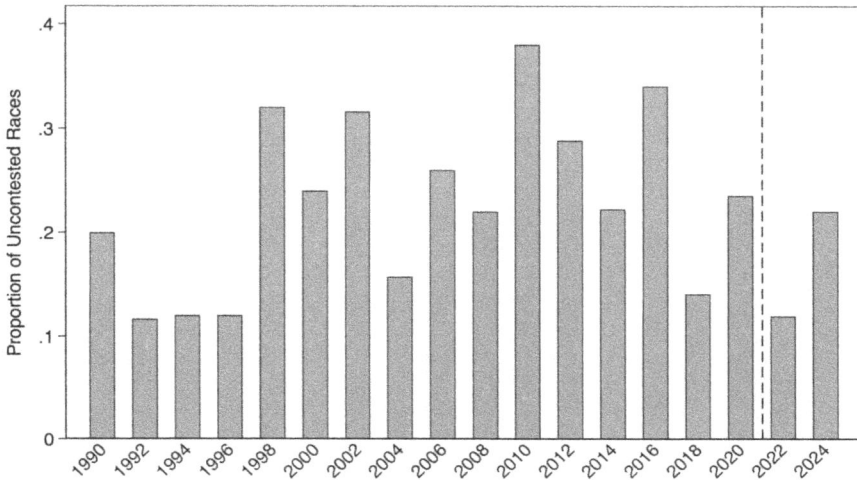

Figure 8.1: Proportion of uncontested state legislative elections in Alaska, 1990 – 2024.

in Figure 8.2. The proportion of races with more than two candidates considerably exceeds that of years prior. There was a substantial uptick in the first cycle under Top-4, and while 2024 witnessed a decrease, the amount was still greater than that of every cycle in the previous two decades. A difference of means test indeed reveals a statistically significant difference after Top-4 implementation. From 1990 to 2020, about fourteen percent of races featured more than two candidates, and that number grew to thirty-one after the implementation of Top-4.

Lastly, we measure competition as the proportion of races decided by ten percentage points or less. The results are presented in Figure 8.3. The two years under Top-4 represent substantially greater numbers of elections decided by narrow margins of victory, especially compared to other elections since 2000. From 1990 to 2020, approximately twenty-one percent of state legislative elections in Alaska were competitive, compared to over thirty percent from 2022 to 2024. A difference of means test generates a statistically significant result.

The implementation of the Top-4 electoral system in Alaska aimed to enhance competition in state legislative elections. Our analysis of elections from 1990 to 2024, using three metrics—proportion of uncontested races, elections with more than two candidates, and races decided by narrow margins—presents mixed results. The proportion of uncontested races decreased from twenty-three percent pre-2022 to 16.5 percent post-implementation, albeit not statistically significantly. However, the proportion of races with more than two candidates nearly doubled to thirty-one percent, indicating a statistically significant increase. Furthermore,

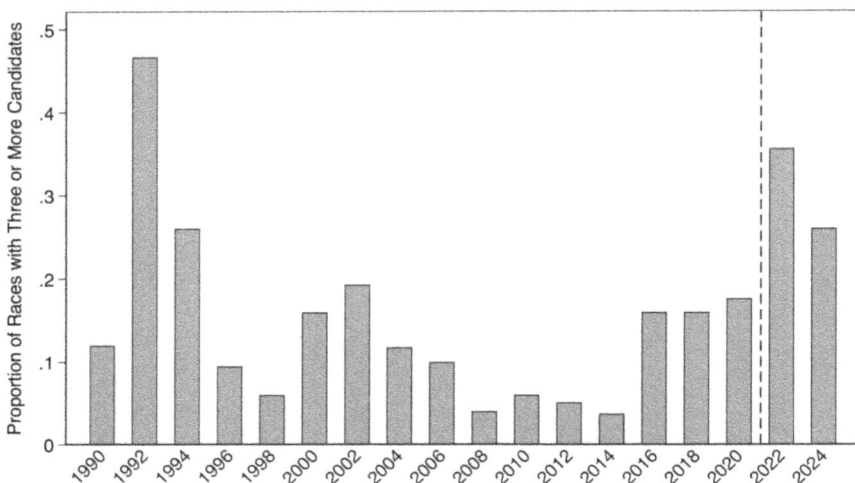

Figure 8.2: Proportion of Alaska state legislative elections with three or more candidates, 1990 – 2024.

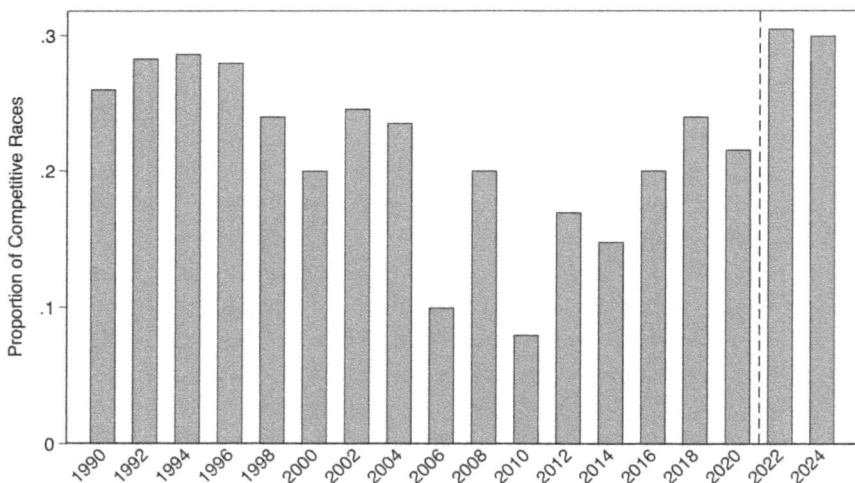

Figure 8.3: Proportion of competitive state legislative elections in Alaska, 1990 – 2024.

elections decided by small margins rose significantly, from twenty-one percent to over thirty percent after the system was introduced. Overall, while the Top-4 system has not uniformly increased competition across all measures, it notably raised the number of candidates and close races, suggesting a positive shift towards more competitive state legislative elections.

Top-4 and the Political Establishment

In this section, we turn to an evaluation of the impact of Top-4 on existing political power dynamics. Specifically, we describe trends in open seat races (those in which the incumbent is not seeking reelection), the reelection rates of incumbents, and the entry and success rates of both Republican and Democratic state legislative candidates. First, in Figure 8.4, we depict the proportion of open seats in each election cycle. While 2022 indeed witnessed the greatest number of open seats in thirty years, it is important to note that redistricting plays a crucial role here. Every cycle under new maps (1992, 2002, 2012, and 2022) sees an increase in open seats relative to the years immediately preceding it. Therefore, while the reform increased uncertainty for incumbents on the best path to victory, it is unlikely that Top-4 uniquely contributed to the larger proportion of open seats seen in 2022. This idea is reinforced by the drastic decrease in 2024, which saw the lowest number of open seats since 2010.

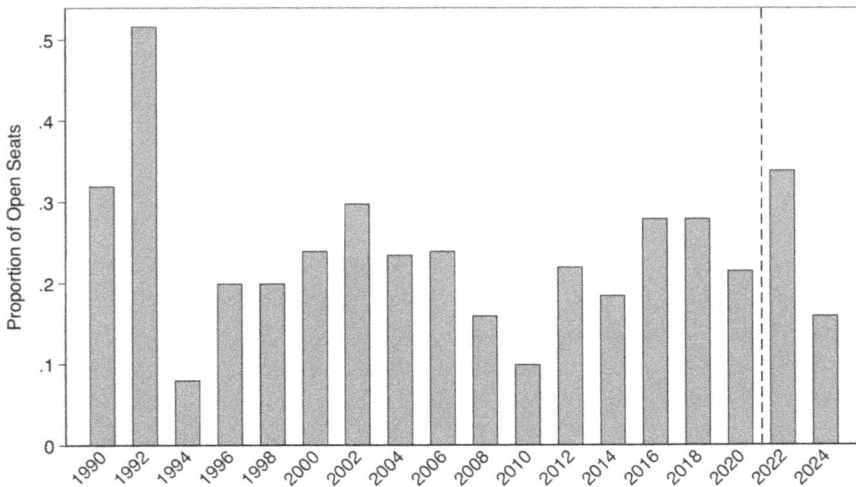

Figure 8.4: Proportion of open seat races in Alaska, 1990–2024.

Next, we analyze incumbent success rates for state legislators between 1990 and 2024. Electoral reforms, by design, introduce uncertainty, which can make it more difficult for incumbents to retain their office. This indeed seems to be the case in Alaska. The reelection rate of incumbents declined after the implementation of Top-4. From 1990 to 2020, incumbents won an average of ninety percent of their races every election cycle. However, in 2022 and 2024, that average dropped to less than eighty-two percent. A difference of means test reveals that this difference is statistically significant. Crosson (2021, 532) suggests, "political elites may maneuver institutional changes to their own benefit." Therefore, it is possible that Alaska may see a reversion to higher incumbent reelection rates in future election cycles.

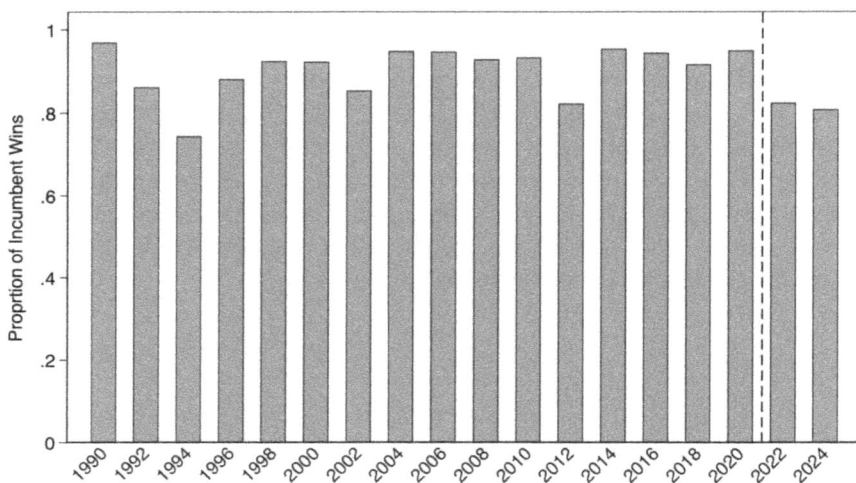

Figure 8.5: Proportion of incumbent wins, 1990–2024.

Lastly, we examine partisan dynamics within Alaska legislative elections. With the opportunity to appear on the general election ballot without placing first in the primary, Top-4 should generate greater participation. And given the strong Republican lean of the state, we should see a disproportionate increase in the number of Republican candidates. This is evident in Figure 8.6. The nonpartisan primary and ranked choice voting allows for intraparty competition unlike traditional primary election systems. By fostering intraparty competition and allowing voters to express nuanced preferences, these systems can lead to outcomes that align more closely with the diverse views of the electorate, ultimately enhancing democratic responsiveness. This increase in intraparty competition may also help explain the decrease in the proportion of Democratic candidates, as depicted on the righthand side of the figure.

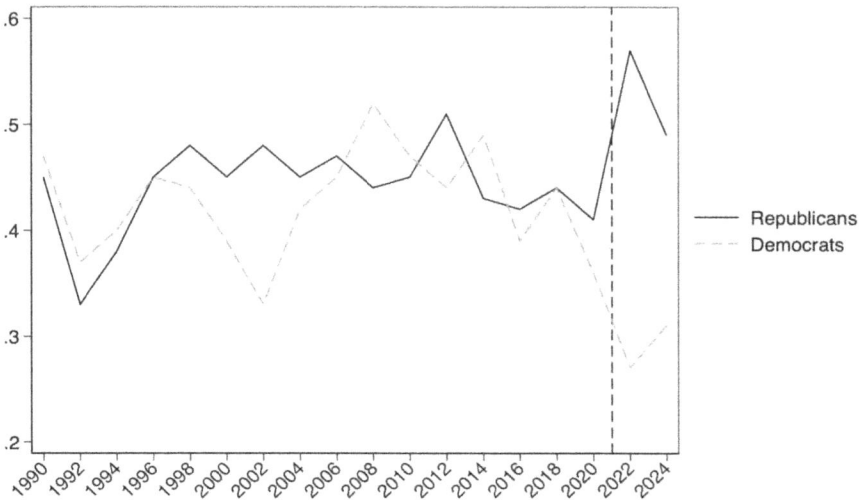

Figure 8.6: Proportion of general election candidates by partisanship, 1990 – 2024.

With this in mind, we plot the success rates of Republican and Democratic candidates in Figure 8.7 with the dashed line again demarcating the elections before and after the reform. Necessarily, given the substantial change in their denominators, the proportion of Republican winners has decreased under Top Four, and the proportion of Democratic winners has increased. It is unclear what the broader implications of this change currently are, but these numbers nonetheless illustrate a shift in the electoral landscape. Importantly, an increase in the number of losing candidates could decrease satisfaction among the electorate (Anderson and LoTempio 2002). It is possible that RCV could mitigate that dissatisfaction.

To summarize, the impact of the Top-4 reform on Alaska's political dynamics reveals significant changes in several electoral trends. The number of open seat races peaked in 2022, largely due to redistricting, not solely the reform, as demonstrated by a reduction in 2024. The reform has nonetheless introduced uncertainty, though, lowering incumbent reelection success rates from an average of ninety percent to under eighty-two percent post-reform. In terms of partisan dynamics, Top-4 encourages greater participation by allowing candidates to reach the general election without winning primaries, seen in a rise in Republican candidates, reflecting Alaska's strong Republican lean. While there has been an increase in Republican participation in elections, the proportion of Republican candidates who emerge victorious has decreased, while the number of Democratic winners has risen. This shift in the electoral landscape suggests that the dynamics within the Republican Party are evolving, potentially leading to more intraparty competition

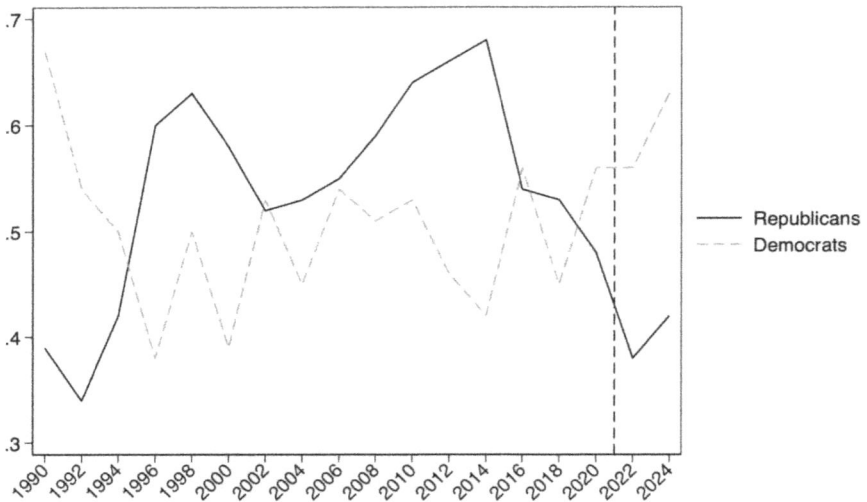

Figure 8.7: Proportion of general election wins by partisanship, 1990–2024.

among Republican candidates. As electoral reforms broaden the pool of Republican candidates who view themselves as viable, these individuals may be encouraged to enter races, thereby increasing competition and promoting more diverse and representative outcomes. However, this increased competition could also lead to voter dissatisfaction if constituents feel that the winning candidates do not adequately reflect their preferences or concerns, highlighting the need for a more thorough analysis of these emerging trends.

Top-4 and Candidate Positioning

Understanding the impact of electoral reform on candidate ideology is crucial for assessing how systemic changes can influence political landscapes. As Alaska implemented its Top-4 primary system, the expectation emerged that this reform would attract more moderate candidates, potentially altering who runs and succeeds in state legislative elections. This anticipated shift presents an opportunity to analyze ideological trends over time, examining whether such a reform can genuinely moderate political extremes and broaden electoral competitiveness. By tracking candidate ideology in recent election cycles, we can evaluate whether Top-4 really reshaped electoral outcomes.

Figure 8.8 depicts the average candidate ideology score for state legislative candidates in Alaska between 1990 and 2022 using campaign finance scores from Adam Bonica's Database on Ideology, Money in Politics, and Elections (2023).[2] Unlike the previous chapter, which uses expert information surveys as well as candidate positions, Bonica's database relies on campaign contributions to estimate ideal points for all candidates. In this case, values closer to zero denote more moderate candidates, with values further away from zero representing greater ideological extremity. Each dot represents an election cycle, and the dashed vertical line represents elections before and after the reform. From this, we see that both parties have polarized over the last three decades as evidenced by candidates from both parties steadily drifting away from zero, yet in opposite directions. However, contrary to expectations, there is not a discernible difference in the ideology of candidates after the adoption of Top-4.

It is important to note that this depicts all candidates who sought office. The purported value of Top-4 is that it would reward candidates for moderating their positions and trying to earn votes from outside their party's base. Therefore, we also examine the average ideology score between those who successfully won a seat in the Alaska legislature and those who did not, again relying on data from Bonica (2023). The results are depicted in Figure 8.9. From this we see that winning candidates are generally more moderate than those who lose their elections—but only among Republicans. This is consistent with Carson and Williamson (2018) and is likely attributable to the fact that extreme candidates are not punished electorally for running in extreme districts. The larger number of seats held by Republicans necessarily means that they were forced to defend themselves in more ideologically diverse, ostensibly more moderate, districts.

A difference of means test reveals a statistically significant difference between winning and losing Republican candidates during this period. However, the same difference does not exist among Democratic candidates—especially in 2020 and 2022 when there is essentially no difference at all between those who earn seats versus those who do not. Related to Top-4, the 2022 election cycle does not differ substantially from the previous ones. Therefore, the figures presented here do not provide any evidence in support of the argument that Alaska's reform efforts changed ideological dynamics within elections.

Anderson et al. (2023, 134) find that "the top-four primary creates opportunities for cross-party voting that can enhance the electoral prospects of moderate candidates." While this remains true, and there is anecdotal evidence in support of this effect (e.g., Leven and Fisher 2023), there does not appear to be a dis-

---

2 Data for the 2024 cycle was not available at the time of this writing.

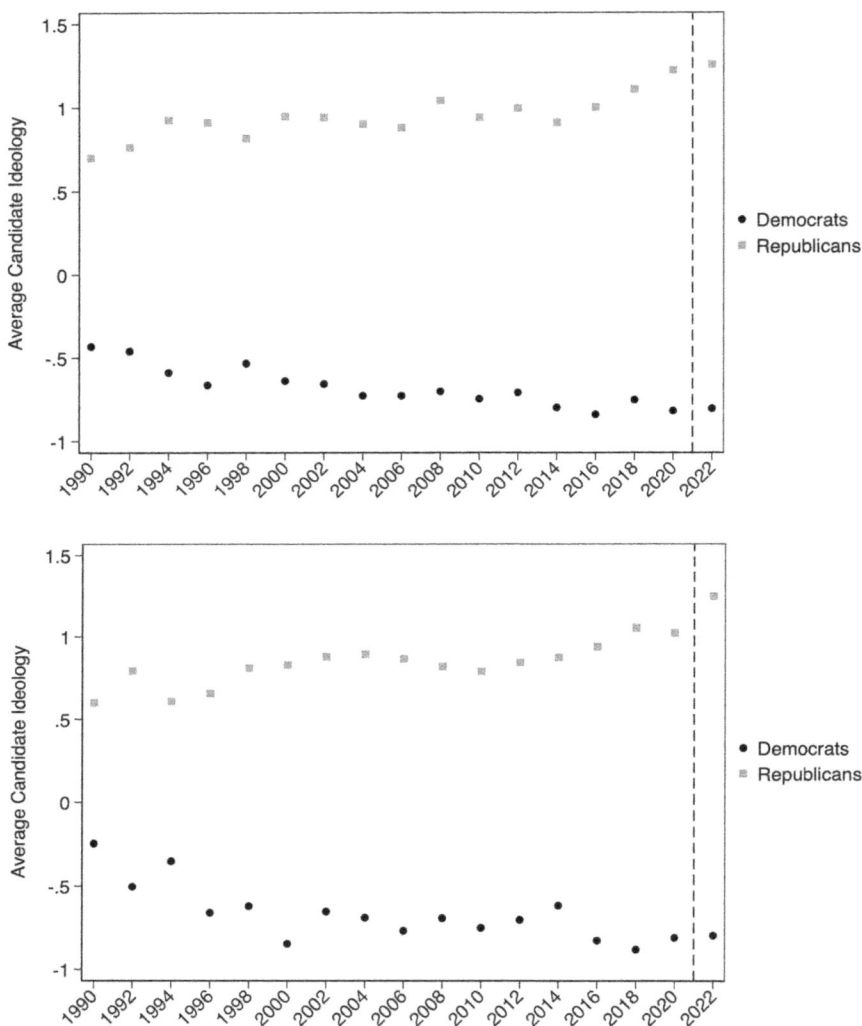

Figure 8.8: Average candidate ideology scores by chamber and party, 1990–2022.

cernible effect in the aggregate. This is consistent with the findings of Ahler et al. (2016, 237) who conclude, "voters failed to distinguish moderate and extreme candidates." However, it is important to note that candidates are politically savvy and unlikely to self-select into a process under which they are unlikely to succeed. Ad-

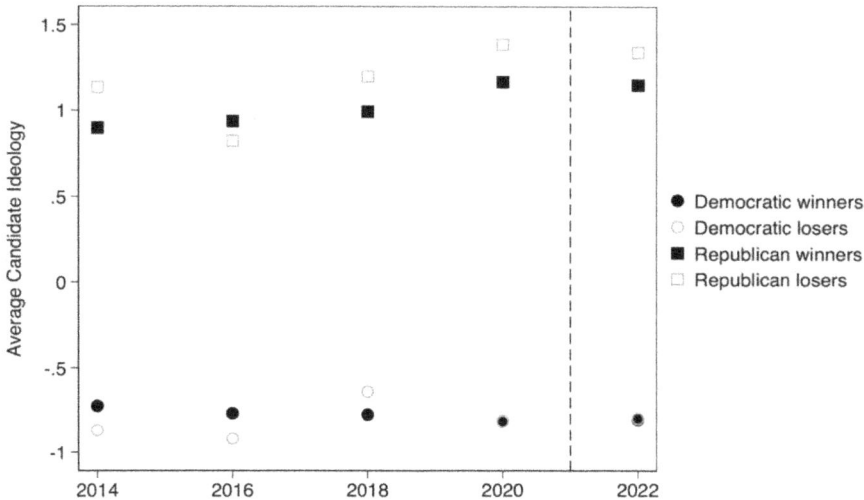

Figure 8.9: Average candidate ideology scores by wins and party, 2014–2022.

ditionally, it may take time for candidates to learn how to fully maximize their chances of success under this system.[3]

Top-4 and Turnout

Electoral reforms hold the potential to significantly influence voter participation in elections. Therefore, we analyze trends in turnout in both primaries and general elections before and after the adoption of Top-4 in Alaska. We expect that by offering a broader slate of candidates and encouraging cross-party appeal, Top-4 could engage a more diverse electorate and incentivize greater voter participation. By examining turnout over time, we can assess whether Top-4 succeeded in broadening democratic engagement, attracting previously disengaged voters, and ultimately transforming the electoral landscape.

Figure 8.10 depicts the voter turnout in primary and general elections in Alaska between 1990 and 2024. Each dot represents an election cycle, and the dashed vertical line represents elections before and after the reform. One of the alleged

---

3 Indeed, while a more observable effect may not yet be present in the data, as discussed in the previous chapter, there are instances of more moderate candidates capitalizing on the new system in order to propel themselves to victory over more ideologically extreme opponents.

benefits of Top-4 was the potential for increased voter engagement. However, this figure does not seem to support that claim. Throughout the thirty-four-year period observed here, Alaska had an average primary election turnout of 29.3 percent. The first election cycle after adoption in 2022 saw a slight increase above the recent average at 32.2 percent, but the second election cycle after adoption witnessed a remarkably—even historically—low turnout level of less than eighteen percent. Although the 2022 primaries did see above average turnout, it is important to note that this cycle was the first election following the death of congressman Don Young, who had served the state as its only member of the House of Representatives for forty-nine years. With such a monumental race having attracted forty-eight candidates seeking to replace him, it is therefore difficult to attribute this uptick exclusively to Top Four (Alaska Division of Elections 2022). Additionally, voters did not seem particularly compelled to cast a ballot in 2024 as there were no ballot measures, no governor's race, and no senate race for the first time since 2000 (Wagner 2024). In total, primary turnout the thirty years prior to Top Four averaged 29.9 percent while the two cycles with Top-4 trailed behind at 25.1 percent, suggesting the reform did not influence voter participation in primaries.

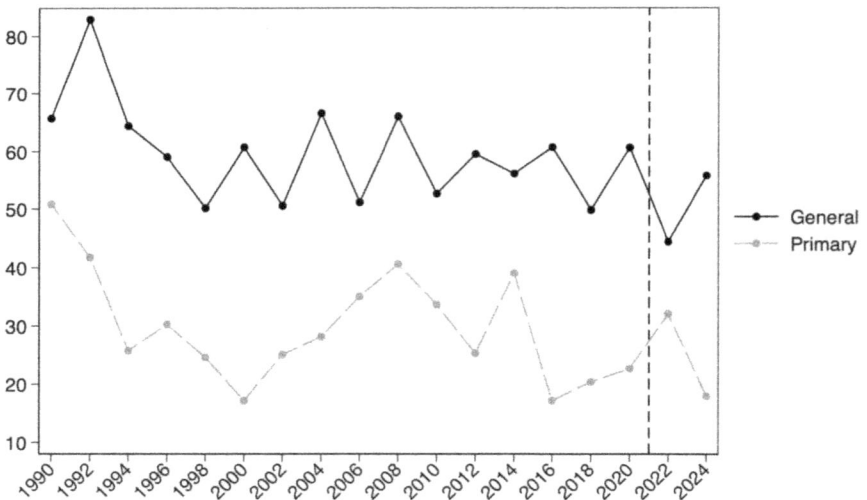

Figure 8.10: Voter turnout in Alaska, 1990–2024.

Although the reform did not appear to improve turnout in Alaska's primaries, Dowling et al. (2024) conclude that ranked-choice voting can improve turnout. Therefore, we now turn our attention to trends in turnout at the general election phase. Throughout the thirty-four-year period examined here, general election turnout averaged around fifty-nine percent. Prior to Top-4, turnout was typically sixty percent, with presidential election years averaging a somewhat higher sixty-four percent. Top-4 did not seem to draw additional voters, though. In fact, the 2022 election cycle witnessed the lowest level of general election turnout during the time period examined at 44.5 percent. Furthermore, the 2024 cycle saw the lowest level of turnout for a presidential election year at 55.7 percent. While it is possible to speculate that turnout could have decreased even further in the absence of Top-4 implementation, our results suggest that the reform did nothing to improve voter turnout in Alaska.

Though Top-4 may not have induced a significant or durable shift in turnout in primary elections, it could have changed the complexion of the electorate. After all, the goal of the reform was to create new incentives for both voters and candidates. Younger voters historically participate less than older voters (Election Lab 2025), are more likely to be dissatisfied with politics (Berthin 2023), and are less likely to identify with one of the two major parties (Pew Research Center 2024). Theoretically, the top four nonpartisan primary system, which, as mentioned earlier, allows voters to choose candidates regardless of party affiliation and advances the top four vote-getters to the general election, could increase engagement among younger voters by offering more diverse and representative choices. This system encourages candidates to appeal to a broader electorate, potentially addressing issues that resonate with younger demographics who feel left out by traditional party politics. By providing a platform for independent or third-party candidates, a Top-4 nonpartisan primary can create a political landscape more aligned with the values and priorities of younger voters, thus incentivizing their participation. Additionally, the act of voting in a more open and flexible system can foster a sense of empowerment and agency among young people, encouraging them to become more active participants in the democratic process.

The Alaska Division of Elections provides turnout data by age group, which we present in Figure 8.11. Each dot represents an election cycle, and the dashed vertical line represents elections before and after the reform. Between 2000 and 2024, we consistently see older age groups participate at considerably higher levels than the youngest group of voters. On average, those between eighteen and twenty-four years of age have twelve percent turnout, with a high of around twenty-one percent. For those aged between twenty-five and forty-four, turnout averages around eighteen percent with a high of 33.5 percent during this period. Around one-third of voters aged forty-five to fifty participate in primary elections, on average, and have a high of just over one-half casting ballots. Lastly, voters aged over sixty have an average turnout of around forty-five percent, with a high water mark of nearly sixty percent turnout. This trend did not change during the 2022 and 2024 elections; the youngest voters lagged behind every other age group.

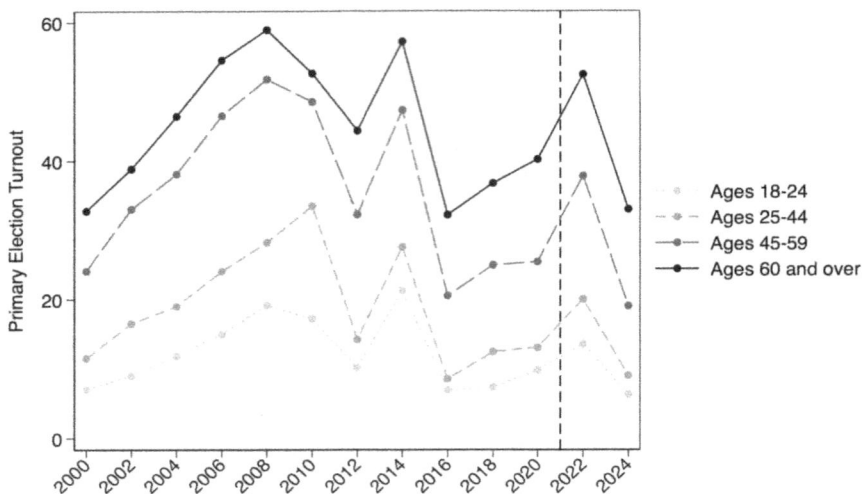

Figure 8.11: Primary election turnout in Alaska by age, 2000–2024.

To evaluate this further, we examine the discrepancy between the oldest and youngest age groups over the same twenty-four-year period. To do this, we divided the turnout percentage of those aged sixty and over by the turnout percentage of those between eighteen and twenty-four years of age. Even if younger voters are not turning out at very high levels, perhaps they are at least making up ground, so to speak, on other age groups. However, this does not appear to be the case. Top-4 does not seem to have inspired greater participation from younger voters. In fact, 2024 witnessed the largest divergence between these two age groups during the period analyzed, as those aged sixty and over turned out at thirty-three percent compared to a mere six percent for those aged between eighteen and twenty-four. Though this may be surprising to some, it is consistent with Berinsky's (2005) observation that electoral reforms often fail to bring new voters into the electorate.

Discussion and Conclusions

The introduction of the Top Four electoral system in Alaska marked a substantial reform in the state's electoral dynamics, aiming to broaden voter choice, enhance competition, and reduce partisanship. Our examination of state legislative elections from 1990 to 2024 shows that the reform did not uniformly increase competition across all metrics, but it did produce some notable shifts. Specifically, the establishment of the new system coincided with a significant increase in the proportion of races featuring more than two candidates and in races decided by narrower margins. This is a positive step towards more competitive elections.

The Top-4 system also prompted noticeable changes in electoral trends concerning incumbency and partisan success. There was a decline in the reelection success rates of incumbents and an increase in Republican candidacies. This may have been a consequence of candidates' ability to participate in general elections without winning primaries. This increase in participation was accompanied by a decrease in the proportion of Republican winners and a rise in Democratic success. Although the full implications of these changes remain unclear, they highlight a transformation in Alaska's political landscape that warrants further exploration, particularly concerning voter satisfaction and the potential for more representative electoral outcomes.

The impact of the Top-4 system on candidate ideology did not meet some reformers' expectations that the system would moderate political extremism or significantly influence the ideological positions of the candidates who run and who win elections. Despite our initial expectation that more moderate candidates would emerge, our analysis revealed no substantial ideological shifts among state legislative candidates following the reform's implementation. While we anticipated that the opportunity for cross-party voting might enhance moderates' prospects, there was no discernible aggregate effect. However, the system may have long-term effects on candidate positioning and electoral outcomes as candidates and parties respond to the new incentives.

Finally, the Top-4 system's influence on voter turnout presented mixed results, as it did not lead to a significant or lasting increase in turnout for either primary or general elections. While the system was designed to engage a broader electorate by providing diverse candidate choices, the turnout data we considered showed few changes. Despite anecdotal evidence suggesting increased voter empowerment due to ranked-choice voting (Alaskans for Better Elections 2024), the overall turnout remained below expectations. This finding underscores the complexity of how electoral reforms like the Top-4 system can impact voter engagement and points to the need for continuous assessment as these changes strive to enhance democratic participation in varying electoral contexts.

These results are not entirely unsurprising considering the existing literature on both the short-term and long-term effects of electoral reforms, which emphasizes that the adaptations made by parties and candidates can take time to materialize. Additionally, these adaptations may dampen the anticipated outcomes of such reforms (Cain 2014; Hill 2022). As highlighted by Albert et al. (2024), this specific reform effort in Alaska may not produce observable differences for several additional cycles while parties, candidates, and voters adjust to the new system.

Despite the mixed results presented here, the introduction of RCV may have changed Alaska's political dynamics in ways that we cannot easily capture through analyses such as the one we have provided. This voting system encourages voters to rank candidates in order of preference, aiming to create a more representative outcome. However, it also introduces complexities that have driven strategic maneuvering among candidates. Many Republican state legislative candidates pledged to withdraw from the general election if they did not secure the top spot in the primary to prevent vote splitting and consolidate support (Downing 2024). This approach aimed to streamline the primary process and enhance the party's chances in the general election, although it was criticized for oversimplifying electoral realities.

A prime example of these dynamics was the race for Alaska's U.S. House seat in 2024. Republican candidate Nick Begich, supported by the House Freedom Caucus, committed to withdrawing if he did not lead among Republicans in the primary (Mollenkamp 2024). In contrast, Lieutenant Governor Nancy Dahlstrom, who had prominent endorsements from figures like Donald Trump, initially refused to make such a pledge. Ultimately, Dahlstrom conceded after finishing third in the primary (Early 2024). Through strategic withdrawals post-primary, Republicans aimed to bolster the strongest contender against incumbent Democratic Representative Mary Peltola. This tactic sought to avoid "exhausted ballots," where votes for eliminated candidates do not transfer to remaining party contenders, thereby failing to consolidate party support effectively. By reducing the field of candidates, Republicans hoped to simplify voter choices in the general election and increase the party's chances of consolidating partisan support in a highly competitive political race. This strategy also enabled the Republican Party to focus their efforts and resources solely on defeating the Democratic incumbent, Peltola, instead of jockeying for second place among co-partisan opponents.

Peltola, who led the primary with over fifty percent of the vote, presented a significant challenge for Republicans seeking to reclaim Alaska's sole House seat (Karni 2024). Her alignment with national Democratic policies was a focal point for Begich, who sought to portray her as less moderate than she claimed. Despite these challenges, the Republican camp, unified behind Begich after Dahlstrom's withdrawal, aimed to capitalize on Alaska's generally conservative electorate. Their strategy involved rallying support around Begich as the sole Republican contender to strengthen their position against Peltola in the general election. The gambit was ultimately successful, culminating in Nick Begich's victory, which demonstrates both the challenges and the potential of the RCV system (Mueller 2024). This strategy was employed by others in Alaska as several state legislative candidates withdrew their candidacies, despite advancing out of the primary, to consolidate support for other conservative Republicans (Acuña Buxton 2024). This outcome highlighted how RCV can influence electoral strategies, allowing candidates to subvert the spirit of the reform through coordinated efforts and strategic withdrawals in an effort to maximize partisan electoral success potentially at the expense of nuanced voter preferences. However, this increased involvement from the state party could foster stronger collaboration and communication among candidates, ensuring that electoral strategies align more closely with broader voter interests and promoting a more inclusive approach to campaigning that values nuanced preferences over strict partisan loyalty.

The impact of the Top-4 system in Alaska remains uncertain as debates continue regarding its effectiveness and impact on both voter engagement and political dynamics. While the system has introduced a more competitive and diverse political landscape, it has also raised questions about its ability to truly represent nuanced voter preferences and effectively increase voter participation. As Alaska navigates these electoral reforms, ongoing assessments will be crucial to understanding their long-term implications. Broader national conversations about electoral reform will likely hinge on outcomes in Alaska, as states across the country seek to learn from its innovation as they look to balance the goals of increasing electoral participation, reducing partisanship, and ensuring fair representation.

Bibliography

Acuña Buxton, Matt. 2024. "A Dozen Candidates Have Dropped Out of Alaska's General Election." *The Alaska Current.* September 4. www.thealaskacurrent.com/a-dozen-candidates-have-dropped-out-of-alaskas-general-election.

Ahler, Douglas J., Jack Citrin, and Gabriel S. Lenz. 2016. "Do Open Primaries Improve Representation? An Experimental Test of California's 2012 Top-Two Primary." *Legislative Studies Quarterly* 41 (2): 237–268.

Alaska Division of Elections. 2022. "2022 Special Primary Election for U.S. Representative: Final Candidate List." August 15. elections.alaska.gov/SpecialPrimaryElection-Candidates. Accessed April 1, 2025.

Alaskans for Better Elections. 2024. "Alaska-Style Elections." Alaskans for Better Elections. www.alaskansforbetterelections.com/alaska-style-elections. Accessed April 1, 2025.

Albert, Zachary, Robert G. Boatright, Lane Cuthbert, Adam Eichen, Wouter van Erve, Raymond J. La Raja, and Meredith Rolfe. 2024. "Election reform and campaign finance: Did Alaska's top 4 nonpartisan primaries and ranked-choice general elections affect political spending?" *Social Science Quarterly* 105: 1668–1690.

Anderson, Christopher J., and Andrew J. LoTempio. 2002. "Winning, Losing and Political Trust in America." *British Journal of Political Science* 32 (2): 335–351.

Anderson, Sarah E., Daniel M. Butler, Laurel Harbridge-Yong, and Renae Marshall. 2023. "Top-Four Primaries Help Moderate Candidates via Crossover Voting: The Case of the 2022 Alaska Election Reforms." *The Forum* 21 (1): 123–136.

Berinsky, Adam J. 2005. "The Perverse Consequences of Electoral Reform in the United States." *American Politics Research* 33 (4): 471–491.

Berthin, Gerardo. 2023. "Why Are Youth Dissatisfied with Democracy?" *Freedom House.* September 14. freedomhouse.org/article/why-are-youth-dissatisfied-democracy.

Bonica, Adam. 2023. Database on Ideology, Money in Politics, and Elections: Public version 3.1 [Computer file]. Stanford University Libraries. data.stanford.edu/dime.

Cain, Bruce E. 2014. *Democracy more or less: America's political reform quandary.* Cambridge University Press.

Carson, Jamie L., and Ryan D. Williamson. 2018. "Candidate Ideology and Electoral Success in Congressional Elections." *Public Choice* 176 (1): 175–192.

Crosson, Jesse. 2021. "Extreme Districts, Moderate Winners: Same- Party Challenges, and Deterrence in Top-Two Primaries." *Political Science Research and Methods* 9 (3): 532–48.

Dowling, Eveline, Caroline Tolbert, Nathan Micatka, and Todd Donovan. 2024. "Does ranked choice voting increase voter turnout and mobilization?" *Electoral Studies* 90, 102816.

Downing, Suzanne. 2024. "Fourth Republican District Passes 'Drop If Not on Top' Resolution Regarding Congressional Race." *Must Read Alaska.* August 13. mustreadalaska.com/fourth-republican-district-passes-drop-if-not-on-top-resolution.

Early, Wesley. 2024. "Nancy Dahlstrom Drops Out of Alaska's U.S. House Race." *Alaska Public Media.* August 23. https://alaskapublic.org/news/2024-08-23/nancy-dahlstrom-drops-out-of-alaskas-u-s-house-race Election Lab. 2025. "Turnout Demographics." University of Florida. election.lab.ufl.edu/turnout-demographics.

Evensen, Jay. 2024. "Opinion: Why Are Utah Lawmakers Set to Abandon Ranked Choice Voting?" *Deseret News.* February 16. https://www.deseret.com/opinion/2024/2/16/24074274/utah-ranked-choice-voting-conservatives/.

FairVote. 2025. "Ranked Choice Voting." FairVote. March. fairvote.org/ranked-choice-voting.

FGA. 2022. "Ranked-Choice Voting: A Disaster in Disguise." Foundation for Government Accountability. August 25. thefga.org/ranked-choice-voting-disaster. Accessed April 1, 2025.

Gerber, Elisabeth R., and Rebecca B. Morton. 1998. "Primary Election Systems and Representation." *Journal of Law, Economics, & Organization* 14 (2): 304–324.

Grose, Christian R. 2020. "Reducing Legislative Polarization: Top-Two and Open Primaries Are Associated with More Moderate Legislators," *Journal of Political Institutions and Political Economy* 1 (2): 267–287.

Hamilton, Katherine. 2021. "3 Reasons Open Primaries Would Transform American Politics." RepresentUs. July 2. https://act.represent.us/sign/3-reasons-open-primaries-transform-politics.

Herz, Nathaniel. 2022. "After Peltola Win in Alaska, a Debate Erupts Over Ranked-Choice Voting." *The Washington Post.* September 1. https://www.washingtonpost.com/politics/2022/09/01/peltola-palin-ranked-choice-voting-alaska/.

Hill, Seth J. 2022. "Sidestepping Primary Reform: Political Action in Response to Institutional Change." *Political Science Research and Methods* 10: 391–407.

John, Sarah, Haley Smith, and Elizabeth Zack. 2018. "The Alternative Vote: Do Changes in Single-Member District Voting Systems Affect Descriptive Representation of Women and Minorities?" *Electoral Studies* 54: 90–102.

Karni, Annie. 2024. "Peltola Finishes First in Alaska House Primary, With Begich as Top Challenger." *The New York Times.* August 21. https://www.nytimes.com/2024/08/21/us/politics/peltola-alaska-house-primary-dahlstrom-begich.html.

Leven, Rachel, and Tyler Fisher. 2023. "Alaska's Election Model." Unite America. October 25. www.uniteamerica.org/articles/alaskas-election-model.

Macomber, Carlo. 2024. "Nonpartisan Primaries Increase Primary Turnout." Unite America. June 28. https://www.uniteamerica.org/articles/nonpartisan-primaries-increase-primary-turnout.

Mollenkamp, Allison. 2024. "GOP Effort to Oust Peltola May Hinge on Who Finishes Second." *Roll Call.* August 15. https://rollcall.com/2024/08/15/gop-effort-to-oust-peltola-may-hinge-on-who-finishes-second/.

Mueller, Julia. 2024. "Peltola Ousted by GOP Opponent in Alaska House Race." *The Hill.* November 16. https://thehill.com/homenews/campaign/4970040-mary-peltola-ousted-nick-begich-alaska-house/.

Pew Research Center. 2024. "Changing Partisan Coalitions in a Politically Divided Nation." April 9. www.pewresearch.org/politics/2024/04/09/changing-partisan-coalitions/.

Sabino, Pascal. 2024. "Native Leaders Organize to Defend Alaska's Ranked Choice Voting System." *Bolts.* September 11. https://boltsmag.org/alaska-ranked-choice-voting-measure-native-organizers/.

Sinclair, J. Andrew, R. Michael Alvarez, Betsy Sinclair, and Christian R. Grose. 2024. "Electoral Innovation and the Alaska System: Partisanship and Populism Are Associated with Support for Top-4/Ranked-Choice Voting Rules." *Political Research Quarterly* 77 (4): 1196–1211.

Squire, Peverill. 2000. "Uncontested Seats in State Legislative Elections." *Legislative Studies Quarterly* 25 (1): 131–146.

Wagner, Zachary. 2024. "Alaska's primary election turnout is on pace to be third lowest in 50 years." *Alaska Beacon.* August 29. alaskabeacon.com/2024/08/29/alaskas-primary-election-turnout-is-on-pace-to-be-third-lowest-in-50-years/.

Williamson, Ryan. 2023. "Evaluating the Effects of the Top-Four System in Alaska." R Street Institute.

Jeremy Gelman, Evan Pritsos, and Benjamin Reilly

Chapter 9
The Consequences of a Top-5/RCV System in Nevada: Advantaging Moderates but Sidelining Third Parties?

Abstract: Electoral reforms that eliminate party primaries and plurality elections are often adopted with the goal of providing voters more options in the general election, advantaging moderate politicians, and providing non-major party candidates a better chance of winning office. In this chapter, we assess these claims in the context of a proposed Top-5 primary and ranked choice general election system in Nevada, which considered but ultimately rejected this voting system in 2024 through a ballot initiative. Using a survey of Nevada voters in four hypothetical primary and general elections, and simulating different potential turnout scenarios, we find mostly confirming evidence for these claims. Moderate candidates from the two major parties, via cross-party rankings transfers, are likely advantaged at the general election. Voters get more choice than at present and should usually be able to choose from candidates in the general election representing both the traditional and insurgent wings of the major parties. However, to the extent that this occurs, the reform leaves less room for third-party and independent candidates and in some scenarios may shut smaller parties out from the general election ballot entirely.

In 2022, Nevadans voted to adopt a Top-5/ranked choice voting system by a 53–47 percent margin. However, the state's ballot initiative process is unique as it requires the same initiative to win support from the public in two consecutive general elections. In 2024, Top-5/ranked choice voting (Top-5/RCV hereafter) failed, coincidentally by the same margin from 2022 but reversed (fifty-three percent opposed, forty-seven percent for).

Between those elections, we sought to understand what effect adopting this system would have on Nevada politics. Among the states considering these sorts of electoral reforms, Nevada was unique as a battleground state and the place a Top-5 model would have been adopted first. We considered the main claims that electoral reform advocates make, namely that Top-5/RCV increases voters' choices, promotes more moderate politics, and gives greater opportunities for third party and independent candidates (Leven and Fisher 2023; Schwarzeneggar and Khanna 2018). In particular, the combination of a Top-5 nonpartisan primary followed by a ranked choice general election is seen as optimal (Gehl 2023; Reilly, Lublin, and Leven 2022). But whether such systems can deliver on these claims is not clear, given their different potential effects as well as the lack of other cases using such institutions.

In this chapter, we evaluate three main claims made about Top-5/RCV: that it provides voters more choice by allowing multiple candidates representing different factions of the major parties to advance to the general election; that it reduces polarization by advantaging moderates in the general election via cross-party voting; and that it enables independent and third-party candidates to be more successful than they would be in a system with party primaries and plurality general elections.

We assessed these arguments in the lead up to the second ballot initiative in Nevada, a state with a very different electorate than other commonly studied RCV cases like Maine and Alaska. Our analysis utilized a survey of Nevada voters in four hypothetical Top-5/RCV elections.[1] Using this data, we adopted a simulation approach to consider how such a system would perform in highly Democratic, Republican, and competitive electorates. In total, we analyzed 20 million simulated elections that include ones dominated by one party and others in which Democrats and Republicans compete at parity.

Our results offer significant support for advocates' claims but with important caveats. On the one hand, we find consistent evidence that moderates are advantaged in a Top-5/RCV system and that crossover voting at the RCV general election is the likely mechanism that facilitates this advantage. When ranking their top choice from the other party, general election voters are far more likely to rate the moderate ahead of the extremist. Yet, a Top-5 system does not inevitably shut out extremists. In some simulations, the most extreme major party candidate in our entire survey wins the general election. Additionally, moderates are already relatively successful in Nevada politics, so it is unclear how much substantive change this reform would produce.

Second, our survey suggests that while a Top-5 primary does indeed expand voter choice, it usually does so by producing multiple candidates from the same party, except when an incumbent is running. In that scenario, the incumbent crowds out co-partisans and leads to multiple challenger candidates on the general election ballot. For parties without an incumbent, most Democratic or Republican voters will be able to choose more than one candidate from their party in the general election, often representing establishment and insurgent wings. While in-

---

1 This study was approved by the UNR Institutional Review Board, Study #2152211–1.

dependent or third-party candidates usually make the final five, they never come close to winning the general election. Additionally, more than one independent or third-party candidate rarely makes the final five. This being the case, a Top-5 system will almost certainly lead to fewer non-major party options for general election voters.

These results highlight the promise and peril of switching electoral institutions (Tolbert 2021). At the statewide level, the main difference voters would experience is selecting between major party factions in the general election. In particular, these races would feature a more moderate Republican candidate in addition to the more extreme option the state GOP often nominates. However, depolarization will require the emergence of even more moderate politicians. Because the Democrats and Republicans who already win elections represent the moderate party factions, and are quite polarized, such candidates winning in a Top-5 system may not significantly change the direction of Nevada politics.

What we Know about Ranked Choice Voting and Nonpartisan Primaries

Since 2008, four states have adopted alternative electoral systems which offer ranked choice voting, nonpartisan primaries, or both.[2] Voters in seven other states (including Nevada) considered ballot initiatives establishing such systems in 2024; all of these initiatives were defeated, although a move to open primaries and RCV was approved in Washington DC. Although the politics within these states and the proposed or adopted voting methods differ, the arguments advocating for these reforms are consistent.

Implementing nonpartisan primaries open to all comers, it is argued, provides three main benefits. First, voters will have more choices in the general election by allowing both moderate and more ideologically extreme candidates from the same party to run on the same ballot. Second, these sorts of primaries, when offered in a Top-4 or Top-5 format, provide minor party and independent candidates a better chance of election (Lublin and Reilly 2023; Schwarzeneggar and Khanna 2018; Troxler 2010). Finally, as was discussed in Chapter 7 and 8, the elimination of partisan primaries discourages candidates from only catering to the more extreme primary voters rather than to the electorate at large.

---

2 Washington State (in 2008) and California (in 2012) adopted a Top-2 primary system. Since 2018, Maine has used ranked choice voting in their partisan primaries and in general elections. In 2022, Alaska implemented a Top-4/RCV system.

Despite these common claims, some of the specific predictions about reforms depend on unique features of the states where they are implemented. For instance, California's top two primary has been described as an antidote to geographic, partisan polarization (Ahler et al. 2016; Crosson 2021; Grose 2020; Highton et al. 2016). In contrast, Maine's ranked choice voting system, which retains closed party primaries, was adopted in response to a history of strong independent candidates and winners securing office with small pluralities (Anderson et al. 2023; Cerrone and McClintock 2021; Nunan 2020; Santucci 2018). Such plurality elections, with votes split between major party and independent candidates, led to unpopular politicians being elected on a small share of the vote. Ranked choice voting was seen as a solution to this problem, as it advantages candidates with wider appeal and reduces the possibility of spoilers (Cerrone and McClintock 2021; Nunan 2020; Reilly 2021).

Research on these specific effects has produced mixed findings. Some studies of California's Top-2 system find it has failed to moderate statewide politics or has decreased the influence of third-party and independent candidates (Highton et al. 2016; McGhee and Shor 2017; Troxler 2010). Others suggest that California's version has increased bipartisanship in the state legislature and stemmed further polarization (Grose 2020; Munger, Jr. 2019), although the effect may be conditional (Crosson 2021). Chapter 10 of this volume summarizes much of the research on the Top-2 system.

The evidence from Maine is also mixed. Some research shows that some legislators' voting records have moderated while others have not (Cerrone and McClintock 2021; Hutchinson and Reilly 2025; Reilly 2021). Analyses from Alaska's Top-4/RCV system (such as those in Chapters 7 and 8 of this volume) suggest that moderate candidates were advantaged in the 2022 statewide elections, especially at the expense of more ideologically extreme Republicans (Anderson et al. 2023; McBeath 2023; Williamson 2023; Reilly et al. 2023). For state legislative elections, some extremists still won in highly partisan districts, but in competitive races moderates tended to prevail, providing a core group of legislators who formed a bipartisan governing coalition (Wright et al. 2025).

These results suggest that the consequences of alternative voting systems depend on a few factors. First, political context matters a great deal. This includes the nature of state-level politics but also the features of an election cycle. Second, the claims about what an alternative voting system should do are varied enough that researchers must address a wide range of potential consequences. As such, our goal is to examine a few common claims about alternative voting systems in Nevada, a state with very distinctive politics and demographics compared to others adopting such reforms. The three claims we focus on, which advocates often cite, are:

1. Multiple Democrats and Republicans, representing different wings of their respective parties, will advance to the general election.
2. Independent and third-party candidates will be more successful in a Top-5
   voting system.
3. In a ranked choice general election, cross-party voting is likely to favor
   moderates.

Nevada Politics

Nevada's proposed reform, much like the Top-4 used in Alaska, would have combined two new systems. The first round would have been a nonpartisan primary,
wherein all candidates appear on the same ballot. The Top-5 vote-getters then advance to the general election, regardless of their respective vote share. In the general election, voters rank the candidates from first to fifth preference. Not all candidates need by ranked for the ballot to be valid, and voters can choose to vote for
only one candidate as under plurality voting. The winner would be the candidate
with a majority, not just a plurality, of votes in the count.

If Nevada had adopted this system, it likely would have produced multiple effects. Like California, it may have facilitated moderates winning in heavily partisan legislative districts. Like Maine, it may have helped candidates with more
widespread support to win seats, rather than extremists nominated by one of
the major parties. Like Alaska, it may have also enabled third parties and independents to gain a slot on the general election ballot.

These potential consequences are shaped by distinctive features of Nevada
politics. Much like California, Nevada's current district lines for both the state legislature and congressional seats heavily favor the Democratic Party. However, unlike California, Washington, and Maine, statewide elections in Nevada tend to be
very close. Since 2010, Nevada has had five elections for US Senator, with each
being decided by less than six percentage points. Recent governor elections
were decided by less than five percentage points. No statewide election in 2022
was decided by more than seven percentage points.

Nevada's voter registration numbers also more closely reflect the nation as a
whole than Maine, California, or Washington. Roughly thirty percent of Nevada
voters are registered Republicans, thirty percent are Democrats, thirty-three percent are registered non-partisan, and seven percent are registered with minor parties. Nevada is also prone to large swings in voter turnout during wave election
years. During the 2014 election, Republicans cast 44.2 percent of votes. Four
years later, in 2018, they only cast 37.1 percent of the vote. These large discrepan-
cies make Nevada a compelling case, as it is reasonable to assume a Top-5/RCV sys-

tem may produce substantially different results given various partisan turnout scenarios.

Nevada's parties also tend to reflect Drutman's (2020) idea of "four parties in two." Both major parties in Nevada are divided between a more moderate establishment wing and a more extreme insurgent wing. For Democrats, the establishment wing is represented by the political machine controlled by allies of the late Senator Harry Reid, while the more insurgent wing is made up of supporters of Bernie Sanders and the Democratic Socialists of America.

The Republican party, like most state Republican parties, is divided between an old-guard wing and a Trump-aligned MAGA wing. Thus, in theory, Nevada should be a case where Top-5 primaries will result in both wings of the major parties advancing to the general election, and where moderates are likely to win in an RCV general due to crossover voting.

Research Design

To assess these arguments, we fielded a survey of 452 registered Nevada voters in February 2024. Four hundred and four respondents were recruited from Dynata's online panel. Dynata, formerly Survey Sampling International, is an online survey firm that recruits representative samples of respondents to participate in research studies. Previous research on Nevada polling indicates that purchased internet-based samples are heavily concentrated in Clark County, and often underrepresent rural and Northern Nevadans (Ladam et al. 2023). This is especially true of rural Republicans, who make up about eight percent of the electorate and currently hold outsize influence in the state Republican party.

As such, the other forty-eight respondents were recruited by confederates of the authors. Specifically, we contacted nine current University of Nevada, Reno students from various backgrounds to recruit five to ten additional respondents each. These students were given instructions on who to contact, with an emphasis on identifying people from different social groups they interact with. These respondents, although only 10.6 percent of the sample, helped geographically and politically balance it.

The sample itself effectively captured Nevadans' current political views. The state's partisan makeup is closely divided between Democrats, Republicans, and those with no party affiliation. Our sample is thirty-five percent Democratic, twenty-six percent Republican, and thirty-one percent Independent. Our simulation approach, which we detail below, means the slight Democratic oversample is not affecting our results. One concern in polling Nevadans is that "Never Trump" Republicans are oversampled, especially in online panels (Ladam et al. 2023).

However, in our data, the median Republican feeling thermometer rating for Trump is very high at 90.

The data is geographically balanced, with seventy-four percent of respondents living in the Las Vegas metro area, sixteen percent in the Reno metro area, and ten percent living in other parts of the state. Relative to registered voters in Nevada, the sample is slightly more female (fifty-seven percent) and has fewer Hispanic or Latino voters (fifteen percent). However, the results we report below are similar when we include more sophisticated weighting schemes in our simulations.

Hypothetical Top-5/RCV Elections

After collecting demographic data, the survey asked respondents to vote in four hypothetical Top-5/RCV elections. For each, they were first provided with a list of candidates and asked to select one. Next, they saw five candidates we selected as likely to advance to the general election and were asked to rank order them. We used the 2022 Alaska ballot's wording for both the primary and general election questions.

Table 9.1 summarizes the four election scenarios. Before proceeding, we highlight five choices we made in constructing this survey. First, the candidate lists for the hypothetical races, the 2024 Senate race and the 2026 Governor race, include only known political figures. Empirically, open primaries always include amateur candidates with little name recognition. As our goal is to understand the partisan and ideological consequences of this electoral system, we opted to select candidates who represent different aspects of the Nevada political landscape.

Second, to better inform respondents about their options in a low-information political environment, we included a candidate's current job, previous political experience, and a list of endorsements.[3] The 2022 endorsements include the ones from that race. For the 2024 and 2026 hypothetical elections, we allocated support based on previous results so that voters could use this information as a heuristic in deciding which wing of a party a candidate represented. For example, in the 2026 hypothetical governor's race, we allocated most of the mainstream Democratic party endorsements to the current Attorney General. However, we assigned left-wing group endorsers (e. g., the Democratic Socialists of America and Justice Democrats) to a closely aligned former state legislator. We only included people and organizations who have recently endorsed in Nevada elections.

---

3 Practically speaking, when a respondent hovered over a candidate's name, a box appeared with this information.

Table 9.1: Election scenarios and general election options.

Scenario	Incumbent	General Election Options
Generic	N/A	A Democratic candidate endorsed by Barack Obama
		A Democratic candidate endorsed by Bernie Sanders
		A Republican candidate endorsed by Donald Trump
		A Republican candidate endorsed by Mitt Romney
		A Libertarian candidate endorsed by Gary Johnson
2022 Governor Election	Democrat	Brandon Davis (Libertarian)
		Joey Gilbert (Republican)
		Dean Heller (Republican)
		Joe Lombardo (Republican)
		Steve Sisolak (Democratic)
2024 Hypothetical US Senate Election	Democrat	Rick Harrison (No Political Party)
		Jim Marchant (Republican)
		Jacky Rosen (Democratic)
		Brian Sandoval (Republican)
		Richard "Tick" Segerblom (Democratic)
2026 Governor Hypothetical Election	Republican	Aaron Ford (Democratic)
		Joey Gilbert (Republican)
		Oscar Goodman (No Political Party)
		Marilyn Kirkpatrick (Democratic)
		Joe Lombardo (Republican)

Third, in all four scenarios we selected the five candidates that advanced to the general election. In making these selections, we balanced realism with intraparty matchups that would help us assess the consequences of Top-5/RCV in various electoral scenarios. We included viable third-party candidates to explore their impact on determining winners.

Fourth, the online respondents were not allowed to exhaust their votes by selecting fewer than five candidates. This was a technical decision made to prevent respondents from simply clicking through the survey.[4] Without doing so, it is unlikely we would have received enough responses to analyze. The consequence is

---

4 Respondents could overvote. For each hypothetical election, about one-quarter of respondents overvoted. Fifteen percent of the sample, sixty-seven respondents, overvoted in all four elections. A closer inspection suggests these were individuals who clicked through the survey. Another 10 percent clicked a ranking twice. Like Alaska's current policy, we counted those ballots until the overvote occurred. Excluding overvotes, genuine or not, does not substantively affect the simulation results, and as we detail below, has a minimal impact on our cross-voting analysis.

that we overestimate the number of second and third choices selected by Nevadans. However, we suspect the overall cross-party voting trend we report later in the chapter to hold for three reasons. First, those most likely to exhaust their ballots are partisans who would not pick an out-party member as their second or third choice to begin with. Second, in actual elections, the percentage of exhausted ballots in each round of counting tends to be low. For instance, in the 2022 Alaska US House of Representatives election, only six percent of voters exhausted their ballots in the third and final round of voting (Alaska Division of Elections 2022). Finally, we verified our substantive results are consistent with scenarios where some Nevadans exhaust their ballots by conducting simulations where we removed some respondents' choices and instead counted them as blank after they selected between one and four candidates. Simulations that include exhausted ballots had no significant effect on the results we report below.

Fifth, throughout the rest of the chapter, we will use the terms moderate and extremist to describe candidates. For Democrats, we use the moderate label to describe individuals in the current party mainstream, or in Nevada parlance, the "Reid Machine." Extremists are those to the left, who generally support more progressive views, and are endorsed by interest groups like the Democratic-Socialists of America or Justice Democrats, who backed Bernie Sanders in the 2016 and 2020 presidential campaigns.

For Republicans, moderates are those largely associated with the Nevada Republican party's mainstream prior to 2016. Extremists are those who practice MAGA-style politics in the party. These individuals question the validity of the Nevada electoral system, heavily emphasize culture war issues, and often support right-wing conspiracy theories. We are quick to note that partisans may disagree with these labels. We merely use them to delineate the major factions in these parties.

The first election respondents vote in is generic. Candidates are denoted by their party and a prominent politician who endorsed them (e. g., a Democratic candidate endorsed by Barack Obama). This approach allows us to just use party ID and the endorsement as cues so we can evaluate broad questions, like whether a certain faction of Democrats or Republicans are more likely to engage in crossover voting.

We included fourteen first round primary options, which are listed in Table 9.2. In selecting major party candidates, we sought to include the most prominent politicians from a specific faction. For minor party candidates, we included the most recent presidential candidate. The slate of independent candidates included some running in the 2024 presidential election, a prominent media personality, and a well-known anti-government politician from Nevada. The other scenarios we analyze include real Nevada politicians running in hypothetical governor and US Senate races. The candidates we selected to advance to the second-round election are listed in Table 9.1. Due to space constraints, we do not list the first-round candidates or describe all of the other election scenarios here.[5]

Table 9.2: First round options in the generic election scenario.

A Democratic candidate endorsed by Barack Obama
A Democratic candidate endorsed by Bernie Sanders
A Democratic candidate endorsed by Joe Manchin
A Democratic candidate endorsed by Marianne Williamson
A Democratic-Socialist candidate endorsed by Alexandria Ocasio-Cortez
A Republican candidate endorsed by Donald Trump
A Republican candidate endorsed by Mitt Romney
A Republican candidate endorsed by Liz Cheney
A Libertarian candidate endorsed by Gary Johnson
An Independent-American candidate endorsed by Don Blankenship
An independent candidate endorsed by Cornel West
An independent candidate endorsed by Robert Kennedy, Jr.
An independent candidate endorsed by Joe Rogan
An independent candidate endorsed by Ammon Bundy

Simulating Elections

A common approach to analyzing an opinion poll is to weight it to create a representative sample and report a predicted winner. However, our interest is not in the outcome of a single election in a Top-5/RCV setting. We seek to understand this reform's likely consequences across many different electoral scenarios, especially if the state's politics shift more Democratic or Republican in the future.

As such, we adopt a simulation approach. First, we create weights for Democratic, Republican, and Independent respondents.[6] For any given simulation, between twenty-five and forty-five percent of the respondents can come from any of these three groups. We include a five percent weight for those who affiliate with minor parties. Once a series of weights have been drawn (e.g., thirty percent Democratic, thirty percent Republican, thirty-five percent Independent and five per-

---

5 The details for the hypothetical elections can be found in the Appendix of our initial working paper on this topic (https://papers.ssrn.com/sol3/papers.cfm?abstract_id=4808131) or by contacting the authors.
6 We do not group independent leaners with partisans. This reflects the political reality that about one-third of Nevadans do not affiliate with a political party, even if most vote similarly to registered partisans.

cent minor parties), we draw a corresponding sample of respondents. Within each group, every respondent has an equal chance of being drawn. Each draw includes seventy percent of our data or 318 respondents. Using this sample, we calculate who would advance to a general election as well as win among our five pre-selected finalists. We analyze 10,000 different partisan weights and draw 500 samples for each. In total, our analysis includes five million potential election outcomes.

As an example, the first partisan split we might analyze is thirty-three percent Democratic, thirty-three percent Republican, twenty-nine percent Independent, and five percent third parties. For that split's first draw, we randomly select 105 Democrats, 105 Republicans, ninety-two Independents, and sixteen third-party voters. Using those respondents, we record the Top-5 vote-getters in the primary and who would win the ranked choice general election. We record the results and redraw 499 more samples of our respondents using that same partisan split. We repeat this same process for 9,999 other partisan splits.

Many of these draws reflect an unlikely combination of Nevada voters. Since we only weight on partisanship, a good portion of these samples are unrepresentative of the electorate in some meaningful way. Is it possible that certain wings of the party, like Sanders' or Romney's endorsed candidates, receive no votes in a single draw? Yes. Even though that is not realistic, it reflects a potential political future that Nevada politics, with or without a final five system, might produce. Our goal is to assess the system's results under many different political scenarios, even those that might be viewed as unrealistic today.

Results

Primary Election

Our first set of analyses focus on the results from the four simulated Top-5 primaries our respondents were asked to vote in. Two of the three claims we are interested in here have to do with primaries: that top-5 primaries allow for multiple candidates from the same party to advance to the general election; and that third party and independent candidates are advantaged by this system. We can begin to address these claims using the aggregated results from our simulations, shown in Table 9.3. Percentages reflect the number of times the candidate advances to the general election divided by the total number of simulated election scenarios.

In all four elections, at least two candidates always secure spots in the general election. Not surprisingly, in every case, it includes the incumbents and most notable politicians in each race. For instance, the two major party candidates in the

Table 9.3: Percent of simulations in which a candidate reaches the general election.

Generic	Governor – 2022	Senate – 2024	Governor – 2026
Always	*Always*	*Always*	*Always*
Obama (D)	Collins (D)	Brown (R)	Ford (D)
Sanders (D)	Lombardo (R)	Rosen (D)	Lombardo (R)
Trump (R)	Sisolak (D)	Sandoval (R)	
Sometimes	*Sometimes*	*Sometimes*	
Kennedy, Jr. (I, 99.9%)	Bridges II (IAP, 99.9%)	Hansen (IAP, 91.7%)	*Sometimes*
Romney (R, 92.1%)	Heller (R, 99.5%)	Becker (R, 77.1%)	Flores (D, 99.9%)
Cheney (R, 6.9%)	Davis (L, 0.3%)	Harrison (I, 18.8%)	Goodman (I, 97.4%)
Ocasio-Cortez (das, 1%)	Whitley (R, 0.2%)	Segerblom (D, 7.4%)	Kirkpatrick (D, 96.9%)
Manchin (D – 0.01%)	Gilbert (R, 0.0008%)	Krause (D, 5%)	Tarkanian (R, 1.9%)
Never	Heck (R, 0.0007%)	Goicoechia (R,	Cox (R, 1.4%)
Blankenship (IAP),	*Never*	0.0002%)	Denis (D, 0.9%)
Johnson (L), Rogan (I),	Evans (R), Evertsen (R),	*Never*	Gilbert (R, 0.8%)
Bundy (I), West (I)	Hamilton (R), Lee (R),	Hardy (R), Krasner (R),	McCurdy II (D, 0.4%)
	Lusak (R), Nohra (R),	Hagan (L), Marchant	Rubison (IAP, 0.08%)
	O'Brian (R), Simon (R),	(R), Root (R)	Schieve (I, 0.002%)
	Walls (R), Zilberberg (R)		*Never*
			Cavanaugh (L), Fiore (R),
			Gansert (R)

Note: Percentages are based on how many simulations, out of 5 million, a candidate was among the top five vote-getters. Minor and independent party labels are: I: Independent; IAP: Independent American Party; L: Libertarian.

2022 Governor and 2024 Senate race always make the final five. The other candidates always securing spots in the general are not surprising. Both the Obama-endorsed and Sanders-endorsed candidates reflect a clear split in the Nevada Democratic party. Collins was the only other Democratic option for governor in 2022. Sandoval is arguably the most prominent Republican politician in the state besides the current governor.

The most notable aspect of these simulated primaries is how often the same five candidates would reach the general election. In the generic race, almost ninety-two percent of the time Nevadans would select between candidates endorsed by Obama, Sanders, Trump, Kennedy Jr., and Romney. In an astounding ninety-nine and ninety-seven percent of simulations, the same five politicians advance in the governors' races. The Senate race is the least predictable, but even then, seventy-seven percent of simulations include the same group.[7]

The first claim, that Top-5 primaries allow for multiple candidates from the same party to advance to the general election, presents mixed results. Table 9.4 shows the percentage of situations where two Democrats or Republicans advance to the general election. In two cases—Democrats in the Senate race and Republicans in the 2026 Governor race—this does not frequently occur. The explanation is straightforward: partisans coalesce around the incumbent. Collins in 2022 is an exception but he is not a liberal ideological alternative to Sisolak that could represent the progressive wing of the party.

Table 9.4: Percentage of simulations in which top two Democratic/Republican candidates advance.

	Generic	Governor, 2022	Senate, 2024	Governor, 2026
% Top Ranked Democrat Makes General	100% (Obama)	100% (Sisolak)	100% (Rosen)	100% (Ford)
% Top Ranked Republican Makes General	100% (Trump)	100% (Lombardo)	100% (Brown)	100% (Lombardo)
% 2nd Ranked Democrat Makes General	100% (Sanders)	100% (Collins)	7.4% (Krause)	99.9% (Flores)
% 2nd Ranked Republican Makes General	92.1% (Romney)	99.5% (Heller)	100% (Sandoval)	1.9% (Tarkanian)

Even if we assume that the more extreme wings would coordinate to support a single candidate to challenge the incumbent and perfect substitution between the first choices in our primary elections, the incumbents still crowd out their co-partisans. For instance, even if progressives coordinated around either extremist in the 2024 hypothetical Senate primary, a more liberal candidate would only advance to the general 12.5 percent of the time. Similarly, a single Republican challenger to Governor Lombardo in 2026, assuming all those votes were aggregated together, only advances in four percent of the simulations.

In almost all our simulations, a third-party or independent candidate made the final five. In all four scenarios, at least one of these candidates was among

---

7 Even with these consistent general election matchups, the make-up of the electorate affects who is likely to advance to the general election. In the Appendix, we include plots that show who would advance to the general election as the electorate becomes more Democratic.

the most frequent candidates to advance to the general election. However, no one from this group always advanced. As such, unlikely scenarios occur where the only five general election candidates are Democrats or Republicans. For instance, in the 2.6 percent of cases Oscar Goodman (I) does not make the 2026 Governor general election, he is almost always replaced with a Republican candidate. In those instances, the ballot would feature three Democrats and two Republicans.

On balance, our analysis suggests that a Top-5 system would lead to multiple Democrats and Republicans on the general election RCV ballot. However, incumbents will likely crowd out challengers from their party. In those elections, the most likely outcome is a 1–3–1 partisan breakdown, with one incumbent from a major party, three challengers from the other major party, and one minor party or independent candidate. Our generic election scenario is the only one without an incumbent but overwhelmingly suggests a statewide race would see two Democrats and two Republicans advance to the general election. Given Nevada's current partisan breakdown, third-party and independent candidates would, on average, be disadvantaged by this system. They will likely be relegated to fighting over one slot in the final five.

General Election

Next, we analyze whether moderates are more likely to win in a ranked choice general election. Recall that we selected the five candidates in our hypothetical elections with the goal of balancing realism with allowing us to test whether a moderate or more extreme Democrat or Republican would win.

In our survey, respondents voted in the same way they would in a real Top-5 general election and we counted ballots just as the state would. We follow the same sampling method we previously outlined, where we randomly draw a weighted seventy percent of our respondents based on their partisanship to simulate different potential electorates. The results reported below again include 5,000,000 simulations (10,000 partisan splits with each split having 500 random draws).

Figure 9.1 plots the proportion of elections a candidate wins in the 2022 Governor election, the closest race of our four hypothetical scenarios, as the percentage of Democrats in our simulations change. The results highlight familiar dynamics in recent Nevada politics, with the Democrat winning more often. However, as the electorate becomes less Democratic, the Republican's chances improve. This reflects recent statewide elections, which have been very close but where Republicans have tended to be less successful. The other three general election scenarios produce similar results.

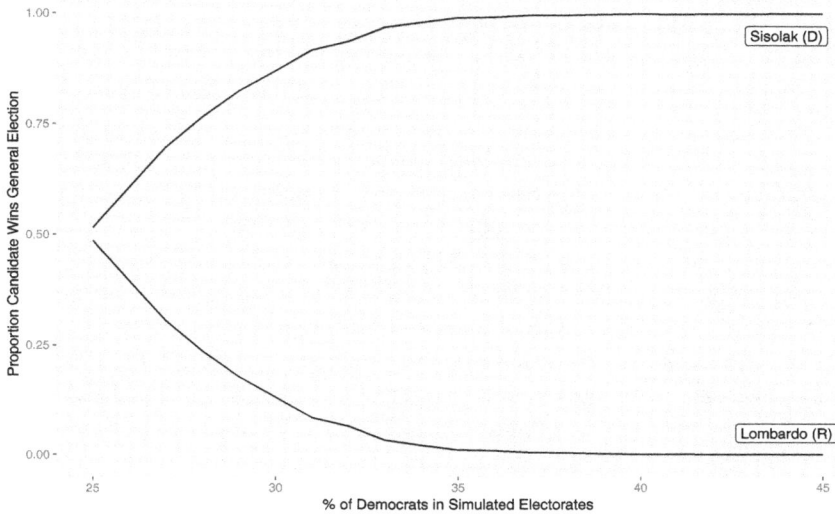

Figure 9.1: Percentage of simulations 2022 Democratic Gubernatorial candidate wins general election, as electorate changes.

Additionally, we consistently find that incumbents and the more moderate candidates win in the general election. The 2022 governor race returns the two candidates who ran in the general election, both mainstream politicians, and not the MAGA-aligned challenger. In the 2024 hypothetical Senate race, the mainstream Democratic incumbent or the moderate Republican (Sandoval) almost always win. However, in a handful of simulations with very Republican-leaning electorates, the much more extreme Republican candidate (Marchant) wins.

The hypothetical 2026 Governor's race is similar. The incumbent (Lombardo) runs against the current, and mainstream, Democratic Attorney-General (Ford). Notably, this race includes another mainstream Democrat (Kirkpatrick) and a well-known independent candidate (Goodman). Neither ever win. The generic election produces a consistent result of the Obama-backed candidate always winning. This is because in the general election, that candidate receives forty-two percent of the first-choice votes. This is likely attributed to Obama being popular in Nevada but also him being a politician no longer running for or holding office. We suspect placing a Biden or Harris-backed candidate would yield different results.

Although these results point to a Top-5/RCV system benefiting moderates, there are important limits imposed by the real world that make drawing a strong conclusion difficult. In particular, Joe Lombardo secured Donald Trump's endorsement in 2022, which we repeat in our hypothetical 2026 election. Lombardo is not a MAGA-styled Republican, and this relationship is often viewed as one of convenience for both. The consequence is that realism limits our ability to present a credible, Trump-backed alternative in the 2026 race.

In the Senate race, the more moderate Sandoval has a much higher profile than Marchant. This disparity in name-recognition likely stacks the deck in his favor. Finally, in the 2026 governor race, we do not include a DSA-aligned candidate. Our expectation was that two party-aligned Democrats would make the general election. Based our results in Table 9.3, we were right. However, we included a MAGA-aligned candidate instead of a DSA candidate, which our primary results suggest is an unlikely combination. The upshot is that we cannot evaluate how a more progressive politician would fare in that hypothetical race.

Even with these caveats, by far the most common outcome is the mainstream or more moderate candidates from both parties do well. Additionally, the simulated results seemingly produce Democratic victories more often than the current system. Importantly, this cannot result from our respondent pool being too Democratic. The simulations subset on partisanship, so a hypothetical election with only twenty-five percent Democratic turnout would represent a significant Republican wave election. In recent elections, this sort of electorate has brought resounding Republican wins. Although the simulations still imply Republicans would be competitive during red wave years, the fact their candidate never wins a majority of the simulations suggests a partisan effect in the general election.

Crossover Voting

Finally, we assess a third claim, one which applies only to the general election. Recall that some advocates of RCV general elections have argued that crossover voting would advantage moderates over extremists. In order to address this claim, we focus here on voters' second and where necessary third choices, and not the factors that predict crossover voting per se. In Table 9.5 we examine voters' second choices, conditional on their first selection.[8] To do so, we consider everyone who, for example, selected a more moderate first choice in the generic election (i. e., Obama-endorsed and Romney-endorsed candidates). Then, we categorize who their second-choice candidates were. In doing so, we contextualize whether

---

8 This analysis includes overvotes. We choose to include them since some occur after the Top-2 rankings. However, excluding all overvotes from a hypothetical election only produces small changes in the percentages and does not change the substantive findings.

crossover voting benefits moderates and whether it comes at the expense of the more extreme candidates.

The most common second ranking, no matter the first-place candidate, goes to the candidate in the same party. Crossover voting never overwhelms voters' partisan preferences. However, crossover voting, with one exception, in the 2022 Governor simulation,[9] always benefits the other party moderate more than the other party extremist. This pattern persists, and is much more important, when we take a more expansive view of crossover voting by analyzing who a voter ranks third after exhausting the candidates from a single party. We examine the scenarios where a voter can rank a major party candidate first and second. This situation assesses whether Democrats/Republicans prefer the other party moderate or extremist if their party's options are eliminated. Table 9.6 shows that in four out of five cases, those who rank candidates from a single party as their top two choices are more likely to rank the out-party moderate, not the extremist, third.

Nevada Democrats, when choosing between MAGA-aligned politicians or the Republican old guard, are overwhelming likely to select the old guard candidate. Republican voters reflect a similar but less dramatic pattern. They rank moderate Democrats third eight to ten percent more often than the extremist in the generic and 2026 governor race. The 2024 Senate race stands out as an exception. There, voters who selected the Republican candidates first and second slightly preferred the Democratic extremist (Segerblom) over the moderate (Rosen).[10]

Taken together, our analysis indicates that crossover voting in a Top-5/RCV system will help moderates, not extremists. This principally occurs when voters run out of co-partisans to vote for. At that point, assuming they do not exhaust their ballot, they are much more likely to select the out-party moderate. For this reason, out-party moderates overperform under RCV and are ranked second or third far more often than out-party extremists.

---

9 We suspect this reflects Democrats' dislike of the two more mainstream, and higher profile, Republicans: Lombardo (who beat Sisolak) and Heller, a former US Senator. Since Democrats could not exhaust their ballots, they may have been inclined to select the lesser-known Gilbert, even though he aligned with the MAGA wing of the party.

10 One possibility is that Rosen was running as an incumbent for that Senate seat. Republican reluctance to rank her third instead of Segerblom may reflect a protest ranking as her candidacy is at the top of mind for more Republican voters.

Table 9.5: Crossover voting at RCV general election, by candidate type.

	% Second Choice	First to Second Place Choices
Generic Moderate Obama (D), Romney (R) Extremist Trump (R), Sanders (D)	61.3% Same Party Extremist 12.1% Other Party Moderate 10% Other Party Extremist	Obama/Romney → Sanders/Trump Obama ↔ Romney Obama/Romney → Trump/Sanders Sanders/Trump → Obama/Romney Sanders/Trump → Romney/Obama Trump ↔ Sanders
	46.5% Same Party Moderate 13.5% Other Party Moderate 9.5% Other Party Extremist	
Governor 2022 Moderate Lombardo (R), Heller (R), Sisolak (D) Extremist Gilbert (R)	53% Same Party Moderate 37% Other Party Extremist 29% Other Party Moderate 6.6% Same Party Extremist	Lombardo ↔ Heller Sisolak → Gilbert Lombardo/Heller ↔ Sisolak Lombardo/Heller → Gilbert Gilbert → Lombardo/Heller Gilbert → Sisolak
	23% Same Party Moderate 33.3% Other Party Moderate	
Senate 2024 Moderate Rosen (D), Sandoval (R) Extremist Segerblom (D), Marchant (R)	56% Same Party Extremist 19.4% Other Party Moderate 6% Other Party Extremist 49.5% Same Party Moderate 12.8% Other Party Moderate 6.4% Other Party Extremist	Rosen/Sandoval → Segerblom/Marchant Rosen ↔ Sandoval Rosen/Sandoval → Marchant/Segerblom Segerblom/Marchant → Rosen/Sandoval Segerblom/Marchant → Sandoval/Rosen Segerblom ↔ Marchant

Table 9.5 *(Continued)*

	% Second Choice	First to Second Place Choices
Governor 2026	62.6 % Same Party	Ford ↔ Kirkpatrick
Moderate	Moderate	Lombardo → Gilbert
Lombardo (R), Ford (D), Kirkpatrick	53.4 % Same Party Ex-	Ford/Kirkpatrick ↔ Lombardo
(D)	tremist	Ford/Kirkpatrick → Gilbert
	13.1 % Other Party	Gilbert → Lombardo
	Moderate	Gilbert → Ford/Kirkpatrick
Extremist	12.1 % Other Party Ex-	
Gilbert (R)	tremist	
	56.7 % Same Party	
	Moderate	
	13.3 % Other Party	
	Moderate	

Table 9.6: Crossover voting after exhausting partisan choices.

	% Other Party Moderate Ranked Third	% Other Party Extremist Ranked Third
Generic: Democratic (Obama/Sanders)	39.2 % (Romney)	8.1 % (Trump)
Generic: Republican (Trump/Romney)	22.4 % (Obama)	16.4 % (Sanders)
Senate 2024: Democratic (Rosen/Segerblom)	42.9 % (Sandoval)	6.1 % (Marchant)
Senate 2024: Republican (Sandoval/Marchant)	15.9 % (Rosen)	17 % (Segerblom)
Governor 2026: Democrat (Ford/Kirkpatrick)	21.1 % (Lombardo)	11.4 % (Gilbert)

Why Nevada's Top-5/RCV Initiative Failed in 2024

As a final question on our survey, we asked these approximately 450 Nevadans the following question: "Compared to the current way Nevadans vote, do you pre-fer this Top-5/ranked choice voting system?" Fifty-six percent said they did, including a significant percentage of Democrats (sixty-nine percent) and Independents (sixty-four percent). Republican support was much lower (thirty-seven percent), and to be clear, our survey sample is small. However, anything near this sort of partisan split, even in a year when Donald Trump won the state's presidential election, would have led the Top-5/RCV initiative to pass. But the second initiative ballot failed decisively. What happened?

We believe that two factors contributed to the initiative's failure. First, both political parties ran vote no campaigns. In particular, state Democrats argued that this reform would lead to one out of every twenty ballots being rejected, which is a rounded up figure from Alaska's 2022 election (Early 2022). Without either party, or at least some prominent politicians, supporting the reform, it faced an uphill battle.

Even with an unsupportive establishment, proposals to shake up politics, especially by reducing polarization, should be appealing to voters in Nevada or elsewhere. Yet, the yes campaign heavily emphasized the open primary, not ranked choice voting. The idea of more choices, including more moderates, on the ballot was never the campaign's emphasis. The lack of attempted persuasion on this point became apparent after Election Day. In post-mortem polling in Nevada and elsewhere, the concepts of ranked choice voting and a desire not to confuse voters were the top reasons cited for opposing these initiatives (West 2024). While it is likely the advocates' polling showed RCV as the weak spot of the reform, not making a case for it at all proved problematic. Instead, arguing that open primaries would somehow fix state politics, even as that part of the reform is the less consequential one (many polarized states have open primaries, after all), did not resonate. In fact, it may have backfired, especially in how the argument for open primaries was made in the Silver State. In his 2024 election predictions, longtime Nevada journalist, news editor, and political observer Jon Ralston (2024) summed up how Nevadans likely saw the Top-5/RCV question:

> Conventional wisdom says it should pass, as proponents have spent a fortune. But something tells me they have oversold and the foes have done enough to create fear of change and chaos. (The pro-[top-5/RCV] ads making it seem as if veterans are disenfranchised may be the most disingenuous ad I have seen in a long time. But maybe it will be rewarded.)

To the extent reformers will continue pursuing these reforms, our data and the 2024 election results in Nevada provide two lessons. On one hand, voters seem to like Top-5/RCV once they experience it, albeit in a simulated election. On the other hand, a lesson from 2024 is that the affirmative case must provide voters a clear vision of what the reform will do. Since most of the reform's effect comes in the second round, not the first, advocates ought to explain why ranking candidates is an improvement over the status quo. Additionally, as Ralston notes and the post-mortem polling shows (West 2024), the scare tactics from the no campaign in Nevada worked. Opponents will surely use similar arguments in the future, so reformers should plan accordingly. We will note that the no campaign's underlying message was that voters are not capable of handling ranked choice voting. Presumably when this is pointed out to voters, that one side thinks they are unable to check five boxes, such messaging will be less effective. But the argument needs to be made.

Discussion

In this chapter, we consider four common arguments about how a Top-5/RCV system may have changed electoral politics in the context of Nevada, a state that considered but ultimately rejected the reform in 2024. Even without a new voting system, Nevada is an interesting case to study as it is more politically competitive than other states that use or are considering similar electoral reforms, with demographics more like the country as a whole. Using a sample of registered voters and, from them, simulating millions of potential Nevada electorates, we find broad but not universal support for arguments made in support of Top-5/RCV.

On the one hand, we find general support for the claim that such a system allows for multiple major party candidates representing different Democratic and Republican factions to advance to the general election. Our simulations suggest this is likely to happen in most cases, except when an incumbent is on the ballot. In that scenario, the more common outcome is that three out-party candidates will run against the incumbent, who will be the only member of that major party. We also find support for the contention that moderates are more likely to prevail in a ranked choice general election. Broadly speaking, we find that this occurs and, as advocates often claim, that crossover voting is essential in facilitating moderates' success.

However, we find mixed evidence that a Top-5 system directly aids independent and third-party candidates. Although non-major party politicians almost always advance to the general election in our primary simulations, they never win a general election. The most frequent scenario only includes one independent or third-party candidate. Simulations with only Democrats and Republicans contesting the general election are more common than one with two independent/third party candidates. Right now, independents, the Independent American Party, and the Libertarian Party all have ballot access and regularly run candidates in Nevada. A Top-5 system would likely lead to fewer independent and third-party options at general elections.

However, this does not necessarily mean non-major party candidates are doomed. Top-5/RCV reduces the incentive for strategic voting that exists under the current system. A shift to it would allow independent voters and weak partisans to support candidates they otherwise might not when voting in a plurality system. Politically popular candidates running as independents or parties subsumed into the Democratic and Republican coalitions by electoral necessity (e. g., the Greens) may eventually emerge and win with enough genuine support. This presents an interesting trade-off. On balance, adopting this electoral reform will mean fewer non-major party candidates in the general election. Yet, it provides those minor party and independent politicians with a substantial support base a better, and frankly more realistic, chance of winning office.

Studies from overseas also suggest that RCV gives minor parties more influence over policymaking if they are part of de facto coalitions (Reilly 2021). While limiting for more quixotic candidates, minor parties with a strong support base can not only compete for office but also influence major parties seeking their supporters' rankings. In this way, Top-5/RCV would likely incentivize minor party and independent party politicians to build competitive electoral coalitions. This provides normative appeal to the reform, by presenting voters with non-Democratic and Republican options that have some chance of winning and, in turn, whose campaigns voters might consider more seriously.

Even as our findings consistently show that major party moderates are advantaged and independent/third party candidates are constrained by a Top-5 system, we provide two notes of caution in interpreting these results. First, our hypothetical statewide elections all include incumbents. Although the majority of statewide elections tend to include one, our analysis cannot directly speak to electoral dynamics in open seat races. More importantly, Nevada currently lacks a high-profile, electorally successful MAGA-aligned politician. Although Trump endorsed Joe Lombardo for governor, this was widely viewed as Trump selecting the likely primary winner.

Second, Nevada polls often underestimate MAGA-aligned voters and oversample Republicans who are skeptical of Trump. At least among Republicans, our data suggests this is not a problem. Trump rates as extremely popular with his partisans in our sample, while other Republicans who have fallen out of the party's favor in recent years do not. However, this may still underestimate Trump's popularity, as one-third of the Nevada electorate is not party affiliated and no benchmark exists to evaluate their partisan lean. As a result, the Democratic advantage we observe may be artificially high because our independent-leaning respondents are too liberal.

Together, these limitations suggest that a better known and liked MAGA Republican and a more MAGA Republican electorate would likely be more electorally successful than our simulations show. Unfortunately, without an actual Nevada politician to include in our analysis, we can only speculate on whether our results paint an overly optimistic scenario for moderates.

Even with these caveats, this study provides multiple contributions to this growing research area. Instead of examining single elections, our simulation approach allows us to consider many possible electoral scenarios in a state where partisan turnout is highly volatile. By evaluating multiple hypothetical elections, we are able to highlight which contextual elements affect how Top-5/RCV will operate. Finally, our results open the door to other questions. We do not analyze open-seat races or highly gerrymandered legislative districts. We only include candidates with reasonably high political profiles. How this system would operate in a state legislative race with candidates who have minimal name recognition in an area with a strong partisan lean is an important question we do not evaluate. Examining a wider array of race types will help political scientists and voters better understand what may happen in a final five system, which will become a critical question if a state adopts it in the coming years.

Bibliography

Ahler, Douglas J., Jack Citrin, and Gabriel S. Lenz. 2016. "Do Open Primaries Improve Representation? An Experimental Test of California's 2012 Top-Two Primary." *Legislative Studies Quarterly* 41 (2): 237–268. https://doi.org/10.1111/lsq.12113.

Alaska Division of Elections. 2022. *RCV Detailed Report, General Election.* https://www.elections.alaska.gov/results/22GENR/rcv/US-REP.pdf.

Anderson, Sarah E., Daniel M. Butler, Laurel Harbridge-Yong, and Renae Marshall. 2023. "Top-Four Primaries Help Moderate Candidates via Crossover Voting: The Case of the 2022 Alaska Election Reforms." *The Forum* 21 (1): 123–136. https://doi.org/10.1515/for-2023-2001.

Cerrone, Joseph, and Cynthia McClintock. 2021. "Ranked-Choice Voting, Runoff, and Democracy: Insights from Maine and Other U.S. States." https://doi.org10.2139/ssrn.3769409.

Crosson, Jesse. 2021. "Extreme Districts, Moderate Winners: Same-Party Challenges, and Deterrence in Top-Two Primaries." *Political Science Research and Methods* 9 (3): 532–548. https://doi.org/10.1017/psrm.2020.7.

Drutman, Lee. 2020. *Breaking the Two-Party Doom Loop: The Case for Multiparty Democracy in America.* Oxford University Press.

Early, Wesley. 2022. "Alaska Rejected More Than 7,500 Ballots in the US House Special Primary. Here's Why." *Alaska Public Media.* https://alaskapublic.org/news/2022-06-29/alaska-rejected-more-than-7500-ballots-in-special-primary-election-heres-why.

Gehl, Katherine. 2023. "The Case for the Five in Final Five Voting." *Constitutional Political Economy* 34: 286–296. https://doi.org/10.1007/s10602-022-09386-6.

Grose, Christian R. 2020. "Reducing Legislative Polarization: Top-Two and Open Primaries Are Associated with More Moderate Legislators." *Journal of Political Institutions and Political Economy* 1 (2): 267–287. https://doi.org/10.1561/113.00000012.

Highton, Benjamin, Robert Huckfeldt, and Isaac Hale. 2016. "Some General Consequences of California's Top-Two Primary System." *California Journal of Politics and Policy* 8 (2): 1–12. https://doi.org/10.5070/P2cjpp8230564.

Hutchinson, Rachel and Benjamin Reilly. 2025. "Does Ranked Choice Voting Promote Legislative Bipartisanship? Using Maine as a Policy Laboratory." *The Forum* 22 (4): 567–584.

Ladam, Christina, Jeremy Gelman, and Carey Stapleton. 2023. "Modern Polling Modalities: A Descriptive Analysis." Presented at the Midwest Political Science Association Conference: Chicago, Illinois.

Leven, Rachel, and Tyler Fisher. 2023. *Alaska's Election Model: How the Top-Four Nonpartisan Primary System Improves Participation, Competition, and Representation.* Unite America Institute. https://www.uniteamericainstitute.org/research/alaskas-election-model-how-the-top-four-non-partisan-primary-system-improves-participation-competition-and-representation.

Lublin, David, and Benjamin Reilly. 2023. "Encouraging Cooperation and Responsibility." *Protect Democracy.* https://protectdemocracy.org/work/encouraging-cooperation-and-responsibility/.

McBeath, Jerry. 2023. "Alaska Electoral Reform: The Top 4 Primary and Ranked-Choice-Voting." *California Journal of Politics and Policy* 15 (1). https://doi.org/10.5070/P2cjpp15160079.

McGhee, Eric, and Boris Shor. 2017. "Has the Top Two Primary Elected More Moderates?" *Perspectives on Politics* 15 (4): 1053–1066.

Munger, Jr., Charles. 2019. "California's Top-Two Primary: A Successful Reform." *USC Schwarzenegger Institute.* https://schwarzenegger.usc.edu/institute_in_action/californias-top-two-primary-a-successful-reform/.

Nunan, Richard. 2020. "As Maine Goes, So Goes the Nation? Ranked Choice Voting and STV as Antidotes to Tribal Populism." In *Democracy, Populism, and Truth*, edited by Mark Christopher Navin and Richard Nunan, 145–160. Springer. https://doi.org/10.1007/978-3-030-43424-3_11.

Ralston, Jon. 2024. "Editor Jon Ralston's 2024 Nevada Election Predictions." *The Nevada Independent.* https://thenevadaindependent.com/article/editor-jon-ralstons-2024-nevada-election-predictions.

Reilly, Benjamin. 2021. "Ranked Choice Voting in Australia and America: Do Voters Follow Party Cues?" *Politics and Governance* 9 (2): 271–279. https://doi.org/10.17645/pag.v9i2.3889.

Reilly, Benjamin, David Lublin, and Rachel Leven. 2022. "Final-Five Voting: Comparative Evidence on a Novel Election System." *The Institute for Political Innovation:* 1–20.

Reilly, Benjamin, David Lublin, and Glenn Wright. 2023. 'Alaska's New Electoral System: Countering Polarization or "Crooked as Hell"? *California Journal of Politics and Policy* 15 (1). https://escholarship.org/uc/item/5k75w7xw.

Santucci, Jack. 2018. "Maine Ranked-Choice Voting as a Case of Electoral-System Change." *Representation* 54 (3): 297–311. https://doi.org/10.1080/00344893.2018.1502208.

Schwarzenegger, Arnold, and Ro Khanna. 2018. "Don't Listen to the Establishment Critics. California's Open Primary Works." *Sacramento Bee.* https://www.sacbee.com/opinion/article213415464.html.

Tolbert, Caroline J., ed. 2021. "The Promise and Peril of Ranked Choice Voting." *Politics and Governance* 9 (2): 265–270. https://doi.org/10.17645/pag.v9i2.4385.

Troxler, Howard. 2010. "Let the Top Two Run, Regardless of Party?" *Tampa Bay Times.*
    https://www.tampabay.com/archive/2010/06/13/let-the-top-two-run-regardless-of-party/.
West, Darrell M. 2024. *The Future of the Instant Runoff Election Reform.* Brookings Institution.
    https://www.brookings.edu/articles/the-future-of-the-instant-runoff-election-reform/.
Williamson, Ryan. 2023. "Evaluating the Effects of the Top-Four System in Alaska." *R Street Shorts*
    122: 1–7.
Wright, Glenn, Benjamin Reilly, and David Lublin. 2025. "Assessing Alaska's Top-4 Primary and
    Ranked Choice Voting Electoral Reform: More Moderate Winners, More Moderate Policy."
    Journal of Political Institutions and Political Economy 6 (1): 59–84. http://dx.doi.org/10.1561/113.
    00000117.

Jesse M. Crosson
Chapter 10
An Affirmative Case for the Top-2 Primary

Over the past several years, election reform in general and primary reform in particular have enjoyed considerable momentum. As Chapters 7, 8, and 9 of this volume discuss, reform advocates have scored major victories in states like Maine and Alaska, as well as major cities like New York City, San Francisco, Washington, D.C., and St. Louis—to name only a few. With Americans increasingly dissatisfied with the polarization and conflict that characterizes modern politics, the moment seems ripe for adopting reforms that might improve accountability linkages and rein in extremism.

Nevertheless, during the 2024 elections, reform efforts encountered some noteworthy setbacks. While the Top-4/Ranked-Choice Voting (RCV) system in Alaska survived a challenge, reform efforts in states like Arizona, Colorado, Idaho, Missouri, Montana, Nevada, Oregon, and South Dakota all fell short (Lieb 2024). Given the recency of these defeats, researchers and commentators still have considerable work ahead to better explain why these efforts failed. However, more than a few analysts have expressed fears that these failures share a common factor: a sense that electoral reform is now perceived as a left-leaning cause du jour—or, worse, a liberal ploy to influence election outcomes.

Inasmuch as voters hold such a position, however misguided, reform efforts are likely to face serious headwinds in the future—especially in Republican-leaning states. This is especially problematic, given that the majority of U.S. states are majority Republican. How, then, might primary reformers proceed? While reformers may well find ways to repackage reforms like RCV and improve public perceptions, I make a case here that one successful, existing reform—the Top-2 primary—deserves a more prominent place among reformers' preferred systems. As I detail below, the Top-2 primary exhibits effectiveness against extremism, operational reliability and practicality, and political feasibility, rendering it an excellent and underappreciated choice for primary reform moving forward.

Effectiveness: The Top-2 Meets its Aims

Largely speaking, the stated goals of the Top-2 when introduced in Washington were similar to those cited in other reform efforts: reformers sought to reduce polarization, enhance accountability, and increase participation. Reformers in

Washington in particular responded to voters who were incensed that they were forced to "pick a ballot" for the first time in seventy years, when a court order led them to replace their blanket primary system with a more typical open primary setup. Seeing the successes of Washington's long-time blanket primary, California sought to copy this system for itself, via Proposition 198 in 1996—a move characterized by political scientists Bruce Cain and Elisabeth Gerber as a political "earthquake" in their edited volume on the change (Cain and Gerber 2002). California's political parties agreed with this characterization and successfully challenged the new law in court, winning a 7–2 decision, as detailed in *California Democratic Party v. Jones (2000)*. In what seemed a decisive blow for advocates of "nonpartisan" primaries, the Supreme Court ruled that participation by non-members in a party's primary violated the party's associational rights.

In response to Washington voters' dismay, and undeterred by the court's decision, Washington's Republican Secretary of State Sam Reed and his allies at the Washington State Grange responded by conceptualizing and promoting a ballot initiative to establish the Top-2 system. Under the system, all candidates for an office compete against one another in a single "primary" election. The top two vote-getters then advance to the general election, regardless of party affiliation. As a result, and similar to the blanket primary originally in place in Washington since the 1930s, voters do not face a need to pick the Republican or Democratic primary. Unlike the blanket primarily, however, Republicans can now face Republicans and Democrats can now face Democrats in the general election. Washington's voters voted in favor of the Top-2 primary in the mid-2000s, and it was implemented in 2008—this time withstanding another court challenge in *Washington State Grange v. Washington State Republican Party* (this time succeeding by a 7–2 vote). Thereafter, just as it had with the blanket primary in the 1990s, California opted to institute Washington's primary system as well, with the Top-2 taking effect in 2012.

As I summarize here, although the system was initially met with skepticism—and challenged extensively in the court system—multiple studies have shown that the Top-2 primary has met its aims. That is to say, the Top-2 provided a path to victory for more moderate candidates, and it has increased primary election turnout over the past decade.

The Top-2 Encourages More Moderate Winners

With respect to limiting extremism and reducing polarization, the logic of the reform is quite straightforward. In typical primary systems across the country, partisan-homogenous legislative districts produce legislators who are, effectively, unaccountable to the general electorate and instead must anticipate how their narrow primary electorates will respond to their actions in office. As multiple chapters in this volume, and countless other pieces of scholarship, have underscored, these dynamics create considerable pressures for legislators to behave in an ideologically extreme fashion. Further still, as scholars such as Danielle Thomsen (2017) have underscored, these conditions can discourage the emergence of moderate candidates altogether.

The Top-2 system fundamentally alters these dynamics via two mechanisms. First, by joining primary elections into a single first-round election, candidates face first-round incentive structures that more closely approximate those of a typical general election—not a single-party primary election. That is to say, with multiple candidates competing all across the left-right spectrum, vying for a small subset of ideological voters is no longer the only viable strategy for advancing to the general election. Indeed, even within the Republican and Democratic coalitions, candidates can find ways to differentiate themselves from one another besides simply appealing to ideological purity. To be clear, this does not mean that candidates will take advantage of these multiple paths to victory: the forces of nationalization (Grumbach 2022; Hopkins 2018) and affective polarization (Iyengar et al. 2019) provide strong reason for candidates to make strong within-party appeals, regardless of the availability of other appeals. However, the Top-2 at the very least provides the opportunity for other appeals—including cross-partisan appeals—to be made.

The second key mechanism behind the Top-2 does not rely upon candidates' first round strategies. Indeed, perhaps the most foundational feature of the Top-2 is that it allows for two candidates of the same party to compete against one another in the general election. In such cases, appeals to negative partisanship or affective polarization are unlikely to present significant advantages: candidates in same-party general-election contests compete against members of their own party—and their own party alone. How, then, can candidates appeal to voters? If we assume that one member of the party holds more moderate policy positions, such candidates should naturally run campaigns by appealing to centrist members of their own party—and even members of the "out" party. In such scenarios, the basic arithmetic of majority coalition-building suggests that the more centrist of the two candidates ought to prevail.

Given the straightforward and (I would argue) quite sound logic behind the Top-2, it is perhaps unsurprising that peer-reviewed scholarship on the Top-2 has generally confirmed the depolarizing effects of the reform, particularly as the system has matured. Even for the early years of the reform, my own research showed that when same-party competition occurs in the general election, more moderate candidates win election to office. As Sam Reed himself described in private communications to his copartisans in the legislature, an important goal of the system was to engender same-party competition in deep blue (and deep red—though, naturally, he didn't emphasize this point) districts. Doing so would allow for the election of more moderate Democrats, with whom he believed Republicans could work productively in the legislature (Crosson 2020). The Top-2 appeared to have delivered—at least in part—on that promise.

A key challenge for the system, however, lay in the occurrence of same-party contests: as my research also found, such competition occurred much less frequently in reality that it ought to have statistically. Thus, my work suggested that the moderating impacts of the Top-2 were blunted, and that future research should examine whether these dynamics abated in future elections. Although no studies have, to my knowledge, returned to the question of same-party competition frequency, other research did incorporate more election studies into their analyses. Perhaps due to elites gaining experience with the new system and better anticipating moderating incentives, these later studies uncovered more widespread moderating effects for the system. Barton (2023), for instance, found that winners in California were more moderate than non-Top-2 counterparts. Likewise, Grose (2020) has found that the Top-2 led to more moderates across political parties. This has been particularly true in California, which had not enjoyed the seventy-year cumulative effects of the blanket primary like Washington had prior to the Top-2.

The Top-2 Encourages Primary Election Participation

For years, scholars and reformers have pointed to low participation as a defining —and concerning—feature of primary elections. In addition to its moderating effects, the Top-2 has also begun to address reformers' low-participation concerns. In the most rigorous study on nonpartisan primaries and turnout to date, Micatka et al. (2024) show that voters in nonpartisan primary states (which include Top-2 primary states) are twelve percentage points more likely to turn out for primary elections than similar voters in other states. These differences are most pronounced for independents and moderates—two groups most put off by pick-a-ballot and (especially) closed primary systems. This evidence is consistent with work on the Top-2 primary specifically. Hill (2022), for instance, found that the introduction of the Top-2 led to a significant increase in voter turnout in California.

From the voter's perspective, it is no mystery why turnout might increase under the Top-2 primary. First and foremost, the Top-2 by definition exhibits no party registration requirements: since voters do not have to select a party ballot, they can participate without concern for party affiliation. Indeed, voting during the Top-2 "primary" is more akin to voting in a typical general election than a typical primary. Voters need not even "know" that much of anything has changed relative to, say, an open primary. They simply select the candidate they would most like to advance to the general election.

Second, voters enjoy true choice in the Top-2 (much as they do in Alaska's Top-4): that is, they need not decide between "conservative" and "ultra conservative" in a Republican primary, or "progressive" and "ultra progressive" in a Democratic primary, as discussed above. Even if voters behave as consistent partisans in today's climate, a third of voters still identify as "independent." The Top-2 primary provides such voters an opportunity to actually pursue the common refrain of "voting for the person and not the party." Whether they do so, of course, remains an empirical question, but a single first-round primary can appeal to those who fashion themselves as "person-first" voters.

A Radical Effect Without Radical Change

Together, the logic—and proven results—of the Top-2 primary leaves reformers with a terrific option for effecting real change. At base, the Top-2 requires only one change to most existing political systems: replacing open/closed primaries with a single, first-round election. The timing of that election can remain the same, and, indeed, the administration of such elections are in many ways simpler than the status quo across the U.S. Moreover, the general election remains the same, both from an administrative perspective and the perspective of the voter: voters select from two "main" candidates vying for victory in November. Voters need not rank candidates, learn about a larger number of candidates, nor think through a strategy for ranking such candidates. They simply cast one vote in the primary and one in the general—the same as many Americans already do.

At the same time, this seemingly small change upends the logic of modern-day American campaigns. Instead of fleeing to the extremes of the political spectrum to win a primary—and then feigning some semblance of centrism during the general (if ever)—candidates must contend with the possibility that they will face an opponent from the same party in the general election. In such cases, simple partisan heuristics break down, and voters must decide on some other basis—including actual policy extremism. Although more research is always warranted, existing empirical scholarship seems to suggest that such dynamics have encouraged moderation among election winners in Washington and California.

As I preface above, the real mechanism behind this success is not the behavior of voters in the majority party in a district. Rather, more moderate candidates can emerge victorious by appealing to voters from the minority party in their district.

In the next section, I underscore how underappreciated this point (and several related to it) has gone in recent years—and how crucial it is if designers of electoral systems wish for their reforms to have effects in the "real world."

Operational Practicality: the Top-2 and the Reality of Voting and Candidate Emergence

The Top-2 primary system meets the base requirements that one should want in a reform: it builds upon a sound logic to meet its ends, and it exhibits actual effectiveness when subject to empirical tests. I am by no means the first to highlight these features. However, I believe the Top-2's success rests on several underappreciated features that not only drive its effectiveness but also render it more likely to succeed across a variety of settings. In particular, the Top-2 leverages more reliable, habitual voters than do systems like open primaries, and it does not rest on potentially unrealistic assumptions about candidate emergence, like Top-4 or Top-5 alternatives.

The Top-2 Leverages Habitual Voting

The first of these features is the means by which the Top-2 builds upon—instead of trying to reinvent—some well-documented "fundamentals" about voter behavior. One major criticism of systems like ranked-choice voting is their complexity, both for voters and election administrators (e. g., Donovan et al. 2022). By contrast to RCV and hybrid systems like the one in Alaska, as I have already argued, the Top-2 is comparatively simple: voters merely select their preferred candidate, and the two candidates with the most votes advance to the general election. This simplicity eliminates the risk of voter error associated with ranking choices incorrectly or leaving portions of the ballot blank. To the voter, in fact, the ballot looks mostly identical to the ones they have encountered for years—meaning that worries about voter confusion or "fear-mongering" (e. g., The Oregonian 2024) are unlikely to threaten voter turnout.

In fact, beyond the simplicity of the system, and perhaps even more importantly, the Top-2 does not require increases in turnout to function effectively. Indeed, unlike reforms like more traditional open primaries that hinge on mobilizing new or independent voters—who are notoriously difficult to predict—the Top-2 leverages habitual voters to drive its moderating effects. More specifically, it makes use of "orphaned" voters as a means for encouraging moderation. In modern-day U.S. politics, millions of Americans are considered "orphaned" within our geographically polarized legislative districts. By "orphaned," political scientists simply mean that millions of voters rarely, if ever, have an opportunity to sincerely vote for the winning candidate in their district or state (Fisk 2020; Noel 2023). By identifying with the "out" party in one of the hundreds of deeply uncompetitive districts (and states) found across the U.S., such voters can go years without any reasonable expectation that their preferred candidate will emerge victorious.

That orphaned voters turn out on Election Day at all is remarkable: individuals who show up to the polls expecting to lose clearly draw upon non-instrumental reasons to motivate their turnout. Such voters, in fact, are emblematic of a core finding in the study of political participation: the greatest predictor of voter turnout is whether or not a given voter has turned out in the past (e.g., Gerber et al. 2003). Rather than turning out to ensure their candidate will win the election, considerable numbers of orphaned voters are "habitual voters," as scholars refer to them—turning out highly reliably, regardless of context.

The Top-2 makes considerable use of habitual orphaned voters. Whereas such voters exert little influence over general elections in lopsided districts, the Top-2 renders them pivotal: should two candidates from the same party advance to the general election, the Top-2 relies upon these voters to ensure that the more moderate of the two candidates will prevail. Indeed, even if out-partisans represent only twenty percent of likely voters, candidates ignore a constituency of this size at their own peril. Moreover, even in cases where candidates avoid same-party competition in the general election, the threat of same-party competition—and the moderating influence of habitual orphaned voters—generates incentives for candidates to pay attention to orphaned voters in a way they rarely do under "normal" circumstances.

Millions of orphaned voters live outside the states of California and Washington. They include Republican voters in deep blue cities and Democratic voters in the ruby red countryside. In fact, by some estimates, approximately one in three voters are partisan orphans, at least at the federal level (Noel 2023). An under-appreciated genius of the Top-2, then, is that the system builds upon the remarkable voting habits of these voters, granting them agency that they so desperately lack under the status quo in most U.S. states.

It is important not to overstate the voting habits of orphaned voters. Some research has shown, in fact, that the turnout of out-party voters declines when a general election features two candidates of the same party (Fisk 2020). In such cases, it seems reasonable to conclude that voters derive some psychological or symbolic benefit from voting for a candidate of their own party, even when such votes are, effectively, wasted. Reformers certainly ought to weigh the normative and expressive value of such actions, as orphaned voters often do not appreciate the pivotality of the position they occupy in the Top-2 system. Nevertheless, as a practical matter, the strategic empowerment of orphaned voters remains a clever and, in my view, underappreciated feature of the Top-2 success.

The Top-2 Makes Reasonable Assumptions about Candidate Emergence

In addition to building upon well-established fundamentals about voting behavior, the Top-2 also builds upon empirical fundamentals of candidate emergence in American politics. To this point, one might argue that many or most of the benefits highlighted here apply to Top-4 (or higher) systems either in place or proposed elsewhere. Candidate emergence, however, represents a challenge for such systems—one for which the Top-2 is more robust than other reforms.

In his groundbreaking book on state legislative elections, Steve Rogers crystallizes a key fundamental about elections in state legislative politics: by his estimate, one in three races for state legislature are uncontested (Rogers 2023). Moreover, virtually all such uncontested races occur in precisely the partisan-homogenous districts that reformers wish to address. By contrast, Top 4-plus systems rely heavily on candidate emergence. Indeed, in order for such systems to encourage moderation via the centripetal forces of ranked-choice voting in the general election, the Top-4 presupposes considerable numbers of candidates in the first round. Rogers' observation—and years of research on state legislative politics in particular—suggests that four or more candidates are unlikely to emerge in many districts.

I do not mean to suggest that prospective candidates cannot respond to systems like the Top-4-plus by adjusting their behavior over time. It seems reasonable to expect that more candidates will run for office, even in one-sided districts, than presently do under more traditional primary-election systems. But it is also by no means guaranteed: the forces of incumbency advantage, for instance, are not specific to a particular primary election system. Such factors discourage candidate emergence for the same reasons in a closed primary as they might in the Top-4-plus. And if fewer than four candidates run in the primary—guaranteeing that they appear on the general election ballot—there is even less guarantee that the most moderate candidate will prevail. In fact, this is precisely the reason why reformers were correct to pair the Top-4 with centripetal voting rules like ranked-choice voting. While the nonpartisan nature of the Top-4 may encourage participation in primary elections (for reasons similar to the Top-2), it itself does not generate moderating incentives in the general election.

The Top-2, by contrast, places no special pressure on candidate emergence: in order to work, in fact, only two total candidates are necessary. Moreover, the Top-2 does not require a special voting rule in order to create centripetal results: voters cast a single vote for their preferred candidate in each of the two rounds, precisely as they do in nearly every other system across the country.

It is this latter point—that the Top-2 does not require a new voting rule—that leads me to the final advantage the Top-2 has over other reform alternatives: political feasibility.

Political Feasibility: The Top-2 is Not Known as a "Progressive" Reform

Electoral reforms must be more than just effective and practical: for a reform to ever see the light of day, it must be politically viable. The Top-2 primary provides at least three dimensions along which it is politically feasible—especially relative to more popular alternatives in reform circles, such as Ranked Choice Voting (RCV) and Top-4/5.

First, research has shown that voters most consistently support reforms that strike them as "more democratic" than the status quo (Boatright 2024). Indeed, while some political scientists pine for a time in which pragmatic, office-focused elites controlled nominations, voters simply do not support changes to primaries that involve restricting access, limiting choices, or, worst of all, eliminating existing elections. One need look no further than voters' responses to the "pick-a-ballot" primaries that Washington attempted to implement in the mid-2000s. Among many other spoiled (and returned) ballots compiled at the Washington State Archive, one voter likened being forced to choose a ballot to communism: "voters should have a choice—this is America not the SOVIET UNION" (emphasis original; Washington State Archive 2004). In point of fact, the open primary that Washington attempted to institute was far more expansive and democratic than most primary election systems across the U.S.

By expanding access to all voters in the first/primary election—and indeed, by not forcing voters to pick a ballot or otherwise reveal a partisan affiliation in any official capacity—the system no doubt meets the "more democracy" litmus test. For that reason alone, the Top-2 should be viewed as equally as viable as a variety of other, more "preferred" reform options.

Yet, there are reasons to believe that the Top-2 primary may enjoy higher levels of political viability than most other reforms. Unfortunately, as the aforementioned political challenges in 2024 have underscored, election reform faces a branding problem: increasingly, voters associate electoral reform with the Left. At worst, some Republicans have attempted to brand systems like RCV as a leftist ploy to control election outcomes. While such claims are nonsensical, it is nevertheless true that many electoral reforms are championed by leaders on the political Left. And indeed, prominent organizations on the Right, such as The Heritage Foundation, have aggressively sought to brand reforms like RCV as "a scheme to disconnect elections from issues and allow candidates with marginal support from voters to win" (von Spakovsky and Adams 2019, n.p.).

The Top-2 is fundamentally different in this regard. Indeed, were it not for one Republican leader—Washington Secretary of State Sam Reed—the reform likely would not exist in the first place. Secretary Reed helped to conceive of the system, but he also defended it time and again in court challenges. The adoption of the system itself underscores how it appealed to voters across the political spectrum: it was the Washington State Grange—hardly a member of the leftist elite—who sponsored and campaigned for the Top-2 system.

Even beyond the Republican roots of the Top-2 in Washington, its adoption in California was also marked by support from the center-right. Famously, Republican Governor Arnold Schwarzenegger advocated for the implementation of the Top-2 in California, but he was not alone among center-right political actors: the California Chamber of Commerce and business interests also supported the reform. Thus, in both Washington and California, high-profile Republicans and centrist or center-right interests played key roles in introducing and defending the reform. Indeed, far from being charged as a left-wing plot, early opponents of the Top-2 in Washington even went so far as to attack the reform as a clandestinely conservative reform, seeking to undercut it by associating the Top-2 with the "jungle" primary in Louisiana. Such efforts were so successful, in fact, that Secretary Reed and his allies intentionally avoided associating the Top-2 with the term "jungle primary." In short, the Top-2 exhibits a major, practical advantage over reforms like RCV, in that it has managed to avoid being branded as a progressive project.

Conclusions

In this chapter, I have sought to articulate an affirmative case for the Top-2 primary. As I have argued here, the Top-2 has not only effectively met its aims of moderation and increased primary election turnout, but it rests upon well-researched regularities of voter behavior and state legislative politics. Just as importantly, at a time when election reform runs the risk of being engulfed by the forces of polarization and issue politicization, the Top-2 provides reformers with a long bi-partisan history of support.

Despite these advantages, I do not mean to suggest that the Top-2 is without its own challenges. Some argue that it undermines partisan representation by en-abling same-party general election matchups, claiming that voters ought to have the right to vote for a party of their choosing in the general election. Given the U.S.'s long tradition of emphasizing candidates over parties—including parties oc-cupying no official place in the Constitution—such concerns do not seem to me to outweigh the benefits of the reform. But reformers and scholars alike certainly should weigh these costs, as same-party competition in the general election will always occupy a central role in the dynamics of the Top Two system.

Others may argue that voters struggle to make informed decisions without ex-plicit partisan cues. But while this may be true in the short term, it is not as though voters lack other sorts of cues entirely. Alternative heuristics—such as can-didate experience, local ties, and affiliations with interest groups—can provide voters with meaningful decision-making tools. Such developments could even in-troduce new dimensions into our rigid two-party system, potentially mitigating the "doom loop" that Drutman has forcefully highlighted (Drutman 2020).

While further debate on these issues is warranted, it seems worthwhile to rec-ognize the undeniable strengths of the Top-2. Unlike other reforms, it has demon-strated effectiveness, operational reliability, and political feasibility, and reform-ers should consider making the Top-2 a more central option in future reform efforts. The twin challenges of hyper-partisanship and deteriorating trust in democracy render electoral reform efforts all the more crucial in the coming years. Recent defeats ought to encourage reformers to reconsider the Top-2 as a system with both proven effectiveness and political tractability across a variety of settings.

Bibliography

Barton, Richard C. 2023. "California's Top Two Primary: The Effects on Electoral Politics and Governance Denver." *Unite America Institute.* search.issuelab.org/resources/42458/42458.pdf.

Boatright, Robert G. 2024. "Primary Elections." In *Electoral Reform in the United States: Proposals for Combating Polarization and Extremism*, edited by Larry Diamond, Edward B. Foley, and Richard H. Pildes, 179–220. Lynne Rienner Publishers.

Cain, Bruce E., and Elisabeth R. Gerber, eds. 2002. *Voting at the Political Fault Line: California's Experiment with the Blanket Primary.* University of California Press.

California Democratic Party v. Jones, 530 U.S. 567 (2000).

Crosson, Jesse. 2020. "Extreme Districts, Moderate Winners: Same-Party Challenges, and Deterrence in Top Two Primaries." *Political Science Research and Methods* 9 (3): 532–548. https://doi.org/10.1017/psrm.2020.7.

Donovan, Todd, Caroline Tolbert, and Samuel Harper. 2022. "Demographic Differences in Understanding and Utilization of Ranked Choice Voting." *Social Science Quarterly* 103 (7): 1539–1550. https://doi.org/10.1111/ssqu.13215.

Drutman, Lee. 2020. *Breaking the Two-Party Doom Loop: The Case for Multiparty Democracy in America.* Oxford University Press.

Fisk, Colin A. 2020. "No Republican, No Vote: Undervoting and Consequences of the Top Two Primary System." *State Politics & Policy Quarterly* 20 (3): 292–312. https://doi.org/10.1177/1532440019893688.

Gerber, Alan S., Donald P. Green, and Ron Shachar. 2003. "Voting May Be Habit-Forming: Evidence from a Randomized Field Experiment." *American Journal of Political Science* 47 (3): 540–550. https://doi.org/10.2307/3186114.

Grose, Christian R. 2020. "Reducing Legislative Polarization: Top Two and Open Primaries Are Associated with More Moderate Legislators." *Journal of Political Institutions and Political Economy* 1 (2): 267–287. https://doi.org/10.1561/113.00000012.

Grumbach, Jacob M. 2022. *Laboratories against Democracy.* Princeton University Press.

Hill, Seth J. 2022. "Sidestepping Primary Reform: Political Action in Response to Institutional Change." *Political Science Research and Methods* 10 (2): 391–407. https://doi.org/10.1017/psrm.2020.42.

Hopkins, Daniel J. 2020. *The Increasingly United States: How and Why American Political Behavior Nationalized.* University of Chicago Press.

Iyengar, Shanto et al. 2019. "The Origins and Consequences of Affective Polarization in the United States." *Annual Review of Political Science* 22 (1): 129–146. https://doi.org/10.1146/annurev-polisci-051117-073034.

Lieb, David A. 2024. "Voters Rejected Historic Election Reforms across the US, despite More than $100 m Push." *AP News.* apnews.com/article/ranked-choice-voting-open-primaries-election-re-form-bc797f209e5f98a18afb2e5f784e63b6.

Micatka, Nathan K., Caroline J. Tolbert, and Robert G. Boatright. 2024. "All Candidate Primaries, Open Primaries, and Voter Turnout." *Journal of Political Institutions and Political Economy* 5 (3): 363–385. https://doi.org/10.1561/113.00000105.

Noel, Hans. 2023. "How Parties Affect Democracy by Redirecting Resources to Competitive Districts." Midwest Political Science Association Annual Meeting, April 2023, Chicago, IL.

Rogers, Steven. 2023. *Accountability in State Legislatures.* University of Chicago Press.

The Oregonian. 2024. "Readers Respond: Stop Fear Mongering about Ranked Choice Voting." *Oregonlive.* www.oregonlive.com/opinion/2024/10/readers-respond-stop-fear-mongering-about-ranked-choice-voting.html.

Thomsen, Danielle M. 2017. *Opting out of Congress: Partisan Polarization and the Decline of Moderate Candidates.* Cambridge University Press.

von Spakovsky, Hans, and J. Adams. 2019. "Ranked choice voting is a bad choice." *The Heritage Foundation.* www.heritage.org/election-integrity/report/ranked-choice-voting-bad-choice.

Washington State Archive. 2004. Constituent to Sam Reed. August 19, 2026. Olympia, WA.

Washington State Grange v. Washington State Republican Party, 552 U.S. 442 (2008).

Part III: **Future Directions and Alternative Reforms**

Hans Noel
Chapter 11
Politics is a Team Sport: Electoral Reform and Political Parties

The purpose of any electoral reform is to change the rules of the game so that the players are compelled to produce different outcomes. Different rules produce different strategies, and different strategies can produce different winners.

In politics, the game in question involves collective action. Voters and politicians form coalitions to achieve their goals—winning an election, passing legislation, enacting policy—or to prevent other coalitions from achieving theirs.

In short, politics is a team sport.

It's an unusual team sport, in which the teams (parties) are themselves fluid, created and recreated on the fly. There may be more than two, and players may have individual incentives at odds with their teams'. But modern democracy is shaped by the performance of those teams, which ones win and what they do with that victory. Many of the failures of modern democracy can be traced back to the inability or unwillingness of parties to play the roles they should.

Reform efforts, then, must at a minimum keep political parties in their vision. More than that, they should be aimed at helping parties do their job. And since parties are made up of individual political actors, reforms should encourage those actors, from politicians to voters, to create, maintain and participate in healthy parties. This is all the more important with reforms aimed at primary elections, since primaries are a tool parties use for their most central decision-making, choosing candidates.

America's political problems are too often diagnosed without reference to parties, or even casting parties as the villain. Polarization, which is centrally a party phenomenon, is presented as "too many extremists in office," rather than "parties are failing to reign in their extremists."

The rest of this chapter will lay out the argument for centering parties in the context of electoral reform, particularly reform of primary elections. Before we intervene in their primaries, we should understand the kind of parties we want. The first section explains how parties organize politics, with special attention to their relationship to ideology and polarization, in both government and in elections. The following section then asks what is necessary for parties to productively do that organizing, identifying some criteria that a party-healthy political system should meet. Together, those two sections shift the diagnosis from "extremism" to "party ineffectiveness." The last section then turns to the role of primary elections, comparing reforms that undermine parties with those that could help them be more effective.

Politics Relies on Parties

The prevailing diagnosis for what ails American politics is "polarization." Our politicians are "too extreme," and thus are unwilling to compromise.

This framing invokes the widely used spatial model of politics (Hotelling 1929; Downs 1957; Black 1958; Enelow and Hinich 1989; Hinich and Munger 1994). We can arrange political outcomes on an ideological spectrum, say from left to right, or liberal to conservative. Voters, politicians, and anyone else can be said to have preferences in that space. With a few more assumptions, we can draw a variety of inferences—the median voter will tend to get what they want, agenda setters can manipulate outcomes, and so on.

Because our understanding of polarization depends so much on this spatial metaphor, it's important that we understand its implications.

In the context of this spatial model, polarization could actually mean several things.[1] Reformers often want to avoid electing members with preferences far from the median voter. This is both because the positions taken are simply too far outside the range of acceptable politics, and also because more moderate members are thought to be better positioned to negotiate with one another.

Of course, there is little agreement on what the range of acceptable is. Yesterday's extreme goals (civil rights, gay marriage, the income tax) are today's status quo. Compromise may be desirable, but it should presumably be compromise from among the full range of opinion. That, in turn, implies a legislature that is representative of that full range of public opinion. A desire for more centrism should flow from a concern that the extreme positions are over-represented, not that they are represented at all.

The focus on extremism versus centrism is easy to confuse with other things that "polarization" can mean. We would call it polarization if the dimensions of politics are increasingly organized around two poles, or if the parties are more clearly sorted between those poles.[2] These forms of polarization do not imply increased extremism but more organization. A lot of the evidence we have of ideological polarization in America is of this type. Politicians or voters are not neces-

---

1 See Masket and Noel (2021, pp. 324–326) for a longer discussion. See also DiMaggio et al. (1996).
2 Some political scientists avoid the term "polarization" for what is "only" sorting. While they are different, sorting still leads to two distinct poles, and is actually closer to the metaphor of "polarized," in the sense that magnets or sunglasses are polarized.

sarily taking more extreme positions, but they are more sorted (Fiorina 2005; Baldassarri and Gelman 2008; Levendusky 2009; Houston 2024).

Meanwhile, political scientists have begun to document what they call "affective polarization" (Iyengar et al. 2012; Mason 2015; Levendusky and Malhotra 2016; Abramowitz and Webster 2016, 2018; Iyengar et al. 2019): the increasing tendency of people from different political camps to dislike and distrust the other side. That is a concern regardless of how "extreme" their policy positions are. Much of the recent alarm about growing incivility and gridlock is more closely related to affective polarization than to extremism in the spatial sense.

This perspective on polarization should make clear that it matters what elected officials, extreme or not, do in office. It is not enough to simply send more moderates to Washington. How will they organize, coordinate, and collaborate once they get there?

Political parties produce the answer to that question. Indeed, political parties are central in how polarization is realized in government, for good and for ill.

Among the relevant roles parties play are:

Communicate ideology: Most voters and even most politicians do not easily know where to position a policy alternative or politician in an ideological space. Which alternative is more conservative? Which candidate is more centrist? Since parties are creating and enforcing coalitions, their decisions provide the necessary information.

Shape ideology: What it means to be liberal and conservative is neither fixed nor certain. The process that determines what goes with what ideologically (Converse 1964) is complicated (Noel 2013), and the coalitions that parties shape play a major role.

Shape policy and procedural coalitions: Once elected, politicians need to bargain with one another to accomplish anything. The primary coalition they have to work with is partisan. The nature of that coalition is more important than any one legislator's own ideology.

Negotiate inter-party compromises: When the many players with many interests in the House, Senate, and White House need to hash out differences, not everyone can be in the room. High-level negotiations involve the majority and minority leadership in Congress, or the chair and ranking member of relevant committees. Parties speak for their members in shaping compromise.

Temper extremism: Party leaders manage intra-party compromise as well. In the legislature, party leaders must hold their coalition together in the face of possible defections from extremists and moderates alike. In nominations, party leaders hope to choose candidates who will have general election appeal in their respective districts.

Provide an avenue of accountability: Because legislating in a collective task, the most effective way to hold legislators accountable is to reward or punish the parties for what they do. Voters can reject incumbents, but they should make sure that their own incumbent is on the team that did the things they don't like. Kicking out a member of the minority for what the majority did would be counter-productive.

Political parties today play these roles, but they do not always play them well. Including parties in our understanding of political ills changes the diagnosis. The problem is not so much "polarization" as "dysfunctional parties"—parties that fail to check extremism or foster compromise.

The rest of this chapter looks more closely at the role that political parties play in governance and in elections, both when they are effective and when they are not.

Governing Relies on Parties

The U.S. Constitution makes no explicit provision for political parties, and so it is plausible to imagine our government without them. The Founders imagined elected officials, representing diverse geographic constituencies, would gather, deliberate, and govern without divisions. James Madison argued that the separation of powers and the large republic would prevent a "faction" of narrow interests from capturing control of the whole government.

It didn't take long for these factions to outmaneuver Madison. His mistake was to assume that since factions are inherently small, they were no match for institutions that empowered politicians to check one another. But as John Aldrich (1995) outlines, some factions teamed up with others and formed larger coalitions —political parties. Early legislators found that when they acted as a team, the members of those teams could do better than they would otherwise (see also Schwartz 1989).

The relative strength of these teams has waxed and waned, but they have always been present. Gary Cox and Mat McCubbins (1993) likened the unstructured House of Representatives to the Hobbesian state of nature, and argued that legislators would turn over some autonomy to a party leader who would serve the interests of those in the party. Leaders can reward and punish members with committee seats and legislative concessions, and most importantly they can control the agenda (Cox and McCubbins 2005) to ensure that the party crafts a record that its members can run on.

The political science literature on Congress in the 1990s and 2000s was particularly focused on how and to what effect party organization shaped Congress. Legislators might be more likely to empower their party leadership when they were more internally homogenous ideologically (Rohde 1991; Aldrich and Rohde 1999, 2000; Aldrich, Rohde and Tofias 2008). Smart leaders might even allow electorally vulnerable members to vote against the party when their votes were not needed (Binder et al. 1999).

Much of this literature focused on demonstrating that parties had observable effects beyond a simple spatial model (e.g. Krehbiel 1998). The current state of the literature is that while spatial models are very useful in understanding policy conflict in Congress, it is necessary to engage with how parties organize politics in that space (e.g. Chiou and Rothenberg 2006; Lawrence et al. 2006; Gailmard and Jenkins 2007; Lee 2010).

In fact, the parties may shape that space itself. Members of Congress rely on party leaders to help them learn what is the "correct" position on legislation (Sinclair 2002). The negotiation and bargaining among party members are a large part of what produces the space that ideological models observe. As Poole and Rosenthal (2007) put it, in many years, "the horizontal dimension can be thought of as both a party-loyalty dimension and an economic dimension" (45).

In short, parties do the work of legislating. They manage internal disagreements and disagreements with the other team. It is party leaders who spearhead discussions with the other house of Congress, and who take the trip to the White House to negotiate with the president.

Parties may not always do this kind of organizing in the best way. There are reasons to worry about overly strong partisan leaders. Gregory Koger and Matthew Lebo (2017), for instance, argue that intense partisan competition in Congress is driven by members' re-election interest in attaching themselves to a strong leader, regardless of whether they agree with the agenda. Similarly, Frances Lee (2016) argues that closely divided party control of government means that neither party has much incentive to compromise in the current legislative term, instead focusing on winning in the next election. Much of the legislative agenda might be filled with messaging votes intended to make the other side look bad (Theriault 2013, 2015).

One way to address such party dysfunction might be to restrain parties. Weaker parties might do less damage. Evidence suggests this backfires. The chaos of the 118th Congress illustrates why.

After narrowly capturing control of the House of Representatives in the 2022 elections, Republicans struggled to choose a leader. Kevin McCarthy, the previous minority leader, faced a revolt from an ideological wing of his party. A group of ideological extremists, led by Florida congressman Matt Gaetz, initially denied McCarthy a majority and later removed him from office. Key to their revolt was not merely their extremism, however. These members had built an independent connection to their districts. They saw that the party needed them more than they needed the party. The publicity from their high-profile clash with leadership generated donations (Montellaro 2024) and further strengthened their independence from their party.

A Republican Party with a more powerful leadership could have reined in its rogue elements. And while most of these defectors were ideologically extreme, many ideologically conservative members did work with the party. The defining characteristic of the defectors was their unwillingness to work with the party, not their ideological preferences.

More comprehensive efforts to undermine parties have concerning consequences. In the early twentieth century, electoral rules in California allowed strong incumbents to run in both the Democratic and Republican primaries, effectively eliminating their partisan identity in the General Assembly. The result was not an enlightened representation of the people but rather an agenda dominated by lobbyists, notably railroad interests (Masket 2009).

This reality of party-organized politics implies an important lesson: Well-functioning government requires healthy parties. It is not enough to just send more moderates (or more progressives or more conservatives, depending on your point of view) to the legislature. The ability and willingness of those members to work with their co-partisans is at least as important as their policy preferences. The most important vote that any member makes is their vote for leadership, because that determines which party gets to lead in organizing the chamber. A moderate who backs a party that advances a more extreme agenda contributes just as much as an extremist. In other words, we need healthy parties, not moderate candidates.

Voters Rely on Parties

Everything we know about how voters make decisions turns on partisanship.

The best predictor of any voting decision is partisan identification or attachment (Campbell et al. 1960; Lewis-Beck et al. 2008; Miller and Shanks 1996). A voter who favors the Democrats will usually vote for the Democratic candidate. A Republican voter will usually vote for the Republican. This partisan attachment is stable over time, and relatively predictable from a voter's demographics, preferences and identity (Bartels 2000; Converse 1962; Green, Palmquist and Schickler 2002; Hetherington 2001).

This partisanship is sometimes decried as closed-mindedness. Why won't a Republican even consider a Democratic candidate, or vice versa? But if parties are what is organizing government, and if voters have correctly chosen their party, then the label is far from meaningless. Voting on the basis of a politician's team is an effective and efficient way to get elected officials who represent you.

The importance of party in voter decisions is easier to see in light of the other factors voters can rely on.

Some Voters Vote on Policy or Ideology

The straightforward spatial model argues that voters will choose the candidate closer to them in the ideological space. On this view, a voter has a pre-existing ideological position, and they then vote for the candidate who is closer to that position. This is the kind of voter that most primary reforms imagine.

But there are limits to using ideology in this way. To begin with, most voters are not ideological. Studies consistently find small percentages of voters are very ideological (Converse 1964) while majorities or pluralities are not ideological at all (Kinder and Kalmoe 2017). Many voters' preferences may not be well described by a simple ideological dimension (Broockman 2016). Even if many voters truly are "moderates," many are also not. (Fowler et al. 2023; Broockman and Lauderdale, forthcoming). They need help organizing politics. Parties provide that help. Without parties helping to anchor the poles, ideology has little meaning for voters.

Indeed, parties may even be responsible for shaping the preferences of those who do think ideologically. Research shows again and again that most policy preferences are disseminated by partisan and other elite political voices (Zaller 1992; Carsey and Layman 2006; Barber and Pope 2019; Dyck and Pearson-Merkowitz 2023). Ideology can and should be understood as independent of parties (Noel 2013), but its transmission to voters involves parties.

Finally, those voters who do have pre-existing ideological views need help figuring out where politicians stand. Again, party is the most useful cue.

Even for a voter who has a perfect sense of their own and all the candidates' locations within a policy space, the information provided by parties is critical. Because parties shape the agenda, knowing a candidate's party is a critical predictor of what they will accomplish in government. Party provides the necessary context for any ideological assessment.

Some Voters Vote on Character or other Traits

We want elected officials with integrity, competence, empathy and so on. It is well-established that many voters filter these judgements through the lens of partisanship, and thus party can muddle our ability to independently assess these qualities. Voters overlook the flaws in a candidate from their own team (Funck and Mc-Cabe 2021; Rothschild et al. 2021).

Fortunately, healthy parties can also provide clarity. For one, they vet candidates. Party leaders know more about them, and their signals can help voters know who is or is not a high-quality candidate. When politicians distance themselves from co-partisans facing scandal, voters respond favorably (Daniele et al. 2020; Hardy 2024). Signals from party actors, both leaders and fellow elected representatives, help shape the success of candidates running for nomination (e. g. Cohen et al. 2008; Dominguez 2011; Kousser et al. 2015; Hassell 2017).

Some Voters Vote in Response to Economic Growth or other Fundamentals

When the economy is doing better, incumbents do better. Or, to be more precise, incumbent parties do better.

The tranche in political science literature on election forecasting has established pretty convincingly that when the economy is doing better, and when voters are in general happier, they reward incumbents (Mayer 1996; Rosenstone 1983; Hibbs 2000; Abramowitz 2008). This mechanism is thought to help hold politicians accountable, although its effectiveness is limited (Achen and Bartels 2016).

The party of the incumbent plays a key role. The president's party tends to lose seats in midterm elections—being in government is costly. But they lose fewer seats when they are more popular (Abramowitz et al. 1986; Erikson 1988; Campbell 1991). The electorate rewards and punishes presidents through their party's success in midterm elections.

In sum, even the non-party ways in which voters evaluate candidates depend very much on parties. Well-functioning elections also require healthy parties.

Parties Struggle to Meet Expectations

The lesson from the previous section is that parties play an integral role in organizing politics. The view that governance or elections can thrive without organizing institutions is simply inaccurate.

But are modern parties healthy enough to do that organizing? Too often they are not.

Modern political parties in the United States and around the world are increasingly mistrusted, often unable to serve the roles expected of them, as several political scientists have shown. Peter Mair (2013) argues in his *Ruling the Void* that political leaders have withdrawn from the electoral arena, leaving ineffective parties in their wake. Daniel Schlozman and Sam Rosenfeld (2024) argue that U.S. political parties are now hollow, hard institutional shells with little effective organization within them. Didi Kuo (2025) similarly finds that parties around the globe lack the means to forge deep connections to communities and citizens.

All of these diagnoses find parties failing to build the kind of robust institutions democracy needs from them. But that doesn't mean parties don't continue to play their central role. They just do it inadequately. As Julia Azari (2016, 2023) has argued, voters and politicians continue to be partisan, even as party institutions struggle to shape the agenda, vet candidates, and provide meaningful guidance on coalitions. Weak parties do a disservice to citizens with strong partisanship.

The weakening of political parties in the United States and around the world is a complex process, tangled up with declining trust in many institutions. The failure of mainstream politics to solve problems leads many to look for other, often more radical solutions. Political leaders thus find it strategically useful to encourage mistrust of the other side. This polarization further alienates all but the most interested citizens, and their mistrust further cedes the domain of politics to ideological activists (e. g. Ladd 2012; Hetherington and Rudolph 2015; Klar and Krupnikov 2016; Barber and McCarty 2016; Ladd and Podkul 2019).

These challenges facing parties probably cannot be overcome with simple institutional changes. Opening or closing primaries will not serve to build robust grass-roots networks. But institutions can help or hinder efforts of parties to serve the role they need to play.

As Seth Masket (2016) argues, political parties are often the target of reformers who see them as corrupting influences on politics. But their efforts to weaken parties do not make them go away.

They can, however, make it harder for parties to be effective.

The now central role of primary campaigns in presidential nominations is an illustrative case. After reforms starting in 1968 required convention delegates to be selected in a manner open to rank-and-file party members, the nominating decision shifted from the party convention to primaries and caucuses, where candidates appealed directly to voters (Shafer 1983). This was widely viewed as locking party leaders out of the process, instead favoring candidates with personal or factional appeals (Polsby 1983).

Party leaders did not just lie down. Cohen et al. (2008) argue that party leaders worked behind the scenes to influence outcomes in the new system. The informal network of party leaders publicly endorsed the sort of candidate a party would have chosen in the old system. And from the 1980s through to the end of the century, those endorsed candidates usually won.

But the tools the party had were blunt and imperfect, and party-preferred candidates did not always win. Perhaps their most significant failure came in 2016, when Republican insiders overwhelmingly preferred not to nominate Donald Trump but were unable to stop him (Cohen et al. 2016; Noel 2016). But they have struggled in other years, too. A more effective party might have successfully encouraged Joe Biden to step aside earlier than the summer of 2024. Most of the frustration Americans have with recent presidential candidates is due to this chaotic system.

This account suggests two features we would like healthy parties to have. Reforms should, at a minimum, not undermine these features, and ideally help foster them.

First, parties should be central to voting. This means voters should be aware of the parties they are voting for. Their decisions should be informed by, and usually driven by, parties. Voters are not simply choosing elected officials. They are choosing among teams.

This doesn't mean voters should always vote blindly for "their" party, mechanistically following their party identification. But it does mean voters should have and use party as a central cue for their decision-making. Knowing the candidates' parties tells you more than anything else, and voting without that cue is so much more difficult.

Second, parties should be robust institutions. They should internally govern themselves, working out what they stand for. They should have control over their nominations and their message. Nominations in particular are central to a party's health—as E.E. Schattschneider (1942) put it, the nomination is "the most important activity of the party. ... if a party cannot make nominations it ceases to be a party" (64).

This doesn't mean voters and other ordinary citizens are not involved in the process. On the contrary, healthy parties incorporate citizen involvement throughout the process. Internal democracy in a party includes primary elections, although it should not be limited to them.

These two conditions are deeply related. Voters cannot rely on parties if the party cannot shape its coalition. And a party has little incentive to shape its coalition if voters are not paying attention.

The Role of Primaries in Party Democracy

Many reforms start from the position that the problem with politics, polarization or otherwise, stems from the effects of party primaries in a two-party system (Gehl and Porter 2020; Troiano 2024). The two parties nominate their candidates, and since the parties are increasingly different, the primary electorates nominate increasingly divergent candidates.

The evidence that primaries themselves are the principal driver for polarization is weak. To begin with, primaries were introduced in the United States over a century ago, but polarization is a much more recent phenomenon. Indeed, research suggests that in their early days, primaries produced more moderate candidates than alternative methods of candidate selection (Hirano and Snyder 2019; Cintolesi 2022).

The voters in those primaries are not, as often assumed, more ideologically extreme than voters in the general election (Boatright 2014; Drutman 2021; Hirano et al. 2010; Hirano and Snyder 2019; Sides et al. 2020; Cowburn 2024). So changing the composition of the primary electorate, as discussed in several chapters of this volume, is unlikely to have much effect.

A particularly useful analysis is Mike Cowburn's *Party Transformation in Congressional Primaries* (2024), essential reading for primary reformers concerned about polarization. Cowburn systematically looks for evidence that primary electorates favor extreme candidates. He finds little, concluding that his findings "cast substantial doubt on the narrative of primary voters as a source of polarization" 160).

But Cowburn does argue that primaries play a role in polarization. This is because politicians do fear "getting primaried," even if that fear is greater than warranted (see also Boatright 2013). In his book, and in Chapter 5 of this volume, Cowburn documents a number of ways in which primaries have changed in the past few decades. He finds ideological messaging and ideological factions are increasingly dominant in congressional primaries, and that candidates often take more extreme positions to defend against these changes.

It is critical to understand that the culprit here is not the party itself. It is a primary environment that is increasingly open to ideological actors, both in and outside the party, who use the primary as a tool of influence. Primaries become the site of conflict among increasingly relevant intra-party factions (see also Bloch Rubin 2017; Clarke 2020; Blum 2020; Blum and Noel 2024). Indeed, party leadership has an incentive to shield its members from the more perverse effects of this environment. But they increasingly struggle to do so, because party leaders do not ultimately hold the power of renomination, primary electorates do.

These intra-party dynamics are not generally the focus of primary reforms. Instead, they tackle the mechanical role that primaries play in narrowing the field of candidates.

In a first-past-the-post electoral system, a large field of candidates can lead to a candidate with only a plurality of support winning. This is one of the central mechanisms of Duverger's Law (1951, 217, literally: "the simple-majority single-ballot system favours the two-party system").[3] Since only the top two candidates are contenders, voters do not want to vote for third- or fourth-place candidates, and candidates do not want to run as a third or fourth candidate. As a consequence, most aspiring lawmakers enter one of the two major parties' primaries, and thus only two major candidates face each other in the general election.

In that environment, the party primaries become the place where a field of many candidates is narrowed to two. But primaries do not exist explicitly for that purpose. From a party perspective, the purpose of the nomination is to ensure that two candidates of the same party do not compete against each other, not to ensure that there are only two parties.

Most efforts to reform the primary process focus on the need to narrow the field. They work not by empowering or encouraging the party to nominate more moderate, pro-compromise candidates, but by eroding the gatekeeping role of parties altogether, replacing it with some other way of narrowing the field.

Party-hostile Reforms

The result is reforms that, even if they do not explicitly target parties, have the effect of undermining them. Such is the case with three particularly popular reforms: non-partisan primaries; ranked-choice voting in single-member districts; and open primaries.

Non-partisan Primaries

One approach is to simply take over from parties their role in narrowing candidates down to a manageable number, usually two in a single-member district (see Chapter 10).

The term "non-partisan primary" should be an oxymoron. A primary election is an election in which partisan voters choose their party's nominee for a general election. This is not simply a semantic objection. Parties turned to primaries to solve an internal problem—how to govern themselves in the selection of their nominee. As noted above, choosing the nominee is an existential matter for a party, and primaries are chosen as a way to do so democratically. If an electoral sys-

---

3 Scholars have demonstrated that Duverger's relationship is hardly an iron law (e.g. Dunleavy and Diwakar 2013; Dunleavy 2012; Rae 1971; Lijphart 1990), but the tendency definitely exists (Reynolds et al. 2005; Clark and Golder 2006).

tem removes a party primary and replaces it with something else, that something else is not really a "primary."

As noted above, a partisan primary *does* narrow the field. The logic behind the non-partisan primary is to do this without parties. Voters first face an all-party field, and then narrow it to two (or more, see below) final candidates who face each other in a run-off.

The evidence that these non-partisan primaries yield moderate candidates is mixed, with most finding small effects clouded by other factors (McGhee et al. 2014; Ahler, Citrin and Lenz 2016; McGhee and Shor 2017). Theoretically, we would only expect moderation to the extent that voting is uniquely about a single ideological dimension, and as noted above, it usually is not.

But top-two primaries do make it harder for parties to meet the goals outlined above. Voters now have party as a mere label at most, often with multiple candidates of the same party competing directly against each other. Even if this did lead to more moderate candidates winning, it would do so at the cost of making party less central for voters.

Under partisan primaries, the party, its leaders and its voters, makes the choice of which candidate it wants. The primary is a place for the party to have an internal debate over its direction. The central question of the primary is what should the party stand for. Under the non-partisan party, the party has lost not only the opportunity to have that debate in a public venue but also the incentive to have the debate at all.

Minority party voters may even be shut out of the general election altogether, as has happened twice for the statewide Senate race in California, as well as in several of the state's House races. This means that voters of one party (usually Republicans in California) had no opportunity to choose someone from their preferred team in the general election; their only opportunity was in in the first stage of voting, where turnout tends to be about half that of the general election.

Parties do not simply step aside in these contexts. They do attempt to coordinate behind their preferred candidate, sometimes in county party meetings or other spaces (Masket 2011; Kousser et al. 2015), and these attempts are often effective.

But informal and indirect endorsement is a blunt tool. It is not the tool of a robust party with connections to voters. It is also not particularly transparent, and it does not embrace a role for voters in shaping the party. Voters are kept at arm's length, only able to vote on candidates, not the direction of the party.

In sum, non-partisan primaries are unlikely to have much effect of polarization, but they do make it harder for parties to build the kind of robust connections to voters that modern democracy expects of them.

Ranked-choice Voting

"Ranked-choice," by itself, is a ballot format, not an electoral system (Rae 1971; Taagepera and Shugart 1989; Santucci 2022). So it might be applied in different ways. But the most common proposals in the United States combine the ranked ballot with a single-member district to, as with the "non-partisan primary," side-step the role parties play in narrowing the field.

The voter is presented with a list of candidates for a single seat and ranks them. When the votes are counted, those who voted for the candidate with the fewest votes have their votes re-allocated to their second choice. The process continues until there is a winner. [4]

This approach can even be combined with the two-stage "non-partisan primary," as above, where the first round narrows the choices to some number greater than two (often four or five), and then the second round employs the ranking. This model is used in Alaska's Top-4 primary system, and variations have been proposed in several other states (see Chapters 7, 8, and 9 of this volume).

Either way, this rule allows the election process to produce a single, majority-supported winner with only a single round of voting, even in the presence of many candidates. Voters are free to vote for candidates with little chance of winning because their second (and third and fourth) choices are also recorded. The vote counters can, in effect, deduce how a voter would vote if their top choices were not available, and so no vote is wasted.

Two potential benefits are expected from this approach. First, a candidate who is not preferred by a majority, but who wins because of a spoiler, will now (most likely) win. And second, such a candidate is thought to be more moderate, since under the median voter theorem, a candidate at the median ought to beat all other candidates (Atkinson and Ganz 2024; Atkinson et al. 2024; Foley 2025; see also Chapter 15 of this volume).

But these benefits depend on some rather strong assumptions. Voters must have complete preferences over a sometimes large field of candidates, and they must provide them. But many voters in ranked-choice systems do not complete their ballot, ranking only their top choice. This is not surprising, given that they may lack the cues given by parties. They simply don't know where the candidates lie (Bawn et al. 2019), and they don't have much incentive to figure it out.

---

4 There are a number of possible variations, including a "Condorcet compliant" approach that conducts a round-robin tournament among candidates (Foley 2023; see also Chapter 15 of this volume) to ensure that the order in which candidates are dropped and their votes reallocated does not lead to the perverse outcome of the Condorcet winner somehow not surviving to the final round (Bailey et al. 2024).

In short, this sort of ballot solution not only expects a lot from voters, but it does so in a world where the main provider of voter information—political parties—is sidelined.

Voters need help navigating both where the candidates stand ideologically, in perhaps a multidimensional space, and which coalitions those candidates will coordinate with once they are elected. Jack Santucci (2022) centers the latter concern in his *More Parties or No Parties*, which traces the efforts to enact and later repeal the single-transferable vote in U.S. municipal elections. Santucci shows that in the U.S. context, the single-transferable vote had the effect of muddling the connection between voter preferences and the coalitions that formed in government.

Even if the parties' coalitions are clearly defined, voters still need to know which coalition they are supporting. And parties need control over their nomination so that the coalition means what they think it means.

Using ranked ballots per se does not prevent parties from playing a central role. Other democracies that use ranked votes, such as Australia, have robust parties. But Australia's parties are not as embattled as American parties are. The method used for the Australian alternative vote may be part of the reason why. Australia's ballot has an explicit option to vote "above the line," for a party's list (Australian Election Commission 2016), giving it some of the features of an open list proportional representation system.

It thus makes little sense to favor or oppose ranked-choice voting itself. It depends on its application. The ballot format can be applied in ways that center parties or sideline them. But current reforms do not include these kinds of features, usually deliberately. It is notable that in the wave of recent attempts to implement RCV across the U.S. states, the reform was often coupled with other anti-party reforms, such as open primaries. So, again, it is not clear that the promised benefits from RCV proposals will develop, but they may serve to make it harder for parties to thrive.

Open Primaries

If a party delegates its candidate selection to a primary electorate, who qualifies to vote in that electorate? The natural answer—that party's voters—is unhelpful, because any party competes to draw in more voters, and voters are allowed to align with a party without making any formal commitment, especially in the United States.

Other democracies that use primaries tend to answer this question narrowly. Only formal members of the party may participate. This is often limited to dues-paying members who may make up only a tiny slice of the electorate. Even this is sometimes seen as too open. When the Labour Party in the United Kingdom chose its leader with an election of dues-paying members, the surge in membership to participate alarmed some, who thought voters were buying access to the contest for a paltry £3 (BBC 2015).

By contrast, party primaries in the United States are the most open in the world. All one must do is declare an affiliation when registering, or even at the time of selecting a primary ballot. In most states, this affiliation is easy to change, although some require it to be done some months in advance. In New Hampshire, for instance, one simply signs a paper to declare a temporary new party status, votes, then reverts back to their previous status. In many states, an affiliation need not even be declared. In no state is party registration binding on a general election vote.

The options in use in the United States might be arranged from the most restrictive, limited to registered party members ("closed"), to the least restrictive, in which any voter may participate ("open"). Various intermediate models ("semi-closed" or "modified open") may allow independents to vote in any primary but restrict partisans to their own primary, or perhaps require that independents automatically register as a partisan for future elections if they elect to vote in a party's primary.

One reform, then, is to make more party primaries "open," to nonpartisan voters—voters who identify as independent and so decline to register as members of one of the two parties. The logic behind the reform would be that independent voters, often located in "the middle," would be a moderating counterweight to the party loyalists who usually make up primary electorates.

There is not much evidence that open versus closed primaries have much effect on nominee extremism (Masket and Noel 2023; Hirano et al. 2010). This is likely because primary electorates are not ideologically that different from the general electorate, as noted above. And the barriers created by "closed" primaries are trivial to overcome, since American parties impose virtually no costs on voters who want to join their primary electorate.

Moreover, independents are not synonymous with moderates, as noted above. In 2016, for example, progressive candidate Bernie Sanders did much better with independent voters than the moderate Hillary Clinton did, likely because many of his voters were independent not because they were in between the two parties but because they felt the Democratic Party was too moderate.

But even if open primaries do not alleviate polarization, there is pressure to move to them on principled grounds. For one, if primaries are important, then all voters should be able to participate in them, but with closed primaries, independents cannot. Of course, "independent" is not an innate characteristic. Voters who decline to choose a party to influence are not disenfranchised. They decide not to avail of that franchise.

Another justification for openness is that in many districts, the winner of the dominant party's primary is almost assured of winning in the general election. So the real decision is made in the primary, and thus voters should be allowed to vote in that contest. The primary is the only place for one to cast a "meaningful vote," which might have a chance of affecting the outcome (Unite America 2025).[5] But allowing those in the political minority to vote in another party's primary doesn't change the fact that they are in the political minority. A single-member district will always fail to represent them.

Finally, open primaries are justified on the grounds that they are paid for by taxpayers, so all taxpayers should be allowed to participate. Laying aside the fact that any taxpayer can participate if they choose to associate with one of the parties, state-run primaries are a consequence of state regulation of parties. Some state parties might not hold primaries at all but for state laws requiring them to do so. It is reasonable for the state to regulate even the inner workings of politically vital organizations such as parties, but it also makes sense that the state covers some of costs of the burdens imposed.

In short, open primaries seem to have little effect on moderation, but they are incompatible with the principles underlying partisan primaries in the first place.

Party-compatible Reforms

If the above reforms are hostile to parties, are there reforms that might accomplish some of the reformers' stated goals that are friendly to parties? There are a number of possibilities.

Campaign Finance Reform

The American campaign finance system is particularly limiting to political parties and particularly encouraging of ideological pressure.

Regulations aimed at promoting equality and avoiding corruption have broadly had to yield to concerns about free expression (Dwyre and Kolodny 2024). Be-

---

5 It is worth noting that by this standard, a primary vote is more "meaningful" than a general election vote in the same way that a tall person is more likely than a short person to bump their head on the moon. (Schwartz 1987).

ginning in 1976 with *Buckley v. Valeo*, which found that restrictions on spending amounted to restrictions on the First Amendment right to free speech, various attempts to restrict the role of money in politics have been struck down on free speech grounds. But the one category of restriction not protected by this shift in priorities has been the limitations imposed by the Bipartisan Campaign Reform Act of 2002 on "soft money" given to directly to political parties and often used for party-building purposes. Meanwhile, ostensibly unaligned independent organizations, focused on ideological goals, are the most protected and thus unrestricted.

This balance of regulations might be expected to encourage polarization, and there is evidence that it does. Ray La Raja and Brian Schaffner (2015) exploit variation across states in how restrictive campaign finance rules are on parties relative to rules on other groups. States where parties are more restricted, they find, let "purists prevail," polarizing winners. This pattern is echoed by Cowburn (2024) who, as noted above, shows that primaries do contribute to polarization, just not through extremism in the primary electorate. Rather, candidates adopt more extreme positions, during and before primaries, to defend against a new environment dominated by ideological factions.

Campaign finance reform focused on strengthening parties may not be enough to reverse what is now decades of polarization, but there is some hope it could arrest it (La Raja 2025). Current campaign finance rules directly hamstring parties hoping to develop the kinds of connections that Kuo or Schlozman and Rosenfeld advocate for.

Multi-member Districts

Extreme elected officials are a problem because they are unrepresentative of their constituencies, which include moderates, independents, and the minority party. Many of the reforms above are designed to give those perspectives more of a voice.

But no single person can ever represent the full diversity of a district. The problem is not the primary but single-member districts. In even a lopsided district, there are many citizens in the minority who will not like their representative. On average, about thirty percent of American voters live in a congressional district represented by someone they voted against (Noel 2023).

The more direct solution is multi-member districts.

Multi-member districts are often associated with multiparty democracy (see below), but multi-member districts would mean better representation even if the two-party system persisted. The moderates and the more ideological of both the majority and the minority of the district could have more representation. Votes would be more "meaningful" because even if the other party is likely to win more seats, the resulting legislature would include more voices (Latner et al. 2021).

Multiparty Democracy

The concern with extremist factions hijacking a party by winning its primary is that once they have won, they get the support of partisan voters who might have preferred a more moderate candidate but who are unwilling to vote for the other side. In a two-party system, the party has little choice but to welcome its extremists.

One way to get around this is to give voters more choices.

Lee Drutman makes this case in his *Breaking the Two-Party Doom Loop* (2020; see also Drutman 2025; Taylor 2025), in which he argues that the United States has the potential for perhaps four parties, but the two-party system prevents the more mainstream factions in the major parties from isolating their extremists into smaller third parties.

There are legitimate questions about whether a multiparty democracy could emerge with our current institutions (Duverger 1951), or whether it would thrive in a presidential system (Mainwaring 1993; Pildes 2025). There are also reasons to believe it could (Mainwaring and Drutman 2024). Reformers have proposed a range of institutions that might encourage multiple parties, from open-list proportional representation to increasing the size of the house (Shugart and Taagepera 2017; Shugart 2021; Santucci 2020; Taylor 2025). Any path to multiparty democracy in the United States would be complicated and would probably not unfold according to any plan.

But it would have two advantages. First, it addresses the problem more directly. It leads to better representation in general, and because of that, it limits extremists to the actual support they can muster. And second, it likely makes it easier for parties to control their coalitions and their agendas. Not only do most institutions make parties more central, but smaller parties are easier to manage and can provide clearer platforms for voters.

Fusion Voting

If true multiparty democracy is too bold of a reform, a much more subtle option is fusion voting.

Under fusion voting, more than one party can nominate the same candidate, and votes for that candidate under different labels are added together in the general election. The practice is currently used in New York, Connecticut, and Mississippi. A candidate can run under a major party label but also under a minor party label. The resulting vote totals reveal a lot about the reasons voters back their chosen candidate. This allows the electorate to send more layered mandates to government in a way that is compatible with the two-party system.

Voters are often torn between supporting a compromise candidate that they do not completely support or voting for their ideal ideological candidate, who is unlikely to win. With fusion, they can vote for the compromise while signaling their support for their own party. Consider a Democrat running a centrist campaign, hoping to appeal to Republican voters who are uncomfortable with an extremist they think has captured their party Those voters would be unwilling to fully embrace a Democrat, but they might be willing to back such a centrist candidate on another ticket.

Meanwhile, minor parties also get traction without being spoilers. If voters do want to send a stronger, more extreme ideological message, they can do so without splitting their party.

Like the other party-friendly reforms discussed above, fusion is not perfect. They all deserve more scrutiny. But by embracing the role of political parties, they are focused on the right problem.

Conclusion

This chapter has argued that many reform efforts have misdiagnosed the problem. They begin with the belief that the United States has too many extremists in government—in Congress, in state legislatures, in executive office—and so the solution is to elect more moderates. Those moderates, once in government, will simply govern better.

But government is organized by someone. Simply sending more moderates will not matter if the parties cannot do their job managing competing interests, moderate and extreme alike. Modern democracy needs parties to meet the moment, and for a variety of reasons, they are not. Some of this is due to hostile rules imposed on parties; some is due to failures of party leadership.

This diagnosis is more serious. Institutional reforms alone probably won't make parties play the role that democracy needs them to play. But weakening parties is the wrong direction. And too many primary reforms do just that.

Some reformers may explicitly argue that parties themselves are the problem, and we should imagine a post-partisan democracy, in which political parties fade away. This is at least impractical, because the partisans who organize parties will not go quietly.

But it is also unwise. Politics requires people to coordinate and cooperate with one another. The people who do that coordination will build teams to make it more effective. And an effective democracy is best when voters know which team they are voting for. Those teams are political parties, so reform efforts should never lose sight of them.

Bibliography

Abramowitz, Alan I. 2008. "Forecasting the 2008 Presidential Election with the Time-for-Change Model." *PS: Political Science and Politics* 38 (3): 691–695.

Abramowitz, Alan I., Albert D. Cover, and Helmut Norpoth. 1986. "The President's Party in Midterm Elections: Going from Bad to Worse." *American Journal of Political Science* 30 (3): 562–576.

Abramowitz, Alan I., and Steven W. Webster. 2018. "Negative partisanship: Why Americans dislike parties but behave like rabid partisans." *Political Psychology* 39 (1): 119–135.

Abramowitz, Alan I., and Steven W. Webster. 2016. "The rise of negative partisanship and the nationalization of U.S. elections in the 21st century." *Electoral Studies* 41 (1): 12–22.

Achen, Christopher, and Larry M. Bartels. 2016. *Democracy for Realists*. Princeton University Press.

Ahler, Douglas J., Jack Citrin, and Gabriel S. Lenz. 2016. "Do Open Primaries Improve Representation? An Experimental Test of California's 2012 Top-Two Primary." *Legislative Studies Quarterly* 41 (2): 237–268.

Aldrich, John. 1995. *Why Parties? The Origin and Transformation of Political Parties in America*. University of Chicago Press.

Aldrich, John, and David Rohde. 1999. "The Consequences of Party Organization in the House: Theory and Evidence on Conditional Party Government." Paper presented at the Conference on Congress and the President in a Partisan Era.

Aldrich, John, and David Rohde. 2000. "The Republican Revolution and the House Appropriations Committee." *Journal of Politics* 62 (1): 1–33.

Aldrich, John, David Rohde, and Michael W. Tofias. 2008. "One D is Not Enough: Measuring Conditional Party Government, 1887–2002." In *Party, Process, and Political Change in Congress: Further New Perspectives on the History of Congress*, edited by David Brady and David McCubbins. Stanford Press.

Atkinson, Nathan, and Scott Ganz. 2024. "Robust Electoral Competition: Rethinking Electoral Systems to Encourage Representative Outcomes." *Maryland Law Review* 84 (1).

Atkinson, Nathan, Scott Ganz, and John Mantus. 2024. "A Simple Agent-Based Model for Simulating Single Winner Elections." Georgetown McDonough School of Business Research Paper No. 4911226.

Australian Election Commission. 2016. "Above the line and below the line voting." Senate Ballot Paper Study 2016.

Azari, Julia. 2016. "Weak parties and strong partisanship are a bad combination." *Vox.* November 3. www.vox.com/mischiefs-of-faction/2016/11/3/13512362/weak-parties-strongpartisanship-bad-combination.

Azari, Julia. 2023. "Weak Parties, Strong Partisanship." In *The Making of the Presidential Candidates 2024*, edited by Jonathan Bernstein and Casey B. K. Dominguez. Rowman and Littlefield.

BBC. 2015. "Labour leadership: Huge increase in party's electorate." *BBC News.* August 12. www.bbc.com/news/uk-politics-33892407.

Bailey, Michael, Theodore Landsman, and Hans Noel. 2024. "Simulating the Impacts of Ranked Choice Voting on the 2020 and 2022 Congressional Elections." Working paper.

Baldassarri, Delila, and Andrew Gelman. 2008. "Partisans without Constraint: Political Polarization and Trends in American Public Opinion." *The American Journal of Sociology* 114 (2): 408–446.

Barber, Michael, and Jeremy C. Pope. 2019. "Does party trump ideology? Disentangling party and ideology in America." *American Political Science Review* 113 (1): 38–54.

Barber, Michael, and Nolan McCarty. 2016. *Causes and Consequences of Polarization.* Brookings Institution Press.

Bartels, Larry. 2000. "Partisanship and Voting Behavior, 1952–1996." *American Journal of Political Science* 44 (1): 35–50.

Bawn, Kathleen, Stephanie L. DeMora, Andrew Dowdle, Spencer Hall, Mark E. Myers, Shawn Patterson and John Zaller. 2019. "Policy voting in U.S. House primaries." *Journal of Elections, Public Opinion and Parties* 29 (4): 533–549.

Binder, Sarah A., Eric D. Lawrence, and Forrest Maltzman. 1999. "Uncovering the hidden effect of party." *Journal of Politics* 61 (4): 815–831.

Black, Duncan. 1958. *The Theory of Committees and Elections.* Cambridge University Press.

Bloch Rubin, Ruth. 2017. *Building the Bloc: Intraparty Organization in the U.S. Congress.* Cambridge University Press.

Blum, Rachel. 2020. *How the Tea Party Captured the GOP: Insurgent Factions in American Politics.* University of Chicago Press.

Blum, Rachel, and Hans Noel. 2024. *Cooperating Factions: A Network Analysis of Party Divisions in U.S. Presidential Nominations.* Cambridge University Press.

Boatright, Robert. 2013. *Getting Primaried: The Changing Politics of Congressional Primary Challenges.* University of Michigan Press.

Boatright, Robert. 2014. *Congressional Primary Elections.* Routledge.

Broockman, David E. 2016. "Approaches to Studying Policy Representation." *Legislative Studies Quarterly* 41 (1): 181–215.

Broockman, David E., and Benjamin E. Lauderdale. Forthcoming. "Moderates." *American Political Science Review.*

Campbell, Angus, Philip E. Converse, Warren E. Miller, and Donald E. Stokes. 1960. *The American Voter.* Wiley.

Campbell, James E. 1991. "The Presidential Surge and its Midterm Decline in Congressional Elections, 1868–1988." *The Journal of Politics* 53 (2): 477–487.

Carsey, Thomas M., and Geoffrey C. Layman. 2006. "Changing Sides or Changing Minds? Party Identification and Policy Preferences in the American Electorate." *American Journal of Political Science* 50 (2): 464–477.

Chiou, Fang-Yi, and Lawrence S. Rothenberg. 2006. "Preferences, Parties, and Legislative Productivity." *American Politics Research* 34 (6): 705–731.

Cintolesi, Andrea. 2022. "Political polarization and primary elections." *Journal of Economic Behavior Organization* 200 (3): 596–617.

Clark, William, and Matt Golder. 2006. "Rehabilitating Duverger's Theory: Testing the Mechanical and Strategic Modifying Effects of Electoral Laws." *Comparative Political Studies* 39: 679–708.

Clarke, Andrew J. 2020. "Party Sub-Brands and American Party Factions." *American Journal of Political Science* 64 (3): 452–470.

Cohen, Marty, David Karol, Hans Noel, and John Zaller. 2008. *The Party Decides: Presidential Nominations Before and After Reform.* University of Chicago Press.

Cohen, Marty, David Karol, Hans Noel, and John Zaller. 2016. "Party versus Faction in the Reformed Presidential Nominating System." *PS: Political Science and Politics* 43 (4): 701–708.

Converse, Philip. 1962. "Information Flow and the Stability of Partisan Attitudes." *Public Opinion Quarterly.* 26 (4): 578–599.

Converse, Philip. 1964. "The Nature of Belief Systems in Mass Publics." In *Ideology and Discontent*, edited by David Apter, 206–261. Free Press.

Cowburn, Mike. 2024. *Party Transformation in Congressional Primaries: Faction and Ideology in the Twenty-First Century.* Cambridge University Press.

Cox, Gary, and Mathew McCubbins. 1993. *Legislative Leviathan.* University of California Press.

Cox, Gary, and Mathew McCubbins. 2005. *Setting the Agenda.* Cambridge University Press.

Daniele, Gianmarco, Sergio Galletta, and Benny Geys. 2020. "Abandon ship? Party brands and politicians' responses to a political scandal." *Journal of Public Economics* 184: 104172.

DiMaggio, Paul, John Evans, and Bethany Bryson. 1996. "Have America's Social Attitudes Become More Polarized." *American Journal of Sociology* 102 (3): 690–755.

Dominguez, Casey B. K. 2011. "Does the Party Matter? Endorsements in Congressional Primaries." *Political Research Quarterly* 64 (3): 534–544.

Downs, Anthony. 1957. *An Economic Theory of Democracy.* HarperCollins Publishers, Inc.

Drutman, Lee. 2020. *Breaking the Two-Party Doom Loop.* Oxford University Press.

Drutman, Lee. 2021. "Theft Perception: Examining the Views of Americans Who Believe the 2020 Election was Stolen." *Democracy Fund Voter Study Group.* www.voterstudygroup.org/publication/theft-perception.

Drutman, Lee. 2025. "Proportional Representation." In *Electoral Reform in the United States: Proposals for Combating Polarization and Extremism*, edited by Larry Diamond, Edward B. Foley and Richard H. Pildes. Lynne Rienner Publishers.

Dunleavy, Patrick. 2012. "Duverger's Law is a dead parrot." LSE European Politics and Policy (EUROPP) Blog (20 Jun 2012). http.s://eprints.lse.ac.uk/46258/.

Dunleavy, Patrick, and Rekha Diwakar. 2013. "Analysing multiparty competition in plurality rule elections." *Party politics* 19 (6): 855–886.

Duverger, Maurice. 1951. *Political Parties: Their Organizations and Activity in the Modern State.* Methuen and Co.

Dwyre, Diana, and Robin Kolodny. 2024. *The Fundamentals of Campaign Finance in the U.S. Why We Have the System We Have.* University of Michigan Press.

Dyck, Joshua J., and Shanna Pearson-Merkowitz. 2023. *The Power of Partisanship.* Oxford University Press.

Enelow, James, and Melvin Hinich. 1989. "The Theory of Predictive Mappings." In *Advances in the Spatial Theory of Voting*, edited by James Enelow and Melvin Hinich, 167–178. Cambridge University Press.

Erikson, Robert S. 1988. "The Puzzle of Midterm Loss." *The Journal of Politics* 50 (4): 1011–1029.

Fiorina, Morris P. 2005. *Culture War? The Myth of a Polarized America.* Pearson Longman.

Foley, Edward B. 2023. "Total Vote Runoff: A Majority-Maximizing Form of Ranked Choice Voting." *University of New Hampshire Law Review* 21.

Foley, Edward B. 2025. "Ballot Structures." In *Electoral Reform in the United States: Proposals for Combating Polarization and Extremism*, edited by Larry Diamond, Edward B. Foley and Richard H. Lynne Rienner Publishers.

Fowler, Anthony, Seth Hill, Jeffrey B. Lewis, Chris Tausanovitch, Lynn Vavreck, and Christopher Warshaw. 2023. "Moderates." *American Political Science Review* 117 (2): 643–660.

Funck, Amy, and Katherine McCabe. 2021. "Partisanship, Information, and the Conditional Effects of Scandal on Voting Decisions." *Political Behavior* 44: 1–21.

Gailmard, Sean, and Jeffery A. Jenkins. 2007. "Negative Agenda Control in the Senate and House: Fingerprints of Majority Party Power." *The Journal of Politics* 69 (3): 689–700.

Gehl, Katherine, and Michael Porter. 2020. *The Politics Industry: How Political Innovation Can Break Partisan Gridlock and Save Our Democracy.* Harvard Business Review Press.

Green, Donald, Bradley Palmquist, and Eric Schickler. 2002. *Partisan Hearts & Minds: Political Parties and the Social Identities of Voters.* Yale University Press.

Hardy, Tranae. 2024. "Managing the Brand: Party Responses to Scandal." Doctoral thesis, Georgetown University.

Hassell, Hans J. G. 2017. *The Party's Primary: Control of Congressional Nomination.* Cambridge University Press.

Hetherington, Marc J. 2001. "Resurgent Mass Partisanship: The Role of Elite Polarization." *American Political Science Review* 95 (3): 619–631.

Hetherington, Marc J., and Thomas J. Rudolph. 2015. *Why Washington Won't Work: Polarization, Political Trust, and the Governing Crisis.* University of Chicago Press.

Hibbs, Douglas. 2000. "Bread and Peace Voting in U.S. Presidential Elections." *Public Choice* 104 (1–2): 149–180.

Hinich, Melvin J., and Michael C. Munger. 1994. *Ideology and the Theory of Political Choice.* University of Michigan Press.

Hirano, Shigeo, and James M. Snyder. 2019. *Primary Elections in the United States.* Cambridge University Press.

Hirano, Shigeo, James M. Snyder Jr., Stephen Daniel Ansolabehere, and John Mark Hansen. 2010. "Primary Elections and Partisan Polarization in the US Congress." *Quarterly Journal of Political Science* 5 (2): 169–191.

Hotelling, Harold. 1929. "Stability in Competition." *Economic Journal* 39 (March): 41–57.

Houston, David M. 2024. "Polarization, Partisan Sorting, and the Politics of Education." *American Educational Research Journal* 61 (3): 508–540.

Iyengar, Shanto, Gaurav Sood, and Yphtach Lelkes. 2012. "Affect, Not Ideology: A Social Identity Perspective on Polarization." *Public Opinion Quarterly* 76 (3): 405–431.

Iyengar, Shanto, Yphtach Lelkes, Matthew Levendusky, Neil Malhotra, and Sean J. Westwood. 2019. "The Origins and Consequences of Affective Polarization in the United States." *Annual Review of Political Science* 22 (1): 129–146.

Kinder, Donald R., and Nathan P. Kalmoe. 2017. *Neither Liberal nor Conservative: Ideological Innocence in the American Public.* University of Chicago Press.

Klar, Samara, and Yanna Krupnikov. 2016. *Independent Politics: How American Disdain for Parties Leads to Political Inaction.* Cambridge University Press.

Koger, Gregory, and Matthew J Lebo. 2017. *Strategic Party Government.* University of Chicago Press.

Kousser, Thad, Scott Lucas, Seth Masket and Eric McGhee. 2015. "Kingmakers or Cheerleaders? Party Power and the Causal Effects of Endorsements." *Political Research Quarterly* 68 (3): 443–456.

Krehbiel, Keith. 1998. *Pivotal Politics: A Theory of U.S. Lawmaking.* University of Chicago Press.

Kuo, Didi. 2025. *The Great Retreat: How Political Parties Should Behave and Why They Don't.* Oxford University Press.

La Raja, Raymond. 2025. "Campaign Finance." In *Electoral Reform in the United States: Proposals for Combating Polarization and Extremism*, edited by Larry Diamond, Edward B. Foley, and Richard H. Lynne Rienner Publishers.

La Raja, Raymond, and Brian Schaffner. 2015. *Campaign Finance and Political Polarization: When Purists Prevail.* University of Michigan Press.

Ladd, Jonathan M. 2012. *Why Americans Hate the Media and How It Matters.* Princeton University Press.

Ladd, Jonathan M., and Alexander R. Podkul. 2019. "Distrust of the News Media as a Symptom and a Further Cause of Partisan Polarization." In *New Directions in Media and Politics*, edited by Travis N. Ridout, 54 – 79. Routledge.

Latner, Michael, Jack Santucci, and Matthew Shugart. 2021. "Multi-seat Districts and Larger Assemblies Produce More Diverse Racial Representation." https://doi.org/10.2139/ssrn.3911532.

Lawrence, Eric. D., Forrest Maltzman, and Steven S. Smith. 2006. "Who Wins? Party Effects in Legislative Voting." *Legislative Studies Quarterly* 31(1): 33 – 69.

Lee, Frances E. 2010. *Beyond Ideology: Politics, Principles, and Partisanship in the U. S. Senate.* University of Chicago Press.

Lee, Frances E. 2016. *Insecure Majorities: Congress and the Perpetual Campaign.* University of Chicago Press.

Levendusky, Matt. 2009. *The Partisan Sort: How Liberals Became Democrats and Conservatives Became Republicans.* University of Chicago Press.

Levendusky, Matthew, and Neil Malhotra. 2016. "Does Media Coverage of Partisan Polarization Affect Political Attitudes?" *Political Communication* 33 (2): 283 – 301.

Lewis-Beck, Michael S., Helmut Norpoth, William Jacoby, and Herbert F Weisberg. 2008. *The American voter revisited.* University of Michigan Press.

Lijphart, Arend. 1990. "The Political Consequences of Electoral Laws, 1945 – 85." *The American Political Science Review* 84 (2): 481 – 496.

Mainwaring, Scott. 1993. "Presidentialism, Multipartism, and Democracy: The Difficult Combination." *Comparative Political Studies* 26 (2): 198 – 228.

Mainwaring, Scott, and Lee Drutman. 2024. *The Case for Multiparty Presidentialism in the US: Why the House Should Adopt Proportional Representation*" Protect Democracy and New America.

Mair, Peter. 2013. *Ruling the Void: The Hollowing of Western Democracy.* Verso.

Masket, Seth. 2009. *No Middle Ground: How Informal Party Organizations Control Nominations and Polarize Legislatures.* The University of Michigan Press.

Masket, Seth. 2011. "The Circus That Wasn't: The Republican Party's Quest for Order in the 2003 California Gubernatorial Recall." *State Politics and Policy Quarterly* 11 (2): 123 – 147.

Masket, Seth. 2016. *The Inevitable Party: Why Attempts to Kill the Party System Fail and How they Weaken Democracy.* Oxford University Press.

Masket, Seth, and Hans Noel. 2021. *Political Parties.* W. W. Norton & Company.

Masket, Seth, and Hans Noel. 2023. "Primaries, Polarization, and Party Control." In *More Than Red and Blue: Political Parties and American Democracy. American Political Science Association and Protect Democracy.* APSA Presidential Task Force on Political Parties.

Mason, Lilliana. 2015. ""I Disrespectfully Agree": The Differential Effects of Partisan Sorting on Social and Issue Polarization." *American Journal of Political Science* 59 (1): 128 – 145.

Mayer, William G. 1996. "Forecasting Presidential Nominations." In *In Pursuit of the White House: How We Choose Our Presidential Nominees*, edited by William G. Mayer. Chatham House.

McGhee, Eric, and Boris Shor. 2017. "Has the Top Two Primary Elected More Moderates?" *Perspectives on Politics* 15 (4): 1053–1066.

McGhee, Eric, Seth Masket, Boris Shor, Steven Rogers, and Nolan McCarty. 2014. "A Primary Cause of Partisanship? Nomination Systems and Legislator Ideology." *American Journal of Political Science* 58 (2): 337–351.

Miller, Warren E., and J. Merrill Shanks. 1996. *The New American Voter.* Harvard University Press.

Montellaro, Zach. 2024. "Matt Gaetz deposed Kevin McCarthy and the donations came pouring in." *Politico.* February 1. https://www.politico.com/news/2024/02/01/matt-gaetz-donations-00139182.

Noel, Hans. 2013. *Political Ideologies and Political Parties in America.* Cambridge University Press.

Noel, Hans. 2016. "Why Can't the G.O.P. Stop Trump?" *The New York Times.* March 1, 2016.

Noel, Hans. 2023. "Carpetbag Democracy: How Parties Shape Representation across Constituencies." Paper prepared for the 2023 American Political Science Convention, September 2023, Los Angeles, California.

Pildes, Richard H. 2025. "Why Proportional Representation Could Make Things Worse." In *Electoral Reform in the United States: Proposals for Combating Polarization and Extremism,* edited by Larry Diamond, Edward B. Foley and Richard H. Pildes. Lynne Rienner Publishers.

Polsby, Nelson. 1983. *Consequences of Party Reform.* Oxford University Press.

Poole, Keith T., and Howard Rosenthal. 2007. *Ideology and Congress.* Transaction Publishers.

Rae, Douglas W. 1971. *The Political Consequences of Electoral Laws.* 2nd edition. Yale University Press.

Reynolds, Andrew, Ben Reilly, and Andrew Ellis. 2005. *Electoral System Design: The New International IDEA Handbook.* International Institute for Democracy and Electoral Assistance.

Rohde, David W. 1991. *Parties and Leaders in the Postreform House.* University of Chicago Press.

Rosenstone, Steven. 1983. *Forecasting Presidential Elections.* Yale University Press.

Rothschild, Zachary K., Lucas A. Keefer, and Julianna Hauri. 2021. "Defensive Partisanship? Evidence that In-Party Scandals Increase Out-Party Hostility." *Political Psychology* 42 (1): 3–21.

Santucci, Jack. 2020. "A Modest and Timely Proposal." *Voteguy.* www.voteguy.com/2020/12/09/a-modest-and-timely-proposal.

Santucci, Jack. 2022. *More Parties or No Parties: The Politics of Electoral Reform in America.* Oxford University Press.

Schattschneider, E.E. 1942. *Party Government.* Greenwood Press.

Schlozman, Daniel, and Sam Rosenfeld. 2024. *The Hollow Parties: The Many Pasts and Disordered Present of American Party Politics.* Princeton University Press.

Schwartz, Thomas. 1987. "Your Vote Counts on Account of How It Is Counted: An Institutional Solution to the Paradox of Not Voting." *Public Choice* 54 (2): 101–121. https://doi.org/10.1007/bf00123001.

Schwartz, Thomas. 1989. Why Parties? Research memorandum UCLA.

Shafer, Byron E. 1983. *Quiet Revolution: Struggle for the Democratic Party and the Shaping of Post-Reform Politics.* Russell Sage Foundation.

Shugart, Matthew S. 2021. "Emergency electoral reform: OLPR for the US House." *Fruits and Votes.* fruitsandvotes.wordpress.com/2021/01/19/emergency-electoral-reform-olpr-forthe-us- house/.

Shugart, Matthew S., and Rein Taagepera. 2017. *Votes from Seats: Logical Models of Electoral Systems.* Cambridge University Press.

Sides, John, Christopher Tausanovitch, Lynn Vavreck, and Christopher Warshaw. 2020. "On the Representativeness of Primary Electorates." *British Journal of Political Science* 50 (2): 677–685.

Sinclair, Barbara. 2002. "Do Parties Matter?" In *Party, Process, and Political Change in Congress: New Perspectives on the History of Congress*, edited by David Brady and Mathew McCubbins. Stanford University Press.

Taagepera, Rein, and Matthew Soberg Shugart. 1989. *Seats and Votes: The Effects and Determinants of Electoral Systems*. Yale University Press.

Taylor, Steven L. 2025. *Trapped in a Two-Party System: How to give Americans more choices at the polls*. Protect Democracy and New America.

Theriault, Sean. 2013. *The Gingrich senators: The roots of partisan warfare in Congress*. Oxford University Press.

Theriault, Sean. 2015. *Party Warriors*. Cambridge University Press.

Troiano, Nick. 2024. *The Primary Solution: Rescuing Our Democracy from the Fringes*. Simon and Schuster.

Unite America. 2025. "Meaningful Votes: A New Metric to Understand American Politics." Research Brief. www.uniteamerica.org/meaningful-vote.

Zaller, John R. 1992. *The Nature and Origins of Mass Opinion*. Cambridge University Press.

Michael J. Ritter and Caroline J. Tolbert

Chapter 12
The Effects of Mail Voting, County Election Administration, and Accessible Primary Rules on Midterm Primary Voter Turnout

Abstract: Can voting reforms and high-quality election administration increase voter turnout and make turnout more equal in primary elections in the United States? This is an important question because, though these elections are critical in determining who will be the candidates in general elections, they are known for low voter turnout rates. This chapter examines how voting reforms and election administration can work independently and together to improve the level of political participation in these elections. More specifically, this research provides an overview of the scholarship on voting reform laws and election administration in relation to American general and primary elections. Then, focusing on U.S. midterm primary elections from 2014 to 2022, this chapter employs qualitative and quantitative research methods and evidence to show how voting reforms and election administration shape voter turnout and turnout equality between different demographic and political groups. Finally, this chapter synthesizes prior research with this study's empirical findings to make a series of policy recommendations. Ultimately, this chapter illustrates how voting reforms and high-quality election administration can serve as curatives to low and unequal political participation in U.S. primary elections.

What if, in the United States, the only elections that mattered were primary elections? While this may seem hyperbolic, some argue this may be an accurate assessment of election circumstances in wide parts of the country. According to Drutman (2021, 21–22), only one-sixth of House general elections are competitive, offering viable candidate choices from different political parties to the general electorate. This means that primaries are the only competitive elections for many Americans in which they can cast meaningful ballots that can make a difference. Yet US primaries typically have very low voter turnout rates. A potential consequence of this problem is that such low voter turnout rates lead to the selection of candidates that are too partisan, particularly because partisan individuals are more likely to vote in primary elections than more moderate individuals. The selection of candidates that are too partisan in primary elections can reduce interest in general elections for moderate Americans (including those on the center-right and center-left), which can deter these Americans from engaging in subsequent general elections. How can this primary turnout problem be addressed? As noted by Drutman (2021), a possible solution is to make primary rules more accessible to a broader segment of the American people. Prior research (Ritter and Tolbert 2020) finds that more accessible voting rules such as mail voting and high-quality election administration can boost turnout in general elections, and this chapter argues that these factors—along with more accessible forms of primary rules, such as open and non-partisan primary rules—increase turnout in a similar manner in midterm primary elections.

A prominent concern with more accessible primary rules, as well as other more accessible voting laws such as no-excuse absentee or mail voting laws (that allow individuals to vote by mail with little or no restrictions) is that they only have minimal effects on voter turnout (Gronke et al. 2008; Drutman 2021; McGhee 2014). Low voting levels are concerning for any democracy, since such levels could decrease perceptions that such governments are representative or legitimate (Powell 1986). This is also a concern with primary elections in the US, when many states have either closed or partially closed rules that prohibit all but registered party members from casting ballots in these elections; such restrictions are known to reduce turnout in these elections. Generally, primary turnout throughout the US is low, at average levels of twenty percent or under in recent midterm elections (Ferrer and Thorning 2023). To rectify this dilemma, a number of states have adopted open and non-partisan primary election reforms in the recent past. These more accessible primary laws essentially remove party registration restrictions for participating in these elections; non-partisan primary reforms take this a step further by consolidating different party primaries into single primaries on single ballots. While one may expect these primary reforms to spark higher turnout, the research that exists on these topics shows mixed evidence that these reforms have this effect (Drutman 2021; McGhee 2014; but see Micatka, Tolbert, and Boatright 2024). Are these reforms without merit, or can they substantially increase turnout in these elections?

This study takes the position that these more accessible primary reform laws can increase voter turnout and bring more political independents into the primary electorate, but further argues that one needs to account for other election institutions—the presence of mail voting, as well as election administration—to best identify such effects. Ritter and Tolbert (2020) find, for example, that the impacts of voting laws are under-identified if one does not control for how well they are administered at the state-level. This chapter takes the Ritter and Tolbert (2020) study a step further by controlling for county election administration, where most election administration actually takes place (Ritter and Tolbert 2024). Within the present study, a key focus is to assess whether more accessible primary election rules (open and non-partisan rules), along with key mediating mechanisms (more mail voting implementation as well as county quality election administration), address the voter turnout problem in American primary elections. This chapter makes the argument that the beneficial aspects of open and non-partisan primary rules, the most accessible state primary rules, will be more clearly identified after controlling for the quality of county election administration and the degree of mail voting implementation in a state. Ultimately, this study shows that open and non-partisan primaries, along with high mail voting implementation and quality election administration, can boost voter turnout in midterm primary elections.

Primary Laws in the U.S.: A Gradual Turn to More Accessibility

An extensive literature on American political development emphasizes the necessity of broad voting rights protections, including in primary elections, for without these protections the overall quality of US democracy is subject to doubt (Keyssar 2009; Kousser 1974). For example, white primaries, prevalent in the American South from the 1870s to 1940s, blocked racial and ethnic minorities—largely Blacks—from casting ballots in the only competitive elections in the one-party American South during this time period (Kousser 1974). Such a restrictive primary system led to questions regarding whether the American South, and America as a whole, was fully a democracy during this era. Today, though closed primary rules may not have the explicit purpose of blocking racial or ethnic minority groups from voting, they place notable constraints on U.S. democracy, as reported by multiple studies (Bipartisan Policy Center Report 2014; Ferrer and Thorning 2023; Macomber and Fischer 2024). By removing party registration restrictions on political participation, open and non-partisan primary rules can be considered ways to dismantle the restrictive elements of the US primary system.

The Bipartisan Policy Center Report (2014) recommended that primary turnout levels should eclipse thirty percent by 2020. Ferring and Thorning (2023, 4, 18, 41) provide descriptive evidence illustrating that more accessible primary rules (open and non-partisan primaries) help states approach such levels of turnout, but in 2022 they found that only twenty percent of the US eligible voting population voted in midterm primary elections. Others challenge the ability of more accessible primary rules to substantially increase voter turnout. Examining total turnout in primary elections, Drutman (2021) says that, at best, "open primaries increase participation by only 2 or 3 percentage points . . ., and top-two primaries by 6 percentage points" (41). Such estimations showing minimal to moderate effects attributable to these laws are buttressed by other studies as well (Geras and Crespin 2018; Hill 2022). However, a recent finding by Micatka, Tolbert, and Boatright (2024) finds that non-partisan primaries increased individual probabilities of voting—the likelihood that individuals vote in these elections—by twelve percent in the 2022 midterm primary elections. Nonetheless, the research on the impacts of open or non-partisan primaries on voter turnout is mixed.

To get a more consistent handle on the impact of primary rules on voter turnout, it may be important to look at factors that can moderate the impacts of such laws. For example, although Drutman (2021, 60) is skeptical about the ability of open and non-partisan primary rules to substantially boost turnout, he suggests that mediating factors—such as the presence of accessible mail voting laws—may have a conditional effect on such rules, possibly making them more positively and significantly related to voter turnout. This literature speaks to a key expectation of this chapter, that the impacts of primary rules on turnout will be enhanced with higher implementation of mail voting and higher quality county election administration.

Primary Laws and Moderating Factors

A set of research findings illustrates that contextual factors condition the impacts of primary rules on voting. Regarding the relevant research literature, Boatright et al. (2020) find that turnout is higher in House primary elections when such contests are listed on the same ballots as presidential primaries. In other work pertaining to the top-two primary in California, Bonneau and Zaleski (2021) show that ballot roll-off rates[1] tend to increase when there are not candidates from each major party on the general election ballot. In a similar vein, Fisk (2020) expounds that, under top-two systems, voter turnout drops in subsequent general elections for individuals who do not have candidates representing their party on the ballot (such as when top-two primaries result in two candidates of the same party winning). Campaign context is also critical: Hill and Kousser (2016) dis-

---

1 Ballot roll-off generally refers to individuals who vote for higher placed positions on a ballot (such as a U.S. presidential or Senate candidate) but then do not vote for lower placed positions. Bonneau and Zaleski (2021) find that roll-off increases on general election ballots when there is an absence of major party candidates for government seats located on such ballots. This can happen when top-two primary outcomes result in only minor party or independent candidates on general election ballots.

cuss how campaign mailers, a reflection of the campaign environment, can raise voting in elections. Jewitt (2014), in a piece of particularly relevant research to the present study, shows that primary rule system context also matters; to this purpose, she finds that states with more open primary rules have higher turnout. Together, these various pieces of research demonstrate that context matters in shaping the impacts of primary rules on voter turnout. However, no study heretofore has probed or analyzed the questions regarding how mail voting and election administration impact the relationship between primary rules and turnout. Our argument is that mail voting and election administration quality can be understood as contextual factors that shape the effects of primary rules on voter turnout.

That being said, perhaps the most similar study—at least in focus—to this one is that of McGhee (2014). In his work, he studies the effects of state-level online voter registration and same-day registration laws on primary election voting over a thirty-year period from 1980 to 2012. His research finds no strong evidence that these measures significantly increased turnout in primary elections (McGhee 2014, 2, 16). While this result suggests that more accessible voting laws do not have a significant effect on primary turnout, this chapter argues that an updated research design—with more recent data from the 2010s and 2020s—provides more leverage for assessing how other accessible voting factors (mail voting and election administration) shape the impact of primary laws on voter turnout.

Moderating Impacts of Mail Voting and County Election Administration

Prior research has found that more accessible voting laws—like mail voting—and higher quality election administration improve turnout in general elections in the U.S., and this chapter expects there to be comparable effects for turnout in primary elections. A substantial literature (Gronke et al. 2008; McDonald et al. 2023; Ritter and Tolbert 2020) explains that a large reason mail voting is expected to increase ballot casting, compared to states with only in-person Election Day voting, is due to mail voting enabling individuals to vote from their own residences, relative to experiencing the time costs associated with going to a polling site. Reducing time and transportation costs linked to voting are prominent reasons why mail voting is related to higher likelihoods of turnout (Bonica et al. 2021; McGhee et al. 2022; Thompson et al. 2020). Ritter (2024) shows that the type of mail voting also matters, with state universal mail, permanent absentee, and no-excuse absentee laws linked to higher levels of turnout, compared to excuse required absentee voting laws; the three former laws attach no legal requirements beyond requesting a mail ballot—and universal mail laws do not require voters to make this request—for individuals to vote by mail, while the latter requires voters to have a state-permitted reason to vote by mail. In another study, McDonald et. al. (2024) uses the percentage of ballots cast via mail as a proxy for mail voting implementation, with higher implementation being more likely to be characteristic of states with the more accessible mail voting laws; they find that higher mail voting implementation is related to higher levels of voter turnout. While the literature on mail voting is extensive, no study has yet evaluated whether mail voting is a key structuring factor relating to voter turnout in primary elections. This study's expectation is that states with more accessible forms of mail voting will have individuals who are more likely to vote in primary elections.

In addition, this chapter also theorizes that election administration is another moderating factor structuring the impacts of primary rules on voter turnout. To provide a metaphorical illustration of this subject, Stewart (2010) likens election administration to a series of chains and links between an election management body (such as a county election office) and the voter; such chains and links include the construction of a ballot, the sending of the ballot to and from the voter, and the tabulation of the ballot at an election office. According to Stewart (2010), if any chain or link in this election administration process is absent or inadequate, a person's ability to cast a countable ballot is reduced. The implication of this concept is that, without accounting for election administration, one cannot accurately isolate the direct effects of mail voting or primary rules on voting (Ritter and Tolbert 2020).

There is much literature that explores how election administration shapes multiple dimensions of federal, state, and local voting systems, including voter access, or the convenience by which individuals are able to vote (Alvarez, Atkeson, and Hall 2013; Ritter and Tolbert 2020). For example, to implement mail voting to promote access, election officials need accurate postal addresses from county or state records to send mail ballots to the proper locations; they need to make informational tools available to voters, such as directions on what identification information is necessary to complete mail ballots; and they also need to make sure that election sites have well-functioning tabulation machines, so mail ballots are quickly and accurately processed and counted.

As a way to assess election administration quality, Ritter and Tolbert (2024) have moved this field of study forward through the creation of the county election administration (CEA) index. This index measures the overall quality of election administration in every county or county-equivalent election jurisdiction in the US. The index is germane because county or county-equivalent election jurisdictions—relative to federal and state governments—are most centrally involved in administering elections in the US. For example, they appoint and locate polling workers and sites, they put together and transmit mail ballots, they secure and maintain election machines, and more. In past research, Ritter and Tolbert (2020) show that higher quality election administration can positively structure the impacts of various voting laws (including mail voting) on voter turnout in general elections.

In this research, the expectation is that higher quality election administration, and higher implementation of mail voting, will boost turnout in midterm primary elections. Under lower quality election administration, there is the expectation that individuals will find it harder to cast ballots. Under such conditions, for example, there is a lower likelihood that a county has enough poll workers, conveniently located polling sites, sufficient quality election machines, and more. On the other hand, when there is higher quality election administration, it is expected that a county will have election administrative features that make the casting of a ballot easier in primary elections. Regarding mail voting, higher mail voting implementation is indicative of state election environments wherein the casting of a ballot is more convenient, so this chapter expects primary election turnout to be enhanced with a wider presence of mail voting. While this chapter argues that more accessible forms of primary voting (open and non-partisan rules) boost turnout, it also argues that turnout will be further enhanced with high-quality election administration and high mail voting implementation.

Expectations on Impacts of More Accessible Primary Rules on Voter Turnout

The accessible voting theoretical framework devised by Ritter and Tolbert (2020) assumes that American states with more accessible electoral systems will promote higher and more equal voter turnout. According to them, more accessible American state electoral systems are represented by the presence of more accessible mail voting laws, as well as higher quality election administration. In their empirical findings, they find that voter turnout is higher in states with these elements of more accessible elections, and they also find that voting is more equal between individuals of different socio-economic statuses and racial/ethnic group categories. To apply this theoretical framework to this chapter, this study expects that more accessible primary rules, more mail voting implementation (a proxy for more accessible mail voting laws), and higher quality county election administration will promote higher turnout in midterm primary elections. Additionally, this research also anticipates that these same factors will help make primary elections more equal by improving the voter turnout probabilities of political Independents, who are disproportionately less likely to vote—compared to Republicans and Democrats—in primary elections (Ferrer and Thorning 2023). More specifically, the following hypotheses are evaluated in this chapter:

H1: More accessible primary rules (open and non-partisan) will promote higher and more equal turnout in primary elections.

H2: More mail voting implementation and higher quality county election administration will promote higher and more equal turnout in primary elections.

To set up the empirical evaluations of these hypotheses, the next section discusses the data and methods for this chapter.

Data and Methods

This chapter employs large voter file data from Catalist (2025), a data analytics firm that takes state vote file data and combines this with other data sources—on demographics, party identification and ideological orientation, news source subscription patterns, and more.[2] In recent years, this data has been employed in numerous studies that examine factors that shape voter turnout (Hersh 2015; Fraga 2018; Ritter and Tolbert 2020), including primary elections (Micatka et al. 2024). The Catalist data includes both registered and unregistered voters, as well as vote histories, enabling the creation of nationally representative panel models to measure the within-person change impacts of various factors on changes in individuals' likelihoods of voting in midterm primary elections. The large nature of the data source also offers superior statistical power compared to other studies that rely on American national election studies, cooperative election studies, or current population survey data, meaning the estimates in this study offer better precision on the impacts of key independent variables on turnout in these elections. The dataset employed in this chapter is a one percent ran-

---

2 Many variables from Catalist are based on hard data, meaning based on evidentiary records, such as state voter files. For thirty states, hard data is available for age, gender, political party, and race or ethnicity. For states where this data is not available in hard form, Catalist employs a statistical matching process to impute them. This procedure is also applied to variables relating to education and income levels. According to the Pew Research Center (Igielnik et al. 2018) and Hersh (2015), the Catalist imputations of these variables are highly accurate and have high predictive validity.

dom sample from the Catalist sampling frame encompassing all American adults from the fifty states and Washington, D.C. More specifically, the data sizes for the study's models include 2,316,161 individuals for the 2014 midterm primary elections, 2,476,044 individuals for the 2018 midterm primary elections, and 2,695,728 individuals for the 2022 primary midterm elections.

The dependent variable in these models is voter turnout in the midterm primary elections (coded 1 for having voted in such elections, 0 for not). Registered and unregistered eligible individuals who did not cast ballots in these elections are counted as non-voters. This coding has been utilized in other studies (Ritter and Tolbert 2020). The 2014, 2018, and 2022 models also included a lagged voter turnout variable, to control for how past voting habits can shape current voting tendencies (Plutzer 2002). These lagged variables are coded 1 for having voted in the preceding midterm election, 0 for having not done so.

As for key independent variables, the first is mail voting. This variable, based on Election Assistance Commission (2024) data, measures what percentage of ballots cast in a state were done so via absentee or mail voting. This is a way of operationalizing the degree to which this mode of voting is implemented (McDonald et al. 2024). Higher implementation is a sign that more voting convenience is available to individuals in such states through absentee or mail voting. Other key independent variables include dummy variables for each of the primary law categories: partially closed, partially open, open, and non-partisan, with closed primary rules the reference category. Within this study's empirical models, if a state has one of these laws, they are coded 1, and states without them are coded 0. For the models, additionally, the partially open category is combined with the open to unaffiliated primary rule category, since these primary rules are similar. Data for primary rules comes from the National Conference of State Legislatures (2023).

The CEA variable measures the quality of county election administration performance, which conceptually represents how well counties administer voting laws (like mail voting) and primary rules (Ritter and Tolbert 2024). For each of the models, this study includes a contemporaneous CEA variable (e. g., CEA 2022 in this instance) as well as a lagged CEA variable (e. g., CEA 2020 for 2022). This is done to capture election administration calibrations made following the most recent major election that could shape voter access (the lagged variable), as well as the degree to which such election administration arrangements were suitable for the given election year (the contemporaneous variable). On a 0 – 100 scale, counties higher on this measure have higher election administration quality. The mean average of this variable increased from 51 to 59 from 2012 to 2022, with standard deviations that ranged from 13 to 18.5. Election administration quality tends to be higher in the Midwest and West, and lower in the South, but the CEA captures considerable within and across state variation in election administration quality throughout the US during these years. As such, the CEA measure provides a lot of leverage for assessing how election administration structures voting in primary elections.

Regarding other key policy variables, two other accessible voting laws—in-person early voting and same-day registration—are included because they also bring more convenience to ballot casting. The former law permits individuals to cast ballots in-person before Election Day, and the latter lets individuals register and vote on the same day. Past research (Ritter and Tolbert 2020) has found that these laws also increase individual turnout probabilities, and this study accounts for these factors by controlling for the degree to which states have implemented these modes of voting. The early voting variable is measured as the percentage of ballots cast in a state via in-person early voting, and the same-day registration (SDR) variable is the percentage of ballots cast in a state via SDR (Election Assistance Commission 2024).

To account for possible spurious relationships or omitted variable bias, we also include several control variables. The political competition variables include the Democratic Governor Fractionalization (for competitiveness of Democratic gubernatorial primaries), Republican Governor Fractionalization (for competitiveness of Republican gubernatorial primaries), Democratic Senate Fractionalization (for competitiveness of Democratic senate primaries), and Republican Senate Fractionalization (for competitiveness of Republican senate primaries) variables. These fractionalization measures, developed by Bradley Canon (1978) and calculated for the 2014–2022 elections by Robert Boatright, are bounded between 0 and 1; they take into account the number of candidates and their vote shares in primary elections, with higher numbers indicating more competitive primary elections (Boatright 2014; Micatka et al. 2024). This accounts for the possibility that the overall competitiveness of primary elections, rather than the rules themselves, is driving turnout. Other control variables include age and age squared, education (the probability that one has a bachelor's degree, ranging from zero to one hundred percent), married (1 = married, 0 = not), and race (Black, Latino, Asian, Other Race; 1 = one of these races/ethnicities, 0 = not, with Whites as the reference group). The income quintile measure calibrates individuals' income to the income distribution within every state (since different states have different living costs), ranging from -2, -1, 0, and 1, to 2, with higher quintiles indicating higher incomes. This income measure was also employed in Ritter and Solt (2019).

The voter file we employ from Catalist includes a variable for the imputed probability that one is a Democrat, ranging from 0 to 100. The imputed partisanship Catalist measure correlates highly with actual records of individuals' party identifications from voter files and hence is considered in this study to be a valid measure of partisanship (see Hersh 2015). Following the variable construction methods employed by Micatka et al. (2024), this study defines Republicans as identified at the 0–25 levels of this imputed partisanship measure, Independents at 26–75 levels, and Democrats at 76–100 levels. Specifically, there are three party identification variables—Republican, Independent, and Democrat—with individuals in these categories coded with a 1 and individuals not in these categories coded with a 0.

This study evaluates the impact of the key independent variables on voter turnout at the individual-level, using logistic regressions models. This is done to examine both the general effects of these variables and how these factors influence turnout among subsamples of Republicans, Independents, and Democrats. What do the results show?

Results

First, the key results for the 2014 midterm primary elections (as displayed in Table 12.1, the 2014 model) show that higher mail voting implementation in the 2014 midterm primary election was related to more turnout. Relative to closed primary elections (the reference category), each of the more accessible primary reform laws (partially closed, partially open, open, and non-partisan) was significantly related to higher turnout. County election administration quality had a null effect on primary turnout during this election year.

Regarding other important results in 2014, higher SDR implementation is positively related to voting, but higher early voting implementation is negatively related to this outcome. Burden et al. (2014) have noted that campaign mobilization tends to be less prevalent in states with only early voting, and this may explain the early voting effect. SDR is broadly known to be the convenience voting law most consistently related to positive effects on voting (Ritter and Tolbert 2020). Most of the political competitiveness variables, except for the Republican Senate Fractionalization primary measure, are significantly related to higher turnout, indicating the importance of having more competitive primaries to spur turnout. As for the control variables, Democrats, but not Independents, are more likely to vote in this election, relative to Republicans. Additionally, non-Hispanic White individuals (the reference racial category) are more likely to vote than individuals from other racial groups. Older individuals are generally more likely to vote, but the significant quadratic age variable indicates there is a ceiling to this relationship. More educated, female, married, but not higher income quintile, individuals are also more likely to vote in the 2014 primary midterm elections.

Table 12.1: Likelihood of voting in 2014, 2018, and 2022 midterm primary elections (controlling for turnout in previous midterm primary elections).

	2014	2018	2022
Lagged Vote	2.249***	2.287***	2.145***
	(0.014)	(0.013)	(0.010)
Mail Voting	0.008***	0.009***	0.013***
	(0.001)	(0.002)	(0.001)
Partially Closed	0.236***	-0.056	-0.250***
	(0.070)	(0.064)	(0.072)
Partially Open	0.245***	-0.213**	-0.277***
	(0.054)	(0.075)	(0.063)
Open	0.204***	0.370***	0.081
	(0.054)	(0.042)	(0.055)
Non-Partisan	0.410***	0.545***	0.163**
	(0.063)	(0.094)	(0.076)
Contemporaneous CEA	-0.0004	-0.002	0.004
	(0.002)	(0.002)	(0.001)
Lagged CEA	-0.0004	0.003*	0.003**
	(0.002)	(0.002)	(0.001)
Early Voting	-0.011**	-0.007***	0.008***
	(0.004)	(0.002)	(0.001)
SDR	0.009**	0.013***	0.037***
	(0.004)	(0.004)	(0.011)
Dem. Gov. Frac.	0.209**	0.592***	-0.299***
	(0.080)	(0.069)	(0.057)
Rep. Gov. Frac.	0.118*	0.085	0.541***
	(0.067)	(0.084)	(0.053)
Dem. Sen. Frac.	1.006***	-0.464***	0.821***
	(0.136)	(0.101)	(0.115)
Rep. Sen. Frac.	-0.285**	0.263**	0.173**
	(0.100)	(0.109)	(0.086)
Income Quintile	-0.008**	0.147***	0.136***
	(0.004)	(0.005)	(0.005)
Independent	-0.252***	-1.222***	-1.374***
	(0.019)	(0.031)	(0.028)
Democrat	0.121***	0.355***	-0.183***
	(0.020)	(0.029)	(0.018)
Black	-0.133***	-0.445***	-0.457***
	(0.033)	(0.036)	(0.022)
Hispanic	-0.341***	-0.458***	-0.597***
	(0.032)	(0.027)	(0.026)
Asian	-0.149**	-0.554***	-0.454***
	(0.070)	(0.058)	(0.056)
Other Race	-0.135**	-0.284***	-0.316***
	(0.058)	(0.025)	(0.029)

Table 12.1 *(Continued)*

	2014	2018	2022
Age	0.079***	0.064***	0.036***
	(0.001)	(0.002)	(0.002)
Age 2	-0.0005***	-0.0004***	-0.0002***
	(0.000)	(0.000)	(0.000)
Pr(Bachelor's Degree)	0.808***	0.006***	0.004***
	(0.071)	(0.001)	(0.001)
Female	0.031***	0.050***	0.044***
	(0.006)	(0.006)	(0.005)
Pr(Married)	0.512***	0.071***	0.039***
	(0.023)	(0.010)	(0.008)
Constant	-6.079***	-4.588***	-3.893***
	(0.099)	(0.120)	(0.089)
Pseudo R^2	0.261	0.268	0.286
Observations	2,316,161	2,482,347	2,695,728

County-level clustered errors in parentheses
* $p < 0.10$, ** $p < 0.05$, *** $p < 0.001$

Moving to the results displayed in the second model of Table 12.1 (the 2018 midterm primary results), do the findings from 2014 hold true for 2018? Except for the lagged county election administration quality variable (CEA 2016), which has a positive effect on primary turnout in the 2018 primary elections, the general answer is yes. The positive effect of the CEA 2016 variable may indicate that election administrators effectively prepared for the 2018 election season (e. g., hiring enough poll workers, having well-functioning election equipment, and having well-located polling sites). Regarding other key variables, states with more implementation of mail voting have higher turnout in this election, as do states with open or non-partisan primary rules. Also, higher implementation of SDR is related to more voting, but higher implementation of early voting results in less turnout. In short, these results demonstrate that mail voting and SDR, more accessible primary rules, and higher quality election administration can improve turnout in midterm primary elections.

As for the control variables in 2018, the political competition variables—except for the Republican Governor Fractionalization and Democratic Senate Fractionalization primary measures—have significant and positive effects on voter turnout. More education, higher income quintile, female, older (though there is a ceiling to this age effect), married, and non-Hispanic Whites (relative to those

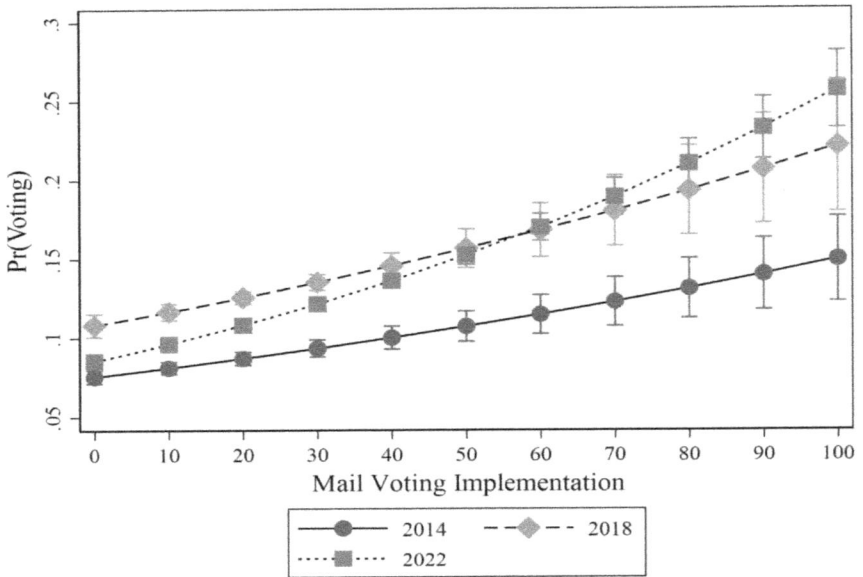

Figure 12.1: impact of mail voting implementation on probability (%) of midterm primary election turnout, 2014, 2018, and 2022.
Note: Probabilities derived from mail voting logistic regression results in first, second, and third models of Table 12.1, while holding other variables at mean values. Vertical lines are ninety-five percent confidence intervals.

from other racial groups) are more likely to vote. Republicans and Democrats, compared to Independents, are more likely to cast ballots in this primary.

To what extent did more accessible primary rules, mail voting, and other key independent variables matter in the 2022 midterm primary elections? As exhibited by the third model, Table 12.1 results (pertaining to the 2022 midterm primary elections), quite a bit. More mail voting implementation is related to higher likelihoods of voting. The same is true of non-partisan primary rules. Higher quality county election administration, represented by the lagged CEA variable, is also positively related to voting. Regarding other voting variables, both higher SDR and early voting implementation are linked to higher propensities of voting.

Regarding the control variables for 2022, except for the Democratic Governor Fractionalization primary election measure, the political competition variables positively relate to turnout. More educated, older, higher income, non-Hispanic White, married, female, and Republican (relative to Independents and Democrats) individuals are more likely to vote.

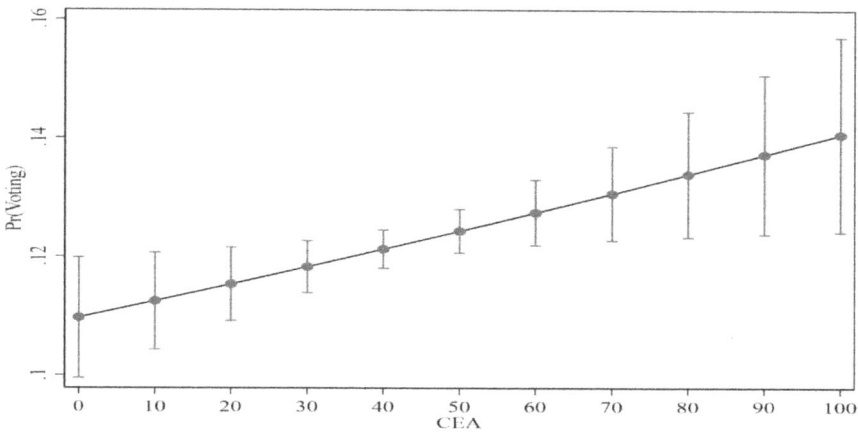

Figure 12.2: Impact of CEA on probability (%) of midterm primary election turnout in 2022. Note: Probabilities derived from the lagged CEA logistic regression result in the third model of Table 12.1, while holding other variables at mean values. Vertical lines are ninety-five percent confidence intervals.

Generally, the 2014 to 2022 midterm primary analyses show that more accessible primary rules, more accessible voting laws, and quality county election administration improve one's probability of voting in these elections.

The Substantive Impacts of Accessible Voting in Midterm Primary Elections

This section translates the key results (mail voting implementation and election administration) from Table 12.1 into more understandable percentages. As illustrated in Figure 12.1, in 2014, the highest mail voting implementation level is related to a 7.39 percent increase in one's probability of voting (from 7.56 to 14.95 percent); in 2018, an 11.31 percent increase (from 10.80 to 22.11 percent); and, in 2022, a 17.15 percent increase (from 8.53 to 25.68 percent). These increases likely reflect the increased popularity of mail voting as a convenient mode of voting in the US (McDonald et al. 2024; Ritter 2024).

What about election administration? For the 2022 midterm primary elections, ranging the lagged CEA variable (CEA 2020) from minimum to maximum levels, as depicted in Figure 12.2, a person's probability of voting increased from 10.97 to 14.06 percent, a 3.09 percent difference. Election administration is also substantively important.

Table 12.2 reports the predicted probabilities pertaining to open and non-partisan primaries. Open primaries significantly boosted the probability of voting by 1.58 and 4.14 percent in 2014 and 2018. Non-partisan primaries increased this probability by 3.4 and 6.7 percent in 2014 and 2018. These results show that these more accessible primary rules have a positive impact on voting.

Table 12.2: Impact of open and non-partisan primary rules on probability (%) of midterm primary election turnout, 2014, 2018, and 2022.

Year	No Open	Open	Open Primary Difference	No Non-Partisan	Non-Partisan	Non-Partisan Difference
2014	7.71	9.29	1.58**	7.54	10.94	3.40**
	(7.31, 8.11)	(8.50, 10.08)		(7.14, 7.93)	(9.89, 11.99)	
2018	10.89	15.03	4.14**	11.26	17.96	6.70**
	(10.42, 11.36)	(14.12, 15.95)		(10.78, 11.74)	(15.52, 20.40)	
2022	11.87	12.74	0.87	11.90	13.72	1.82
	(11.39, 12.36)	(11.88, 13.61)		(11.49, 12.31)	(12.21, 15.24)	

Note: Probabilities derived from open and non-partisan primary rule logistic regression results in first, second, and third models of Table 12.1, while holding other variables at mean values. Numbers in parentheses are ninety-five percent confidence intervals.
** indicates difference estimates, comparing turnout probabilities without versus with examined primary rules, are statistically distinct because the estimates' confidence intervals do not intersect.

Overall, these substantive findings illustrate that more accessible primary rules, mail voting, and effective election administration can positively shape turnout rates for midterm primary elections.

How Do More Accessible Election Rules and Election Administration Impact Midterm Primary Election Turnout among Republicans, Independents, and Democrats?

Table 12.3 displays the percentage probability impacts of open and non-partisan primary rules for Republicans, Independents, and Democrats. These are derived from three subsample logistic regression models, with the same variables as the earlier models in this study, except that these subsample models are applied separately to Republican, Independent, and Democratic individuals (models available in online appendix). The results reveal that open and non-partisan rules improve voter turnout for individuals from all three party categories.

More accessible primary rules can play a key role in generating higher turnout among Independents. In 2014, open primary rules increased the probability of voting for Independents by 2.05 percent, and non-partisan primary rules by 3.22 percent. For 2018, open primary rules boosted the probability of an Independent voting by 2.94 percent, and non-partisan rules raised the probability by 4.85 percent. Regarding 2022, open primary rules increased the likelihood of Independents voting by 1.72 percent.

For Republicans, open primary rules increased their probability of voting by 6.25 percent in 2018. In 2014, 2018, and 2022, respectively, non-partisan primary rules increased Republican probability of voting by 6.51, 17.05, and 3.89 percent. For Democrats, in 2014 and 2018, open primary rules increased the probability of voting by 1.44 and 2.79 percent. In these same years, non-partisan primary rules improved the probability of Democrats voting by 3.89 and 7.45 percent. More accessible primary rules boost turnout probabilities for Republicans, Democrats, and Independents in midterm primary elections.

Mail voting implementation has a larger percentage impact on individual voting probabilities in midterm primary elections than either open or non-partisan rules by themselves. For Republicans, in 2014, the maximum level of mail voting implementation was related to an 11.1 percent increase in an individual's probability of voting, from 15.41 to 26.51 percent. In 2018, the probability increase was from 22.64 to 45.99 percent; and, in 2022, this increase was from 24.95 to 50.36 percent.

In 2014, for Independents, the boost in probability of voting attributable to mail voting implementation varied from 6.62 (at the minimum implementation) to 14.14 percent (at the maximum implementation), an increase of 7.52 percent. In 2018, this increase was 5.52 percent, bumping up from 3.05 to 8.27 percent. Among Independents in 2022, the highest mail voting implementation was related to an 8.32 percent boost in one's probability of voting, from 2.62 to 10.94 percent.

For Democrats in 2014, mail voting increased turnout probability positively by 7.65 percent, from a minimum of 7.98 to a maximum of 15.63 percent. For 2018, the maximum implementation of mail voting was linked to a 26.5 percent probability of voting, while the minimum implementation to a 19.03 percent probability, a 7.47 percent difference. For Democrats in 2022, this overall positive effect was 24.75 percent, from 11.54 to 36.29 percent.

Higher mail voting implementation appears to benefit individuals in all party categories, although those associated with the major parties benefit more.

As for the impact of county election administration, the general findings are that higher performing county election administration increases the likelihood of

Table 12.3: Impact of open and non-partisan primary rules on probability (%) of Republicans, Independents, and Democrats in midterm primary elections, 2014, 2018, and 2022.

	No Open Primary	Open Primary	Impact of Open Primaries	No Non-Partisan Primary	Non-Partisan Primary	Impact of Non-Partisan Primaries
Republican 2014	16.19 (15.60, 16.78)	17.17 (15.85, 18.05)	0.98	15.23 (14.63, 15.82)	21.74 (20.00, 23.47)	6.51**
Republican 2018	23.91 (23.22, 24.60)	30.16 (28.74, 31.58)	6.25**	23.74 (22.99, 24.49)	40.79 (36.34, 45.26)	17.05**
Republican 2022	31.48 (30.67, 32.29)	31.28 (29.71, 32.86)	-0.2	30.96 (30.3, 31.62)	34.85 (31.37, 38.03)	3.89**
Independent 2014	6.46 (6.09, 6.83)	8.51 (7.74, 9.27)	2.05**	6.71 (6.38, 7.04)	9.93 (8.88, 10.97)	3.22**
Independent 2018	2.54 (2.36, 2.72)	5.48 (4.94, 6.03)	2.94**	3.13 (2.93, 3.34)	7.98 (6.47, 9.50)	4.85**
Independent 2022	3.34 (3.08, 3.59)	5.06 (4.61, 5.51)	1.72**	3.91 (3.70, 4.12)	4.49 (3.73, 5.25)	0.58
Democrat 2014	8.26 (7.81, 8.72)	9.70 (8.80, 10.59)	1.44**	7.79 (7.37, 8.22)	11.68 (10.18, 13.17)	3.89**
Democrat 2018	19.48 (18.63, 20.33)	22.27 (20.81, 23.72)	2.79**	18.82 (18.01, 19.64)	26.27 (22.75, 29.79)	7.45**
Democrat 2022	17.91 (17.16, 18.66)	16.17 (14.82, 17.51)	-1.74	17.23 (16.51, 17.95)	18.78 (16.39, 21.16)	1.55

Note: Probabilities derived from open and non-partisan primary rule logistic regression results from Appendix Tables 1, 2, and 3 (online appendix), while holding other variables at mean values. Numbers in parentheses are ninety-five percent confidence intervals.
** indicates difference estimates, comparing turnout probabilities without versus with examined primary rules, are statistically distinct because the estimates' confidence intervals do not intersect.

voting for Republicans and Independents. In 2014, higher contemporaneous county election administration quality (CEA in 2014) was related to higher likelihoods of voting among Republicans. In 2018, higher contemporaneous county election administration quality (CEA in 2018) was related to higher likelihoods of voting among Independents. And, in 2022, higher lagged county election administration quality (CEA in 2020) was related to higher turnout probabilities among Independents, and higher contemporaneous county election administration quality (CEA in 2022) was related to higher turnout among Republicans. These positive CEA results suggest that countries generally prepare well for administering primary elections, particularly in the cases of Republicans and Independents. There are, however, two negative relationships between CEA and turnout: one, a negative relationship between contemporaneous county election administration quality and turnout among Democrats in 2014, and, two, between lagged county election administration quality and turnout among Republicans in 2018. These negative findings suggest that, during these years, county election administration quality may not have perfectly conformed to the needs of Democratic or Republican primary voters. Nevertheless, the general pattern of findings is that higher quality county election administration can enhance turnout in midterm primary elections.

The ancillary findings (on the other primary rules, as well as in-person early voting and SDR) are available in the online appendix. To briefly summarize these results, partially closed and partially open rules are more inconsistently related to higher turnout than open or non-partisan primary rules among individuals across the party subsample categories. Additionally, SDR, in 2014, 2018, and 2022, is more typically related to higher turnout among individuals across the party subsample categories (for Republicans, Democrats, and Independents). Early voting, on the other hand, only has a positive effect on turnout for Republicans and Democrats in 2022, and more often has negative or null impacts on turnout among Republicans, Democrats, and Independents in 2018 and 2020.

In sum, these subsample results indicate that Republicans, Independents, and Democrats mutually benefit from more accessible primary rules, more mail voting implementation, and—to some extent—from better quality election administration.

Conclusion

In conclusion, this chapter has illustrated how more accessible primary rules, paired with high mail voting implementation and quality election administration, can enhance voter turnout probabilities generally among prospective midterm primary voters, as well as individuals indexed by their party identification, including Independents. Regarding the impacts of open and non-partisan primary rules, the study shows estimates that are in line with past studies that have indicated that these laws can have moderate impacts on primary turnout (Geras and Crespin 2018; Hill 2022). Importantly, the study also shows that these laws can boost turnout among Independents, a usually low turnout group in these elections (Ferrer and Thorning 2023).

For possible prescriptive guidance, states that combine open or non-partisan primary rules with high mail voting implementation and high average county election administration quality may act as policy benchmarks. As of 2022, states with open primary rules and above mean average mail voting implementation and above mean average county election administration quality include Hawaii, Michigan, and Vermont. As of this same year, states with non-partisan primary rules and above mean average mail voting implementation and above mean average county election administration quality include California, Nebraska, and Washington.

Ultimately, breaking new ground, this chapter demonstrates the critical role that mail voting implementation and county election administration play in building turnout in midterm primary elections, with mail voting in particular having large substantive impacts on voter turnout among the overall primary electorate, as well as among Republicans, Democrats, and Independents. This chapter has also shown that combining accessible primary rules, such as open and non-partisan primary rules, along with high mail voting implementation and quality election administration, can optimize turnout in these elections.

Bibliography

Alvarez, R. Michael, Lonna Rae Atkeson, and Thad E. Hall. 2013. *Evaluating Elections: A Handbook of Methods and Standards.* Cambridge University Press.

Bipartisan Policy Center Report. 2014. "Governing in a Polarized America: A Bipartisan Blueprint to Strengthen Our Democracy." https://bipartisanpolicy.org/download/?file=/wp-content/uploads/2019/03/BPC-CPR-Report.pdf.

Boatright, Robert G. 2014. *Congressional Primary Elections.* Routledge.

Boatright, Robert G., Vincent G. Moscardelli, and Clifford D. Vickrey. 2020. "Primary Election Timing and Voter Turnout." *Election Law Journal* 19 (4): 472–485.

Bonica, Adam, Jacob M. Grumbach, Charlotte Hill, and Hakeem Jefferson. 2021. "All-Mail Voting in Colorado Increase Turnout and Reduces Turnout Inequality." *Electoral Studies* 72: 102363.

Bonneau, Daniel P., and John Zaleski. 2021. "The Effect of California's Top-Two Primary System on Voter Turnout in U.S. House Elections." *Economics of Governance* 22 (1): 1–21.

Burden, Barry C., David T. Canon, Kenneth R. Mayer, and Donald P. Moynihan. 2014. "Election Laws, Mobilization, and Turnout: The Unanticipated Consequences of Election Reform." *American Journal of Political Science* 58 (1): 95–109.

Canon, Bradley C. 1978. "Factionalism in the South: A Test of Theory and a Revisitation of V. O. Key." *American Journal of Political Science* 22 (4): 833–848.

Catalist. 2025. Homepage. https://catalist.us/.

Chu, C., Y. Cyrus, S. Y. Lin, and Wen-Jen Tsay. 2021. "Estimating the Willingness to Pay for Voting when Absentee Voting is Not Allowed." *Social Science Quarterly* 102 (4): 1380–1393.

Drutman, Lee. 2021. "What We Know about Congressional Primaries and Congressional Primary Reform." New America. https://search.issuelab.org/resources/38554/38554.pdf.

Election Assistance Commission. 2024. "Studies and Reports." https://www.eac.gov/research-and-data/studies-and-reports.

Ferrer, Joshua, and Michael Thorning. 2023. "2022 Primary Turnout: Trends and Lessons for Boosting Participation." Bipartisan Policy Center. https://bipartisanpolicy.org/download/?file=/wp-content/uploads/2023/03/Primary-Turnout-Report_R03.pdf.

Fisk, Colin A. 2020. "Executive Summary." New America. https://www.newamerica.org/political-reform/reports/what-we-know-about-congressional-primaries-and-congressional-primary-reform/executive-summary.

Fraga, Bernard L. 2018. *The Turnout Gap: Race, Ethnicity, and Political Inequality in a Diversifying America.* Cambridge University Press.

Geras, Matthew J., and Michael H. Crespin. 2018. "The Effect of Open and Closed Primaries on Voter Turnout." In *Routledge Handbook of Primary Elections*, edited by Robert G. Boatright. Routledge Handbooks.

Gronke, Paul, Eva Galanes-Rosenbaum, Peter A. Miller, and Daniel Toffey. 2008. "Convenience Voting." *Annual Review of Political Science* 11 (1): 437–455.

Hersh, Eitan D. 2015. *Hacking the Electorate: How Campaigns Perceive Voters.* Cambridge University Press.

Hill, Seth J. 2022. "Sidestepping Primary Reform: Political Action in Response to Institutional Change." *Political Science Research and Methods* 10 (2): 391–407.

Hill, Seth J., and Thad Kousser. 2016. "Turning Out Unlikely Voters? A Field Experiment in the Top-Two Primary." *Political Behavior* 38 (2): 413–432.

Igielnik, Ruth, Scott Keeter, Courtney Kennedy, and Bradly Spahn. 2018. "Commercial Voter Files and the Study of U.S. Politics." Pew Research Center. www.pewresearch.org/methods/2018/02/15/commercial-voter-files-and-the-study-of-u-s-politics/.

Jewitt, Caitlin E. 2014. "Packed Primaries and Empty Caucuses: Voter Turnout in Presidential Nominations." *Public Choice* 160 (2): 295–312.

Keyssar, Alexander. 2009. *The Right to Vote: The Contested History of Democracy in the United States.* Basic Books.

Kousser, J. Morgan. 1974. *The Shaping of Southern Politics: Suffrage Restriction and the Establishment of the One-Party South.* Yale University Press.

Macomber, Carlo, and Tyler Fisher. 2024. "Not Invited to the Party Primary: Independent Voters and the Problem with Closed Primaries." Unite America Institute. https://docsend.com/view/kz8jkfxixy727fds.

McDonald, Michael P., Juliana K. Mucci, Enrijeta Shino, and Daniel A. Smith. 2024. "Mail Voting and Voter Turnout." *Election Law Journal* 23 (1): 1–18.

McGhee, Eric. 2014. "Voter Turnout in Primary Elections." Public Policy Institute of California. https://www.ppic.org/publication/voter-turnout-in-primary-elections/.McGhee, Eric, Jennifer Paluch, and Mindy Romero. 2022. "Vote-by-Mail Policy and the 2020 Presidential Election." *Research & Politics* 9 (2): 20531680221089197.

Micatka, Nathan K., Caroline J. Tolbert, and Robert G. Boatright. 2024. "All Candidate Primaries, Open Primaries, and Voter Turnout." *Journal of Political Institutions and Political Economy* 5 (3): 363–385.

National Conference of State Legislatures. 2023. "Changes in State Primary Elections Since 2000." www.ncsl.org/elections-and-campaigns/changes-to-state-primary-elections-since-2000.

Plutzer, Eric. 2002. "Becoming a Habitual Voter: Inertia, Resources, and Growth in Young Adulthood." *American Political Science Review* 96 (1): 41–56.

Powell, G. Bingham, Jr. 1986. "American Voter Turnout in a Comparative Perspective." *American Political Science Review* 80 (1): 17–43.

Ritter, Michael. 2024. "Assessing the Impact of the United States Postal System and Election Administration on Absentee and Mail Voting in the 2012 to 2020 US Midterm and Presidential Elections." *Election Law Journal* 22 (2): 166–184.

Ritter, Michael, and Frederick Solt. 2019. "Economic Inequality and Campaign Participation." *Social Science Quarterly* 100 (3): 678–688.

Ritter, Michael, and Caroline J. Tolbert. 2020. *Accessible Elections: How the States Can Help Americans Vote*. Oxford University Press.

Ritter, Michael J., and Caroline J. Tolbert. 2024. "Measuring County Election Administration in the United States." *Election Law Journal* 23 (3): 258–276.

Stewart, Charles, III. 2010. "Losing Votes by Mail." *N.Y.U. Journal of Legislation and Public Policy* 13: 573.

Thompson, Daniel M., Jennifer A. Wu, Jesse Yoder, and Andrew B. Hall. 2020. "Universal Vote-by-Mail has No Impact on Partisan Turnout or Vote Share." *PNAS Nexus* 117 (25).

Deb Otis and Rachel Hutchinson

Chapter 13
Optimizing Nonpartisan Primaries with Ranked Choice Voting and Proportional Representation

Abstract: Individual election reforms should not just be evaluated in isolation but also in the context of how they contribute to the larger election reform agenda. In this chapter, we take this approach with nonpartisan primaries. Nonpartisan primaries are a popular election reform; as of 2024, five states use them in some form. Nonpartisan primaries can invite more voters into the electoral process and make general elections more competitive. However, nonpartisan primaries come in different forms; some are more transformative than others, and some have considerable drawbacks. Incorporating ranked choice voting (RCV) into nonpartisan primaries and/or general elections can address issues associated with nonpartisan primaries, such as vote-splitting and limited choice in general elections. Using a top-four primary followed by an RCV general election (the "Alaska model") particularly optimizes for competition and choice. Like nonpartisan primaries generally, the Alaska model has been criticized for diminishing the role of parties in the nomination process. However, the model can be adjusted by allowing party endorsements to appear next to candidates' names on the ballot, giving parties greater influence and making the reform more sustainable. Finally, only proportional representation can foster robust competition and fair outcomes in every election. Of the proportional systems under consideration in the United States, the proportional form of RCV is most compatible with nonpartisan primaries.

There is no shortage of evidence that the U.S. political system is struggling—from toxic campaign rhetoric to gridlock (Binder 2015) to public dissatisfaction with democracy (Riccardi and Sanders 2023). As the problem grows, so does the number of ideas and organizations emerging to solve it. There is a proliferation, perhaps even oversaturation, of ideas and goals in the democracy reform space. Most of us can agree that our government should be more functional and representative, but what does that mean, and how do we get there? Much of today's reform energy centers on electoral system changes, such as nonpartisan primaries and ranked choice voting (RCV).

So far, this book has analyzed primary elections and primary election reforms. Given the increasing momentum (as well as competition) in the election reform space, in this chapter we explore how an election reform like nonpartisan primaries can be evaluated not just on its own merits but also on how it fits into the broader election reform agenda. We first review what advocates of nonpartisan primaries hope to achieve, how the reform has worked in practice, and where it falls short. We then consider how nonpartisan primaries can be strengthened with other reforms and if/how they can lead to more transformative changes.

We argue here that as a type of "open" primary, nonpartisan primaries may allow more voters to participate, but we argue that the most common variant ("top two") falls short on other important democratic criteria. For example, "top two" is vulnerable to vote splitting and can shut opposition and minor parties out of the general election entirely. We argue that using RCV in the general election addresses these vulnerabilities, particularly as part of a "top four" or "top five" package. Still, the "top four" model has drawbacks in its current implementation, in that it muddies the significance of party nominations, recognition, and rights. We suggest further modifications, such as equal and reasonable ballot access, and allowing parties to endorse candidates on the ballot.

Finally, any system based on single-winner elections cannot foster accurate representation as well as a system of proportional representation can. While there will always be some single-winner elections (such as for a state governor or U.S. Senator) for which nonpartisan primaries may be a meaningful innovation, efforts toward proportional representation should continue for legislative offices. Proportional RCV, the only proportional system ever adopted and used in the U.S., can easily be combined with nonpartisan primaries, providing for a seamless transition from single-winner reforms to multi-winner reforms.

Our analysis and recommendations are consistent with the notion that no reform alone can "fix" democracy. We focus on nonpartisan primaries (NPPs) here, among all of the reforms being proposed today, because NPPs have immediate demonstrated interest from voters, advocates, and funders, while also drawing ire from political parties. At the same time, it would be an injustice to analyze, and propose improvements to, NPPs in a vacuum. NPPs are part of a larger reform ecosystem, and we take care to consider how they could better interact with other reforms.

The Promises and Pitfalls of Nonpartisan Primaries

Historically, "primary" reform has been centered around opening the partisan nominating process to more voters. Nominees used to be selected at closed conventions, in smoke-filled rooms by party bosses. In the 1900s, reformers pushed for primary elections in order to establish a more open nominating process (Boatright 2024). More recently, reformers have pushed for "open primaries" (Home 2021, n.p.) in which any voter can vote in a primary, though they may have to declare a party affiliation in order to do so. Today, many reformers (Nonpartisan primaries—Unite America n.d.) are advocating for nonpartisan primaries, in which all candidates run on the same primary ballot, and all voters can participate regardless of party affiliation. California and Washington use "top two" nonpartisan primaries (meaning the two candidates with the most votes advance to the general election), and Alaska uses a "top four" nonpartisan primary. Alaskans voted to retain this system in 2024 in the face of a repeal attempt.

Advocates for nonpartisan primaries argue that the system will advance more popular, representative candidates. Politicians may be more incentivized to reach out to independents and voters of the opposite party, potentially reducing polarization. It is also possible for multiple candidates from the same party to advance to the general election, meaning in safe seats, the primary is no longer the decisive election, and legislators may be less fearful of being "primaried" by a more extreme partisan.

We have seen some evidence in previous chapters of this book that these dynamics work in practice. As Crosson discussed in Chapter 10, some studies suggest that "top two," in addition to and/or in combination with two other reforms, modestly increased moderation in the California legislature (McGhee 2018) although other research does not find the same effect (Kousser et al. 2015). Another report shows that general elections became more competitive in California following the adoption of top two (Olson and Ali 2015). At the same time, nonpartisan primaries can cause "vote-splitting" and unrepresentative outcomes. Consider the 2012 race for California's 31st Congressional District, a Democratic-leaning district in Southern California (Ballotpedia n.d.). In the nonpartisan primary, the Democratic vote was split between four candidates. Two Republican candidates advanced to the general election, and Democrats were shut out of the general election ballot, even though they collectively received forty-nine percent of the vote. Vote-splitting often harms Republicans as well. For example, in the 2022 race for California State Senate District 4, almost sixty percent of the primary electorate voted for a Republican. However, because that vote was split between six candidates, no Republican advanced. Instead, two Democrats advanced with a combined forty percent.

Top two can also result in strategic campaigning. In the 2024 California U.S. Senate election, Democrat Adam Schiff's campaign spent millions (Reston 2024) of dollars on ads boosting Republican Steve Garvey to help keep a potentially more challenging opponent (Democratic Reps. Katie Porter or Barbara Lee) off of the November ballot. Schiff's plan worked—he kept his fellow Democrats off the ballot and won by eighteen points.

Top two voting punishes parties when many candidates run, incentivizes candidates to play games, and pushes parties to "clear the field." These dynamics can lead to suboptimal choices for voters in the general election, since the outcome of the primary may depend more on how votes were split rather than which candidates were the most preferred. Admittedly, partisan primaries can lead to similar tactics and outcomes. However, even if/when top two advances better choices than partisan primaries would (because in theory, a broader electorate decides who advances), it does nothing to give voters more choices in the general election. When "top two" produces a same-party general election, it may make the general election more competitive, but it entirely shuts the opposing party out. Third party and independent candidates almost never advance (Gehl 2023).

Whether the benefits of top two nonpartisan primaries outweigh the drawbacks may depend on what one values. However, improvements such as "top four" and the changes suggested here can achieve better results for voters, candidates, and parties.

Improving Nonpartisan Primaries with Ranked Choice Voting: The Top-4/5 Model

Ranked choice voting (RCV) can be used in the general election to allow for more than two choices. With RCV, voters rank the candidates in order of preference. In the single-winner version of RCV, if a candidate receives more than fifty percent of first choices, they win. If not, candidates are eliminated successively in a series of instant runoffs. If a voter's first choice is eliminated, their vote counts toward their next choice. This process continues until a candidate wins with more than fifty percent of the vote. Because RCV solves the vote-splitting problem, it can identify a majority winner even when three or more candidates compete. As we saw in Chapters 7 and 8 of this volume, Alaska's top four primary plus the RCV general election has had some interesting early results, but it is too soon to know how parties and candidates will adapt.

Top four or five makes room for both major parties, and potentially third party and independent candidates, to compete in the general election (Gehl 2023). Using RCV in the general election ensures the winner has broad support. The system enjoys the other benefits of RCV too, such as positive campaigning and coalition building (Williamson 2023; Chapter 8 of this volume). Take this quote from Alaska U.S. Senator Lisa Murkowski, for example:

> We like the fact that candidates were actually perhaps a little bit more civil to their opponents, when I knew that I needed to get [an opponent's] second place vote. So I'm not going to trash talk her in our debates or in my public encounters because I want to pick up some of that support, too... I think what we demonstrated in Alaska was the possibility that electoral reform can happen and it can deliver outcomes that are less partisan and perhaps less politically rancorous. (PBS 2023)

However, some have argued that in light of "Alaska-style" ballot measures failing in Nevada, Idaho, and Colorado in 2024, there should be greater separation between nonpartisan primaries and RCV (Gruber 2024; see also Chapter 9 of this volume). Ranked choice voting has indeed faced increasing opposition; opponents have claimed it leads to ballot error and voter confusion (FGA 2022). However, in reality, polling reveals that voters who use RCV almost universally support and understand it (Dowling et al 2025). Some research finds that RCV increases ballot errors (Pettigrew and Radley 2025), other research finds that it does not (Kimball and Anthony 2016; Neely and McDaniel 2015). Of note, opposition to the "Alaska-style" ballot measures mainly came from the major parties (Daley 2024). This hints that the resistance was driven by the model's threat to entrenched interests, not necessarily material concerns about RCV.

Optimizing the Top-4/5 Model

Top four or five has disadvantages for political parties; whether that is desirable or not depends on who one asks. In Alaska, parties have essentially lost their nominating process. Their "nominees" (i.e. candidates who appear on the ballot with their label) are not necessarily chosen by members of their own party.

While some voters appreciate seeing multiple members of their preferred party on the ballot (Lucky 2024), party leaders and candidates have sometimes found it challenging. When multiple candidates from the same party advance, intra-party conflict can get dragged into the general election—though RCV may mitigate some of that. Republicans Nick Begich and Sarah Palin were quite hostile toward one another during their special election bids for Alaska's House seat in 2022 (Ruskin 2022), and Democrat Mary Peltola won in the end. However, if they had embraced the logic of RCV and strongly cross-endorsed one another, the result may have differed. Indeed, candidates and other actors may learn and adapt to institutional incentives over time. In fact, Palin and Begich lightly encouraged voters to "rank the red" come their rematch for the regular general election, and Palin received a greater portion of "transfer ballots" from Begich's voters than she did in the special election (Hutchinson and Fitzgerald 2025).

In 2024, in contrast, both major parties in Alaska attempted to clear the field of multiple candidates from their party, essentially staging internal primaries with the nominees chosen by party leaders. For political parties, having a single nominee can make it easier to engage their base, present a single message, and get out the vote, and it can in some circumstances allow parties to redirect resources toward other elections. Sometimes, an informal agreement within the party can be effective. In the 2024 race for Alaska's U.S. House seat, Nick Begich was the top Republican vote-getter in the primary. The Republicans who placed third and fourth both dropped out of the general election, and Begich went on to win.

But it might not always be this easy. On the Democratic side, the state party backed incumbent Representative Mary Peltola, who came in second place in the primary. Another Democrat, Eric Hafner, won a spot on the general election ballot as a result of the two Republicans dropping out. The Alaska Democratic Party asked a judge to remove Hafner from the ballot, on the grounds that Hafner was imprisoned in New Jersey and did not fulfill the requirement of living in Alaska at the time of the election. The lawyers for the Alaska Democrats also said that "Hafner's presence on the ballot will damage the competitive prospects of the Alaska Democratic Party's preferred candidate, Congresswoman Peltola, because it will confuse voters by presenting them with an additional candidate on the ballot who is not entitled to be there and would not be entitled to serve if elected" (Stone 2024). The Alaska Democrats were ultimately unsuccessful, and Hafner appeared on the general election ballot.

In sum, while party attempts to consolidate around their perceived strongest competitor may be beneficial to the party, they can deprive voters of the choices they selected in the primary election. We see the policies proposed in this chapter as a way to balance these two values. As long as nonpartisan primary proposals are designed in a way that makes campaign activities more difficult for political parties, parties potentially present an ongoing source of opposition.

We should also be mindful of minor parties' concerns about nonpartisan primaries. Stein (2024) has suggested that minor parties risk losing ballot access and/or party recognition in a top four system. Most states grant minor parties ballot access if they win a certain number or share of votes in a previous election, and/or gather a certain number of signatures or registrants. With top four, the only way to get on the general election ballot is to be in the top four primary vote-getters. Minor parties might find this attainable for elections in which fewer candidates typically run, such as for state representative or senator. The Nevada-based survey experiment discussed in Chapter 9 suggested that a top five primary might reduce the number of third party and independent candidates, and in some scenarios shut smaller parties out of the general election ballot altogether.

As dissatisfied as voters are with the major parties (Igielnik 2023), it is simultaneously true that political parties are a vital part of modern democracy. They are an essential feature of how voters and campaigns organize to win elections, and how elected officials organize and govern when in office. Party nominations also give voters important information about candidates. In addition, party support is necessary to make any reform easier to win and more sustainable. Therefore, the top four model can and should be further modified to concretely respond to the above concerns, and help ensure enduring success.

First, ballot access requirements (such as signature requirements and/or filing fees) should be equal and reasonable for all candidates filing to run in the primary election. This is how top four voting was implemented in Alaska, where all candidates pay a $100 filing fee. As a result, all candidates of all partisan affiliations have an equal, reasonable opportunity to compete in the first stage.

Party recognition rules could also be keyed to several meaningful and reasonable levels of public support to ensure that more parties are capable of forming, growing, and competing on a level playing field. For example, parties could become "qualified" (i.e., able to identify their nominee on the ballot) based on meeting any of the following criteria:
– Running candidates in at least X primary election contests
– Advancing candidates to at least X general election contests
– Attaining at least X percent of the vote in any round of a statewide primary or general election tabulation
– Electing a candidate in any state or federal general election contest
– Registering at least X voters as party members

These criteria could encourage minor parties to develop and run candidates in less-competitive seats in order to build their power and support. This may increase choices for voters, diversity on the ballot, and turnout from minor-party voters. In fact, Lee and Lee (2024) recorded a turnout boost in Alaska's state legislative primaries post-top-four-adoption, which they suspect had something to do with the increased number of races that featured multiple candidates.

Second, parties should be able to endorse a candidate on the ballot. Parties could nominate a candidate (or candidates) through a mechanism of their choosing (with that candidate's consent), and only that candidate would receive the "Party Nominee" label on the ballot. For example, parties could hold a private-ly-funded convention or caucus before or after the first round. This would empower parties to lift up candidate(s) of their choice, if they wish to. Parties are, after all, private organizations, and if they wish to operate as such, they need a private nomination process. This is the norm internationally. However, at times parties might prefer to see who emerges as a strong candidate in the first round before making an endorsement, or they might prefer not to endorse at all.

These two provisions address the concerns of both "open primary" advocates (i.e. that taxpayers should not have to fund primary elections in which nonpartisans cannot participate) and parties (i.e. that only partisans/party members should have a say in who their party's nominee is). With these tweaks, we can reconceptualize the reform as getting rid of primaries, returning nominating processes back to parties, and introducing an all-candidate winnowing/preliminary round.

These provisions can also help minor parties align their voters around a clear preference to maximize their odds of reaching the general election. Privatizing party nominating contests also introduces an additional element of fairness for minor parties. Under the "publicly funded party primary + general election" model that most states use, major parties are effectively subsidized by tax dollars; and minor parties are not subsidized unless they qualify for the primary ballot (and in most states, minor parties already face higher ballot access requirements). Under the top four or five system recommended here, all parties would be responsible for funding their own nominating contests—if they choose to hold an internal party contest separate from the public primary election.

Multiple parties could also be allowed to endorse the same candidate (with that candidate's consent) using aggregated fusion voting. Under this approach, parties would have the ability to endorse a new candidate in the general election if, for example, a party's nominee does not advance to the general election.

There are several ways to address notations for non-endorsed candidates. In states with party registration, non-endorsed candidates can choose to have their party registration (or lack thereof) by their name (e.g., "Registered Republican"). Allowing both party endorsements and registration to appear on the ballot creates greater options for candidates who prefer the same party to offer different visions for "what the party is or should be." Figure 13.1 shows an example of this.

Alternatively, non-endorsed candidates could express their affiliation in (non-party) language of their choosing, subject to a word and/or letter limit, e.g. "Liberal," "Progressive," "Conservative," "Constitutionalist," "MAGA," etc. With this option, candidates could run under more targeted party banners befitting their ideologies. There would be less risk of confusion between party-endorsed and party-identified/registered candidates, since only the former would be noted on the ballot, unlike option #1. This may also decrease vote-splitting between minor-party

Figure 13.1: Sample RCV ballot with party endorsements.

Sample Ballot					
Candidate	1st Choice	2nd Choice	3rd Choice	4th Choice	5th Choice
BUGS BUNNY Libertarian Party Nominee	◯	◯	◯	◯	◯
DAFFY DUCK Republican Party Nominee	◯	◯	◯	◯	◯
PORKY PIG Registered Democrat	◯	◯	◯	◯	◯
ELMER FUDD Registered Republican	◯	◯	◯	◯	◯
TWEETY BIRD Democratic Party Nominee & Working Families Party Nominee	◯	◯	◯	◯	◯
Write-in _____	◯	◯	◯	◯	◯

candidates in the primary, increasing their chances of advancing a candidate. This option is the "strongest party" version of top four/five voting, and arguably the most aligned with existing political science literature on the importance of fostering coherent and responsible parties (Muirhead 2006; Muirhead and Rosenblum 2020; Rosenbluth and Shapiro 2018; Rosenblum 2010). This option is shown in Figure 13.2.

As far as electoral system design goes, at least for a single-winner contest, a top four or five system—modified according to our suggestions above—offers a way for competing interests (such as voters, reformers, parties, political scientists) to see something they support included in an already-popular reform. Voters would have more meaningful voice and choice in the general election, all voters could participate in taxpayer-funded elections, and parties would have a(n optional) renewed role in vetting and nominating candidates.

Figure 13.2: Sample RCV ballot with candidate self-descriptions.

Candidate	1st Choice	2nd Choice	3rd Choice	4th Choice	5th Choice
Sample Ballot					
BUGS BUNNY Libertarian Party Nominee	◯	◯	◯	◯	◯
DAFFY DUCK Republican Party Nominee	◯	◯	◯	◯	◯
PORKY PIG Progressive	◯	◯	◯	◯	◯
ELMER FUDD Constitutionalist	◯	◯	◯	◯	◯
TWEETY BIRD Democratic Party Nominee & Working Families Party Nominee	◯	◯	◯	◯	◯
Write-in _____	◯	◯	◯	◯	◯

Toward Comprehensive Reform: Nonpartisan Primaries and Proportional Representation

The top four system is a meaningful innovation, as far as single-winner systems go. There will always be some inherently single-winner elections in the U.S. (such as state governor, or U.S. Representative in smaller states like Alaska), and it is worthwhile to discuss the most democratic way to elect those offices. At the same time, as long as single-winner contests are the norm, there are some democratic ideals that cannot be fully met. A top four or five system may allow more voters to decide who wins a seat, but still, only one candidate can win and represent that electorate. If a district is sixty percent Republican and forty percent Democratic, a Republican candidate will probably win (and can feasibly do so by pandering only to Republican voters), and a significant minority of the district will likely feel that their representative does not represent their views or legislate on their behalf. The top four or five system may be a more open and democratic way of electing that Republican, but it does not solve this fundamental problem. Though it is arguably optimal in its own right for, say, electing a U.S. Senator, it can also lay the groundwork for more transformational change for offices that do not necessarily have to be single-winner, such as for the U.S. House.

Among the democratic ideals for which reformers and thought leaders advocate, fair representation is a consistent and inescapable theme (Apau 2024; Brennan Center for Justice n.d.; Mantell 2024). Adopting a proportional representation (PR) system—a system that awards seats to parties and/or candidates in proportion to the share of votes they receive—is the most obvious way to get there. Some countries that use PR allocate seats based on the national vote share, but given the size and state-oriented nature of the United States, PR proposals here typically use multi-member districts within states.

For instance, consider Nebraska, which currently has three single-member districts, and a statewide partisan composition of sixty-two percent Republican and thirty-eight percent Democratic. In 2024, two seats were considered safely Republican, and one was considered a toss-up (Cook Political 2023). As of 2024, Republicans represent all three seats. With PR, Republicans would likely still win two seats, but Democrats would likely win the third seat. PR would preserve the delegation's Republican majority while also awarding a fair share of representation to Democrats in the state.

The only proportional system that has ever been adopted and used in the U.S. is proportional RCV (Sumpter and Parsons 2024). The "proportional" version of RCV implements a specific threshold-to-elect (i.e. percent of votes needed to win) based on the number of winners, and eliminates candidates until the desired number of winners/nominees have reached the threshold. The system is currently in place in Cambridge, Massachusetts; Minneapolis, Minnesota; Albany, California; Portland, Oregon; and other municipalities. Proportional RCV should result in proportional outcomes for parties when implemented for partisan elections. However, other (nonpartisan) groups, such as racial or cultural communities or issue constituencies, can also elect candidates of their choice if they reach the threshold to elect.

By electing legislators in proportion to the share of votes they receive, political, racial, and other groups can gain more accurate representation. Such systems can also curb gerrymandering; with multi-member districts, there are simply fewer lines to draw. It becomes nearly impossible to gerrymander for partisan advantage if the system inherently awards seats fairly.

There are several organizations working to expand PR in the United States, but the effort faces an uphill battle. Naturally, legislators are hesitant to change the system under which they were elected. The Fair Representation Act (FRA), which would implement multi-member districts and proportional RCV for congressional elections, as well as single-winner RCV for U.S. Senate elections, has been introduced in Congress several times but never made it out of committee. The FRA was last introduced in the 118th Congress by Representative Don Beyer. The bill was referred to the House Judiciary Committee but did not get a hearing or vote. Perhaps more legislators would be willing to sign on if the effective date were further in the future.

Proportional RCV can accommodate nonpartisan primaries. In a state that uses traditional partisan primaries, the FRA allows parties to nominate as many candidates as there are seats per district. In a state that uses nonpartisan primaries, the NPPs would advance twice as many candidates as there are seats (e. g. in a three-member district, six candidates would advance). The recommendations outlined above (e. g. parties can endorse/cross-endorse on the ballot) would still apply.

Now, imagine a state that uses top four/five for single-winner elections (e. g. governor and senators) and proportional RCV for multi-winner elections (e. g. Congress and state legislators). The voter experience would be consistent across all contests: Voters simply rank the candidates in order of preference.

Nonpartisan primaries are not inherently compatible with other proportional systems, like list PR. List PR requires that the parties produce a list of candidates, which requires some partisan nomination process that directly affects whose name(s) appear on the general election ballot. An NPP-List PR hybrid is possible (imagine, for example, a nonpartisan preliminary round winnows the field, and then parties can decide which advancing candidates to put on their list), but it is neither intuitive nor currently used anywhere in the world.

Additionally, since any reform would need some level of major party support to pass, it is important to note that proportional RCV would potentially be less disruptive to the two-party system than other proportional systems. As written in the FRA, the smallest "threshold-to-elect" in any district would be seventeen percent (in a five-member district), a higher threshold than that used in most European countries' PR systems, making it less vulnerable to party fracturing. In Australia, which has long used proportional RCV to elect members to its Senate, the two major parties continue to hold most of the influence.

It also should be noted that Congress would have to repeal the Uniform Congressional District Act of 1967 before we could even use PR in a congressional election. The Act mandates the use of single-member districts for Congress. However, the movements for NPP, PR,[1] and a host of other reforms are each earning increasing attention, funding, and legislative wins, and will be more sustainable when they pursue their aims within the context of other proposed reforms.

Conclusion

We should not think about each reform proposal in a vacuum. Reformers and scholars should take care to consider the greater ecosystem of the democratic reform movement, i.e. where the current energy is, what the end goal is, and how we get from A to B. At the same time, it is unrealistic to expect every player to abandon their own preferred reform in favor of a common/higher goal, given every group might have slightly different goals and different theories on how to effect change. For example, if the end goal is to give voters a more meaningful opportunity to participate in elections, nonpartisan primaries may not be as transformative as PR, but passing them is an easier win in the short term. On the flip side, advocates for PR typically desire a stronger party system, and nonpartisan primaries (as they have been implemented thus far) may be counter-conducive to that goal.

In this chapter we have suggested ways in which nonpartisan primaries can be improved and adapted to meet the goals of different actors and how to make the reform more politically sustainable, such as by allowing parties to endorse candidates on the ballot. We have also suggested ways in which PR advocates might meet the reform energy where it is at—for example, by embracing a system like proportional RCV that can accommodate nonpartisan primaries. To conclude, while it can be valuable to attempt to isolate the impact of a particular reform, the impact is never truly isolated to the affected elections/electorate. Election reforms like nonpartisan primaries impact the prospects for further reform; we believe the tweaks we have proposed can ensure that impact is positive.

Bibliography

Apau, Deborah. 2024. "Proportional Representation: Boosting Voter Turnout and Strengthening Democracy." *Protect Democracy*.
protectdemocracy.org/work/proportional-representation-voter-turnout/.

---

1 For example, since 2022, the cities of Arlington, VA; Charlottesville, VA; Portland, ME; Portland, OR; and Oak Park, IL have all advanced proportional RCV measures.

Binder, Sarah. 2015. "The Dysfunctional Congress." *Annual review of political science* 18 (1): 85–101. https://doi.org/10.1146/annurev-polisci-110813-032156.

Boatright, Robert G. 2024. *Reform and Retrenchment: A Century of Efforts to Fix Primary Elections.* Oxford University Press.

"California's 31st Congressional District Elections, 2012." *Ballotpedia.* ballotpedia.org/California%27s_31st_Congressional_District_elections,_2012.

Cook Policial. 2023. "2023 Cook PVI[SM]: District Map and List (118th Congress)." www.cookpolitical.com/cook-pvi/2023-partisan-voting-index/118-district-map-and-list.

Daley, David. 2024. "The Republican and Democratic Parties Are Killing Electoral Reform across the US." *The Guardian.* www.theguardian.com/commentisfree/2024/nov/16/republicans-democrats-electoral-reform.

Dowling, Eveline, Caroline Tolbert, Nathan Micatka, and Todd Donovan. 2025. "Is Ranked-Choice Voting Associated with Turnout Across Race/Ethnic Groups?" *Social Science Quarterly* 106 (3), doi.org/10.1111/ssqu.70025.

FGA. 2022. "Ranked-Choice Voting: A Disaster in Disguise." thefga.org/research/ranked-choice-voting-a-disaster-in-disguise/.

Gehl, Katherine. 2023. "The Case for the Five in Final Five Voting." *Constitutional Political Economy* 34 (3): 286–296. https://doing.org/10.1007/s10602-022-09386-6.

"Gerrymandering & Fair Representation." *Brennan Center for Justice.* www.brennancenter.org/issues/gerrymandering-fair-representation.

Gruber, Jeremy. 2024. "Open Primary Advocates Must Embrace the Historic Principles of Change." *The Fulcrum.* thefulcrum.us/electoral-reforms/open-primaries-campaigns.

Hirano, Shigeo, and James M. Snyder Jr. 2019. *Primary Elections in the United States.* Cambridge University Press.

Hutchinson, Rachel, and Ben Fitzgerald. 2025. "Impact of Cross-Endorsements in Ranked Choice Voting Elections." *Fair Vote.* fairvote.org/report/rcv-cross-endorsements-report/#executive-summary.

Igielnik, Ruth. 2023. "Discontent With Party Politics Reaches New Heights." *The New York Times.* www.nytimes.com/2023/09/21/us/politics/politics-discontent.html.

Kimball, David, and Joseph Anthony. 2016. "Voter Participation with Ranked Choice Voting in the United States." Unpublished manuscript, University of Missouri, St, Louis. www.umsl.edu/~kimballd/KimballRCV.pdf.

Kousser, Thad, Justin Phillips, and Boris Shor. 2015. "Reform and Representation: A New Method Applied to Recent Electoral Changes." *SSRN.* ssrn.com/abstract=2260083.

Lee, Jeannette, and Jay Lee. 2024. "Voter Participation Jumped When Alaska Opened Its Primaries." *Sightline Institute.* www.sightline.org/2024/06/03/voter-participation-jumped-when-alaska-opened-its-primaries/.

Lucky, Juli. 2024. "Exit Polling Shows Alaskans Found Ranked Choice Voting Simple." *Alaskans for Better Elections.* www.alaskansforbetterelections.com/exit-polling-shows-alaskans-found-ranked-choice-voting-simple/.

Mantell, Will. 2024. "Fair Representation Act Would Transform Congressional Elections, Stop Gerrymandering." *Fair Vote.* fairvote.org/press/fair-rep-act-24/.

McGhee, Eric. 2018. *Political Reform and Moderation in California's Legislature: Did Electoral Reforms Make State Representatives More Moderate?* Public Policy Institute of California. www.ppic.org/wp-content/uploads/r-0517emr.pdf.

Muirhead, Russell. 2006. "A Defense of Party Spirit." *Perspectives on politics* 4 (4). https://doi.org/10.1017/s1537592706060452.

Muirhead, Russell, and Nancy L. Rosenblum. 2020. "The Political Theory of Parties and Partisanship: Catching Up." *Annual Review of Political Science* 23 (1): 95–110. https://doi.org/10.1146/annurev-polisci-041916-020727.

Neely, Francis, and Jason McDaniel. 2015. "Overvoting and the Equality of Voice under Instant-Runoff Voting in San Francisco." *California Journal of Politics and Policy* 7 (4). https://doi.org/10.5070/p2cjpp7428929.

"Nonpartisan Primaries — Unite America." *Uniteamerica.org.* www.uniteamerica.org/nonpartisan-primaries.

Olson, Jason, and Omar Ali. 2015. *A Quiet Revolution: The Early Successes of California's Top Two Nonpartisan Primary.* d3n8a8pro7vhmx.cloudfront.net/openprimaries/pages/418/attachments/original/1440450728/CaliforniaReportFinal8.24small.pdf?1440450728.

Open Primaries. 2021. Homepage. openprimaries.org.

PBS. 2023. "Lisa Murkowski." www.pbs.org/wnet/firing-line/video/lisa-murkowski-e7kt6r/.

Pettigrew, Stephen, and Dylan Radley. 2025. "Overranks, and Skips: Mismarked and Rejected Votes in Ranked Choice Voting." *Political Behavior.* https://doi.org/10.1007/s11109-025-10028-4.

Reston, Maeve. 2024. "Why Two Democratic Senate Hopefuls Are Boosting Republica Rivals in Calif." *The Washington Post.* www.washingtonpost.com/elections/2024/02/29/adam-schiff-katie-porter-steve-garvey-california-senate-race/.

Riccardi, Nicholas, and Linley Sanders. 2023. "Americans Are Widely Pessimistic about Democracy in the United States, an AP-NORC Poll Finds." *AP News.* apnews.com/article/poll-democracy-partisan-ship-trump-biden-trust-221f2b4f6cf9805f766c9a8395b9539d?utm_campaign=TrueAnthem&utm_medium=AP&utm_source=Twitter.

Rosenblum, Nancy L. 2010. *On the Side of the Angels: An Appreciation of Parties and Partisanship.* Princeton University Press.

Rosenbluth, Frances, and Ian Shapiro. 2018. *Responsible Parties: Saving Democracy from Itself.* Yale University Press.

Ruskin, Liz. 2022. "Why Republicans in Alaska's First Ranked Choice Election Reserve Their Venom for Each Other." *Alaska Public Media.* alaskapublic.org/2022/08/11/why-republicans-in-alaskas-first-ranked-choice-election-re-serve-their-venom-for-each-other/.

Stein, Jill. 2024. www.facebook.com/drjillstein/posts/we-fully-support-ranked-choice-voting-as-the-movement-for-rcv-gains-momentum-how/1109133827248139/.

Stone, Eric. 2024. "Alaska Democrats Ask Judge to Remove Imprisoned Out-of-State U.S. House Candidate from November Ballot." *KTOO.* www.ktoo.org/2024/09/05/alaska-democrats-ask-judge-to-remove-imprisoned-out-of-state-u-s-house-candidate-from-november-ballot/.

Sumpter, Meredith, and Michael Parsons. 2024. "Ranked Choice Voting: What Happened & What's next." *Democracy Takes.* democracytakes.substack.com/p/ranked-choice-voting-what-happened.

Williamson, Ryan. 2023. *Evaluating the Effects of the Top-Four System in Alaska.* https://www.rstreet.org/wp-content/uploads/2023/01/REALFINAL_policy-short-no-122-no-embargo.pdf.

Derek Monson
Chapter 14
A Constitutional Perspective on American Elections

Abstract: Primary election research focuses on empirical outcomes. This elevation of outcomes, however, fuels polarization, which hinders the advancement of constructive primary election reform. An appeal to broadly resonant first principles is a necessary complement to empirical outcomes to create the necessary political space and time to advance reform. The U.S. Constitution, as understood by *The Federalist Papers*, suggests the following first principles: (1) faction can undermine governance in the public interest; (2) there is a need for elected officials to be regularly held to account by voters for their decisions; and (3) large, diverse constituencies in elections have the power to combat the problem of faction. These principles point to open primary election systems that allow unaffiliated voters to participate.

American elections today often feel like extreme turbulence on an airplane: a disturbing experience that induces a strong desire for it to end as soon as possible. For instance, a recent poll taken one month after the 2024 election reported that sixty-five percent of American adults limited their political news consumption due to overload or fatigue (Associated Press-NORC 2024). The tendency of elections to turn off voters is understandable given the polarized partisan messaging that permeates them.

Some scholars argue that American polarization is driven by growing prejudice among Americans toward those with a different ideological or partisan identity (Lewis and Lewis 2023, 81–82). A difference in ideological or partisan identity is interpreted as a moral or intellectual deficiency, not simply a difference of opinion, and transforms every even-year election into a high-stakes war for the soul of the nation. Winning at all costs becomes justified due to the moral evil represented by political opponents.

This polarized framing of elections elevates the defeat of opposing candidates and their ideas as the highest priority. Traditional political goals, such as advancing one's own policy agenda or ensuring the capacity to govern post-election, become secondary. An "ends justify the means" mentality among partisans is the result. Partisan leaders abandon basic republican principles like submitting to the will of the people expressed by election outcomes and instead seek to control those outcomes through means such as legislative redistricting and extreme partisan management of Congressional process, with the goal of ensuring that the most partisan ballot (i. e., primary elections) becomes the deciding vote in as many districts as possible.

The outcome-obsessed, polarized approach to elections has its parallel in the primary election research literature. While driven by different motivations than partisan leaders, the focus of primary election research is empirical outcomes in elections—competitive primaries, less extreme primary winners, Condorcet winners, and so on. This leads to an important question: Can empirical primary election research successfully drive reforms that lessen polarization when it elevates a focus on outcomes that, in a partisan context, deepen polarization? The likely answer is no, for two reasons.

First, by elevating electoral outcomes as the principal focus of empirical analysis, it affirms the intuition of polarization: The measurement of a primary election policy is the likely outcomes it produces. Therefore, in the polarized viewpoint, engineering primary elections with desired outcomes in mind is justified.

Second, the empirical literature's findings regarding likely electoral outcomes of different primary election approaches act as a signal to polarized partisans regarding which election systems pose the greatest threat to the end of defeating political opponents. The primary system's purpose in the partisan view is to ensure the ideological commitment of the primary winner rather than building consensus support for the victor with general election victory in mind. When empirical primary election research highlights as its main finding that a particular system is designed to produce winners with the broadest support, it shows polarized partisans the primary election approaches that ought to be most strongly opposed.

While entirely necessary and valuable for understanding primary election policies, research on primary election outcomes is an insufficient foundation for primary election reform. What is needed beyond empirical insight is an effort that can delay or eliminate the gridlock of polarized politics by presenting an appeal to both sides that creates political space to move forward with constructive primary election reforms. A complementary effort that directly challenges the typical signaling systems of polarized politics can give empirical insights political room to breathe and to influence policy deliberations.

I argue in this chapter that an appeal to broadly resonant first principles can accomplish this goal. First principles that hold appeal to both political progressives and political conservatives can short-circuit the fast-forming political alignments that produce polarized disagreement, allowing time for a possible consensus to form around primary election reform.

The U.S. Constitution, as understood by *The Federalist Papers*, offers such a set of first principles. These principles are applicable to primary elections today and include: (1) concern with excessive empowerment of political factions; (2) the need to hold those in power to account by a regular vote of the people; and (3) broad-based elections check undue influence from political factions. As applied to debates around how best to structure our state-based primary election systems, these principles point to open primaries that allow independent voters to participate as the approach most consistent with the U.S. Constitution. Further intellectual work and debate will likely produce additional compelling and broadly resonant sets of first principles.

The Problem of Faction

The framers of the American Constitution, including the authors of *The Federalist Papers*, held grave concerns about the inevitability of a political problem they called "faction." For instance, Federalist No. 81 describes the "pestilential breath of faction" poisoning the "fountains of justice" (Hamilton et al. 1961, 484). Similarly, Federalist No. 39 expresses worry about the potential power of a "handful of tyrannical nobles" and Federalist No. 40 notes the risk that the "perverseness or corruption" of a tiny fraction of the country could hold the fate of the overwhelming majority of the nation in its hands (Hamilton et al. 1961, 241, 251).

But the greatest articulation of the problem of faction that concerned the framers is perhaps Federalist No. 10. It offers a definition of "faction":

> By a faction, I understand a number of citizens, whether amounting to a majority or a minority of the whole, who are united and actuated by some common impulse of passion, or of interest, adversed to the rights of other citizens, or to the permanent and aggregate interests of the community. (Hamilton et al. 1961, 78)

In contemporary political science terms, we might say that the framers were concerned about interest groups, which are defined as "any association of individuals or organizations, usually formally organized, that, on the basis of one or more shared concerns, attempts to influence public policy in its favor" (Thomas 2024, n.p.). In other words, the animating concerns of the framers mirror the worries of many in our politics today from all sides of the spectrum. For example, just as the framers were concerned about the influence of factions on Founding Era politics and government, today's American progressives worry about the influence of large businesses on democracy, and today's American conservatives are concerned about the influence of unions.

The problems created by factions noted in Federalist No. 10 include "clog[ging] the administration" of government and "convuls[ing] society" (Hamilton et al. 1961, 80). This is an apt description of what we often see coming out of Congress today. The only possible responses are twofold: (1) eliminate the cause of faction; or (2) control the effects of faction (Hamilton et al. 1961, 78). The first can only be accomplished by undesirable or impossible means, such as eliminating the liberty and diversity of opinion that allows factions to form. Limiting the impact of faction on politics, government, and society as a whole is the only practical way to combat the problem of faction.

The People and Elections: The Ultimate Check on Faction

As they did with other problems inherent in government by, for, and of the people, the framers turn to the power of the people as a primary means to check the problem of faction. The people are referred to as having "the whole power" of the Constitution in their hands, as a "complete barrier against the oppressive use" of political power, and as the source of the Constitution's legitimacy in Federalist No. 8, No. 32, and No. 43, respectively (Hamilton et al. 1961, 68, 197, 279). When a faction is a political minority, Federalist No. 10 notes how elections serve as a check on the problem of faction since "the majority will defeat its sinister views by regular vote" (Hamilton et al. 1961, 80).

When a faction represents a political majority, the breadth of the constituency in an election is the key. As Federalist No. 10 notes, "the greater number of citizens" brought under the sphere of representative government creates the "circumstance principally which renders factious combinations less to be dreaded" (Hamilton et al. 1961, 83).

By contrast:

> The smaller the society, the fewer probably will be the distinct parties and interests composing it; the fewer the distinct parties and interests, the more frequently will a majority be found of the same party; and the smaller the number of individuals composing a majority, and the smaller the compass within which they are placed, the more easily will they concert and execute their plans of oppression. Extend the sphere, and you take in a greater variety of parties and interests; you make it less probable that a majority of the whole will have a common motive to invade the rights of other citizens; or if such a common motive exists, it will be more difficult for all who feel it to discover their own strength, and to act in unison with each other. Besides other impediments, it may be remarked that, where there is a consciousness of unjust or dishonorable purposes, communication is always checked by distrust in proportion to the number whose concurrence is necessary. (Hamilton et al. 1961, 83)

In other words, the same diversity of interests, passions, perspectives, etc. that leads all politically organized societies to form factions/interest groups can check the problem of faction if the voting constituency is large enough—the variety of factions in a broad constituency will make competing demands of a single representative, challenging governance for a single set of interests. As Federalist No. 10 argues:

> Does it consist in the greater security afforded by a greater variety of parties, against the event of any one party being able to outnumber and oppress the rest? In an equal degree does the increased variety of parties comprised within the Union, increase this security[?] Does it, in fine, consist in the greater obstacles opposed to the concert and accomplishment of the secret wishes of an unjust and interested majority? Here, again, the extent of the Union gives it the most palpable advantage. (Hamilton et al. 1961, 83–84)

The author of Federalist No. 10 immediately applied the application of these ideas to elections, arguing that:

> As each representative will be chosen by a greater number of citizens in the large than in the small republic, it will be more difficult for unworthy candidates to practice with success the vicious arts by which elections are too often carried; and the suffrages of the people being more free, will be more likely to centre in men who possess the most attractive merit and the most diffusive and established characters. (Hamilton et al. 1961, 82–83)

Just as the framers immediately saw an application of constitutional principles to the practice and policy of elections generally, so too can we apply them to primary elections.

Applying First Principles to Elections

The Federalist Papers argue that numerically large and diverse constituencies for elected representatives can be an effective antidote to undue influence from factions, and therefore limit the negative impact on governance that factions can have. It follows that primary elections should be structured to produce meaningfully large and diverse constituencies.

Constitution-reinforcing primary elections can take multiple forms. Partisan primaries can be constitution-reinforcing when they broaden the primary voter base by inviting independent voters to participate. Semi-open primaries accomplish this by allowing independent voters to select which partisan primary they would like to vote in. Open primaries do the same by decoupling party membership from primary participation.

The only partisan primary structure that seems to go against these constitutional principles is closed primaries, in which only party members may vote in a primary election. Closed primaries, by design, seek to limit participation in primary elections to the most partisan voters. By narrowing the primary constituency in this manner, closed primaries increase the ability of a faction of the party to sway the outcome of the primary in one direction or another. When combined with modern redistricting techniques that can often make the primary election the only competitive election, this makes it feasible for an elected official to govern based on the interests of one or a small number of factions within the political party—immune to the desired effect of regular elections of holding an elected representatively meaningfully accountable to a broad group of diverse interests among their general voting constituency.

By the same token, nonpartisan primary election systems would seem to be constitution-enforcing. By putting all candidates for office into the same primary election in which any voter can participate regardless of partisan affiliation or non-affiliation, nonpartisan primaries produce the largest, most diverse constituency possible. A faction of one political party may be able to organize to get a desired candidate through the primary and into the general election. However, the possibility for additional candidates of the same partisan affiliation making it through to the general election—a likelihood when districts are engineered to be as safely Republican or Democrat as possible—lessens the capacity of that faction to determine the outcome of the general election with the result from the primary election.

Only primary systems that allow independent voters to participate seem to produce the large and diverse constituencies necessary to check the problem of faction. Therefore, only semi-open, open, and nonpartisan primaries seem to reinforce the principles of the U.S. Constitution.

Also worth noting briefly is the potential for redistricting policy to be constitutionally reinforcing. A constitution-reinforcing redistricting system would draw legislative and congressional districts with numerically large and geographically diverse constituencies. However, there are hard limits to what redistricting can accomplish to check the problem of faction in this regard. For instance, in many areas of the country where population density is high (e. g., cities and many suburbs), producing sufficient geographic diversity is a practical challenge. Similarly, in many states there is a distinct partisan lean among voters statewide. So while some districts could be drawn to ensure partisan or ideological diversity, many could not simply because the political diversity of the underlying voter pool is limited. Therefore, while both policies are important for addressing polarization, the structure of primary elections would seem to be the more impactful of the two.

Conclusion

Unlocking the power of empirical insight for policy reform requires a complementary effort designed to scramble typical polarized disagreement that prevents constructive reform from advancing. This complementary effort can be achieved through an elevation of broadly resonant first principles, such as those found in the debate over ratifying the U.S. Constitution.

An appeal to first principles grounded in *The Federalist Papers* has a clear resonance with political conservatives, who often cite this source in public arguments. However, the principle of large and diverse constituencies should also appeal to political progressives who see attempts to shrink the voter base as targeting the minorities that they seek to empower. Additionally, both progressives and conservatives have clear concerns with the influence of interest groups that mirror the framers' concerns about faction articulated in *The Federalist Papers.*

A broadly compelling appeal through *The Federalist Papers* offers a concrete example of how finding broadly resonant first principles is possible, and how it can be used to pause polarized politics long enough for election reform to move forward. The sooner we can get there, the better.

Bibliography

Associated Press-NORC. 2024. "Most adults feel the need to limit political news consumption due to fatigue and information overload." AP-NORC News and Media. December 26. apnorc.org/projects/most-adults-feel-the-need-to-limit-political-news-consumption-due-to-fatigue-and-information-overload/.

Hamilton, Alexander, James Madison, John Jay, and Clinton Rossiter. [1788] 1961. *The Federalist Papers.* New American Library. https://archive.org/details/federalistpapers1961hami/page/n5/mode/2up.

Lewis, Hyrum, and Verlan Lewis. 2023. *The Myth of Left and Right – How the Political Spectrum Misleads and Harms America.* Oxford University Press.

Thomas, Clive. 2024. "Interest group." Britannica. December 17. www.britannica.com/topic/interest-group.

Edward B. Foley
Chapter 15
Holding a Round-robin Tournament Among All the Candidates: Optimizing Round One of a Two-round Electoral System

Abstract: Partisan primaries combined with "sore loser" laws prevent general election voters from electing the candidate whom a majority of them prefer. This occurs whenever the majority of general election voters would prefer a candidate who was eliminated from contention in the partisan primary. Eliminating "sore loser" laws, however, would not solve the problem because that would risk too many candidates on the general election ballot. The solution instead is to restructure primary elections so that they function as a preliminary tournament among all the candidates running for the office in question regardless of their party affiliation. Because primary elections are paid for and operated by the government, they need to serve the public and not merely partisan purposes, and the best way for primaries to serve the public interest is for them to operate as preliminary tournaments. The form of a preliminary tournament among all candidates that would be most conducive to the purpose of holding a democratic election is one in which the voters evaluate each candidate in comparison to each other candidate. This head-to-head comparison for each pair of candidates is equivalent to a round-robin sports tournament. As in those sports tournaments, the two candidates who do best in these head-to-head comparisons (by being preferred by a majority of voters over most other candidates, with a suitable tiebreaker as necessary when two or more candidates have the same number of head-to-head victories) advance to a final round of the competition, where an ultimate winner is determined.

In Ohio's 2024 U.S. Senate race, four candidates appeared on the ballot for the primary election that the state held on March 19. The incumbent, Sherrod Brown, was the only Democrat running in the primary. There were three Republicans: businessman Bernie Moreno, the candidate endorsed by Donald Trump and most associated with the MAGA wing of the Republican party; Frank LaRose, Ohio's secretary of state who earlier in his career had distanced himself from Trump but who increasingly aligned himself with Trump, hoping that he rather than Moreno would have received Trump's endorsement; and Matt Dolan, a state senator and a traditional Republican, endorsed by Governor Mike DeWine and former Senator Rob Portman. Of the three Republicans, Dolan was the GOP candidate who most clearly was associated with what was left of the non-MAGA, business-oriented branch of the party.

Because Ohio conducted its March 19 primary on a partisan basis, Senator Brown ran unopposed as the only Democrat and thus advanced to the November general election. Among the three Republican candidates, Trump-endorsed Moreno came in first with just over half of the votes (50.48 percent), and thus he too advanced to the general election. Matt Dolan came in second, with a third of the votes (32.86 percent), but he was precluded from the November ballot because he was somewhat less popular among Republican voters than Moreno. LaRose came in last, with only a sixth of the Republican votes.

In the general election, Moreno beat Brown, 50.09 percent to 46.47 percent. A Libertarian candidate, Don Kissick, received 3.43 percent (with write-ins receiving the remaining 0.01 percent).[1]

Did Ohio's primary serve the state's voters well by confining the November ballot to Moreno, Brown, and Kissick, while excluding Dolan and LaRose? There is a good reason to think not. It is likely than Dolan was more popular among all of Ohio's voters than each of the other candidates in the race. In other words, if all the state's voters had been given a chance to compare Dolan one-on-one against each of the other candidates, it is likely that a majority of the state's voters would have preferred Dolan to each of them. Brown's voters most probably would have preferred Dolan to each of the other Republicans as the least objectionable among the three and also preferred Dolan over the Libertarian. Republican voters who preferred Moreno or LaRose over Dolan still most likely would have preferred Dolan over Brown, the Democrat. The relatively few Libertarian voters also presumably would have preferred Dolan as more fiscally conservative than Brown. Thus, even though we can safely assume that Dolan would have beaten any of the other candidates running for Ohio's U.S. Senate seat if Dolan had been given a chance to compete against them one-on-one in November, Ohio's primary election blocked Dolan from being on the November general election ballot and prevented the state's voters from expressing this preference for him over each of the others.

There are ways to restructure primary elections so that they do not defeat the will of the voters in this way. Specifically, as will be explained in this chapter, a primary election can be structured in the form of a round-robin tournament

---

1 For both the primary and general election see Ohio Secretary of State (2024).

among all candidates of all political parties.[2] This idea is related to, but different from, the kind of all-candidates primaries that some states, like Alaska and California, currently use (see Chapters 7, 8, and 10). In those states, a simple plurality-winner electoral procedure is used in their all-candidates primaries: the ballot only enables voters to identify their most-preferred candidate with a single vote, and these ballots are tallied to determine which candidates receive the most votes and thus advance to the general election. A round-robin primary, by contrast, enables voters to express their preference for each pair of candidates to determine which candidates are preferred by a majority of voters compared to each opponent. The candidates with the most round-robin victories are the ones to advance to the general election.

To understand why it would be better to structure primaries in this way, it is necessary first to consider why the government conducts primary elections at all.

Why Have a State-run Primary? The Significance of "Sore Loser" Laws

The most important fact about a primary election is that it is operated by the state at its own expense. While primaries are largely perceived as partisan procedures, because they usually exist to determine a political party's nominee so that the nominee appears on the general election ballot, primaries in fact are government-run affairs. Thus, they need to serve appropriate government purposes related to the overall conduct of the government's electoral system.

It is possible for the government to operate an electoral system without itself operating and paying for any primary elections, as occurred in nineteenth-century American elections. States again could choose to conduct only the November general election, setting the rules for how candidates qualify for the general election ballot—presumably by gathering enough signatures. The political parties could then decide for themselves how they want to go about nominating candidates to appear on the state's general election ballot. If a political party wanted to pay for and operate a primary election in order to choose its nominee, it certainly could do that. But whether or not a candidate won a party's primary would have no bearing one way or the other on whether the candidate qualified for the state's general election ballot; that separate issue would be determined exclusively by the state's signature-gathering rules.

---

2 For further elaboration of this concept beyond what is presented in this chapter, see Foley (2021).

But if a state operates only a general election, without some form of preliminary round of voting to narrow the field of candidates on the general election ballot, the state runs the risk that too many candidates on the general election ballot defeat the will of the majority. A state can hope that the incentives of a plurality-winner rule for the general election—meaning that the candidates with the most votes wins even if not a majority—will create a stable two-party system, such that even without state-run primaries there will be only two major-party candidates on the general election ballot, and the state can essentially ignore minor-party candidates as irrelevant.[3] The problem with this hope is that it ignores the possibility that more than one candidate from the same major party might want to appear on the general election ballot. Even if only one of these candidates can appear on the general election ballot as the party's chosen nominee, the other candidate might want a chance to convince the state's general election voters that they would be the better choice and be willing to appear on the general election ballot as an independent candidate without any party's nomination. For example, we might imagine Matt Dolan wanting to appear on Ohio's general election ballot after being unable to secure the Republican party's nomination.[4]

Most states currently prohibit more than one candidate affiliated with the same political party from appearing on the general election ballot as candidates for the same office. This prohibition is known as a "sore loser" law. It bars a candidate who runs in a primary election from being on the general election ballot in the same race (Kang 2011). But if a state got out of the business of operating primary elections, it could not enforce this kind of "sore loser" law. It would be unconstitutional to deny a candidate like Matt Dolan the right to appear on the general election ballot as an independent or third-party candidate just because he was unable to secure the Republican nomination in an internal party procedure that wasn't the first stage of a two-stage electoral process operated by the government itself.[5] So, if the state didn't operate primaries or some other sort of first stage of a two-stage electoral process, the state would confront the serious problem of having too many additional candidates beyond the two major-party nominees.

---

3 The incentives of plurality-winner elections to create a two-party system are known among political scientists as Duverger's Law (Duverger 1954).
4 In 2010, incumbent U.S. Senator Lisa Murkowski ran and won a write-in campaign after losing the Republican Party nomination to a challenger associated with the insurgent "Tea Party" movement within the GOP (Alaska Division of Elections 2010).
5 *Storer v. Brown* 415 U.S. 724 (1974) (upholding a "sore loser" law only because it was part of the state's own procedures for winnowing the field of candidates).

In short, there is the compelling justification of practicality for states to operate and pay for a two-stage, rather than single-stage, electoral system. But the first stage need not exist in the specific form of a partisan primary. Instead, the first stage could be conducted in the so-called nonpartisan form that Alaska and California currently use, in which all candidates regardless of party affiliation appear on the primary ballot. But this model is only one alternative that a state could consider. Thus, we are back to the basic question: assuming the government is going to operate some sort of two-round electoral system, in which the purpose of the first round is to narrow the field of candidates so that there aren't too many in the second round, what are sensible rules and procedures for this first round, so that it operates in the best interest of the state's voters as a whole and does not deprive them of the opportunity to vote in the second round for the candidate whom a majority prefer compared to each other candidate running in the race?

Elections as Tournaments

The goal of the state's electoral process overall is to elect the candidate whom a majority of voters prefer over all the others running in the race. The goal of the first round of a two-round process, then, is to narrow the field so that the majority of voters can pick their most-preferred candidate in the second round. It's easiest for the majority of voters to do this if the second round is limited to just two candidates.

In this sense, we can think of an electoral process as analogous to a sports tournament. The goal of the tournament's final round is to have the two strongest competitors face off against each other in order to identify the winner. The purpose of the tournament's preliminary rounds is to narrow the field of competitors so that the two strongest competitors remain for the final round.

In the context of elections, it is possible to structure the final round of voting so that there are more than two candidates remaining. One can have the second round of a two-round voting system be the "final four" candidates, for example, and then structure the second round of voting as an instant mini-tournament among these four finalists to determine which one the majority of voters prefer most.[6] But it is simplest if the second round of voting has only two final candidates, with the voters choosing which of the two they prefer. In any event, wheth-

---

6 Alaska currently structures its electoral process to include a four-candidate general election in which ranked-choice voting is used to determine the winner. See Alaska Division of Elections (2025).

er the second round of a two-round electoral system has two, four, or some other number of candidates, the same question remains about how best to structure the first round so that it advances the strongest set of candidates from whom the voters will choose the winner in the second round.

Structuring a Round-robin Tournament to Identify the Top Two Candidates

Given the goal of having the strongest candidates in the second and final round of a two-round electoral process, it makes the most sense to structure the first round in the form of a round-robin tournament. The essence of a round-robin tournament is that each competitor has a head-to-head match against each other competitor, and the strength of the competitors relative to the field as a whole is determined by their number of head-to-head victories. Round-robin tournaments are used for many sporting events, especially in the preliminary stages of multistage competitions, like the "group" stage of World Cup soccer.

In the context of an election, the round-robin format could be used at the first stage of a two-stage electoral system to identify the top two, or top four, candidates entitled to advance to the second and final stage. In an election in which there are only four or five candidates to begin with, as in the case of Ohio's 2024 U.S. Senate race, it may seem silly to have a separate preliminary round that advances four candidates to the second and final round. But many primary elections involve more than four or five candidates. Just two years earlier, for example, Ohio's 2022 U.S. Senate race had a total of ten candidates, seven Republicans and three Democrats. In any event, let us assume for purposes of further discussion in this chapter that the first round of the two-round process might have a variable number of candidates—as few as three or four and as many as a dozen or so—and regardless of the number of candidates at the first stage, only two advance to the second stage for a final head-to-head match to determine the winner.

In order to conduct a round-robin tournament among all the candidates at the first-stage of the two-stage process, it is necessary to use ranked-choice ballots if there are any more than three candidates, as there are likely to be. Otherwise, the voters would be indicating their preferences in too many head-to-head matches, and the ballot would be too long and time-consuming. But if voters rank candidates in order of preference, the round-robin tournament can be conducted based on these rankings because on every ballot for each pair of candidates one will be ranked higher than the other, and thus the head-to-head match between the two candidates can be conducted. Moreover, voters can be permitted to rank as many or as few candidates as they wish, since any unranked candidates can be considered as less favored by the voter than any ranked candidate, and the voter can also be considered as abstaining from the head-to-head match between two unranked candidates.

Once the round-robin tournament is conducted based on the rankings on all the ballots, the standings of the candidates can be determined based on the number of head-to-head victories for each candidate in the round-robin tournament. If two candidates are entitled to advance to the final round of the election, then the two candidates with the most head-to-head victories in the first round will be the two to advance. Just as in sporting events that use round-robin tournaments to determine which competitors advance to the next stage of the competition, it may be necessary to employ a tiebreaker if two or more candidates have the same number of head-to-head victories.[7] In the case of elections, there are two straightforward options for this tiebreaker. One is the total number of votes that each candidate receives across all their round-robin matches—that is, each time a candidate is ranked higher than another candidate on a ballot. The other is the candidate whose worst round-robin defeat has the narrowest margin of defeat and thus comes closest to a round-robin victory.

There are theoretical advantages to each of these two tiebreaker options. The advantage of the "total votes" tiebreaker is that it selects the candidate (among those in contention for the relevant position, in this case one of the two spots in the final round of the election) who is most preferred overall relative to the rest of the candidates. Selecting this candidate maximizes the preference of the average voter in the electorate.[8]

The advantage of the "slimmest worst defeat" tiebreaker is that it selects the candidate who has the broadest support within the electorate. This candidate is the one for whom the fewest voters would prefer a different candidate to prevail (Foley 2024). Of course, sometimes both tiebreakers will yield the same result: the candidate with the most total votes also having the slimmest worst defeat. But in the event that the two tiebreakers diverge, it's necessary to choose one, and either one will work. Given the goal of having the round-robin tournament identify the two candidates best positioned to represent the whole electorate if elected to the

---

7 If two candidates tie for first place in the number of round-robin victories, then there would be no need for a tiebreaker, as two candidates advance to the final round of the electoral process. But if two (or more) candidates tie for second place , or three (or more) candidates tie for first place, then a tiebreaker is necessary to determine which two candidates advance to the final round.

8 In the theoretical literature of electoral methods, this "total votes" tiebreaker is known as a Borda count. See Black (1958).

office in question, I would argue that slimmest worst defeat is the better tiebreaker precisely because it guarantees that one of the two candidates in the final round of the election will be the candidate who, based on the votes in the first round, has the broadest support among voters compared to each other candidate.

Imagining Ohio's 2024 U.S. Senate Election as a Round-robin Tournament

If Ohio had operated a round-robin tournament instead of a partisan primary as the first stage of its 2024 U.S. Senate election, it is most likely that Matt Dolan and Bernie Moreno would have advanced to the November general election as the two candidates with the most round-robin victories. For reasons we have already discussed, Dolan would have had round-robin victories against each of the other candidates, while Moreno would have had round-robin victories against everyone except Dolan.[9] All the state's voters then would have made their choice between these two candidates after they conducted a final round of campaigning in advance of the vote in November.

Democrats might object to the exclusion of their nominee, Brown, from the November ballot in a round-robin system. But that exclusion reflects the relative weakness of Brown and the Democratic party in Ohio right now. Brown would not have won a head-to-head contest against any of the three Republican candidates, and indeed might not even have won a head-to-head contest against the Libertarian candidate, Kissick. Letting all the state's voters choose in November between Dolan and Moreno, as the two strongest candidates in the state against the rest of the competition, makes much more sense than having the voters choose between Brown and Moreno with Kissick—but not Dolan—also on the ballot as a third option.

Some might argue that having only two Republicans on the ballot in November, and no Democrat or candidate from any other party, is bad for the political system because it weakens the competition between political parties and dilutes

---

9 This assumes that supporters of both Brown and Dolan would have been indifferent between Moreno and LaRose as equally representative of the MAGA wing of the Republican party, even though Moreno rather than LaRose secured Trump's endorsement. If supporters of both Brown and Dolan preferred LaRose over Moreno for being less associated with Trump, then LaRose would replace Moreno as the candidate with the second most round-robin victories. Either way, the two finalists would have been one non-MAGA and one MAGA Republican for all the state's voters to choose between after the two went head-to-head in November.

the Republican brand in the general election. But this argument is unsound. The round robin can be structured so that the political parties make their nominations in advance by whatever method they choose, including a traditional partisan primary at their own expense. Then, only one Republican candidate (Moreno) will appear on the round-robin ballot with the Republican label, and Dolan will have to appear on the round-robin ballot as an independent or as the nominee of some other party. The same point is true for LaRose. Brown will be on the round-robin ballot as the nominee of the Democrats, and Kissick as the Libertarian nominee. Therefore, each party will be represented in the election by a single voice. If a majority of voters still favor Dolan over each opponent despite Dolan being an independent (or minor-party nominee), that is only because the voters find the major-party nominees insufficiently attractive. In that case, the nature of the round-robin tournament is likely to induce a new party to enter the competition to capture the support of the voters who will enable Dolan to prevail over each competitor. Alternatively, the previously "minor" party that nominated Dolan, because he could not win the GOP nomination, would no longer be so minor. It effectively would replace the Democrats as the second major-party in the state.[10]

Thus, the round-robin electoral system is not anti-party; it just doesn't necessarily benefit the two existing major parties. The measure of an electoral system's value for a democracy is not whether it benefits existing parties but instead whether it creates healthy electoral competition among parties and candidates, enabling voters to choose whichever candidate they collectively most want to win. The round-robin system does just that, by advancing to the general election the two candidates whom the voters prefer more when compared to each of the others. A party's nominee—whether Republican or Democrat or otherwise—will appropriately earn one of those two spots on the November ballot if, but only if, they demonstrate that a majority of voters prefer them more than each of the other candidates competing for the same spot.

The argument is sometimes made that the first round of a two-round electoral system should not be so consequential as to limit the second round to only two

---

10 If this round-robin electoral system led to the election of Senators and Representatives from new parties, along with still dominant Democrats and Republicans in Congress, then these new parties would need to decide which major party to join with in order to form a majority in each legislative chamber. This situation would be similar to what occurred in the nineteenth-century when occasionally the formation of a coalition with minor parties, like the Free Soilers, was necessary. The existences of such coalitions to create a legislative majority within the chamber does not negate the fact that the minor party within the coalition is a separate political party distinct from the majority party within the coalition.

candidates if voter turnout is especially low, as it is for most primaries in the U.S. This argument, however, rests on a false premise insofar as the turnout for a round-robin tournament need not be especially low. France conducts a two-round electoral system for its legislative as well as presidential elections, and turnout for its first round is much higher than for U.S. primaries (BBC News 2016). The key is holding the first round much closer to the second round than U.S. primaries are held in relation to the November general election. Ohio's primary for its 2024 U.S. Senate election was held on March 19—231 days and over seven months before the November 5 general election. Admittedly, 2024 was a presidential election year, and presidential primaries need to be held before the presidential nominating conventions. But a round-robin tournament as the first stage of a two-stage U.S. Senate (or U.S. House of Representatives) election need not (and perhaps should not) be held on the same day as a state's presidential primary. A state could hold the round-robin tournament in September, to select two candidates for the November ballot, and that relatively short gap between the September and November votes combined with the structure of the round-robin format—in which all qualifying candidates from all parties would appear on the September ballot for the round-robin tournament—would substantially increase turnout relative to a partisan primary held in March (see Chapters 4 and 16 of this volume). Further, if all states held a preliminary round-robin tournament on the same day in September for their congressional elections every two years, with all states using these round-robin tournaments to select two candidates for the November ballot, voter turnout in September would likely rival turnout in November.

Conclusion: Moving Forward With This Reform

If we want states to conduct two-round electoral systems that best serve the interests of the voters, we must change the first round of these systems so that it no longer is a partisan primary. Indeed, we would be better served if we didn't even call it a "primary"—let that term be used exclusively for elections that a party may choose to hold to select its nominee for an election, but let the party and not the state operate that primary. The first round that the state conducts for its two-round system can be called a "preliminary" or "first-stage" ballot. This antecedent vote, to determine which candidates are entitled to advance to the second and final round of the election, should be conducted in the form of a round-robin tournament. This is the best way to identify the candidates most worthy to advance and compete for ultimate victory—just as round-robins are used to determine which competitors advance in sporting events.

The idea of conducting elections in the form of a round-robin tournament isn't new. On the contrary, it dates at least as far back as the thirteenth century, when a Majorcan monk proposed this method for electing the leader of a monastery (Colomer 2013). The idea resurfaced in the eighteenth century, when a French mathematician developed it again (McLean 2015). Prior to the invention of computers in the second half of the twentieth century, it would have been impossible as a practical matter to conduct a large-scale election involving millions of ballots with multiple candidates—realistically, any more than three candidates would have doomed the enterprise. But modern computing makes this a breeze. All voters need to do is rank as many candidates as they wish in order of preference, and the computers can do the rest to set up the round-robin tournament among all the candidates and determine which candidates win the most round-robin matches and are entitled to advance to the next stage of the election. If there needs to be a tiebreaker based on either the total number of votes each candidate received in their round-robin matches, or which candidate's worst round-robin defeat was by the slimmest margin, the computer can easily make this calculation as well.

The basic idea of having a preliminary stage of the electoral process in which all candidates regardless of political party compete against each other in order to determine which are the strongest candidates deserving to advance to the final stage of the election is also not a novel proposition. As mentioned in Chapters 7, 8, and 10, Alaska and California are among the states that already have adopted this format. But this format can be improved upon. The best way to determine the strongest candidates deserving to advance to the general election is not the simply plurality-winner procedure that Alaska and California use. Instead, it is the kind of round-robin procedure identified here. The round-robin method, by comparing each candidate one-on-one against every opponent, enables an assessment of the relative strength of each candidate against the entire field.

There should be nothing holding us back from adopting this much better method for conducting the first round of the state's two-round electoral system. It would be perfectly permissible for any state to choose this method for conducting its congressional, including Senate, elections. If the parties still want to choose their nominees by means of partisan primaries, they can hold these primaries before the round-robin tournament and do that on their own.

The defeat of other types of reform in 2024 (discussed in Chapter 9) should not be considered an impediment to pursuing this reform. There was no public discussion of structuring elections to function like tournaments, an idea that will resonate with many voters. The opposition to ranked-choice voting that caused the defeat of these reform proposals was due to the fact that the specific way ranked-choice voting operated in Alaska disadvantaged Republicans, whereas using ranked-choice ballots to structure a round-robin tournament among the candidates would not have had this effect—and indeed would have elected a Republican instead of a Democrat (Foley and Maskin 2022). It is time to consider this alternative approach of round-robin primaries in order to make elections work for the benefit of the voters themselves.

Bibliography

Alaska Division of Elections. 2010. "2010 General Election Results." https://www.elections.alaska. gov/results/10GENR/index.php.

Alaska Division of Elections. 2025. "Ranked Choice Voting." https://www.elections.alaska.gov/ election-information/#RankedChoice.

BBC News. 2016. "US Election: Why Does the US Have Such Low Voter Turnout?" *BBC News.* October 28. https://www.bbc.com/news/election-us-2016-37634526.

Black, Duncan. 1958. *The Theory of Committee and Elections.* Cambridge University Press.

Colomer, Josep M. 2013. "Ramon Llull: From 'Ars Electionis' to Social Choice Theory." *Social Choice and Welfare* 40: 317–328.

Duverger, Maurice. 1954. *Political Parties: Their Organization and Activity in the Modern State.* Translated by Barbara and Robert North. Methuen.

Foley, Edward B. 2021. "Tournament Elections with Round-Robin Primaries: A Sports Analogy for Electoral Reform." *Wisconsin Law Review:* 1188–1227.

Foley, Edward B. 2024."Maximum Convergence Voting." *Florida Law Review* 76: 1751–1805.

Foley, Edward B., and Eric Maskin. 2022. "Alaska's ranked-choice voting is flawed. But there's an easy fix." *The Washington Post.* November 1. www.washingtonpost.com/opinions/2022/11/01/ alaska-final-four-primary-begich-palin-peltola/.

Kang, Michael S. 2011. "Sore Loser Laws and Democratic Contestation." *Georgetown Law Journal* 99: 1013–1075.

McLean, Iain. 2015. "The Strange History of Social Choice." In *Handbook of Social Choice and Voting,* edited by Jac C. Heckelman and Nicholas R. Miller, 15–34. Edward Elgar.

Ohio Secretary of State. 2024. "2024 Official Election Results." www.ohiosos.gov/elections/election-results-and-data/2024-official-election-results/

Storer v. Brown 415 U.S. 724 (1974).

Robert G. Boatright and Caroline J. Tolbert

Chapter 16
What Would a National Primary Day Look Like, and How Would we Get There?

Abstract: Some primary election reform advocates have argued in favor of consolidating all nonpresidential primaries on the same day, or among a small number of days. A National Primary Day could, among other things, focus the attention of interest groups, parties, the media, and the general public on the national issues at stake in the election, and could result in substantially increased turnout. This reform has never been attempted, however, so it is difficult to know how it would work in practice. In this chapter we evaluate arguments in favor of establishing a National Primary Day, explore evidence about the effects of consolidating election dates in the U.S. and other countries, and discuss the potential consequences of increased primary turnout for representation and candidate behavior. Finally, we discuss the ways in which such a reform could be established.

Currently, primaries for state and federal office are held throughout the spring and summer; the earliest tend to occur on the first Tuesday in March, while the latest are held during the first half of September. As Unite America's Nick Troiano (2024, 77) notes, in 2022 there were eighteen different dates on which congressional primaries were held. In a survey we conducted in 2023 (Boatright et al. 2024), over seventy percent of respondents who expressed an opinion stated that they were in favor of having a one-day national primary. Unlike the responses to most of our other survey questions, there were no significant differences in responses according to state primary type, level of political interest, or partisanship. This high level of public support does not in itself mean it is necessarily a good idea. We think, however, that having a National Primary Day is politically feasible and has more potential to solve the problems raised in this book than do other proposed reforms. Accordingly, in this chapter we describe the very brief history of the national congressional primary idea; the potential consequences of it for voter engagement and for campaign strategy; and the ways in which a single-day congressional primary might be established.

The Brief History of the National Primary Day Idea

The concept of a National Primary Day has received scant attention. In a 1902 study, Ernst Meyer argued that primaries should be given the same "dignity" as general elections (405) and concluded that it would be less expensive, fairer, and more attractive to voters to consolidate primaries on the same day. At the time, there was substantial concern that if parties held their primaries on different dates it would be easy for one party to meddle in the other's primary, and Meyer sems likely to have been referring in part to the practice of separating parties' primaries. However, he does indicate that the same logic held for variations in when nearby states or areas of states used different primary dates.

Since that time, discussions about consolidating primary dates have appeared sporadically. For most of the twentieth century, it was assumed that states had the authority to schedule their primaries whenever they wished. There have been, as Boatright et al. (2020) have noted, several arguments made about the optimal timing for primaries, some of which have to do with voter turnout. It was held that summer primaries would yield low turnout due to vacations and agricultural schedules, that spring primaries might yield low turnout because voters would not yet have started to pay attention to the election, and that therefore fall primaries might yield the highest turnout.[1] There is limited empirical support for this claim. Nonetheless, in 1951 a National Municipal League report called for states to hold fall primaries. It proposed a filing deadline of September 1 and an October 1 primary. The report does not go into detail about the effects of clustering primaries or of having a single-day primary; rather, it is concerned solely with the timing of primaries. Yet this is implicitly a call to have all primaries on one date.

The merits of consolidating primaries have been invoked in pursuit of other goals, as well. There is a lengthy literature on the merits of having a national presidential primary (see, e.g., Mazo 2020; Norrander 2020). Similarly, studies of the Presidential "Super Tuesday" primary have emphasized the value of clustering primaries as a way to increase turnout (Norrander 1992). More recently, some scholars of municipal elections have called for moving off-year municipal elections to even-numbered years (Hajnal 2009; Anzia 2014). Although there are numerous other issues raised about this type of consolidation that go beyond the

---

1 For a sampling of these see Horack (1923); Merriam (1908), 137–39. For state-specific accounts see Craig and Austin (2008), Sabato (1977), and Zimmerman (2008).

scope of this chapter, the logic is the same—having more elections on the same day is expected to increase voter participation and improve the representativeness of the electorate.

As was discussed in the foreword to this book, the Bipartisan Policy Center (2018; see also Ferrer and Thorning 2023) has argued in favor of establishing a single-day state primary of the sort that we are proposing here. It has noted that states which hold primaries on the same day as adjacent states have turnout approximately two to three percentage points higher than would otherwise be predicted, and that states that have moved their primaries to coincide with those of neighboring states have also seen increases. Although the number of states included in these categories is small, it notes that "the effect could scale" with a greater consolidation of primary dates. Kamarck (2014) summarizes many of the challenges posed by variations in primary turnout, including the election of extreme candidates and the inability of political parties to adequately plan for primaries.

And this is all—in our research on primary elections, we have found no other detailed explanations of what a single-day primary might do. Although Kamarck and the Bipartisan Policy Center team have written extensively on primaries and have evaluated many different proposed reforms, their support for the single-day primary mostly involves adding it to lists of changes that could be adopted. Contemporary primary reform advocacy groups, such as Issue One, Open Primaries, or Unite America, have considered this as well but without offering details (see Troiano 2024, 77). To our knowledge, no one has sketched out the results of such a change. It is our task here, then, to present some very preliminary predictions about what might transpire.

Consequences of a National Primary Day

Effects on Turnout and Representation

Let us first consider first-order effects—the ways in which holding all primaries on the same day might influence voter turnout. We suspect that many voters are not aware of the date of their state primary. In addition, many states move their primaries on a regular basis. In some instances this has been the result of legislation (see Boatright 2024, ch. 8) while in others it is a regular occurrence. Currently nine states hold their state primaries at least one month earlier during presidential election years than they do in midterm election years. This requires a mobilization effort on the part of statewide, congressional, or legislative primary candidates to inform voters of when the primary is. In states with onerous voter registration requirements, of course, this adds yet another barrier. A single-day primary would thus be more memorable for voters.

A single-day primary would also garner more media coverage. Northwestern University's State of Local News Project has documented a decline in local newspapers and the growth of "news deserts" in many American states and counties (Abernathy 2023). It is increasingly difficult for citizens to be informed about local or statewide political issues. Were there a single-day national primary, national newspapers and cable news outlets would draw attention to primary races. Furthermore, an estimated fifty-eight percent of citizens receive their news from digital platforms—news websites, social media, web searches, or podcasts (Pew Research Center 2023). Many of these sources are undoubtedly national, not local, in their focus, and many of the average citizen's social media contacts may well reside in other states. An awareness that other Americans are voting in a primary may well inspire some citizens to vote in their own local primary.

A national primary would also simplify mobilization efforts by parties or interest groups. An organization seeking to increase turnout by a particular demographic group or to highlight the salience of a particular issue could engage in a nationwide advocacy campaign or publicize lists of endorsed candidates. Political parties could also benefit from having a single day to focus on. As Kamarck (2014) notes, parties have benefited in the high-turnout early presidential primary states from the attention placed on these states' primaries but have had little success in states that draw less attention. She speculates that the two parties might be able to collaborate either in the establishment of a single primary day or in establishing separate national party primary dates, one for Democrats and another for Republicans.

For all of these reasons, it seems to us that a single-day primary might increase turnout, and it might increase turnout among lower propensity voters— people who tend to be younger, less wealthy, and more moderate than regular primary voters. It would increase the likelihood that the primary electorate would look more like the American population. The electorate would be less extreme and more representative.

Some might respond that such an increase would likely bring to the polls many voters who know very little about the candidates, and that it would in fact decrease the likelihood that the selection of nominees would be an informed choice. We would offer two responses to this claim. First, as other chapters in this book (particularly Chapters 7 and 8 on Alaska) suggest, an expanded electorate would compel candidates to campaign among different types of voters. If candidates change the way they campaign, the themes they raise in their campaigns, or the audiences they seek out, it is likely that they will be able to make a stronger claim to represent the view of their potential constituents. Ultimately it would be the responsibility of the candidates to help voters make an informed choice.

Second, we are skeptical that under the current system voters in down-ballot races know very much about the candidates. If turnout is indeed driven by the most consequential races on the ballot, then except in instances where there is very substantial rolloff, many voters in House primaries, state legislative primaries, and other such races are already casting votes based on limited information. Studies of congressional elections have estimated that rolloff ranges between four and six percent in general elections (Miller 2022). While primaries may have higher levels of rolloff given that voters cannot use a party as a voting cue, these studies still suggest that many low information voters are still making choices.

Secondary Effects of a Single-day Primary

There are many secondary effects from having a single-day primary as well—things that might improve primaries but are not necessarily related to turnout or representation. A single-day primary would limit the power of organized interests. It is not a bad thing for interest groups to become active in primaries, but the sequential nature of contemporary primaries gives undue power to interest groups that have sought to encourage extreme candidates. As one of us has argued (Boatright 2013), ideological groups with small but dedicated national membership bases have become adept at using the sequential nature of primaries to create a narrative about their challenges to moderate Democrats and Republicans. Groups that use their resources and their membership base strategically can have multiple chances through the year for such attacks. Such efforts also succeed because incumbents can be caught unawares and because the very low turnout in some of these elections ensures that a group can succeed by mobilizing only a very small percentage of voters.

Apart from these organized efforts, the sequential nature of primaries can cause such events to take place even without extensive group involvement. In one of the best-known cases of a successfully "primarying," in 2014 House Majority Leader Eric Cantor was defeated by a little-known challenger, David Brat, in a primary where approximately ten percent of eligible voters took part, in a state where voters are not accustomed to voting in primaries because primary elections are often not held at all.[2] Brat's victory on June 10 resonated throughout the primary season, ensuring that immigration, the issue Brat campaigned on, played a

---

2 For details on this election see Bell, Meyer, and Gaddie (2015).

role in later primaries. One could make a similar argument about Alexandria Ocasio-Cortez's unexpected primary on June 26, 2018, that it was a consequence of many factors, including the efforts of the advocacy group Justice Democrats, the inattention of the incumbent representative to his district given his role in the Democratic Party House leadership, and the gradual change in the racial demographics of the district. Ocasio-Cortez's victory helped to fuel a narrative about the rise of the progressive wing of the party.[3]

A single-day primary would not necessarily lead to fewer challenges like these. Such challenges would, however, require the candidates to reach out to a larger number of voters. If all primaries were happening on the same day, post hoc explanations of the election would be more accurate. An increase in turnout might advantage insurgent candidates, but it would ensure that insurgent candidates' victories would be a consequence of voter mobilization as opposed to voter inattention. Upsets such as these would also be seen in context—as one or two interesting outcomes among several hundred, as opposed to being harbingers of what might or might not take place in primaries later in the year.

Although we have frequently heard that legislators would not go along with the single-day primary idea, we believe that a single-day primary could in fact be advantageous for politicians, and that from a practical standpoint, a single-day primary would improve the quality of lawmaking during the election year. Congress could adjourn for a week or two prior to the primary in order to make it easier for members to return to their districts to campaign. This might be seen as providing an advantage to incumbents, but it seems reasonable that incumbents facing opposition not be in a position where they have to choose between campaigning and attending to congressional legislation. That is, it seems problematic for incumbents to be put at a disadvantage because they were in Washington doing their jobs, or that in a closely divided Congress, the spring and summer schedule would need to accommodate idiosyncrasies in state primary dates in order to pass crucial legislation.

One potential criticism of this argument is that a single-day primary might effectively nationalize the election. There is some truth to this, although the extent of nationalization might well depend on where parties and groups choose to spend their money and what they chose to talk about. State legislators are responsible for choosing primary dates in most states; they can be expected to be prioritize their own renomination or reelection prospects over those of federal politicians, and they might have their own beliefs about what timing is best or about the pros and cons of higher turnout. Jewitt (2019, 60–61) asserts that state legisla-

---

3 For details on these elections see Freedlander (2021).

tors tend to have a preference for later primaries and that they have been an obstacle to reform plans for presidential primaries. We would contend that state legislators may be even more susceptible to problems introduced by variations in
turnout than are federal candidates. The lower down the ballot one goes, the
less control candidates might be perceived to have over primary turnout. If
state legislators really want lower turnout, they have the option of separating
state primaries from congressional primaries (as New York did), but this also is
normatively troubling and it can make state legislators subject to variations in gubernatorial primary turnout.

Another response might simply be either that there is nothing objectionable
about nationalizing elections or that they are in effect nationalized already.
Many recent studies of state elections (e.g. Hopkins 2018) have shown that state
legislative elections are increasingly becoming referenda on developments in federal politics. While it is not clear that state legislative primaries should necessarily
be subject to these patterns, some recent studies have contended that Republican
candidates' connections to Donald Trump have been consequential in some Republican primaries (Hood and McKee 2023). Manento and Testa (2022) argue
that voters increasingly use views on national political figures as cues in primaries. Higher turnout primaries, in part because they would attract more moderate voters and in part because they would attract a more consistent group of voters, might therefore also help state legislators, even though these legislators might
not initially see matters this way.

How A National Primary Day Might be Established

There are three possible ways in which a National Primary Day might be established; they resemble the agenda for establishing a national single day presidential primary (Mazo 2020). First, Congress might pass a law establishing a national
primary. It is debatable whether Congress has this authority—the Constitution
grants to state legislatures the power of determining the "times, places, and manner of holding elections for Senators and Representatives" (Article I, Section 4) but
then goes on to note that Congress may "at any time alter such regulations." Most
scholars who have taken up the subject conclude that *United States v. Classic* (313
U.S. 299 (1941)) gives Congress the authority to regulate primaries in this way (Briffault 2020, 72). However, Congress has generally been reluctant to consider legislation that affects state administration of primaries unless it is doing so as a response to corruption or civil rights violations. There have been some recent

efforts to create national rules for primaries—for instance, Rep. John Delaney (D-Maryland) introduced bills in 2015 and 2017 requiring nonpartisan top two primaries in all House races.[4] Both of these bills died in committee.

A second approach would be for Congress to offer financial incentives for states to hold their primaries on a designated date, or provide other incentives to consolidate the primary calendar. Such proposals would not be out of place among the slate of what are billed as pro-democracy reforms contained in the For the People Act, which Democrats have introduced at the start of the past three Congresses. The problem with an approach such as this is that it yokes the establishment of a National Primary Day to a partisan agenda.

Third, states could agree amongst themselves to move toward adopting a shared primary date. The National Popular Vote Interstate Compact is a possible model here. States could agree to move to a shared date only when a threshold number of states have done so. Unlike the National Popular Vote Compact, however, there is not particular level at which the threshold need be set. As noted above, the effects of clustering are likely also to be beneficial. An agreement among some states to compress their primaries into a time period of weeks rather than months, advocacy for one date on which many but not all states held their primaries, or a series of dates of which groups of states held primaries would all be superior to the status quo.

What might matter here is the introduction of the concept of a National Primary Day. If that framing were to draw media attention, it could create momentum on its own, or at least spark a conversation about the primary calendar. There is still room, in this framing, for some articulation of regional concerns. A shared primary date for midwestern industrial states, for instance, might be framed as a statement about the challenges facing those states and might accordingly draw media attention in a manner that would be less idiosyncratic than trying to interpret results one state at a time. There is already some regional variation in primary dates—Southern states tend to vote early and many vote on Super Tuesday in presidential years, while New England states disproportionately vote in the Fall. What is missing, however, is a national discussion of primary results. Further consolidation of primary dates, accompanied by a rhetoric about the value of doing so, could spur other states to follow.

Any effort to establish a single day primary by any of these means would require a pressure campaign. It would require advocacy groups to take seriously the benefits a National Primary Day would provide. We have not fully spelled out the idea here; we are political scientists, not activists, and we fully concede that an

---

4 https://www.govinfo.gov/app/details/BILLS-114hr2655ih.

advocacy campaign would require money, a media strategy, national grassroots organizing, a more serious consideration of state constitutions and state laws, and a host of other things. There would need to be some agreement on what day this might be. Organizations that have put work into advocacy for open primaries, ranked-choice voting, or other such reforms would need to take up this cause. We believe that a National Primary Day is more feasible and would be more consequential than other projects that have received ample attention and funding.

Conclusions

Even if our proposal were not realized, the nation and the reform community might benefit from a new conversation such as the one we have sought to offer. We need to talk more about the causes and consequences of very low primary turnout. Some surveys have shown that social norms about whether one should vote in primaries are weaker than those regarding voting in general elections (Gerber et al 2017). This conversation could help change beliefs about the importance of voting in primaries.

We recognize that there is an established agenda of other types of election reforms. Many of these topics are worthy endeavors, and many reform advocates share our concern over the state of American democracy today. We are skeptical, however, that some of the most popular reform proposals are worth the effort. As we have demonstrated elsewhere (Boatright, Tolbert, and Micatka 2024), much of the reform agenda is stymied by partisan conflict and is likely to remain so. A well-financed, participatory effort to establish open primaries or ranked choice voting in a few states risks producing underwhelming results which may demobilize supporters or just lead to the cascading reform cycles and further cynicism about the democratic process (see Cain 2015). Ultimately, however, we would argue, following Sarah Anzia's (2014) logic, that many of the reforms on the table promise results, at least in regards to turnout, that are far smaller than a change in election timing and a consolidation of primaries might offer.

And what if we are wrong? It is difficult to predict any particular harms that might come from the consolidation of primary dates. There are valid arguments for spreading out presidential primary elections, but there are no compelling arguments in favor of spreading out primary election dates for other offices. The common early twentieth century arguments about harvest schedules or summer travel seem antiquated today, and of course could be addressed through the use of absentee ballots or by settling on a date that posed no problems. At worst, we would be left with a new civic holiday that, unlike the general election date, did not pit partisans of one side against another. We see this as a way to empower voters while also enabling political parties to rebuild.

We note, finally, that our proposal could be seen as an entry into discussions about how to rebuild a sense of community in America. Americans are more skeptical of elections and democracy than at any point in our lifetimes. According to one survey, a majority of younger Americans believe that democracy in America is "in trouble" or "failing" (Institute of Politics 2023). Some organizations have responded to this by calling for more civic attention to the celebration of Election Day–by, for instance, making Election Day a national holiday, or holding the election on a weekend. Such proposals are indicative of a desire to make Election Day an event we celebrate, not something we dread. We see the establishment of a National Primary Day as an idea that fits within this ambit—but it may even be better or more achievable in some ways. Whereas general elections will remain matters of conflict and anxiety as long as the nation remains as polarized as it is today, a National Primary Day can be more of a civic celebration. Members of both parties can select their candidates without directly competing with each other. Some candidates will lose, but the parties will not. A National Primary Day can be a celebration of democracy. Although the direct primary has not always lived up to its initial proponents' hopes, creating a National Primary Day, or even having a larger national conversation about it, seems likely to be a way to improve our elections and perhaps to improve our democracy.

Bibliography

Abernathy, Penelope Muse. 2023. "The State of Local News: The 2023 Report." Northwestern Medill Local News Initiative. localnewsinitiative.northwestern.edu/projects/state-of-local-news/2023/report/.

Anzia, Sarah. 2014. *Timing and Turnout: How Off-Cycle Elections Favor Organized Groups.* University of Chicago Press.

Bell, Lauren Cohen, David Elliott Meyer, and Keith Gaddie. 2015. *Slingshot: The Defeat of Eric Cantor.* Sage Publishing.

Bipartisan Policy Center. 2018. "2018 Primary Turnout and Reforms." Bipartisan Policy Center,

Boatright, Robert G. 2013. *Getting Primaried: The Changing Politics of Congressional Primary Challenges.* University of Michigan Press.

Boatright, Robert G. 2024. *Reform and Retrenchment.* Oxford University Press.

Boatright, Robert G., Vincent G. Moscardelli, and Clifford Vickrey. 2020. "Primary Election Timing and Voter Turnout." *Election Law Journal* 19 (4): 472–485.

Boatright, Robert G., Caroline J. Tolbert, and Nathan Micatka. 2024. "Public Opinion on Reforming U.S. Primaries." *Social Science Quarterly* 105 (3): 876–893.

Briffault, Richard. 2020. "Constitutional Law and the Presidential Nomination Process." In *The Best Candidate*, edited by Eugene D. Mazo and Michael R. Dimino, 54–79. Cambridge University Press.

Cain, Bruce E. 2015. *Democracy More or Less: America's Political Reform Quandary*. Cambridge University Press.

Craig, Stephen C., and Roger Austin. 2008. "Elections and Partisan Change in Florida." In *Government and Politics in Florida*, 3rd ed., edited by J. Edwin Benton, 48–89. University Press of Florida.

Ferrer, Joshua, and Michael Thorning. 2023. "2022 Primary Turnout: Trends and Lessons for Boosting Participation." Bipartisan Policy Center.

Freedlander, David. 2021. *The AOC Generation*. Beacon Press.

Gerber, Alan S., Gregory A. Huber, Daniel R. Biggers, and David J. Hendry. 2017. "Why Don't People Vote in U.S. Primary Elections? Assessing Theoretical Explanations for Reduced Participation." *Electoral Studies* 45: 119–129.

Hajnal, Zoltan L. 2009. *America's Uneven Democracy: Race, Turnout, and Representation in City Politics*. Cambridge University Press.

Hood, Marni V., and Seth C. McKee. 2023. "How Much Is a Trump Endorsement Worth?" *State Politics & Policy Quarterly* 23 (4): 380–395.

Hopkins, Daniel. 2018. *The Increasingly United States*. University of Chicago Press.

Horack, Frank E. 1923. "The Workings of the Direct Primary in Iowa, 1908–1922." *Annals of the American Academy of Political and Social Sciences* 106: 148–157.

Institute of Politics. 2023. *Harvard Youth Poll*. Harvard Kenney School Institute of Politics. https://iop.harvard.edu/youth-poll/46th-edition-fall-2023.

Jewitt, Caitlin E. 2019. *The Primary Rules: Parties, Voters, and Presidential Nominations*. University of Michigan Press.

Kamarck, Elaine. 2014. "Increasing Turnout in Congressional Primaries." Brookings Institution, Center for Effective Public Management. www.brookings.edu/research/increasing-turnout-in-congressional-primaries/.

Manento, Cory, and Testa, Paul F. 2022. "In Party We Trust? Voter Support for Party-Backed Candidates in Primary Elections." *Political Behavior* 44 (4): 1633–1656.

Mazo, Eugene D. 2020. "Primary Day: Why Presidential Nominees Should be Chosen on a Single Day." In *The Best Candidate*, edited by Eugene D. Mazo and Michael R. Dimino, 145–183. Cambridge University Press.

Merriam, Charles. 1908. *Primary Elections*. University of Chicago Press.

Meyer, Ernst Christopher. 1902. *Nominating Systems*. Self-published.

Miller, Michael G. 2022. "Candidate Extremism and Voter Roll-Off in US House Elections." *Legislative Studies Quarterly* 47 (4): 791–821.

National Municipal League. 1951. *A Model Direct Primary Election System: Report of the Committee on the Direct Primary*. National Municipal League.

Norrander, Barbara. 1992. *Super Tuesday: Regional Politics and Presidential Primaries*. University of Kentucky Press.

Norrander, Barbara. 2020. *The Imperfect Primary*. Routledge.

Pew Research Center. 2023. "News Platform Fact Sheet." Pew Research Center. www.pewresearch.org/journalism/fact-sheet/news-platform-fact-sheet/.

Sabato, Larry. 1977. *The Democratic Party Primary in Virginia*. University of Virginia Press.

Troiano, Nick. 2024. *The Primary Solution*. Simon and Schuster.

United States v. Classic, 313 U.S. 299 (1941).

U.S. Constitution, Article I, Section 4.

Zimmerman, Joseph P. 2008. *The Government and Politics of New York State*, 2nd ed. State University of New York Press.

Index

Note: Page numbers in *italics* indicate figures, **bold** indicate tables in the text, and references following "n" refer notes.

www.ingramcontent.com/pod-product-compliance
Lightning Source LLC
Chambersburg PA
CBHW032342280326
41935CB00008B/424